Glasgow

Footprint

The travel guide

Handbook

Alan Murphy and Rebecca Ford

Oh ye cannae fling pieces oot a twenty-storey flat,
Seven hundred hungry weans'll testify to that.
If it's butter, cheese or jeely, if the breid is plain or pan,
The odds against it reaching earth are ninety-nine tae wan...

from "The Jeely Piece Song" by
Adam McNaughtan, 1967

Glasgow Handbook
First edition
© Footprint Handbooks Ltd 2002

Published by Footprint Handbooks
6 Riverside Court
Lower Bristol Road
Bath BA2 3DZ. England
T +44 (0)1225 469141
F +44 (0)1225 469461
Email discover@footprintbooks.com
Web www.footprintbooks.com

ISBN 1 903471 24 9
CIP DATA: A catalogue record for this
book is available from the British Library

Distributed in the USA by
Publishers Group West

ois Ordnance Survey®
This product includes mapping data
licensed from Ordnance Survey® with
the permission of the Controller of Her
Majesty's Stationery Office. © Crown
Copyright. All rights reserved. Licence
No. 43501U.

Credits

Series editors
Patrick Dawson and Rachel Fielding

Editorial
Editor: Ian Emery
Maps: Sarah Sorensen

Production
Page layout: Mark Thomas
Typesetting: Leona Bailey, Emma Bryers
and Davina Rungasamy
Maps: Claire Benison and Robert Lunn
Colour maps: Kevin Feeney
Cover: Camilla Ford

Design
Mytton Williams

Photography
Front cover: Scotland In Focus
Back cover: Scotland in Focus
Inside colour section: Edinburgh
Photographic Library, Scotland in Focus,
The Travel Library

Print
Manufactured in Italy by LEGOPRINT

A foot in the door

Right It may look like the Doge's Palace in Venice, but the Templeton Business Centre was originally built as a carpet factory
Centre Kelvingrove Art Gallery and Museum not only houses one of the finest collections in the country but is perhaps the only major art gallery entered by the back door, leading to the urban myth that the architect leapt from the tower and killed himself because it had been built back to front
Previous page The sun has set on Glasgow's heavy industries but the city has re-invented itself as a major tourist attraction

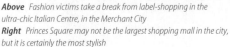

Above Fashion victims take a break from label-shopping in the ultra-chic Italian Centre, in the Merchant City
Right Princes Square may not be the largest shopping mall in the city, but it is certainly the most stylish

Introduction

Glasgow is hard to define. This spontaneous free-spirit has cast off its industrial past to become a modern, design-conscious city with an energy and exuberance that is simply not found anywhere else in Scotland. It even looks different. None of that sober grey stone that gives other Scottish cities a restrained, slightly austere appearance. Glasgow is a beguiling blend of old red sandstone and quirky ironwork, laced with glinting contemporary glass and steel. It is often described as Scotland's most European city, but it could also be compared to Manhattan, with its grid of streets, its tall, narrow buildings, and its wisecracking citizens. And then it has an air of Celtic edginess like Liverpool, a distinctive city swagger like London, and a lingering sense of Victorian civic pride like Manchester. Definitely a different place.

The Empire strikes back

There's an old saying that Edinburgh is the capital but Glasgow has the capital. This dates back to the late 19th century, when Glasgow proclaimed itself the 'Second City of the Empire'. It was a thriving, cultivated city grown rich on the profits from its cotton mills, coal mines and shipyards, and a city that knew how to flaunt its wealth. The legacy of Glasgow's prosperous past is all around: in the magnificent City Chambers in George Square; the neoclassical architecture of the Merchant City; the sweeping terraces of the West End and honey-coloured villas of South Side; and its galleries full to bursting with priceless art treasures, from Rodin to Rembrandt.

Citizen vain

Glasgow is definitely among the coolest of cities – and that's not just because it stands at 56° North, the same latitude as Moscow. Those expecting some kind of cloth-capped heritage theme park may be disappointed by the city today. Its present inhabitants possess a style and swagger that makes their Edinburgh counterparts look staid and stuffy by comparison. Just take a stroll round the Merchant City or along Byres Road in the West End and sit in one of the many stylish bars and cafés and you'll witness a degree of posing that is almost continental in its fervency. The country's caffeine capital is really more Barcelona or Greenwich Village than west coast of Scotland.

Designs on success

Glasgow is unusual among great cities in that it has no single defining monument: no Eiffel Tower; no Trafalgar Square; no Empire State Building; nor an Edinburgh Castle for that matter. Ironically, though, this city has picked itself up from the near terminal trauma of economic wipe-out, dusted itself down and re-invented itself as a major European tourist attraction, thanks mainly to its buildings. Glasgow may not have been the architect of its own downfall, but its great designers have risen from beyond the grave to breathe new life back into the city. Foremost among them is, of course, Charles Rennie Mackintosh. To say that Barcelona has Gaudí and Glasgow has Rennie Mackintosh is not over-stating the case. He is not only one of Scotland's most celebrated architects, but also one of the creative geniuses of modern architecture. It is only in the past few decades, however, that his talent has been fully recognised and serious efforts made to preserve his artistic legacy. The restoration of the Willow Tea Rooms, Scotland Street School, Queen's Cross Church and the Mackintosh House at the Hunterian Art Gallery, are all testimony to his prodigious talents, but it is his great masterpiece, the Glasgow School of Art, that really stands out.

Survival of the wittiest

Glasgow has been many things to many people over the years. It has variously been named 'Dear Green Place', 'Second City of the Empire', 'Workshop of the World' and 'No Mean City'. Today, it is simply one of the most interesting cities to visit in Britain. Yet for most of the 20th century people would have laughed if anyone had suggested visiting it for pleasure. The city had a reputation for both violence and poverty and the conditions in its sprawling slums (ironically a legacy of the very industries that had made the city wealthy) were amongst the worst in Britain. It is a reputation that has been slow to shift. As late as 1996 a survey by *The Scotsman* newspaper asking residents of Edinburgh (only 40 miles away) what they associated with Glasgow, came up with: deep fried pizzas, rickets, Rangers and Celtic, Irn Bru and Billy Connolly. Hardly a ringing endorsement.

A clean break In the face of such entrenched attitudes other, less gutsy cities might have given up and spiralled further into decline, but Glasgow refused to accept the seemingly inevitable. Under the banner of its 'Glasgow's Miles Better' campaign, the city began to reinvent itself. Someone once said that all Glasgow needed was a good bath, and they were right. Buildings, blackened by years of pollution, were scrubbed clean, creative talent was nurtured, smart shops and restaurants encouraged to open up in the city. Designers, realising that Glaswegians loved clothes and were prepared to pay for good ones, opened outlets here and soon the city's Italian Centre was the home of both *Armani* and *Versace*. The campaign was so successful that in 1990 the city was nominated European City of Culture, a success it followed by becoming European City of Architecture and Design in 1999. Not only were these triumphs, to the delight of many Glaswegians, the nominations also put Edinburgh's nose severely out of joint. A few rough edges remain, of course, to provide the essential urban grit and the backdrop for the occasional TV detective.

Glasgow smiles better Yes, we know, it's a cliché to say that Glasgow people are friendly, but it's true. This is, without doubt, the friendliest of Britain's large cities. Writer William McIlvanney once said that Glasgow wasn't a city, it was a twenty-four hour cabaret, and this sums up perfectly one of the city's greatest attractions – its sense of humour. The city that gave us Billy Connolly, Jerry Sadowitz and Rab C Nesbit does not take itself too seriously – and cannot be serious for very long. Humour is integral to life here and Glaswegians find it in everything – particularly people from Edinburgh, who they traditionally see as cold, humourless and full of their own importance.

Fighting qualities The Glasgow people are the city's driving force, with their distinctive blend of restless energy, guts and determination, thrawn bloody-mindedness and remarkable fighting qualities. They seem to thrive on adversity, which is just as well, as they've had plenty of it. Glasgow has suffered more economic setbacks than you could shake a closed shipyard at: everything from the American Independence, which effectively put an end to the lucrative tobacco trade, to post-war depression. But it has recovered each time and can now claim with some credibility to be the world's first successful post-industrial city.

Left *Glasgow's medieval cathedral, built on the site of St Mungo's original church. It was Mungo who first brought Christianity to the city and, centuries later, David Livingstone (whose statue is seen here) exported it to Africa*
Centre *The Clyde Auditorium, or 'Armadillo', as it's better known, is one of the symbols of Glasgow's bright, shiny future*
Next page *The wonderfully atmospheric library is one of the highlights of theGlasgow School of Art, Charles Rennie Mackintosh's great masterpiece*

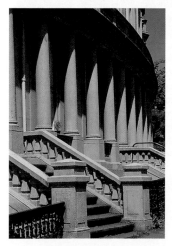

Left *Parts of the West End are characterized by sweeping terraces of elegant neoclaccicism*
Above *The Central Station viaduct was known as the 'Highlandman's Umbrella', as locals used to joke that economic migrants used it to shelter from the rain rather than buy their own umbrella*

Glasgow in a nutshell

The finest examples of Glasgow's rich Victorian architectural legacy can be found in the commercial centre, stretching from George Square west to the M8. Here, in the streets around Blytheswood Hill, great canyons of stone were constructed, transforming the city into a Scottish equivalent of New York or Chicago – a city of high testosterone architecture. While George Square is the heart of modern Glasgow, the area around the medieval cathedral was the heart of the old city. In fact, until the 18th century Glasgow consisted only of a narrow ribbon of streets running north from the river past the Glasgow Cross and up the High Street to the cathedral. Then came the city's rapid expansion west and the High Street became a dilapidated backwater.

East Enders To the east of George Square is the Merchant City, where the elegant warehouses of the 18th century tobacco and sugar merchants are in the process of being cleaned up and reclaimed by the professional classes, not only as the latest des res, but also as a fashionable place to eat, drink, shop and play. Further east is Glasgow's East End, a traditional working-class stronghold which is gradually giving way to the relentless drive of urban gentrification. Here chic café-bars and art galleries rub shoulders with no-nonsense pubs, artery-hardening greasy spoons and sprawling markets selling everything from dodgy video games to second-hand clothes.

West Side Story On the other side of the M8 is the West End, an area which contains many of the city's major museums, as well some of its finest examples of Victorian architecture. During the course of the 19th century the West End grew in importance as wealthy merchants moved there, away from the dirt and grime of the industrial city. Soon after, in 1870, the university also moved west, to its present site overlooking Kelvingrove Park, and in 1896 the Glasgow District Subway was extended west. Now, Glasgow's West End is a mix of youthful hedonsim and suburban calm. The streets between Kelvingrove Park and the Great Western Road, around Hillhead Underground and Byres Road, are alive to the sound of students, shoppers and late-night revellers. Here you'll find the city's most interesting shops, and best pubs and restaurants. Within a stone's throw are the Hunterian Museum, Kelvingrove Art Gallery and Museum and Transport Museum, as well as some dear green spaces, namely Kelvingrove Park and the Botanic Garden. Head further along the Great Western Road, however, and the wild west becomes the mild west as you enter the residential districts of Kelvinside, Anniesland and Knightswood, all bywords for genteel respectability.

Southern comforts South of the River Clyde is a part of Glasgow largely unknown to most tourists, except perhaps for the Gorbals, a name once synonymous with urban violence, but now more likely to inspire ennui rather than fear. Venture further south and you enter a different world, of sedate suburbs known as South Side. Here you'll find two of the city's most notable attractions, the Burrell Collection and Pollok House, both set in the sylvan surrounds of Pollok Country Park. There are other reasons to venture south of the river, not least of these being to see Charles Rennie Mackintosh's House for an Art Lover in nearby Bellahouston Park. Further east is another stop on the Mackintosh trail, the Scotland Street School Museum, and to the south, in Cathcart, is Holmwood House, Alexander 'Greek' Thomson's great architectural masterpiece.

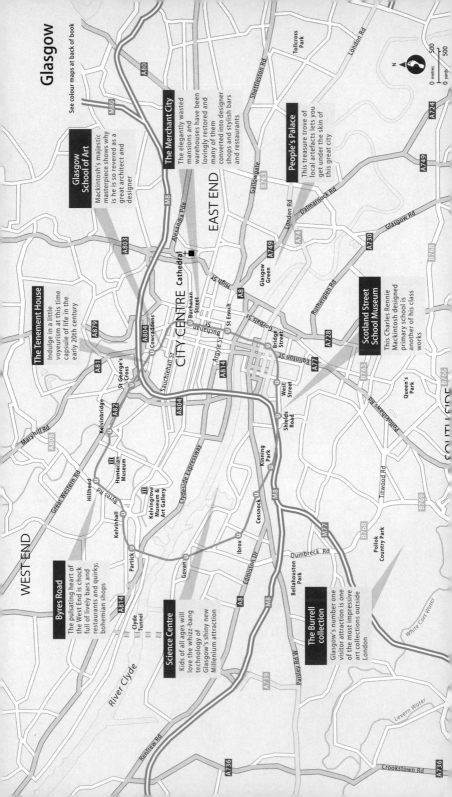

Glasgow

See colour maps at back of book

Glasgow School of Art
Mackintosh's majestic masterpiece shows why is he is so revered as a great architect and designer

The Merchant City
The elegantly wasted mansions and warehouses have been lovingly restored and many of them converted into designer shops and stylish bars and restaurants

The Tenement House
Indulge in a little voyeurism at this time capsule of life in the early 20th century

People's Palace
This treasure trove of local artefacts lets you get under the skin of this great city

Scotland Street School Museum
This Charles Rennie Mackintosh designed primary school is another of his class works

Byres Road
The pulsating heart of the West End is chock full of lively bars and restaurants and quirky, bohemian shops

Science Centre
Kids of all ages will love the whizz-bang technology of Glasgow's shiny new Millenium attraction

The Burrell collection
Glasgow's number one visitor attraction is one of the most impressive art collections outside London

WEST END

CITY CENTRE

EAST END

SOUTH SIDE

River Clyde

Contents

9

10

11

Essentials

Essentials

Planning your trip

Where to go

To get the most out of Glasgow bring a sense of humour and a rainproof jacket. Okay, you may not need the latter, but you will need the former to appreciate one of this city's greatest attractions – its wisecracking citizens. You could spend a great few days simply wandering round soaking up the atmosphere and the renowned Glasgow 'patter'. This the birthplace of comedian Billy Connolly, who always maintained that he knew lots of people who were funnier than him. As William McIlvanney, one of Glasgow's great contemporary novelists, famously remarked, this isn't so much a city as a twenty-four hour cabaret.

Around the city

Glasgow city centre covers the large area from Charing Cross train station and the M8 in the west to Glasgow Green in the east, near the cathedral. It is built on a grid system across some steep hills on the north side of the River Clyde. The heart of the city is **George Square**. Here you'll find the Tourist Information Centre (TIC), and the two main train stations (Central station and Queen Street station), as well as the Buchanan bus station; are all within a couple of blocks. Immediately to the east of George Square is the rejuvenated **Merchant City** which, together with the streets west of George Square, forms the commercial and business centre. The main shopping streets in the city centre are Sauchiehall Street, which runs parallel to the river, west as far as Kelvingrove Park, the pedestianized Buchanan Street, which runs south from the east end of Sauchiehall Street, and Argyle Street, at the south end of Buchanan Street.

The **West End** begins on the other side of the M8, which cuts a swathe through the city. This is the home of Glasgow University and is the city's main student quarter, with many of its best bars, cafés and restaurants. The West End is well connected with the city centre by the Underground. **South of the Clyde** are the more sedate suburbs, know as the South Side. To the southwest are two of Glasgow's main tourist attractions, Pollock House and the Burrell Collection, which can easily be reached from the city centre by train or bus.

The **River Clyde** itself has been added to the list of visitor attractions in recent years. The Clydeside Walkway, which runs all the way from the Scottish Exhibition and Conference Centre (SECC) beyond the city limits to Bothwell Castle in Uddingston, is an attempt to direct Glasgow's great river towards a post-industrial future of leisure and tourism. There are also trips up and down the river in a variety of craft – everything from an ancient paddle steamer to a big blue amphibious car.

Not surprisingly for a city whose name is said to mean 'dear green place', Glasgow boasts quite a few green spaces – more per head of population than any other city in Europe. There are more than 70 parks in all, from **Glasgow Green** in the East End to **Kelvingrove Park** in the West End, and **Queen's Park** and **Pollock Country Park**, both in the South Side. As well as the many green spaces, there are several scenic **walkways** and **cycle paths** in and around the city, giving visitors the opportunity to escape the noise and traffic and to stretch their legs. There are also several long-distance walkways and cycle routes which start in Glasgow. The tourist office has a wide range of maps and leaflets detailing these routes, which follow quiet back streets, public parks and disued railway lines for much of the way.

Best sights

Those who have come to see the sights won't be disappointed, for there are some world-class museums and galleries, many of which are free. To see and do everything recommended below would take five or six days, without rushing around too much.

Top of everyone's list, and the city's most popular visitor attraction, is the **Burrell Collection**, a state-of-the-art building stuffed with priceless antiquities from around the world. In the West End are the **Kelvinhall Museum and Art Gallery** and the **Transport Museum**. Across the other side of town, in the East End, is the fascinating **People's Palace**, which tells the story of this great city, while on the north side of the city centre is the strangely beguiling **Tenement House**, a time capsule of life in pre-war Glasgow.

And then, of course, there's Charles Rennie Mackintosh, Glasgow's answer to Gaudí. Many visitors come solely to admire the genius of the man, and his master-piece, the **Glasgow School of Art**, is not to be missed. Most of the Mackintosh sights are in and around the city centre, with the exception of Hill House in Helensburgh, and can be visited comfortably in two or three days. Lovers of fine buildings will also want to see some examples of Alexander 'Greek' Thomson, Glasgow's other great architect, especially **Holmwood House**, which has been described as a 'sonnet in stone'.

Glasgow is also a great city for shopping, and once you've tired of sightseeing you can head for **The Barras** in the East End, Glasgow's biggest market, where you can hear the patter as well as possibly unearthing a bargain or two. At the other extreme are the chic boutiques and expensive designer stores of the **Merchant City**, and somewhere in between there are the quirky, bohemian shops in the little cobbled lanes around **Byres Road** in the West End.

When to go

Glasgow is worth visiting at any time of the year, but the **high season** is from May to September – when the weather tends to be at its best – and this is when the city receives the vast majority of visitors. Prices at this time of year will also be higher. Another busy time is Hogmanay, or New Year to sassenachs.

Climate — Glasgow is one of the wettest cities in the UK and there are times when the cloud cover is so pervasive it feels like being enclosed in a Tupperware box. The Scottish climate is notoriously unpredictable, and a bright, sunny morning can turn into a downpour in the time it takes to butter your toast. Predicting the weather is not an exact science and tables of statistics are most likely a waste of time. There's an old saying in Scotland that if you don't like the weather, then wait 20 minutes. Generally speaking, May to September are the warmest months, with an average summer high of around 18-19°C, and though they are often the driest months, you can expect rain at any time of the year, even in high summer. So, you'll need to come prepared, and remember the old hikers' adage that there's no such thing as bad weather, only inadequate clothing. Two excellent weather forecast websites are www.met-office.gov.uk and www.bbc.co.uk/weather

Tours and tour operators

There are numerous organized tours on offer, from bus or walking tours of the city to more personalized special-interest tours. There are also a number of **cruises on the Clyde**, see page 120 for details. In addition, for those who want to escape the city, there are coach and mini-bus tours covering all parts of Scotland.

City bus tours — One of the best ways to see the city sights is to take a **guided bus tour** on board an
Tickets for city open-top, double-decker bus with a multi-lingual guide. They stop at the main tour-
bus tours are also ist sights including the cathedral, Tall Ship, Botanic Gardens, Kelvingrove Art Gallery,
available at the Hunterian Museum and Glasgow School of Art. Tickets are valid for the full day and
tourist office you can hop on and off any of the company's buses at any of the stops. Adult £7.50,

OAPs and students £6, children (5-12 years) £2.50, family ticket £19.50 (two adults and up to four children).

Guide Friday Tours, 2nd Floor, St Georges Buildings, 5 St Vincent Place, T2487644, www.guidefriday.com Buses depart from George Square every 30 minutes, from 0930 till 1530, March-October. Tour lasts 1 hour 20 minutes. Tickets also allow discounts on many of the city's main attractions, they can be bought from the bus driver or at the Guide Friday Tourism Centre. *City Sightseeing Glasgow Ltd*, 153 Queen St, T2040444, www.scotguide.com Buses depart every 10-15 minutes in summer (less frequently in winter) from George Square, the first one leaving around 0900 and the last one between 1730 and 2000, depending on the time of year. The complete tour lasts one hour. Tickets can be purchased from driver, the TIC or at the Buchanan bus station. They also run tours to some of Scotland's major destinations such as Loch Lomond and Loch Ness.

There are various **guided walks** around the city. The *Scottish Tourist Guides Association*, T/F01786-447784, offer a variety of entertaining and informative tours. *Mercat Tours*, T7720022, www.mercattours.com, offer the chilling 'Gruesome Glasgow Tour', daily at 1900, and 'Ghosts and Ghouls Tour', daily 2100, which leave from outside the TIC in George Square, from April to October. They also offer themed on walks on various aspects of Glasgow's history.

City walking tours

Lovers of literature, or those who like a good laugh, should try *The Glasgow Literary Tour*, a witty and fascinating journey through the city's famous and forgotten novelists, and contemporary and controversial writers. They run in June Thursday-Sunday at 1800, July-August daily at 1800 and 2030, and September Thursday-Sunday and should be booked in advance, T0131-2266665. Tickets cost £5, £3.50 concession. All these walking tours last 1½ hours.

Essentials

British Tourist Authority offices overseas

The BTA represents the STB abroad. More information can be obtained from their website (www.bta.org.uk), or from the offices listed below:

Australia *Level 16, The Gateway, 1 Macquarie Pl, Circular Quay, Sydney NSW 2000, T02-93774400, F02-93774499.*

Belgium and Luxembourg *306 Av Louise, 1050 Brussels, T2-6463510, F2-6463986.*

Canada *111 Avenue Rd, Suite 450, Toronto, Ontario MR5 3J8, T416-9256326, F416-9612175.*

Denmark *Montergade 3, 1116 Copenhagen K, T33-339188, F33-140136.*

France *Maison de la Grande-Bretagne, 19 Rue des Mathurins, 75009 Paris, T1-44515620, F1-44515621.*

Germany, Austria and Switzerland *Taunustrasse 52-60, 60329 Frankfurt, T69-2380711.*

Ireland *18/19 College Green, Dublin 2, T1-6708000, F1-6708244.*

Italy *Corso Vittorio Emanuele II No 337, 00186 Rome, T6-68806821, F6-6879095.*

Netherlands *Stadhouderskade 2 (5e), 1054 ES Amsterdam, T20-6855051, F20-6186868.*

New Zealand *17th Flr, Fay Richwhite Building, 151 Queen St, Auckland 1, T09-3031446, F09-3776965.*

South Africa *Lancaster Gate, Hyde Park Lane, Hyde Park 2196, Johannesburg, T011-3250342.*

USA *7th Flr, 551 Fifth Av, New York, NY 10176-0799, T212-986-2200/ 1-800-GO-2-BRITAIN. 10880 Wilshire Blvd, Suite 570, Los Angeles, CA 90024, T310-4702782.*

Alternatively, try a self guided tour with *Walkabout Tours*. You pick up one of their audio machines from the Tourist Information Centre in George Square, then use it to guide you around the city centre and Cathedral Precinct. £5. For details visit www.walkabout-tours.com

Mackintosh tours The *Charles Rennie Mackintosh Society* runs 'Mackintosh in Style Weekends' through-out the year. They visit the main sights around the city, and Hill House in Helensburgh, and the tour includes two nights dinner, bed and breakfast, plus lunch in the *Willow Tea Rooms*. From £212 for shared accommodation. For more information and dates contact the Mackintosh Society (see page).

Special interest & taxi tours *Glasgow Stadttouren Auf Deutsch* (GSD Tours), 14 Inverewe Drive, Deaconsbank, Glasgow, T6210417, James.Moore1@tesco.net run tours of the Merchant City and other parts of the city for German-speaking visitors, as well as themed nights. *Taxi Owner's Association (TOA)*, T4297070, www.gwtoa.co.uk runs city and country tours on request. Tours of historical places of interest last from one to three hours. Most taxis have wheelchair facilities.

Tours around Scotland There are many companies offering general-interest or special-interest tours of Scotland. Travel agents will have details, or you can check the small ads in the travel sections of news-papers, or contact the *British Tourist Authority* or *Scottish Tourist Board* for a list of opera-tors (see boxes on this page and page 17 for contact details).

If you are travelling with friends or family and would prefer your own, tailor-made itin-erary, perhaps to include visits to Glasgow or Edinburgh, golf, sightseeing, castles, dis-tilleries, festivals or highland games, contact *Scotland Tours*, www.scot-land-tours.com

Two recommended British companies aimed at the more mature traveller are *Saga Holidays*, Saga Building, Middelburg Square, Folkestone, Kent CT20 1AZ, T0800-

Scottish Tourist Boards

Scottish Tourist Board Central
Information Department *23 Ravelston*
Terr, Edinburgh EH4 3EU, T0131-3322433,
www.visitscotland.com
In London *19 Cockspur St, London*
SW1 5BL, T020-7930 2812.

Area Tourist Boards
Argyll, the Isles, Loch Lomond, Stirling
& Trossachs Tourist Board *7 Alexandra*
Par, Dunoon, Argyll PA23 8AB,
T01369-701000,

www.scottish.heartlands.org
Ayrshire & Arran Tourist Board
Burns House, Burns Statue Sq, Ayr KA7 1UP,
T01292-288688,
www.ayrshire-arran.com
Dumfries & Galloway Tourist Board
64 Whitesands, Dumfries
DG1 2RS, T01387-253862,
www.galloway.co.uk
Edinburgh & Lothians Tourist Board
3 Princes St, Edinburgh EH2 2QP,
T0131-4733800, www.edinburgh.org

Essentials

300500 and *Shearings Holidays*, Miry Lane, Wigan, Lancs WN3 4AG, T01942-824824. Saga also operates in the USA, 222 Berkeley Street, Boston, MA 02116; and in Australia, Level 1, 10-14 Paul Street, Milsons Point, Sydney 2061.

Other **specialist tour operators in the USA** are *Abercrombie & Kent*, T1-800-323 7308, www.abercrombiekent.com, *Especially Britian*, T1-800-869 0538, *Prestige Tours*, T1-800-890 7375, *Sterling Tours*, T1-800-727 4359, www.sterlingtours.com and *Cross-Culture*, 52 High Point Dr, Amherst, MA 01002-1224, T800-491 1148, www.crosscultureinc.com

Scot-Trek, 9 Lawrence Street, T/F3349232, organizes guided walks and holidays for all   Trekking tours
levels of walkers, from day rambles to seven-day mountain treks. *Travel-lite at 'McFarlanes'*, 5 Mugdock Road, Milngavie, Glasgow, T9567890, will collect and drop your rucksack at convenient locations along the West Highland Way, from mid-April till the end of September.

Finding out more

The best way of finding out more information for your trip to Glasgow is to contact the **Greater Glasgow & Clyde Valley Tourist Board**. You can also contact the **British Tourist Authority** (BTA) in your country or write (or email) direct to the head office of the **Scottish Tourist Board** (STB). (see boxes above and on page 16 for contact details). The BTA and STB can provide a wealth of free literature and information such as maps, city guides, events calendars and accommodation brochures. Travellers with special needs should also contact their nearest BTA office.

The main **Tourist Information Centre** is at 11 George Square, T2044400, F2213524, www.seeglasgow.com open May daily 0900-1800; June and September daily 0900-1900; July and August daily 0900-2000; October-April Monday-Saturday 0900-1800. They provide an excellent service, including a wide selection of maps and leaflets and a free accommodation booking service. You can also buy travel passes, theatre tickets, arrange car rental and exchange currency at their *bureau de change*.

Various maps of the city are available, including the Tourist Board's useful free city cen-   Maps
tre map and the very handy *Glasgow Popout Map*. A much more detailed and comprehensive map for those wishing to explore the nooks and crannies of the city is the *Ordnance Survey Glasgow Street Atlas* (£5.99).

Essentials

Useful websites   The official Scottish Tourist Board site and the various area tourist board sites provide information on accommodation, transport and tourist sights as well as on outdoor activities such as walking, skiing, fishing amongst others. **www.britannia.com**   is a huge UK travel site. Click on 'Scotland Guide' for a massive selection of subjects plus links to other useful sites including newspapers. Also useful is **www.bbc.co.uk**   the UK's most popular site with an excellent 'What's On' guide.

www.electricscotland.com   Massive directory with lots of information on clans, travel etc. Also with in-depth history pages.

www.scotland.gov.uk   Updates on government affairs in Scotland.

www.scottish.parliament.uk   Easy-to-use guide to the Scottish Parliament.

www.geo.ed.ac.uk/home/scotland/scotland/html   Background information on history, politics and geography.

www.scotland.net   Scotland online; offers good information on golf, walking and climbing and also features **www.travelscotland.co.uk**   run in conjunction with the STB, offering magazine-style features and reviews.

www.scotland-info.co.uk   Good for local information on hotels, shops and restaurants.

www.aboutscotland.co.uk   Useful for accommodation.

www.walkscotland.com   Suggested walks, contacts and practical information for hikers and climbers.

www.golfscotland.co.uk   Everything you need to know on golf in Scotland.

www.ski.scotland.net   Information on ski conditions at all centres, updated daily.

www.born2ski.com and **www.ifyouski.com**   Both sites have Scotland pages with useful ratings of ski sites.

www.ceolas.org   Celtic music site with lots of information and sounds.

www.scotchwhisky.net   Everything you ever wanted to know about the "water of life".

www.clyde-valley.com/glasgow   Covers all Glasgow sights and is updated regularly.

www.whatsonwhen.com   For a good selection of events and venues.

www.glasgowlife.com   News and schedule of events, plus much more.

www.rangers.co.uk   Official site of Glasgow Rangers FC.

www.celtic.co.uk   Official site for Glasgow Celtic FC.

www.gigguide.co.uk   Lists live music events and includes chat rooms.

www.crmsociety.com   Official site of the Charles Rennie Mackintosh Society, with details of all the sites, forthcoming events and a virtual tour of Queen's Cross Church.

Language

For a more detailed discussion, plus a glossary of words and phrases, see page206   Glaswegian is one of the most distinctive regional dialects in Britain, having evolved over the centuries to become almost a complete language with its own extensive vocabulary and grammar. As in other large industrial cities such as Liverpool and London, social change and instability has been reflected in linguistic development, though it is only recently that the local dialect has been considered worthy of academic study and as a medium for serious literature.

Disabled travellers

For travellers with disabilities visiting Glasgow, and the rest of Scotland, independently can be a difficult business. While most theatres, cinemas and modern tourist attractions are accessible to wheelchairs, **accommodation** is more problematic. Many large, new hotels do have disabled suites, but will charge more, and most B&Bs, guesthouses and smaller hotels are not designed to cater for people with disabilities. **Public**

transport is just as bad, though newer buses have lower steps for easier access and some *ScotRail* intercity services now accommodate wheelchair-users in comfort. Glasgow Underground is currently inaccessible to wheelchair users. Govan, Partick and St Enoch stations are accessible by escalator only, though these can be switched off, on request, for use by the visually impaired and guide-dog users. Staff are in general are very helpful. Taxis, as opposed to minicabs, all carry wheelchair ramps, and if a driver says he or she can't take a wheelchair, it's because they're too lazy to fetch the ramp.

Wheelchair users and blind or partially sighted people are automatically given 30-50% discount on train fares, and those with other disabilities are eligible for the **Disabled Person's Railcard**, which costs £14 per year and gives a third off most tickets. There are no reductions on buses, however.

If you are disabled you should contact the travel officer of your national support organization. They can provide literature or put you in touch with travel agents specializing in tours for the disabled. The Scottish Tourist Board produces a guide, *Accessible Scotland*, for disabled travellers, and many local tourist offices can provide accessibility details for their area. For more information, contact **Disability Scotland**, Princes House, 5 Shandwick Place, Edinburgh EH2 4RG, T0131-2298632. The **Royal Association for Disability and Rehabilitation** (RADAR), Unit 12, City Forum, 250 City Road, London, EC1V 8AF, T020-72503222, www.radar.org.uk, is a good source of advice and information, and produces an annual guide on travelling in the UK (£7.50 including P&P). The **Holiday Care Service**, 2nd Floor, Imperial Building, Victoria Road, Horley, Surrey, RH6 7PZ, T-1293-774535, provides free lists of accessible accommodation and travel in the UK.

The **Ultimate Guide to Disability Access & Transport Within Glasgow** provides access transport information and includes eating out, shopping, places of interest, entertainment, places of worship and accommodation. For more information contact The Glasgoe Access Panel, c/o GCVS, 11 Queens Crescent, Glasgow, G4 9AS, T3322444, gcvs@cqm.co.uk

Information & organizations (margin)

Gay and lesbian travellers

In the past, Glasgow had a reputation for being violent (where the 'hard man' originated from), yet its inhabitants are known for being friendly, unpretentious and extremely talkative. Gay Glasgow is fun, thriving, visible and full of diversity. There are plenty of pubs, clubs and cafes to choose from, many of them downtown at the 'gay village' in the Merchant City. You can dip into them briefly , until you find out which one you like. And with them being open all hours, there is something for everyone.

Glasgow is easy to get round, either by clockwork orange subway, bus or on foot, so it is worth venturing beyond the gay village. The city is beautiful with a gay presence all over. Byres Road in the fashionable West End has a coffee shop every 10 yards, many with full-length windows facing onto the street so you can watch the gay shoppers parade by. In the summer Kelvingrove Park and Queens Park are ideal for gay sunbathing. Culturally, there's plenty happening in terms of great theatre, stimulating movies, live music, and impressive art galleries (most of them free). Each year **Glasgay**, the lesbian and gay arts festival, running from late October to November, becomes stronger , while **Scottish Gay Pride** is in late June. Enjoy.

For a list of gay venues, ▶▶ go to page 133

Bi-G-Les, c/o LGBT, 11 Dixon Street, 221 7203. Youth group for bisexuals, lesbians and gay men that meets weekly. **Body Positive**, 3 Park Quadrant, 3325010. HIV/AIDS support and advice. **Centre for Women's Health** 2 Sandyford Place, 2116700. Centre providing information and services to women. Specific services for lesbians. Glasgow Women's Library ,109 Trongate, T5528345. Open Tuesday-Friday 1300-1800; Saturday

Gay contacts (margin)

1400-1700. Lesbian archive and information centre. **Lesbian Line**, PO Box 686, G3 7TL, T5523355. Lesbian support line.

PHACE West, 49 Bath Street, T3323838. Information and support for those affected by HIV/AIDS. **Steve Retson Project**, 2 Sandyford Place, T2218601. Open Tuesday and Thursday 1730-2030. Sexual health clinic for gay men. **Stonewall Scotland**, LGBT Centre, 11 Dixon Street, T2040022. Campaigning equality group for lesbians and gay men. **Strathclyde Lesbian & Gay Switchboard**, PO Box 38, G2 2QE, T3328372. Open 1900-2200 daily. Helpline for gay men and lesbians.

Gay outlets   *Clone Zone*, 11 Dixon Street, T2484485. In the foyer of the LGBT centre, a small shop crammed full of gay goodies. *EasyEverything Internet Café*, 57-61 St Vincent Street. Open 24 hours. After the clubs, this centrally located café gets filled with gay punters surfing on the internet.

Saunas   *Centurion Sauna*, 19 Dixon Street, T2484485. 1200-2200. Ring the buzzer, then ascend the steps to this sauna on the first floor, above Somerfield supermarket. It used to be an office complex, and the sticky floor still hints at its past. It has sauna cabins, a steam room, rest areas, and attracts a mixed age range. *The Lane*, 60 Robertson Street Lane. T2211802. 1200-2200. £10/8. Small out-of-the-way sauna with lockers and private cabins.

Accommodation   *Glasgow Guest House*, 56 Dumbreck Rd, T4270129. Six twin bedrooms, gay friendly guest house, 5 minutes from the city centre by bus.

Magazines &   *Gay Scotland* magazine, T5572625, is a good source of information, and *The List*, the
websites   Edinburgh and Glasgow listings magazine, is also useful. There's also the UK gay-scene index at **www.queenscene.com** which has information on clubs, gay groups, accommodation, events, HIV/AIDS and cultural and ethical issues. Other good sites include: **www.gaybritain.co.uk**; **www.gaytravel.co.uk www.rainbownetwork .com** and **www.gaypride.co.uk**

Student travellers

See also the Getting   There are various official youth/student ID cards available. The most useful is the **Inter-**
there and Getting   **national Student ID Card** (ISIC). For a mere £6 the ISIC card gains you access to the
around sections for   exclusive world of student travel with a series of discounts, including most forms of
information on   local transport, up to 30% off international airfares, cheap or free admission to muse-
student/youth travel   ums, theatres and other attractions, and cheap meals in some restaurants. You'll also
discounts   receive the ISIC handbook, which ensures you get the most out of the services available. For more details contact T08708-413224, www.isiccard.com, or call in to *STA Travel*, the country's leading student travel centre (see page 27). They are more than happy to seek out the best travel bargains and will help with flights and insurance. Contact manager.glasgow@statravel.co.uk to receive mailing of the latest deals.

Citizens of Canada and the USA are entitled to emergency medical coverage, and there's a 24-hour hotline to call in the event of medical, legal or financial emergencies.

If you're aged under 26 but not a student, you can apply for a **Federation of Inter-national Youth Travel Organisations** (FIYTO) card, or a **Euro 26 Card**, which give you much the same discounts. If you're 25 or younger you can qualify for a **Go-25 Card**, which gives you the same benefits as an ISIC card. These discount cards are issued by STA and hostelling organizations (see page 144).

Studying in   If you want to study in Scotland you must first prove you can financially support and
Scotland   accommodate yourself without working and without recourse to public support. Your

A day out for the family

Start with a visit to the **Glasgow Science Centre** on the South Bank of the Clyde (there's a café here too), then take the path that runs to the right of the centre, along the Clyde. It brings you to Bell's Bridge, a pedestrian swing bridge over the river. Cross this, then walk along to your left, down to the **Tall Ship at Glasgow Harbour**. When you've visited this, you can walk a little further down to your left to see (if you're in luck) the helicopters land on the nearby helipad (kids love this). Afterwards you can walk back to the Tall Ship, from where you can take a trip down the river, or walk back to the Science Centre, where you can join a **glasgowducks** tour in an amphibious vehicle. You can then head off to **Harry Ramsden's**, 251 Paisley Road (T4293700) for fish and chips and lashings of ginger.

Essentials

studies should take up at least 15 hours a week for a minimum of six months. Once you are studying, you are allowed to do 20 hours of casual work per week in the term time and you can work full-time during the holidays. In **North America** full-time students can obtain temporary work or study permits through the **Council of International Education Exchange** (CIEE), 205 E 42nd Street, New York, NY 10017, T212-8222600, www.ciee.org

Travelling with children

Inform the airline in advance that you're travelling with a baby or toddler and check out the facilities when booking as these vary with each aircraft. **British Airways** now has a special seat for under-twos; check which aircraft have been fitted with them when booking. Pushchairs can be taken on as hand luggage or stored in the hold. Skycots are available on long-haul flights. Take snacks and toys for in-flight entertainment and remember that swallowing food or drinks during take-off and landing will help prevent ear problems.

Visit www.babygoes2.com for in-depth advice

A large number of hotels and guesthouses welcome children and offer a babysitting/listening service. Some hotels that actively encourage families with toddlers are: *Novotel*, 181 Pitt Street, T2222775, www.accorhotels.com; *Bewleys Hotel*, 100 Bath Street, T3530800, www.bewleyshotel.com; and *Jurys Glasgow Hotel*, Great Western Road, T3348161, www.jurysdoyle.com

Sleeping *For full details and listings* ▶▶ *go to page 139*

Two particularly child-friendly restaurants in the city centre are: *TGI Fridays*, 113 Buchanan Street, T2216996, open daily 1100-2330; and *Di Maggio's Pizzeria*, 21 Royal Exchange Square, T2482111, which has other branches throughout the city. If you want to eat out with younger children one place worth trying is *Alphabet Yard*, 15 Millbrae, T6496861, in South Side. It has a play barn for kids and is always full of families. Open Sunday-Thursday 1200-2145, Friday and Saturday 1200-2200.

Eating *All 3 restaurants are in the mid-range category*

Keeping the kids occupied is a great deal easier in Glasgow than in many other cities. Not only do many museums and attractions make a real effort to cater for children, there are also plenty of leisure centres and parks in which they can let off steam. One place that is sure to please both small children and surly teenagers (as well as their fathers) is the glistening new **Glasgow Science Centre** (T4205010, www.gsc.org.uk) on the Clyde. It has loads of interactive exhibits and looks at all aspects of science, from the workings of the human body, to genetic modification and the internet. There's even a lab where visitors can examine specimens under microscopes. It's bright, lively and, if you go up the tower, has great views over Glasgow.

Places to go

Other museums worth visiting include the **Transport Museum** (T2872720) – boys seem to love the old fire engines and trains – the **Tall Ship at Glasgow Harbour** (T3390631), and the **Scottish National Football Museum** at Hampden Park (T6204000). A trip here also gives you the opportunity to take a tour of the ground. Then there's **The People's Palace** (T5540223), one of those museums which really does seem to have something to please the whole family. Kids love exhibits like the old 'cludgie' or outside toilet, as well as the funny old bathing suits worn on holidays 'Doon the Watter' at resorts like Saltcoats and Rothesay (there's even a knitted bikini c. 1930). The original 'steamie' (communal laundry) that once stood on Ingram Street has old clothes and a washboard, and kids are encouraged to have a go at doing the washing in the old-fashioned way.

More nostalgia is on offer at **Scotland Street School Museum**, which has reconstructed classrooms from the Victorian era, the 1940s and the 1960s. Kids used to the informality of the modern school find the rigid severity of these early classrooms intriguing. The museum also has computer activities and games.

It's also really worth making the journey out to **New Lanark** (T01555-661345, www.newlanark.org), the industrial village,planned and built in the 18th century which has loads of atmosphere and gives children a vivid insight into life 200 years ago.

In **The Lighthouse**, Scotland's Centre for Architecture and Design (T2258414), there's an Education Centre that includes a Young Designers Gallery and a Wee People's City, which is aimed at children aged three to eight and encourages them to learn about the city in an unusual way. While this is aimed at schools, you can often gain access if you book beforehand.

For theatre aimed at children you can try the **Sharmanka Gallery** in King Street, where kinetic sculptures made from scrap perform to music. It has been variously described as ghoulish, hilarious and unforgettable, and there are special children's performances.

Places to let off steam There are plenty of leisure facilities in the city where kids can let off steam. The St Enoch and Braehead shopping centres both have skating rinks, while out of the city at Coatbridge is **The Time Capsule** (T01236 449572), a huge, water leisure complex where kids can swim and slide until they're exhausted. Glasgow also has over 70 parks and gardens including **Strathclyde Country Park** (T01698 266155), which has facilities for watersports. Out at Lochwinnoch is **Muirshiel Country Park** (T01505 842803, www.scottishpark.com), which has several walks and trails, and there is also an **RSPB Nature Reserve** (T01505-842663, www.rspb.org.uk) where kids get the chance to observe birds in the wild. There are also a number of cycle ways and walkways in and around the city. Trips along the river are also popular with kids and the choice ranges from a trip on the paddle steamer **Waverley** to a powerboat ride (see page 119).

Women travellers

Travelling in Scotland is neither easier nor more difficult for women than travelling in other other parts of the UK. Generally speaking, Scots are friendly and courteous and even lone women travellers should experience nothing unpleasant. In the main cities and larger towns, the usual precautions need to be taken and you should avoid walking in quiet, unlit streets and parks at night. See also Safety on page 34

Overseas consulates

The following consulates are in Glasgow (Phone code: 0141):

Germany 158 West Regent Street, T2210304.

Italy 24 St Enoch Square, T2263000.
Norway 80 Oswald Street, T2041353.
Spain 389 Argyle Street, T2216943.
Sweden 16 Robertson Street, T2217845.

Working in Scotland

Citizens of **European Union** (EU) countries can live and work in Britain freely without a visa, but **non-EU residents** need a permit to work legally. This can be difficult to obtain without the backing of an established company or employer in the UK. Also, visitors from Commonwealth countries who are aged between 17 and 27 may apply for a working holiday-maker's visa which permits them to stay in the UK for up to two years and work on a casual basis (ie non-career oriented). These certificates are only available from British embassies and consulates abroad, and you must have proof of a valid return or onward ticket, as well as means of support during your stay. **Commonwealth** citizens with a parent or grandparent born in the UK can apply for a **Certificate of Entitlement to the Right of Abode**, allowing them to work in Britain.

An option for citizens of some **non-commonwealth** countries is to visit on an 'au pair' placement in order to learn English by living with an English-speaking family for a maximum of two years. Au pairs must be aged between 17 and 27, and come from one of the following countries: Andorra, Bosnia-Herzegovina, Croatia, Cyprus, Czech Republic, The Faroes, Greenland, Hungary, Macedonia, Malta, Monaco, San Marino, Slovak Republic, Slovenia, Switzerland or Turkey. This can be a good way to learn English, but check out the precise conditions of your placement before taking it up. For more details, contact your nearest British embassy, consulate or high commission, or the **Foreign and Commonwealth Office** in London (see below).

Pick up a copy of What Scotland, a free guide for independent travellers living and working in Scotland, T020-73849330

Before you travel

Getting in

Visa regulations are subject to change, so it is essential to check with your local British embassy, high commission or consulate before leaving home. Citizens of all European countries – except Albania, Bosnia-Herzegovina, Bulgaria, Macedonia, Romania, Slovak Republic, Yugoslavia and all former Soviet republics (other than the Baltic states) – require only a passport to enter Britain and can generally stay for up to three months. Citizens of Australia, Canada, New Zealand, South Africa or the USA can stay for up to six months, providing they have a return ticket and sufficient funds to cover their stay. Citizens of most other countries require a visa from the commission or consular office in the country of application.

For **visa extensions** contact the Home Office, Immigration and Nationality Department, Lunar House, Wellesley Road, Croydon, London CR9 2BY, T020-86860688, before your existing visa expires. Citizens of **Australia**, **Canada**, **New Zealand**, **South Africa** or the **USA** wishing to stay longer than six months will need an Entry Clearance Certificate from the British High Commission in their country. For more details, contact your nearest British embassy, consulate or high commission, or the Foreign and Commonwealth Office in London, T020-72701500. Also, the **Immigration Advisory Service** (IAS) offers free and confidential advice to anyone

Visas
The Foreign Office's website (www.fco.gov.uk) provides details of British immigration and visa requirements

British embassies abroad

Australia High Commission: Commonwealth Av, Yarralumla, Canberra, ACT 2600, T02-62706666, www.uk.emb.gov.au

Canada High Commission: 80 Elgin St, Ottowa, K1P 5K7, T613-2371530, www.bis-canada.org

France 9 Av Hoche, 8e, Paris, T01-42663810.

Germany Friedrich-Ebert-Allee 77, 53113, Bonn, T0228-234061.

Ireland 29 Merrion Rd, Ballsbridge, Dublin 4, T01-2053700.

Israel 192 Hayarkon St, Tel Aviv, T3-7251222, www.britemb.org.il/

Netherlands Koningslaan 44, 1075AE Amsterdam, T20-6764343.

New Zealand High Commission: 44 Hill St, Wellington, T04-4726049, www.brithighcomm.org.nz

South Africa High Commission: 91 Parliament St, Cape Town 8001, T21-4617220.

USA 3100 Massachusetts Av NW, Washington DC 20008, T202-4621340, www.britain-info.org

applying for entry clearance into the UK: County House, 190 Great Dover Street, London SE1 4YB, T020-73576917, www.vois.org.uk

Customs regulations & tax

For more information on British import regulations, contact HM Customs and Excise, Dorset House, Stamford Street, London, SE1 9PJ, T020-79283344, www.hmce. gov.uk

Visitors from EU countries do not have to make a declaration to customs on entry into the UK. The limits for **duty-paid goods** from within the EU are 800 cigarettes, or 1kg of tobacco, 10 litres of spirits, 20 litres of fortified wine, 90 litres of wine and 110 litres of beer. There is no longer any duty-free shopping. Visitors from non-EU countries are allowed to import 200 cigarettes, or 250 g of tobacco, two litres of wine, and two litres of fortified wine or one litre of spirits. There are various import restrictions, most of which should not affect the average tourist. There are tight **quarantine restrictions** which apply to animals brought from overseas (except for Ireland). Many goods in Britain are subject to a **Value Added Tax** (VAT) of 17.5%, with the major exception of books and food. Visitors from non-EU countries can save money through the Retail Export Scheme, which allows a refund of VAT on goods that are to be taken out of the country. Note that not all shops are participants in the scheme and that VAT cannot be reclaimed on hotel bills or other services.

What to take

You'll be able to find everything you could possibly need for your trip in Glasgow, so you can pack light and buy stuff as you go along. Given the climate, however, you should bring warm and waterproof clothing, whatever the time of year. Also bring light clothes in the summer.

A **sleeping bag** is useful in hostels. A **sleeping sheet** with a pillow cover is needed for staying in **Scottish Youth Hostel Association** (SYHA) hostels to save you the cost of having to hire one. A padlock can also be handy for locking your bag if it has to be stored in a hostel for any length of time. Other useful items include an alarm clock (for those early ferry departures), an adaptor plug for electrical appliances, an elastic clothes line and, if you're hill-walking or camping, a Swiss Army knife, torch (flashlight) and compass.

Insurance

It's a good idea to take out some form of travel insurance, wherever you're travelling from. This should cover you for theft or loss of possessions and money, the cost of all medical and dental treatment, cancellation of flights, delays in travel arrangements, accidents, missed departures, lost baggage, lost passport, and personal liability and legal expenses.

There are a variety of policies to choose from, so it's best to shop around to get the best price. Your travel agent can also advise you on the best deals available. *STA Travel* and other reputable student travel organizations often offer good-value travel policies. Travellers from North America can try the *International Student Insurance Service* (ISIS), which is available through *STA Travel*, T1-800-7770112, www.sta-travel.com Some other recommended travel insurance companies in North America include: *Travel Guard*, T1-800-8261300, www.noelgroup.com; *Access America*, T1-800- 2848300; *Travel Insurance Services*, 1-800-9371387; *Travel Assistance International*, T1-800-8212828; and *Council Travel*, 1-888-COUNCIL, www.counciltravel.com Another company worth calling for a quote is *Columbus Direct*, T020-7375 0011. **Older travellers** should note that some companies either won't cover people over 65 years old, or may charge high premiums. The best policies for older travellers are offered by *Age Concern*, T01883-346964.

Points to note: you should always read the small print carefully. Some policies exclude 'dangerous activities' such as scuba diving, skiing, horse riding or even trekking. Not all policies cover ambulance, helicopter rescue or emergency flights home. Find out if your policy pays medical expenses direct to the hospital or doctor, or if you have to pay and then claim the money back later. If the latter applies, make sure you keep all records. Whatever your policy, if you are unfortunate enough to have something stolen, make sure you get a copy of the police report, as you will need this to substantiate your claim.

Money

The British currency is the pound sterling (£), divided into 100 pence (p). Coins come in denominations of 1p, 2p, 5p, 10p, 20p, 50p, £1 and £2. *Bank of England* banknotes are legal tender in Scotland, in addition to those issued by the *Bank of Scotland*, *Royal Bank of Scotland* and *Clydesdale Bank*. These Scottish banknotes (bills) come in denominations of £1, £5, £10, £20, £50 and £100 and are legal tender in the rest of Britain, though some shopkeepers south of the border may be reluctant to accept them.

Credit cards & ATMs Most hotels, shops and restaurants in Scotland accept the major credit cards (*Access/MasterCard*, *Visa* and *Amex*), though some places may charge for using them. They may be less useful in more remote rural areas and smaller establishments such as B&Bs which will often only accept cash. You can withdraw cash from selected banks and Automatic Telling Machines – ATMs, or 'cashpoints' as they are called in Britain – with your cash card. Your bank or credit card company will be able to give you a list of locations where you can use your card.

Visa card holders can use the *Bank of Scotland*, *Clydesdale Bank*, *Royal Bank of Scotland* and *TSB* ATMs; *Access/MasterCard* holders can use the *Royal Bank* and *Clydesdale*; *Amex* card holders can use the *Bank of Scotland*.

If you have an account with a high-street bank in England or Wales, you can use your cashpoint card in Scotland. *Bank of Scotland* and *Royal Bank* accept *Lloyds* and *Barclays* cash cards; *Clydesdale* accepts *HSBC/Midland* and *National Westminster* cards. *Bank of Scotland*, *Clydesdale* and most building society cashpoints are part of the Link network and accept all affiliated cards.

Travellers' cheques The safest way to carry money is in the form of travellers' cheques. These are available for a small commission from all major banks. *American Express (Amex)*, *Visa* and *Thomas Cook* cheques are widely accepted and are the most commonly issued by banks. You'll normally have to pay commission again when you cash each cheque. This will usually be one percent, or a flat rate. No commission is payable on *Amex* cheques cashed at *Amex* offices. Make sure to keep a record of the cheque numbers and the cheques you've cashed separate from the cheques themselves, so that you can get a full refund of all uncashed cheques should you lose them. It's best to bring sterling cheques to avoid changing currencies twice. Also note that in Britain travellers' cheques are rarely accepted outside banks, so you'll need to cash them in advance and keep a good supply of ready cash.

Money transfers If you need money urgently, the quickest way to have it sent to you is to have it **wired** to the nearest bank via *Western Union* (T0800-833833) or *Moneygram* (T0800-894887). Charges are on a sliding scale – so it costs proportionately less to wire out larger sums money. Money can also be wired by *Thomas Cook* or *American Express*, though this may take a day or two, or transferred via a bank draft, but this can take up to a week.

Banks & bureaux de change Bank opening hours are Monday-Friday from 0930 to between 1600 and 1700. Some larger branches may also be open later on Thursdays and on Saturday mornings. Banks are usually the best places to change money and cheques. Outside banking hours you'll have to use a **bureau de change**, which can be found in the city centre and also at the airport and train stations. **NB** Some *bureaux* charge high commission rates for changing cheques. Avoid changing money or cheques in hotels, as the rates are usually very poor.

The major Scottish banks have branches throughout the city, those with cashpoints (ATMs) in the centre of town are: *Bank of Scotland*, 235 Sauchiehall Street, 110 Queen Street, 55 Bath Street and 63 Waterloo Street. *Royal Bank of Scotland*, 98 Buchanan Street, 22 St Enoch Square, 140 St Vincent Street and 393 Sauchiehall Street. *Clydesdale Bank*, 14 Bothwell Street, 7 St Enoch Square, 30 St Vincent Place, 344 Argyle Street and 120 Bath Street. The major **English clearing banks** all have branches in the city, and are open Monday-Friday only (phone for opening times): they include *Barclays*, 90 St Vincent Street and *Lloyds TSB*, 12 Bothwell Street.

For **currency exchange**: *American Express*, 115 Hope Street, T2214366, open Monday-Friday 0830-1730, Saturday 0900-1200. *Thomas Cook*, Central station, T2044496, open Monday-Wednesday and Saturday 0800-1900, Thursday and Friday 0800-2000, Sunday 1000-1800.

Cost of living/ travelling Glasgow needn't be an expensive city to visit. Cheap accommodation is available in hostels or B&Bs, transport is relatively cheap and you can get by on £20-25 per day if you eat in cafés and pubs or cheap restaurants. Also, most of the museums and galleries are free. If you want to enjoy the city's better restaurants and go out at night, then you'll need at least £50-60 per day, without being extravagant. Single travellers will have to pay more than half the cost of a double room in most places and should budget on spending around 60% of what a couple would spend.

Getting there

Air

Generally speaking, the cheapest and quickest way to travel to Scotland from outside the UK is by air. There are good links to Glasgow, with direct flights from many European cities and from North America. There are also daily flights from Ireland and regular flights from other parts of the UK. There are no direct flights to Scotland from Australia, New Zealand, South Africa or Japan, so it's necessary to get a connection from London.

Airlines in Britain and Ireland

Aer Lingus, Ireland, T01-8444777; UK,
T0645-737747, www.aerlingus.ie
British Airways, T08457-733377,
www.britishairways.com
British European, T08705-676676.
British Midland, T0870-6070555,
www.iflybritishmidland.com
Eastern Airways, T01955-603914.

easyJet, T0870-6000000,
www.easyjet.com
Go, T0845-6054321, www.go-fly.com
KLM UK, T08705-074074, www.klm.com
Manx Airlines, T08457-256256.
Ryanair , T08701-569569; Ireland,
T01-6097800, www.ryanair.com
Scot Airways, T0870-6060707.

Discount travel agents in Britain and Ireland

Council Travel, 28a Poland St, London,
W1V 3DB, T020-74377767,
www.destinations-group.com
STA Travel, Strathclyde University
Students' Association, 90 John St, Glasgow,
T5528808; also 184 Byres Rd, T3386000.
Their main London branch is at 86 Old
Brompton Rd, SW7 3LH, T020-73616161,
www.statravel.co.uk They have other

branches in London, as well as in Brighton,
Bristol, Cambridge, Leeds, Manchester,
Newcastle-upon-Tyne and Oxford and on
many university campuses.
Trailfinders, 254-284 Sauchiehall St,
Glasgow, G2 3EH, T3532224. Main London
branch, 194 Kensington High St, W8 6FT,
T020-79383939.

Essentials

There are a mind-boggling number of outlets for buying your plane ticket, and finding the best deal can be a confusing business. **Fares** will depend on the season. Ticket prices to Scotland are highest from around early June to mid-September, which is the tourist high season. Fares drop in the months either side of the peak season – mid-September to early November and mid-April to early June. They are cheapest in the low season, from November to April, when very few visitors are willing to brave the Scottish winter. The exception is during Christmas and New Year when seats are at a premium and prices rise sharply. It's also worth noting that flying at the weekend is normally more expensive.

Buying a ticket
Also worth trying are:
www.expedia.co.uk
www.lastminute.com
www.cheapflights
.co.uk
www.e-bookers.com
www.deckchair.com
www.flynow.com
www.dialaflight.co.uk

It is always worth spending a bit of time researching the various options available and starting early, as some of the cheapest tickets have to be bought months in advance and the most popular flights sell out quickly. One of the best ways of finding a good deal is to use the internet. There are a number of sites where you can check out prices and even book tickets. You can search in the travel sections of your web browser or try the sites of the discount travel companies and agents listed in this section.

There are direct flights to **Glasgow International** airport almost hourly from London's **Heathrow**, **Gatwick**, **Stansted** and **Luton** airports. There are also daily flights from provincial UK airports and from **Dublin**. The cheapest flights leave from London Luton or Stansted, plus a few provincial airports, with *Ryanair*, *easyJet* and *Go*. If you book on-line, fares with these carriers can be as little as £5 one-way during promotions, but usually you can expect to fly for under £50 return. These tickets are often subject to rigid restrictions, but the savings can make the extra effort worthwhile. Cheaper tickets usually have to be bought at least a week in advance, apply to only a few midweek flights, and must include a Saturday night stayover. They are also non-refundable, or only partly refundable, and non-transferable. A standard flexible and refundable fare from London to Glasgow or Edinburgh will cost at least £150-200 return. There are direct flights from several European cities to Glasgow International: including **Amsterdam**, **Brussels**, **Copenhagen**, **Gothenberg**, **Madrid** and **Zurich**.

Flights from
Britain, Ireland
& Europe

Airlines flying from North America

Air Canada, T1-800-7763000,
www.aircanada.ca
American Airlines, T1-800-4337300,
www.americanair.com
Continental Airlines ,T1-800-2310856,
www.flycontinental.com
Delta Airlines, T1-800-2414141,
www.delta-air.com
Icelandair, T1-800-2235500,

www.icelandair.com
Northwest Airlines, T1-800-4474747,
www.nwa.com
TWA, T1-800-2212000, www.twa.com
United Airlines, T1-800-5382929,
www.ual.com
Virgin Atlantic Airways, T1-800-8628621,
www.fly.virgin.com

Discount travel agents in North America

*Air Brokers International, 323 Geary St,
Suite 411, San Francisco, CA94102,
T1-800-8833273,
www.airbrokers.com Consolidator and
specialist in Round-the-world and Circle
Pacific tickets.*
Council Travel, *205 E 42nd St, New York,
NY 10017, T1-888-COUNCIL,
www.counciltravel.com Student/budget
agency with branches in many other US
cities.*
Discount Airfares Worldwide On-Line,
*www.etn.nl/discount.htm A hub of
consolidator and discount agent links.*
**International Travel Network/Airlines
of the Web**, *www.itn.net/airlines Online
air travel information and reservations.*

STA Travel, *5900 Wiltshire Blvd, Suite
2110, Los Angeles, CA 90036,
T1-800-7770112,
www.sta-travel.com Discount
student/youth travel discount company
with branches in New York, San Francisco,
Boston, Miami, Chicago, Seattle and
Washington DC.*
Travel CUTS, *187 College St, Toronto, ON
M5T 1P7, T1-800-6672887,
www.travelcuts.com Specialist in
student discount fares, IDs and other
travel services. Branches in other
Canadian cities.*
Travelocity, *www.travelocity.com Online
consolidator.*

Ryanair flies to Glasgow's second airport, **Prestwick**, from **London Stansted**, **Frankfurt Hahn**, **Dublin**, **Brussels** and **Paris Beauvois**.

Flights from North America — There are direct flights to **Glasgow International** from **New York Newark** (*Continental Airlines*), **Chicago** (*American Airlines*) and **Toronto** (*Air Canada*). There are also flights from many other US and Canadian cities via London with the Transatlantic carriers listed in the box above. *Icelandair* flies to Glasgow via Reykjavik from **Boston**, **Halifax**, **Minneapolis**, **New York**, **Orlando** and **Washington**. *Northwest Airlines* flies via Amsterdam to Glasgow from **Detroit**, **Memphis** and **Minneapolis**, with onward flights operated by *KLM UK*. Because of the much larger number of flights to London, it is generally cheaper to fly there first and get an onward flight (see box above for airlines offering the best deals).

For low-season Apex fares expect to pay around US$400-600 from New York and other East Coast cities, and around US$500-700 from the West Coast. Prices rise to around US$700-900 from New York, and up to US$1,000 from the West Coast in the summer months. Low-season Apex fares from Toronto and Montreal cost around CAN$600-700, and from Vancouver around CAN$800-900, rising to CAN$750-950 and CAN$950-1150 respectively during the summer.

Road

Essentials

Road links to Scotland are excellent, and a number of companies offer express coach services day and night. This is the cheapest form of travel to Scotland: the two main operators are *National Express*, T08705-808080, www.gobycoach.com and its sister company *Scottish Citylink*, T08705-505050, www.city.link.co.uk There are direct buses from most British cities to Glasgow. Tickets can be bought at bus stations or from a huge number of agents throughout the country. Fares from London with *National* Express are between £28 and £36 return. The journey takes around eight hours. There are several services daily, with links to other major English cities, including: **Manchester** (four hours); **Birmingham** (5½ hours); **Newcastle** (four hours) and **York** (6½ hours).

Bus & coach

All long-distance buses to and from Glasgow arrive and depart from Buchanan bus station, on Killermont Street, T3327133, three blocks north of George Square. There's a left-luggage office at Buchanan bus station, open daily 0630-2230.

Bus travel passes Full-time students or those aged under 25 or over 50, can buy a **Coach Card** for £9 which is valid for one year and gets you up to one-third off all National Express fares within the UK. A **Family card** costs £15 and allows two children to travel free with two adults, but children normally travel for half price. Full-time students and under 25s can buy a **Citylink Smart Card** for £6 which gives 30% discount on *Citylink* and *National Express* journeys within Scotland. The **Tourist Trail Pass** offers unlimited travel on all *Scottish Citylink* and *National Express* services throughout Britain. Passes cost from £49 for two days' travel out of three consecutive days, up to £190 for 14 days' travel out of 30 consecutive days. Passes can be bought at travel agents and at the booking office at Buchanan bus station, T0121-4238499 for details. In **North America** these passes are available from *British Travel International*, T1-800-327 6097, www.britishtravel.com or from *US National Express*, T502-298 1395.

The main route if driving to Glasgow from the south is the M6, which becomes the A74(M) in Scotland and is dual carriageway all the way from the border. The journey north from London takes around eight to 10 hours. There's an *Autoshuttle Express* service to transport your car overnight between England and Scotland and vice versa while you travel by rail or air. For further information T08705-133714; reservations T08705-502309.

Car

To drive in Scotland you must have a current driving licence. Foreign nationals also need an **international driving permit**, available from state and national motoring organizations for a small fee. Those importing their own vehicle should also have their vehicle registration or ownership documentation. Make sure you're adequately insured. Throughout the UK you **drive on the left. Speed limits** are 30 miles per hour (mph) in built-up areas, 70 mph on motorways and dual carriageways and 60 mph on most other roads.

It's advisable to join one of the main UK motoring organizations during your visit for their **24-hour breakdown assistance**. The two main ones in Britain are the *Automobile Association* (*AA*), T0800-448866, www.theaa.co.uk, and the *Royal Automobile Club* (*RAC*), T0800-550550, rac.co.uk One year's membership of the *AA* starts at £46, and £39 for the *RAC*. They also provide many other services, including a reciprocal agreement for free assistance with many overseas motoring organizations. Check to see if your organization is included. Both companies can also extend their cover to include "other European countries". Their **emergency numbers** are: *AA* T0800-887766; *RAC* T0800-828282. You can call these numbers for breakdown assistance even if you're not a member, but you'll have to a pay a large fee.

Railcards

There are a variety of railcards which give discounts on fares for certain groups. Cards are valid for one year and most are available from main stations. You need two passport photos and proof of age or status.

Young Person's Railcard: for those aged 16-25 or full-time students in the UK. Costs £18 and gives 33% discount on most train tickets and some ferry services.

Senior Citizen's Railcard: for those aged over 60. Same price and discount as above.

Disabled Person's Railcard: costs £14 and gives 33% discount to a disabled person and one other. Pick up application form from stations and send it to: Disabled Person's Railcard Office, PO Box 1YT, Newcastle-upon-Tyne, NE99 1YT. It may take up to 21 days to process, so apply in advance.

Family Railcard: costs £20 and gives 33% discount on most tickets (20% on others) for up to four adults travelling together, and 81% discount for up to four children.

Car hire/rental is expensive and you may be better off making arrangements in your home country for a fly/drive deal through one of the main multi-national companies. The minimum you can expect to pay is around £150-180 per week for a small car. Small, local hire companies often offer better deals than the larger multi-nationals. Most companies prefer payment with a credit card, otherwise you'll have to leave a large deposit (£100 or more). You'll need your driver's licence and to be aged between 21 and 70. **Motorcycle hire** is very expensive, ranging from around £200 up to £350 per week.

Sea

Ferries from Northern Ireland

Larne to Cairnryan: *P&O Irish Sea*, T0870-2424777, www.poirishsea.com, has several crossings daily to Cairnryan. The journey takes one hour. **Belfast to Stranraer:** *Stena Line,* T0870-707070, www.stenaline.co.uk run numerous ferries (three hours) and high-speed catamarans (1½ hours). **Belfast to Troon**: *Seacat Scotland* run daily services (2½ hours; £250 for two adults and a car), T08705-523523, www.seacat.co.uk

There are several trains daily from Stranraer to Glasgow Central (2¼ hours) and regular services from Troon (45 minutes).

Train

A shuttle bus (No 398) runs every 10 mins between Central station (Gordon St entrance), Queen St station and Buchanan bus station (£0.50)

Glasgow has two main train stations: Glasgow Central station is the terminus for all trains to southern Scotland, England and Wales; and Queen Street station serves the north and east of Scotland. There are fast and frequent rail services to and from **London Euston** (five hours). There are also daily services to **Birmingham** (four hours) and **Manchester** (3½ hours) and other main towns and cities in England. Two companies operate direct services from London to Scotland: *GNER* trains leave from Kings' Cross and run up the east coast to Edinburgh, Aberdeen and Inverness; and *Virgin* trains leave from Euston and run up the west coast to Glasgow. *Scotrail* operate the **Caledonian Sleeper** service if you wish to travel overnight from London Euston to Glasgow. This runs nightly from Sunday to Friday. There are left-luggage lockers at Glasgow Central and Queen Street train stations (£2 per day).

Eurostar, T08705-186186, www.eurostar.com operates high-speed trains through the Channel Tunnel to London Waterloo from Paris (three hours), Brussels (two hours 40 minutes) and Lille (two hours). You then have to change trains, and stations, for the onward journey north to Scotland. If you're driving from continental Europe you could take **Le Shuttle**, which runs 24 hours a day, 365 days a year, and takes you and your car from Calais to Folkestone in 35-45 minutes. Fares range from £84 to £165 per car, depending on how far in advance you book or when you travel (T08705-353535 for bookings).

National Rail Enquiries, T08457-484950, www.railtrack.co.uk For information on all rail services and fares. For advance credit/debit card bookings, T08457-550033. *GNER*, T08457-225225, www.gner.co.uk *Virgin*, T08457-222333; *ScotRail*, T08457-550033, www.scotrail.co.uk

Enquiries

To describe the system of rail ticket pricing as complicated is a huge understatement and impossible to explain here. There are many and various discounted fares, but restrictions are often prohibitive, which explains the long queues and delays at ticket counters in railway stations. The cheapest ticket is a **Super Apex**, which must be booked at least two weeks in advance, though this is not available on all journeys. Next cheapest is an **Apex** ticket which has to be booked at least seven days before travelling. Other discount tickets include a **Saver** return, which can be used on all trains, and a **Super Saver**, which costs slightly less but cannot be used on a Friday or during peak times. All discount tickets should be booked as early as possible as they are often sold out weeks, or even months, in advance, especially Apex and Super Apex tickets. The latter tickets guarantee seat reservations, but Saver and Super Saver tickets do not. Seats can be secured by paying an extra £1.

Fares
For details of various discount rail passes and rail services within Scotland, see page 37

Essentials

Touching down

Glasgow airports

Glasgow International airport, T8871111, is eight miles west of the city, at junction 28 on the M8. It handles domestic and international flights. All main national and international car hire firms are by the luggage carousel in Domestic Arrivals. Also here is the **SPT** (Strathclyde Passenger Transport) desk, T8484330 (open Monday-Saturday 0800-1800, Sunday 0900-1800), where you can pick up the very useful *Travel Options Guide*, which explains how to get to and from the airport. At the Interarontional Arrivals area is a *Thomas Cook* and *Travelex* bureau de change and a **Tourist Information Centre**, T8484440 (open Monday-Saturday 0730-1700, Sunday 0800-1530). There's also a travel agent for late bookings and ticket sales. On the first floor are lots of shops, cafés and restaurants and smoking areas, and another *Thomas Cook* bureau de change (open till 2230) and *Travelex*. Both charge 1.5 % commission. There's also a post office (open Monday-Friday 0900-1730, Saturday 0900-1330). There are internet facilities by the main check-in and wheelchair services at the main entrance. Note that *Go* and *AirTours* check-in is currently in the St Andrews building, to the right of Domestic Arrivals. The car park pay-stations are by the babbage carousels. Parking costs £7 per day for the first four days, and £10 per day thereafter. There is an *Express by Holiday Inn* and *Posthouse* hotel opposite the terminal.

Glasgow
International
For all UK airports, visit www.baa.co.uk

Airport to city centre To get into town take one of two buses which leave from bus stops 1 and 2 opposite the Departures building. Bus No 905 departs every 10-15 minutes 0600-1800, and then every 30 minutes from 1800 till 2300. Bus No 200 is a 24-hour service which leaves every 20 minutes from 0600 till 2000, then every hour from 2000 till 0600. They both go as far as Buchanan bus station, with drop-off points at Glasgow Central and Queen Street train stations. Journey time is 25-30 minutes and costs £3.30 single, £5 return. Tickets can be bought from the driver. A taxi from the airport to the city centre costs around £12.

Touching down

Electricity The current in Britain is 240V AC. Plugs have three square pins and adapters are widely available.

Emergencies For **police**, **fire brigade**, **ambulance** and, in certain areas, **mountain rescue** or **coastguard**, dial 999.

Laundry Most towns have coin-operated launderettes. The average cost for a wash and tumble dry is about £3. A service wash, where someone will do your washing for you, costs around £4-5. In more remote areas, you'll have to rely on hostel and campsite facilities.

Time Greenwich Mean Time (GMT) is used from late October to late March, after which time the clocks go forward an hour to British Summer Time (BST). GMT is five hours ahead of US Eastern Standard Time and 10 hours behind Australian Eastern Standard Time.

Toilets Public toilets are found at all train and bus stations and motorway service stations. They may charge 20p, but are generally clean, with disabled and baby-changing facilities. Those in town centres are often pretty grim.

Weights and measures Imperial and metric systems are both currently in use. Distances on roads are measured in miles and yards, drinks are poured in pints and gills, but in most other instances, the metric system is used.

City centre to airport Buses to the airport leave from Buchanan bus station and stop outside the Tourist Information Centre on George Square, as well as a few other bus stops in the city centre (look for the Airport logo).

Prestwick Prestwick airport, T01292-511006, www.gpia.co.uk, is 30 miles southwest of the city. It is used by **Ryanair** flying from London Stansted, also for flights from Paris Beauvais, Dublin, Franfurt Hahn and Brussels. Trains run to and from Central Station every 30 minutes (45 minute journey; £2.50 single). There's also a bus service which leaves from Buchanan Bus Station every 30 minutes from 0715 till 2220 Monday-Saturday, and every hour on Sunday. It takes 1½ hours and costs £0.50 for passengers with a valid airline ticket.

Other Scottish airports **Edinburgh**, T0131-3331000, has all the necessary facilities, including a tourist information desk, currency exchange, ATMs, car hire, restaurants and bars (first floor) and shops (ground floor and first floor). Scotland's other main airports are **Aberdeen**, T01224-722331, **Inverness**, T01463-232471, **Prestwick**, T01292-511006, **Dundee**, T01382-643242, and **Wick**, T01955-602215.

Airport tax Departure tax is included in the price of air tickets. For economy fare flights within the UK and from EU countries it is £5. For all other flights it is £20. Taxes on first or club class flights are £10 for the UK and EU and £40 for other destinations.

Tourist information

Tourist offices – called Tourist Information Centres (TICs) – are found in Glasgow city centre (see page 17) and International airport and in most of the surrounding towns. Their addresses, phone numbers and opening hours are listed in the relevant sections of this book. Opening hours vary depending on the time of year, and many of the smaller offices are closed during the winter months. All tourist offices provide information on accommodation, public transport, local attractions and restaurants, as well as selling books, local guides, maps and souvenirs. Many also have free street plans and leaflets describing local walks. They can also book accommodation for you (see page

How big is your footprint?

- *Drive carefully and behave courteously to other motorists and cyclists on narrow, winding roads. Park vehicles where they will not be a hazard or disruption to other motorists, residents or businesses.*
- *Keep to public paths through farmland to minimise crop damage, and avoid 'short-cuts' on steep terrain to prevent soil erosion and damage to natural vegetation.*
- *Litter is an eye-sore, harmful to farm animals, wildlife and the water supply – leave no waste and take all your rubbish home.*
- *Protect wildlife, plants and trees.*
- *Respect ancient monuments, buildings and sites of religious importance – do not vandalise or cause graffiti.*
- *Avoid damaging crops, walls, fences and farm equipment and fasten all gates.*
- *Do not collect wildflowers, seabird eggs or historical artefacts for souvenirs.*
- *Avoid pollution of water supplies - there are few toilets outside of villages so when walking in the countryside bury human waste and toilet paper in the ground and at least 30 metres from water courses.*
- *Guard against all risk of fire from matches, cigarettes, cooking stoves and campfires.*
- *Keep dogs under careful control, especially when near sheep at lambing-time, seabird nesting sites and cliff edges; and avoid dog-fouling in public places.*
- *Stay away from working areas on the moors and hills during grouse-shooting, lambing season, deer culling and heather burning, and respect other locally or nationally imposed access restrictions.*
- *Report any damage or environmental concerns to the landowner or the Scottish Environment Protection Agency (SEPA) in Stornoway (T01851-706477).*
- *Be adequately prepared when you walk in the hills – check the weather forecast, carry warm, waterproof clothing and adequate food and water supplies, and know how to use a map and compass.*

Essentials

---

35), for a small fee. Addresses of the main office of the *Scottish Tourist Board* and the *Area Tourist Boards* are given on page 17.

Entry to most municipal **art galleries and museums** is free, as well as to most **Museums,** state-owned museums. Most fee-paying attractions give a discount or concession for **galleries &** senior citizens, the unemployed, full-time students and children under 16 (those under **monuments** five are admitted free everywhere). Proof of age or status must be shown. Apart from the large, main galleries listed in the travelling text , there are many small, independent galleries showcasing contemporary local, Scottish and international artists. The *Glasgow Galleries Guide*, free from any of the galleries, lists all current exhibitions.

Over 100 of the country's most prestigious sights, and 185,000 acres of beautiful countryside, are cared for by the **National Trust for Scotland** (NTS), 26-31 Charlotte Square, Edinburgh EH2 4ET, T0131-2439300, www.nts.org.uk If you're going to be visiting several sights during your stay, then it's worth taking out an annual membership. This costs £28, £12 if you're aged under 26 and £47 for a family, and gives free access to all NTS and NT properties. The *National Trust Touring Pass* costs £18 per adult and £28 for a family, and gives free admission to its properties for seven days. A 14-day adult or family pass costs £26 and £44 respectively. YHA and HI members and student-card holders get 50% discount on NTS admission charges.

Historic Scotland (HS), Longmore House, Salisbury Place, Edinburgh EH9 1SH, T0131-6688800, www.historic-scotland.gov.uk manages more than 330 of Scotland's most important castles, monuments and other historic sites. Historic Scotland offers an *Explorer Ticket* which allows free entry to 70 of their properties including Edinburgh and Stirling castles. It costs £17 per adult and £35 for a family for seven days, and £22/£42 for 14 days. It can save a lot of money, as entry to Edinburgh Castle alone is £7.50 per adult.

Local customs and laws

Visitors will generally find their Glaswegian hosts to be friendly and obliging. Glasgow people are famed for their warmth and humour and the level of hospitality should be a significant part of the enjoyment of your trip.

Tipping Tipping is at the customer's discretion. In a restaurant you should leave a tip of 10-15% if you are satisfied with the service. If the bill already includes a service charge, you needn't add a further tip. Tipping is not normal in pubs or bars. Taxi drivers will expect a tip for longer journeys, usually of around 10%, and most hairdressers will also expect a tip. As in most other countries, porters, bellboys and waiters in more upmarket hotels rely on tips to supplement their meagre wages.

Religion Religion is a very touchy subject here and is inextricably linked with the city's two main football teams. Any discussion is best avoided.

Responsible tourism

Sustainable or eco-tourism has been described as: "…ethical, considerate or informed tourism where visitors can enjoy the natural, historical and social heritage of an area without causing adverse environmental, socio-economic or cultural impacts that compromise the long-term ability of that area and its people to provide a recreational resource for future generations and an income for themselves…"

The Highlands and Islands of Scotland, which are easily accessed from the city centre, are beautiful, dramatic and wild, but also a living, working landscape and a fragile and vulnerable place. By observing the simple guidelines set out in the box on the previous page and behaving responsibly, you can help to minimise your impact and protect the natural and cultural heritage of this unique island environment so that it can continue to be appreciated by other visitors.

For further information on what action is being taken either in Scotland, throughout UK or across the world to guard against the negative aspects of tourism on the natural environment and traditional cultures, contact **Tourism Concern** in London (T020-7753 3330) or the **Tourism and Environment Forum** (www.greentourism.org.uk).

Safety

Glasgow is, in general, a reasonably safe and civilized place, and the vast majority of people are almost preternaturally friendly. Aside from the ubiquitous nuisance of drunks on public transport and around the city centre at the weekend, most visitors should encounter few problems. In saying that, however, some precautions should be taken. As in all large cities, you should avoid walking alone at night in quiet unlit streets and parks. If you are robbed or assaulted and need to report the crime, phone the police on 999. **Strathclyde Police** Headquarters are at 173 Pitt Street, T2042626, 24 hours; lost property open 0900-1700. For free legal advice contact the **Citizen's Advice Bureau**, 3rd Floor, Hellenic House, 87 Bath Street.

Where to stay

Glasgow has a good range of accommodation. Most of the hotels, guest houses, B&Bs and hostels are in the city centre and the West End or south of the river, around Queen's Park. The best area to find good value mid-range accommodation is the West End, around Kelvingrove Park and the university. Many of the hotels and guest houses here are restored Victorian townhouses This is a good area to stay in, as it's convenient for several of the city's major sights as well as many of the best bars and restaurants. *For a full list of accommodation ➤ go to page 139*

Finding a decent room for the night can be difficult during the peak season in July and August and it's best to book ahead at these times. The **Tourist Information Centre (TIC)** can help find somewhere to stay and also publishes a free accommodation guide. Many of the expensive business hotels offer substantial discounts at weekends, making them excellent value for a weekend break. Details of these are also available at theTIC.

For a full list of accommodation ➤ go to page 139

Getting around

The best way to explore the city centre sights is by walking, although some of the hills are very steep. If you want to explore the West End or South Side, you'll need to use the public transport system, which is efficient and comprehensive. The best way to get from the city centre to the West End is to use the city's **Underground**, or subway as it's also known, whose stations are marked with a huge orange 'U' sign. This is less effective for the South Side but there's a vast range of buses from the city centre. There's also an extensive suburban train network which is a fast and efficient way to reach the suburbs south of the Clyde.

South of George Square, in front of the giant St Enoch Centre, is the **Strathclyde Travel Centre**, T2264826 (open Monday-Saturday 0830-1730). They can provide maps, leaflets and timetables. Their free *Visitor's Transport Guide* includes a particularly useful map of the city. There are other **travel information centres** at Buchanan bus station, T3327133 (open Monday-Saturday 0630-2230, Sunday 0700-2230), Hillhead Underground station, on Byres Road, T3333673 (open Monday 0800-1730, Tuesday-Saturday 0830-1730), and at Glasgow airport (see page 31). For enquiries about public transport call *Traveline* on T0870-6082608. **Transport information**

Bus services are operated by *First Glasgow* and *Arriva*. Full details of bus routes and timetables are available from the Travel Centre in St Enoch Square. Short trips in the city start from £0.80. On most buses you'll need to have the exact change. After midnight, till 0400-0430, there's a limited night bus service (more frequent at weekends). All the sights outside the city centre listed in this book include details of how to get there by bus. **Bus**

Amongst the most popular are: Nos **45/47/57** to Pollockshaws train station for the Burrell Collection, from Union Street or Jamaica Street; No **57** also goes to Bellahouston Park for House for an Art Lover; Nos **23/24** to the Science Centre from Jamaica Street; No **66** runs from Anniesland Cross, through the West End and City Centre and south to Holmwood House; Nos **44A/44D** go to Cathcart train station (for Holmwood) from Sauchiehall Street. For an unofficial tour of the outlying districts like Rutherglen and Ruchill, try the No **89/90** Inner Circle bus which also goes through the Clyde Tunnel and stops at the Science Centre, Botanic Gardens, Mount Florida (for Hampden) and Parkhead (Celtic FC).

A good way to get around town is to buy a ticket for one of the official **guided bus tours** (see page 14). **FirstDay** is an all-day travel ticket which allows you to travel on all *FirstGlasgow* buses in and around the city centre for £1.85 (or £2.20 before 0930). Tickets can be purchased on the buses.

Essentials

Running like clockwork

*The Underground is particularly useful for getting to and from the West End and the city centre. **St George's Cross** is handy for Woodlands Road and the Park Conservation area; **Kelvinbridge** for Great Western Road and Kelvingrove Park. **Hillhead** is perfect for the shops and restaurants around Byres Road, as well as the Hunterian Museum and Botanic Garden, while **Kelvinhall** is close to the Transport Museum and Kelvingrove Art Gallery & Museum. South of the Clyde the Underground is less convenient for the tourist, though **Govan** is handy for Govan Old Parish Church, **Shields Road** is directly opposite the Scotland Street Musuem and **Bridge Street** is not far from the Citizens Theatre.*

Car   It is relatively easy to get around Glasgow by car, especially as the M8 runs right through the heart of the city. Parking is not a problem either. There are sufficient street meters and 24-hour multi-storey car parks dotted around the centre, at the St Enoch Centre, Mitchell Street, Oswald Street, Waterloo Street and Cambridge Street. For car hire companies, see box on next page.

Taxi   Taxis are plentiful and reasonably priced and can be hailed from anywhere in the city. There are taxi ranks at Central and Queen Street train stations and Buchanan bus station, and outside *Curlers* on Byres Road. The main cab operator in the city is *TOA* (Taxi Owner's Association) who can be contacted 24 hours a day on T4297070. They also run city tours (see page 16). Minimum fare around the city centre is £2. To the Burrell Collection from the city centre (about three miles) should cost around £7-8. There are lots of smaller firms who offer cheaper fares if you phone and book.

Train   Trains leave from **Glasgow Central** mainline station to all destinations south of the Clyde, including to Greenock (for ferries to Dunoon), Wemyss Bay (for ferries to Rothesay), Ardrossan (for ferries to Arran) and to Prestwick airport. There's a low-level station below Central station which connects the southeast of the city with the northwest. This cross-city line serves the SECC and a branch runs north to Milngavie, at the start of the West Highland Way. There's also a line from **Queen Street** station which runs west all the way to Helensburgh, via Partick and Dumbarton. Branches of this line run to Balloch, at the south end of Loch Lomond, and to Milngavie.

Underground
A map of the circuit is included in the full colour map at the front of the book, page 8

Locals affectionately refer to it as the 'Clockwork Orange', as there's only one circular route serving 15 stops and the trains are bright orange. It's easy to use and there's a flat-rate fare of £0.90 per journey. Better value is the **Discovery** ticket, which offers unlimited travel for one day for £1.60 after 0930 Monday-Saturday and all day Sunday. Trains run roughly every four minutes during peak times and every six to eight minutes at other times. Trains run from 0635till 2310 Monday-Saturday and from 1100 till 1750 on Sunday.

The **Roundabout Glasgow** ticket covers all Underground and train transport in and around the city for one day and costs £3.50 (child £1.75). The ticket also gives a £1.50 discount on a city bus tour. It's valid Monday-Friday after 0900 and all day at weekends. There's also a **Daytripper** ticket which gives unlimited travel on all transport networks throughout Glasgow, the Clyde coast and Clyde valley. It's valid for one day and costs £7.50 for one adult and two children, or £13 for two adults and up to four children.

Car hire companies

Arnold Clark, 10-24 Vinicombe St,
T3349501 (also at the airport,
T8480202). Avis, 161 North St, T2212877
(also at the airport, T8872261).
Budget, 101 Waterloo St, T2264141
(also at the airport, T8870501).
easyCar, www.easycar.com
EuroDollar, T01895-233300.
Europcar, T08457-222525.
First European, T8861072.

Hertz, 106 Waterloo St, T2487736
(also at the airport, T8877845).
Holiday Autos, T8705-300400,
www.holidayautos.com
Melvilles, 555 Sauchiehall St, 192
Battlefield Rd, Langside and
at airport, T0345-525354.
National Car Rental, T08705-365365.
Thrifty, T0141-4454440.

Essentials

Leaving town

Travelling around Scotland by bus takes longer than the train but is much cheaper. There **Bus**
are numerous local bus companies but the main operator is *Scottish Citylink*, part of the
National Express group. From Glasgow there are buses to **Edinburgh** every 15 minutes
(1½ hours, £5 return); hourly buses to **Stirling** (45 minutes, £6.10 return); 15 buses daily to
Aberdeen (four hours, £25 return); three buses daily to **Portree** (seven hours, £30 return);
and hourly to to **Dundee** (2½ hours, £13 return). Bus No 119 runs to **Milngavie**, at the start
of the West Highland Way (30 minutes) and Nos 204/205/216 go to **Balloch** at the southern end of Loch Lomond, via **Helensburgh** (for Hill House).

Travelling using your own private transport allows you to cover a lot of the country out- **Car**
side of Glasgow in a short space of time. Roads in Scotland are generally a lot less busy
than those in England and driving is relatively stress-free, especially on the B-roads and
minor roads.

The majority of ferry services on the west coast are operated by *Caledonian* **Ferry**
MacBrayne, or *CalMac* as they're more commonly known; The Ferry Terminal,
Gourock, PA19 1QP, T01475-650100, reservations T08705-650000, www.calmac.co.uk
They run services on the **Firth of Clyde**, sailing from Gourock to Dunoon and Wenyss
Bay to Rothesay. Fares are expensive, especially with a car, but if you're planning on
using ferries a lot, you can save a lot of money with an **Island Hopscotch** ticket, which
offers reduced fares on 17 set routes. The ticket is valid for one month and you need to
follow your set itinerary, though this can be changed en route without too much fuss.
For more details and some sample fares, see under the relevant destination. *Western*
Ferries, T0141-3329766, also runs services between **Gourock** and **Dunoon**.

As in the rest of the UK, hitch-hiking is never entirely safe, and is certainly not advised **Hitching**
for anyone travelling alone, particularly women travellers. Those prepared to take the
risk should not find it too difficult to get a lift.

The rail network in Scotland is limited and train travel is comparatively expensive, but **Train**
trains are a fast and effective way to get around and also provide some beautifully sce- *Cyclists should note*
nic journeys. Services in the central belt, between Glasgow, Edinburgh and Stirling, are *that reservations*
for bikes (£3.50)
fast and frequent. *ScotRail* operates most train services, including to **Edinburgh** (every *are required on*
15-30 minutes, 50 minutes), **Perth**, **Dundee** and **Aberdeen** (hourly), **Stirling** (hourly, *some services*
30 minutes), **Helensburgh** (every 30 minutes) and **Balloch** (every 30 minutes), and
Lanark (hourly). They also operate the West Highland line from Queen Street north to
Oban (three daily, three hours).

For information on fares and timetables, contact *National Rail Enquiries*, T08457-484950, open 24 hours. You can buy train tickets at the stations, from major travel agents, or over the phone with a credit/debit card. For advance credit/debit card bookings call T08457-550033, or www.scotrail.co.uk For busy, long-distance routes it's best to reserve a seat. Seat reservations to Edinburgh are included in the price of the ticket when you book in advance. If the ticket office is closed, there's usually a machine on the platform. If this isn't working, you can buy your ticket on the train. Details of the different railcards available are given in the box on page 30. Details of the different types of tickets are on page 31.

Eurorail passes are not valid for use in Britain, but *ScotRail* offers a couple of worthwhile travel passes. The most flexible is the **Freedom of Scotland Travelpass**, which gives unlimited rail travel within Scotland. It is also valid on some regional buses and Glasgow Underground. It costs £69 for four days' travel out of eight consecutive days, £99 for any eight out of 15 consecutive days and £119 for any 12 out of 15 consecutive days. Holders of a **Senior Citizen's** or **Young Person's Railcard** get a 30% discount on these passes.

Keeping in touch

Communications

Internet   It is now almost de rigueur amongst travellers to get an email address that can be accessed anywhere through the internet, using, for example a Hotmail or Yahoo account. As in many places, internet access in Scotland is extensive and often easier and more reliable than the phone. Every major town now has at least one internet café, with more springing up daily. Email works out much, much cheaper than phoning home and is also useful for booking hotels and tours and for checking out information on the web. Many hotels now have internet and many hostels also offer internet access to their guests. Websites and email addresses are listed where appropriate in this guide. The Scottish Tourist Board and area tourist boards have their own websites and these are given on page 17.

There are too many internet cafes in Glasgow to list here. A few of the more central ones include: *easyEverything*, 57 St Vincent Street, a huge facility and the cheapest service in town; *The Internet Café*, 569 Sauchiehall St, T5641052, charges £2-2.50 per ½ hour on-line; *Internet Exchange*, 136 Sauchiehall St, T3530535; *Café Internet*, 153-157 Sauchiehall Street, T3532484.

Post   Post offices are open Monday-Friday 0900 to 1730 and Saturday 0900 to 1230 or 1300. Smaller, sub-post offices are closed for an hour at lunch (1300-1400) and many of them located in shops. The main **post office** is at 47 St Vincent St, T0345-222344. Services include poste restante, currency exchange and cash withdrawal at the *German Savings Bank*. Open Monday-Friday 0830-1745, Saturday 0900-1900. There are also branches at 85-89 Bothwell Street, 216 Hope Street and 533 Sauchiehall Street. Post offices in some supermarkets are open on Sunday.

Stamps can be bought at post offices, but also from vending machines outside, and at many newsagents. A first-class letter to anywhere in the UK costs £0.26 and should arrive the following day, while second-class letters cost £0.19 and take between two to four days. Airmail letters of less than 20g cost £0.37 to Europe. To the USA and Australia the costs are £0.45 for 10g and £0.65 for 20g.

Most public **payphones** are operated by *British Telecom* (*BT*) and take either coins (10p, 20p, 50p or £1) or **phonecards**, which are available at newsagents and post offices displaying the *BT* logo. These cards come in denominations of £2, £3, £5 and £10. Some payphones also accept credit cards. Note that 20p is the minimum charge from a payphone, 50p if using a credit card.

For most countries (including Europe, USA and Canada) calls are cheapest between 1800 and 0800 Monday-Friday and all day Saturday and Sunday. For Australia and New Zealand it's cheapest to call from 1430 to 1930 and from midnight to 0700 on any day.

Phone codes for towns and cities outside Glasgow are given in the margin by the town's heading in the Trips from Glasgow chapter. You don't need to use the area code if calling from the same area. Any number prefixed by 0800 or 0500 is free to the caller; 0345 numbers are charged at local rates and 0990 numbers at the national rate.

To **call Scotland** from overseas, dial 011 from the USA and Canada, 0011 from Australia and 00 from New Zealand, followed by 44, then the area code, minus the first zero, then the number. To **call overseas from Scotland** dial 00 followed by the country code. Country codes include: **Australia** 61; **France** 33; **Germany** 49; **Ireland** 353; **Italy** 39; **Japan** 81; **New Zealand** 64; **South Africa** 27; **Spain** 31; **USA** and **Canada** 1.

Telephone
Operator: T100
International operator: T155
Directory enquiries: T192
Overseas directory enquiries: T153

Essentials

Media

The main British daily and Sunday newspapers are widely available in Scotland and some of them publish special Scottish editions, among them the *Scottish Daily Mail*, *Scottish Daily Express* and Rupert Murdoch's notorious scandal sheet, *The Sun*.

The **Scottish press** produces two main 'quality' newspapers, the liberal-leaning *The Scotsman*, published in Edinburgh, and *The Herald*, published in Glasgow, which is the oldest daily newspaper in the English-speaking world, dating from 1783. The biggest-selling daily is the *Daily Record*, a tabloid paper (or red top as they are known). The Sunday equivalents of the dailies are *Scotland on Sunday* from the *Scotsman* stable, the *Sunday Herald* and the *Sunday Mail*, published by the *Daily Record*. Visitors to Glasgow should buy a copy of the fortnightly listings magazine, *The List*, with lively features and previews, and reviews of all events in both cities. The *Evening Times*, the city's evening newspaper, is also a good source of information on local events.

Foreign newspapers and magazines, including *USA Today* and the *International Herald Tribune*, are available in larger newsagents in central Glasgow. *Time* and *Newsweek* are also available in larger newsagents and bookstores.

Newspapers & magazines

There are five main **television channels** in Scotland; the publicly funded *BBC 1* and *BBC2*, and the independent commercial stations, *Channel 4*, *Channel 5* and *ITV*. The *ITV* network in Scotland comprises *STV*, which serves central Scotland and parts of the West Highlands, the Aberdeen-based *Grampian TV*, which produces a lot of Gaelic programmes, and *Border TV*, which covers Dumfries and Galloway and northwest England.

The BBC network also broadcasts several **radio channels**, most of which are based in London. These include: *Radio 1*, aimed at a young audience; *Radio 2*, targeting a more mature audience; *Radio 3*, which plays mostly classical music; *Radio 4*, which is talk-based and features arts, drama and current affairs; and *Radio 5 Live*, which is a mix of sport and news. *Radio Scotland* (92-95FM, 810MW) provides a Scottish-based diet of news, sport, current affairs, travel and music. There are also a large number of local **commercial radio stations**, stretching from Shetland in the north to the Borders in the south. The local Glasgow station is *Clyde 1* (102.5FM), while in Edinburgh it is *Radio Forth* (97.3FM).

TV & radio

Internet news Up-to-the-minute news can be found at **www.bbc.co.uk/news** which offers its service in a variety of languages, and **www.sky.co.uk/news** For local and national news
check out **www.theherald.co.uk**

Food and drink

*Places to eat are
marked on maps in
this book with the
symbol* ●

Look, forget the deep-fried Mars bar. Okay, it was invented here – and is still available in
some establishments – along with other Caledonian culinary delights like the deep-fried
pizza, deep-fried black pudding and the deep-fried *Cadbury's creme egg* (honest!). These
may be the headline-grabbing foods that everyone associates with Glasgow, but they
really don't reflect the quality and variety of food that the city has to offer.

Glasgow has undergone a culinary renaissance and the last few years has seen a
proliferation of classy restaurants combining the finest of cuisine with all the style and
cool you'd expect from this most design-conscious of cities. With celebrity chefs Nick
Nairn and Gordon Ramsay now competing – and bitching – for the top slot in the city,
dining out in Glasgow has become a serious business. There of plenty of places where
being seen is nearly as important as the food – although Glaswegians won't put up
with being ripped off, so you nearly always get good value for money.

Glasgow has always boasted a wide selection of ethnic eateries, particularly
Indian, **Chinese** and **Italian** restaurants, and these have been joined by a growing
number of cuisines from around the globe. You can eat almost any kind of food here
from Australian to Yugoslavian. **Scottish** cuisine is also well represented, reflecting
the growing trend of marrying traditional Scottish ingredients with continental and
international flavours and styles. Meats like venison, pheasant, lamb and beef are
often on the menu, and haggis may feature too – often as a starter so as not to
frighten the uninitiated. Fresh local fish is also widely available, sometimes fashion-
ably seared, sometimes served in an unusual sauce, and sometimes just fried with
big-fat chips. Look out for salmon, halibut, scallops, langoustines, mackerel and Loch
Fyne kippers.

Vegetarians are also well catered for. Though there aren't too many exclusively
vegetarian or vegan restaurants, most places now offer substantial and imaginative
vegetarian menus. As is the case for veggies in all cities, the more upmarket (or do we
mean snooty?) restaurants tend to be less veggie friendly and are still inclined to think
that fish is a veggie choice. To be fair, these places often have very short menus too,
because they are trying to produce higher quality food. So if you're wanting to splash
out and eat somewhere special you're well advised to book in advance and warn
them that you're coming. They're generally very helpful then – and you might even
end up having the choice of more than one main course!

Glasgow also reflects the move away from strict culinary national boundaries and
towards a more international style. Fusion food is currently in vogue, though that
could well change in a few months' time. The city's many bistros and brasseries feature wide-ranging menus incorporating everything from Mediterranean cooking to
Pacific Rim specialities. They also tend to be more lively and informal places to eat, as
well as offering good value for money – nd this is one of the city's great strengths.
Compared to other cities (for example, London), you can eat well and in some style
without breaking the bank.

Eating categories

In this book places to eat are divided into three categories: **expensive** *(over £20 a head);* **mid-range** *(£10-20 a head); and* **cheap** *(under £10 a head). These prices are based on a two-course meal (main course plus starter or dessert) without drinks. We have tried to include an equal number of choices in each category, though this is not always possible. All places listed are recommended as offering relatively good value, quality and standards of service within their respective price category.*

The greatest concentration of cheap eating places is around **Byres Road** in the West End, which is heavily populated by students and therefore the best area for cheap, trendy places to eat. The **Merchant City** contains most of the designer brasseries, which are more expensive, but many of the **bars** serve good food at reasonable prices. In fact it's becoming harder and harder to distinguish bars from restaurants, as more places offer flexible menus and all-day dining. Some of the places listed in the 'Eating and drinking' sections also appear in the **Bars** section. **Cafés** are often good-value places to eat, and these are also listed.

Where to eat *Places to eat in this guide are grouped according to price and location, while pages 229-231 offer a quick guide by type of cuisine*

For those on a tight budget, many city restaurants offer cheap business lunches. These can be brilliant value, particularly in the Indian restaurants where you can often fill up for about £7. Pre-theatre dinner menus also provide an opportunity to sample some of the finest food at affordable prices, if you don't mind eating before 1900. Most of the restaurants serve from 1200-1430 and 1800-2200, but bars and brasseries tend to be more flexible. Also note that many of Glasgow's restaurants are open seven days a week.

BYOB is a commonly used abbreviation meaning bring your own bottle

Glasgow also prides itself on its café society and many of the new, trendy designer cafés make it seem more like Barcelona or Greenwich Village than the west coast of Scotland (though it's admittedly a bit chillier). Glasgow is full of authentic Italian cafés where you can enjoy a cheap fry-up washed down with a frothy cappuccino, or a gorgeous pastry followed by a strong, dark espresso. These are still the best places to get decent coffee and are worth seeking out.

Cafés

Unfortunately, they are in danger of being outnumbered by the big chains that have sprung up throughout the city, offering their ubiquitous brands of bland lattes and overly frothy capps. Whatever your preference, you won't have any trouble finding the right place for that essential caffeine shot during a hard day's sightseeing or shopping. Glasgow is also the home of the tearoom and those who insist on their mid-afternoon infusion won't be disappointed. Most of the city cafes also serve good food or substantial snacks and can be the most economical option for a hungry traveller. Many have drinks licences and are also open at night.

Drinks

Forget all the tired old clichés about Glasgow and Glaswegians, a night out in Scotland's largest city is a memorable experience – for all the right reasons. There are bars and pubs to suit all tastes, from ornate Victorian watering holes to the coolest of designer bars, where you can listen to thumping dance beats before heading off to a club. Even the trendiest of places, though, are saved from being pretentious by the never-ending warmth and humour that pervades this city.

Essentials

Which whisky?

*Opinions vary as to what are the best single malts and as to when you should drink them. As a rough guide, we would recommend a Speyside malt such as Glenmorangie or Glenlivet **before dinner** and one of the Islay malts – Ardbeg, Bowmore, Bunnahabhain (pronounced 'bun-a-haven'), Lagavulin, or the very wonderful Laphroaig (pronounced 'la-froig') – **after dinner**.*

If the Islays are not to your taste, then you could try instead Highland Park from Orkney or perhaps Tamdhu or Aberlour from Speyside. Those eternal favourites, Glenfiddich and The Macallan, can be enjoyed at any time.

The city centre is packed full of bars of every description, from the continental style of the **Merchant City**, to the authentic spit-and-sawdust of the **East End**. One of the best areas for the sheer number and variety of pubs and bars is the **West End**, with its large student population. A number of style bars have also opened up along Bath Street.

Glasgow's famously liberal licensing laws have unfortunately been repealed and there now exists a restrictive **curfew**. At the time of writing, most pubs and bars open till 2400, though a few are open later, and many of them close at 2300 on weekdays and Sunday.

Note that there's bound to be some overlap between bars, cafés, bistros and restaurants. Many of the bars listed below, especially those in the Merchant City and West End, serve very good food at reasonable prices, and the best of these are also included in the respective Eating and drinking sections. Similarly, many of the **cafés** and **bistros** listed under their respective sections are among the best places to enjoy a drink. Also note that many bars feature regular **live bands** and **comedy nights**, and the most notable of these are listed separately in the Entertainment & nightlife chapter.

Beer   Beer is the staple alcoholic drink in Scotland. The most popular type of beer is lager, but connoisseurs should sample one of the many excellent types of **heavy**, which is a thick, dark ale served at room temperature with a full, creamy head. Types of heavy are graded by the shilling, which indicates its strength; the higher the number the stronger the beer. The usual range is 60 to 80 shillings (written 80/-). The best ales are hand-pumped from the cask. Beer is served in pints, or half pints, and you'll pay between £1.50 and £2.50 for a pint, depending on the brew and location of the pub.

The market is dominated by the large brewers – *Youngers, McEwan's, Scottish and Newcastle* and *Tennet's*. They produce smooth, strong beers, but the country's best seller is, strangely enough, *Tartan Special*, which is weak and tasteless by comparison. For the best of Scottish beers, however, you should try one of the small **local breweries**. Edinburgh's *Caledonian* produces a wide range of excellent cask ales. Others worth trying are *Belhaven*, brewed in Dunbar, *Maclays*, brewed in Alloa, and the very wonderful *Greenmantle*, brewed in the Borders.

Whisky   No visit to Scotland would be complete without availing oneself of a 'wee dram'. A popular tipple amongst the more mature Glasgow residents is a 'hauf an' hauf', which is a half pint of beer and a nip (measure) of whisky. The roots of Scotland's national drink (*uisge beatha*, or 'water of life' in Gaelic) date back to the late 15th century, but it wasn't until the invention of a patent still in the early 19th century that distilling began to develop from small, family-run operations to the large manufacturing business it has become today. Now more than 700 million bottles a year are exported, mainly to the USA, France, Japan and Spain.

There are two types of whisky: **single malt**, made only from malted barley; and **grain**, which is made from malted barley together with unmalted barley, maize or other cereals, and is faster and cheaper to produce. Most of the popular brands are blends of both types of whisky – usually 60-70 % grain to 30-40 % malt. These **blended** whiskies account for over 90% of all sales worldwide and most of the production of single malts is used to add flavour to a blended whisky. Among the best known brands of blended whisky are *Johnnie Walker*, *Bells*, *Teachers* and *Famous Grouse*. There's not much between them in terms of flavour and they are usually drunk with a mixer, such as water or soda.

Single malts are a different matter altogether. Each is distinctive and should be drunk neat to fully appreciate its subtle flavours. Single malts vary enormously. Their distinctive flavours and aromas are derived from the peat used for drying, the water used for mashing, the type of oak cask used and the location of the distillery.

Single malts fall into four groups: Highland, Lowland, Campbeltown and Islay. There are over 40 distilleries to choose from, the majority located around Speyside, in the northeast. The region's many distilleries include that perennial favourite, *Glenfiddich*, producing a malt which is sold in 185 countries. A recommended alternative is the produce of the beautiful and peaceful Isle of Islay, whose malts are lovingly described in terms of their peaty quality. Scots tend to favour the 10 year-old *Glenmorangie*, while the most popular in the USA is *The Macallan*.

Soft drinks The soft drink most closely associated with the city is *Irn Bru*. It is to Glasgow what *Coca Cola* is to the USA. In fact, *Irn Bru* is drunk by more people in the city than *Coke*. This rust-coloured, sweet beverage, said to be 'made from girders', is even used as a mixer for various spirits and if you over indulge it provides the perfect hangover cure the next morning.

Shopping

Glasgow is a great city for shopping. Here you'll find the main designer stores such as *Emporio Armani*, *Versace* and *Diesel* as well as *Hobbs*, *Jigsaw*, *Karen Millen*, *Monsoon* and *Cruise*. Buchanan Street is the main shopping street and is lined with good clothes shops as well as boasting some of the city's best shopping malls. The **Buchanan Galleries** is a vast retail complex where you could quite happily exceed your credit limit, while **Princes Square**, further south near Argyle Street, is a tad more chic.

Near the foot of Buchanan Street is **Argyll Arcade**, one of Britain's oldest covered shopping arcades, which is almost a little jewellery quarter in itself with lots of jewellery shops. Opposite the bottom of Buchanan Street, in St Enoch Square, is the **St Enoch Centre**, claimed to be the largest all-glass building in Europe, which has numerous high-street chains.

East of Buchanan Street, the rejuvenated **Merchant City**, with its beautifully restored 18th-century warehouses, is home to many expensive designer shops, bars and cafés. A shopping trip here could inflict some serious damage on your wallet or purse.

In the East End is *The Barras*, Glasgow's largest market with over 800 stalls, where you can find everything you could ever want, from electronic goods to second-hand clothes. Back in the city centre is the *Victorian Village*, on West Regent Street, home to some good antique stalls.

The West End is the best place for quirky, independent shops, especially Ruthven Lane and Cresswell Lane, two cobbled streets off Byres Road which are worth exploring. Close by is *De Courcy's*, an unusual shopping arcade which has good gift shops and outlets selling everything from second-hand CDs to dried flowers.

Entertainment and nightlife

For a full listings of events & venues, ▶▶ *go to page 125*

It's been a few years now since Glasgow was chosen as 'European City of Culture' but the legacy lives on and the city continues to play host to a wide span of art, theatre, film and music. The majority of the larger theatres, concert halls and cinemas are concentrated in the city centre, though its two most renowned theatres, the *Citizens'* and the *Tramway*, are to be found south of the Clyde.

When it comes to nightlife, Glasgow is a city of energy and passion. Its club scene is amongst the most vibrant in the UK. Most of the nightclubs are clustered around the main shopping streets of the city centre, within easy walking distance of each other, and are open from 2230/2300 to between 0300 and 0400. Club nights and venues often change, so check current details in *The List* (see below) and also look for flyers in bars and pubs.

Details of all the city's events are listed in the two local newspapers, *The Herald* and the *Evening Times*. Another excellent source of information is the fortnightly listings magazine *The List*, which also covers Edinburgh and which is on sale in most newsagents. To book tickets for concerts or theatre productions, call at the Ticket Centre, City Hall, Candleriggs (open Monday-Saturday 0900-1800; Sunday 1200-1700) phone bookings T2874000 (Monday-Saturday 0900-2100; Sunday 0900-1800). Note that some of the live music venues don't have their own box office. For tickets and information go to Tower Records, on Argyle Street, T2045788. Tickets and information on all events are available at the Tourist Information Centre in George Square. You can also find flyers (promotional leaflets) for various events at the main concert halls and theatres and in many of the bars and cafés in the centre of town.

On-line information can be found at **www.whatsonwhen.com**, a world events guide, and **www.bigmouth.co.uk**, a comprehensive gig guide to the UK. It has an excellent search engine and you can buy tickets on-line.

Holidays and festivals

Bank holidays **New Year's Day** and **2 January**, **Good Friday** and **Easter Monday**, **May Day** (the first Monday in May), **Victoria Day** (the last Monday in May), **Christmas Day**, **Boxing Day** (25 and 26 December) are the main bank holidays. There are also local public holidays in spring and autumn. Dates vary from place to place. Banks are closed during these holidays, and sights and shops may be affected to varying degrees.

Events
For details of local festivals ▶▶ *go to page 134*
There is a huge variety of organized events held in Glasgow every year, ranging in size and spectacle from the massive New Year celebrations to the more traditional local Highland Games. The **Scottish Tourist Board** publishes a comprehensive list, *Events in Scotland*, twice a year. It's free and is available from the main tourist offices.

There are various special exhibitions staged at Charles Rennie Mackintosh properties throughout the year. For a list of those planned for 2002 contact the CRM Society (see page 93).

Sport and special interest travel

Cycling

There are numerous paths and cycle routes through the centre of Glasgow out into the surrounding countryside. One of these starts from Bell's Bridge (by the SECC) and runs to Erskine Bridge and back to the city centre via Paisley. It's a total distance of 31 miles and *OS Landranger sheet 64* covers the entire route. The **Clyde Coast Cycle Route** runs from Bell's Bridge, through some of the city's parks, and closely follows the old Pais-ley-Ardrossan Canal to Greenock, Gourock and on to Ardrossan, for ferries to the Isle of Arran. It's 28 miles one-way as far as Gourock and the route is covered by the *Glasgow and Clyde Coast Cycle Routes* leaflets, Glasgow to Paisley and Paisley to Greenock sections.
Cycle routes

   The **Glasgow Loch Lomond Cycle Way** is for both walkers and cyclists. It runs from the centre of Glasgow, following a disused railway track to Clydebank, the Forth and Clyde Canal towpath to Bowling, then a disused railway to Dumbarton, finally reaching Loch Lomond by way of the River Leven. The route continues all the way to Killin, in the heart of the Perthshire Highlands, via Balloch, Aberfoyle and Callander. An alternative route turns back at Clydebank and follows the Forth and Clyde Canal towpath all the way to the Firhill Basin and from there back to the cuty centre. *OS Landranger sheet 64* covers the route. There's also a new **Glasgow-Edinburgh** route, which incorporates part of the Clyde Walkway (see page 120).

For the most up-to-date information on the expanding network of cycle routes in the area, and throughout the country, contact **Sustrans**, 53 Cochrane Street, T5720234, www.sustrans.org.uk A useful book is *25 Cycle Routes In and Around Glasgow*, by EB Wilkie, HMSO, price £8.99. The *Cyclists' Touring Club (CTC)*, Cotterell House, 69 Meadrow, Godalming, Surrey, GU7 3HS, T01483-417217, www.ctc.org.uk the largest cycling organization in the UK, providing a wide range of services and information on transport, cycle hire and routes, from day rides to longer tours.
Information & organizations

   Bikes can be taken free on most local rail services on a first-come-first-served basis (call *ScotRail* bookings, T08457-550033). On long-distance routes you'll have to make a reservation and pay a small charge (£3.50). Space is limited on trains so it's a good idea to book as far in advance as possible. **Bus and coach** companies will not carry bikes, unless they are dismantled and boxed. **Ferries** transport bikes for a small fee and **airlines** will often accept them as part of your baggage allowance. Check with the ferry company or airline about any restrictions. There's also the option of a **cycling holiday package**, which includes transport of your luggage, pre-booked accommo-dation, route instructions and food and backup support.

   The Scottish Tourist Board (STB) publishes a free booklet, *Cycling in Scotland*, which is useful and suggests routes in various parts of the country, as well as accommoda-tion and repair shops. Many area tourist boards also provide cycling guides for their own areas.

Dales, 150 Dobbies Loan, T3322705. Close to Buchanan bus station. *West End Cycles*, 16 Chancellor Street, T3571344. At the south end of Byres Road. £12 per day for moun-tain bikes, £50 per week. ID and £50 deposit required. This is also an excellent place to buy bikes and is a BMX specialist.
Bike hire

Essentials

Fishing

Scotland's rivers, streams, lochs and estuaries are among the cleanest waterways in Europe and are filled with salmon, trout (sea, brown and rainbow) and pike. Not surprisingly, then, fishing (coarse, game and sea) is hugely popular in Scotland.

There is no close season for **coarse fishing** or **sea angling**. For **wild brown trout** the close season is early October to mid-March. The close season for **salmon** and **sea trout** varies from area to area and between net and rod fishing. It is generally from late August to early February for net fishing, and from early November to early February for rod fishing.

No licence is required to fish in Scotland, but most of the land and rivers are privately owned so you must obtain a **permit** from the owners or their agents. These are often readily available at the local fishing tackle shop and usually cost from around £15, though some rivers, such as the Tweed, can be far more expensive.

The STB's booklet *Fish Scotland* is a good introduction and a source of all kinds of information. It is available free from tourist offices, or by post (see page 17). You can also contact the *Scottish Federation of Sea Anglers*, Brian Burn, Flat 2, 16 Bellevue Road, Ayr, KA7 2SA, T01292-264735; or *Scottish National Anglers Association*, David Wilkie, Administration Office, Caledonia House, South Gyle, Edinburgh, EH12 9DQ, T0131- 3398808.

Games and activities

AMF Bowling, Elliot Street, Finnieston, T2484478. Monday-Thursday 1100-2400. Ten-pin bowling alley, where you can also eat fast food and drink beer for that all-American experience.

Bedlam Paintball, Wares Wood, Houston, T07000-233526. If your idea of fun is getting shot in the testicles from close range with a small sphere full of paint, then paintballing is for you. An emulsional experience guaranteed.

Braehead Ice Rink, King's Inch Road, Renfrew, T8854600. Public skating rink open daily. Six-sheet curling rink for those who wish to emulate Scotland's Olympic gold medalists.

Cloudbusters Paragliding, 2 Inchmurrin Drive, Cathkin, T6346688.

Glasgow Ski and Snowboard Centre, Bellahouston Park, 16 Drumbreck Road, T4274991. Monday-Thursday 0930-2230, Friday 0930-2100, Saturday and Sunday 0930-1800. Floodlit artificial snow slope. Only £10 per day, including equipment hire and use of the tow.

Laserquest 2000, 177 Trongate, T5527667. Monday-Sunday 1030-2230. Shoot and be shot at in the dark while trying to avoid running into walls. Sounds great.

Scotkart Indoor Kart Racing, Westburn Road, Cambuslang, T6410222; John Knox Street, Clydebank, T0800-6895278. Two of the biggest indoor race tracks in Scotland. If you're flexible you can take advantage of some good price deals.

Shawfield Dog Track, Shawfield Stadium, T6474121. Tuesday, Thursday and Friday from 2000, Saturday from 1945. £3 admission. Cheap booze, greasy food, great atmosphere and the chance of winning money. What more could you wish for?

West of Scotland Cricket Club, 40-42 Peel Street, T3390688. For those who prefer more relaxed pursuits, why not saunter on over here for a civilized afternoon of drinking, sitting in a deckchair and waiting for the rain to stop so that the covers can come off?

Golf

Scotland has over 400 golf courses, with more being built all the time, and, therefore *To arrange golfing* has more courses per head of population than any other country in the world. Any *holidays visit* decent-sized town in Scotland will have a golf course nearby and most, if not all, are *www.scotland-golf-* available for play. There are many public courses, which tend to be both cheap and *tours.co.uk* extremely busy, and are often excellently laid out. The majority of private clubs allow visitors, although many have restrictions as to on what days visitors can play. Weekends are usually reserved for club competitions for the members so it is best to try to play on a weekday. All private clubs have a dress code and it is inadvisable to turn up for a round in a collarless shirt and jeans. These minor caveats aside, you are more than likely to receive a warm and courteous welcome. **Green fees** for one of the top championship courses will cost from around £40 upwards. Many clubs offer a daily or weekly ticket. A **Golf Pass Scotland** costs between £46 and £70 for five days (Monday-Friday), depending on the area. *Golf in Scotland* is a free brochure listing 400 courses and clubs with accommodation details. For a copy contact the STB. The *British Tourist Authority* (BTA) has a very useful *Golfing Holidays* booklet which provides details of golfing holidays and major golf tournaments in Britain. (BTA and STB addresses are on pages 16 and 17). Golfing tours are organized from the USA by *Golf International Inc*, T1-800-833 1389 and *Jerry Quinlan's Celtic Golf*, T1-800-535 6148, www.jqcelticgolf.com

There are many municipal courses in and around Glasgow, as well as several top class championship courses within easy reach of the city. These include: **Haggs Castle**, 70 Dumbreck Road, T4270480; **Loch Lomond**, Rossdhu House, Luss, T01436-860223, www.lochlomond.com; **Prestwick Golf Club**, 2 Links Road, T01292-477404, www.prestwickgc.co.uk; **Royal Troon**, Craigend Road, Troon, T01292-311555; **Turnberry Hotel**, Turnberry, Ayrshire, T01655-331000, wwww.turnberry.co.uk

Hiking and climbing

There are numerous marked trails in and around the city, including the **Kelvin Walkway** (see page 94 for a full route description) and the **Clyde Walkway** (see page 120). There is also some excellent walking to be had in Mugdock Country Park, at Milngavie, to the north of the city. Here also is the starting point for Scotland's busiest and best-known long-distance trail, the **West Highland Way**, which runs for 92 miles to Fort William. The route progresses steadily from the Lowlands, along the eastern shore of **Loch Lomond** and the traverse of the western edge of **Rannoch Moor**, to enter **Glencoe** at White Corries. It continues over the Devil's Staircase, past Kinlochleven, and through **Glen Nevis** to Fort William. Many walkers finish off with an ascent of **Ben Nevis** 4,406ft, the highest mountain in Britain. **Further information**, including a trail leaflet with accommodation and facilities guide, is available from *West Highland Way Ranger Service*, Balloch Castle, Balloch, G53 8LX, T01389-758216.

Some of the walk descriptions given in this guidebook should ideally be used in conjunction with a good map, such as the *Ordnance Survey* (OS) *Landranger* series. The relevant map numbers have been listed, where possible, with the route description. OS maps can be found at Tourist Information Centres and also at **outdoor activity shops**, which are usually staffed by experienced climbers and walkers who can give good advice about the right equipment. The best-equipped shops are *Tiso*, www.tiso.co.uk whose *Glasgow Outdoor Experience*, Couper Street, off Kyle Street, T5595450, is Europe's largest outdoor shop and includes features such as the 15 m 'North Face Pinnacle' the 'Chill Zone', a refrigerated room with temperatures down to -20°C; and *Glasgow Climbing Centre*, Ibrox Church, 534 Paisley Road West, T4279550, which stocks no fewer than 65 different routes for the beginner to the expert.

Essentials

The best time for hiking is usually from May to September, though in the more low-lying parts April to October should be safe. The **Scottish Tourist Board** is a useful source of information for walkers (address on page 17). Local tourist offices have details of interesting local walks.

Visitors to Scotland should be aware of the need for caution and safety preparations when walking or climbing in the mountains. The nature of Scottish weather is such that a fine sunny day can turn into driving rain or snow in a matter of minutes. Remember that a blizzard can be raging on the summit when the car park at the foot of the mountain is bathed in sunshine. It is essential to get an up-to-date weather forecast before setting off on any walk or climb. Whatever the time of year, or conditions when you set off, you should always carry or wear essential items of clothing. A basic list for summer conditions would be: **boots** with a good tread and ankle support and a thick pair of socks; **waterproof jacket and trousers**, even on a sunny day; **hat and gloves** are important if the weather turns bad; **warm trousers** should be worn or carried, tracksuit bottoms are okay if you also have waterproof trousers; **spare woolly jumper or fleece jacket** will provide an extra layer; **map and compass** are essential to carry and to know how to use. Other essentials are **food and drink**, a simple **first aid kit**, a **whistle** and a **torch**. A small 25-30 litre rucksack should be adequate for carrying the above items. Also remember to leave details of your route and expected time of return with someone, and remember to inform them on your return.

Spectator sports

American football **Scottish Claymores** play in the NFL Europe League, with their home games at Hampden Park. Tickets £12. Contact them at 205 St Vincent Street, T2223800, www.claymores.co.uk

Football

Football news and information can be found online at www.footballnews. co.uk and www.football365.co.uk

Football (soccer) is Scotland's most popular spectator sport. The *Scottish Football League*, established in 1874, is the main competition. Scottish football is dominated, and always has been, by the two main Glasgow teams, Rangers and Celtic, known collectively as the 'Old Firm', who regularly attract crowds of over 50,000 and are amongst the wealthiest clubs in Britain. For a brief period in the 1980s this stranglehold was broken by Aberdeen and Dundee United, but events since have proved this an aberration rather than a trend. For more on the Old Firm, see page 207.

The domestic football **season** runs from early August to mid-May. Most matches are played on Saturdays at 1500, and there are often games through the week, on Tuesday and Wednesday evenings at 1930. There is usually a match on a Sunday afternoon, which is broadcast live on satellite TV. **Ticket prices** range from £15 up to £25 for big games.

Celtic Football Club are based at Celtic Park, 95 Kerrydale St, T5562611, off the London Road in the East End. *Clyde Football Club*, Broadwood Stadium, Cumbernauld, T01236-451511. *Partick Thistle Football Club*, Firhill Stadium, 80 Firhill Road, T5791971. *Queens Park Football Club*, Hampden Park, Mount Florida, T6321275. *Rangers Football Club*, Ibrox Stadium, 150 Edmiston Drive, T4278500, in the South Side.

The **national** team play at Hampden Park, T6204000. Refurbished at a cost of £63 million, Hampden has reopened with a much reduced capacity of 52,000 but now boasting UEFA five-star facilities. Stadium tours are available and also housed here is the Scottish Football Museum (see page 108).

Sports and leisure centres

If you're staying more than a few weeks and intend keeping in shape, then it's worth investing in the Glasgow Club Leisure Pass. It costs £30 per month and allows unlimited access to all council-owned leisure centres and swimming pools. For more information T2872000.

Alexandra *Sports Hall*, Alexandra Parade (northeast of the cathedral), T5561695. Monday-Wednesday 1000-2200, Thursday and Friday 1400-2200, Saturday and Sunday 1000-1700. Gym, badminton and short tennis courts, and sunbeds for the terminally lazy.

Kelvinhall International Sports Arena, Argyle St, T3572525. Monday-Sunday 0900-2230. Excellently equipped complex with a gym, athletics track, a variety of aerobics classes and a dance studio. Free access for those with Glasgow Club memberships.

North Woodside Leisure Centre, 10 Braid Square, St George's Cross, T3328102. Monday 0800-2000, Wednesday and Friday 0730-2130, Tuesday and Thursday 0900-2100, Saturday and Sunday 1000-1600. Women-only Wednesday 1130-2130 and Sunday 1400-1600. Swimming pool and gym but also suitable for less-enthusiastic fitness types, with sunbeds, yoga classes, steam rooms and a sauna.

Pony trekking and horse riding

Pony Trekking is a long-established activity in Scotland and miles of beautiful coastline, lochsides, and moorland are accessible on horseback. There are numerous equestrian centres around the country catering to all levels of riders. The STB produces a *Trekking & Riding* brochure listing riding centres around the country, all of them approved by the **Trekking and Riding Society of Scotland** (*TRSS*) or the **British Horse Society** (*BHS*).

Centres offer **pony trekking** (leisurely strolls at walking pace for novices), **hacks** (short rides at a fast pace for experienced riders) and **trail riding** (long-distance rides at no more than a canter). These include: *Ardgowan Riding Centre*, Bankfoot Farm, Inverkip, T01475-521390, riding@ardgowan.co.uk and *Carmichael Trekking & Madtrax* (*Scotland*)*@Carmichael*, A73 Clyde Valley Tourism Route, Carmichael, Thankerton, Biggar, T01899-308336, www.carmichael.co.uk

For general information contact the **TRSS**, Horse Trials Office, Blair Atholl, Perthshire, T01796-481543, or the **BHS**, British Equestrian Centre, Stoneleigh Park, Kenilworth, Warwicks CV8 2LR, T01203-414288.

Health

No vaccinations are required for entry into Britain. Citizens of **EU** countries are entitled to free medical treatment at National Health Service hospitals on production of an E111 form. Also, Australia, New Zealand and several other non-EU European countries have reciprocal health-care arrangements with Britain.

In the event of a medical emergency: dial 999 or 112 (both free) for an ambulance

Citizens of other countries will have to pay for all medical services, except accident and emergency care given at Accident and Emergency (A&E) Units at most (but not all) National Health hospitals. Health insurance is therefore strongly advised for citizens of non-EU countries.

Pharmacists can dispense only a limited range of drugs without a doctor's prescription. Most are open during normal shopping hours, though some are open late, especially in larger towns. Local newspapers will carry lists of which are open late.

Doctors' surgeries are usually open from around 0830-0900 till 1730-1800, though times vary. Outside surgery hours you can go to the casualty department of the local hospital for any complaint requiring urgent attention. For the address of the nearest hospital or doctors' surgery, T0800-665 544.

Hospitals & medical services

For STD clinics & HIV information, see page 19

Glasgow Royal Infirmary is at 84 Castle Street, T2114000, near the cathedral. Open 24-hours. The *Southern General Hospital* on Govan Road, T2011100, is the main South Side hospital. For **dental emergencies** go to the *Glasgow Dental Hospital*, 378 Sauchiehall Street, T2119600. Monday-Friday 0900-1500. **Pharmacies**: *Boots*, 200 Sauchiehall Street, 18 Union Street and St Enoch Centre. *Superdrug*, Central station, T2218197; open Monday-Wednesday and Sunday till 2000, Thursday-Saturday till 2100. *Munroes'*, 693 Great Western Rd, T3390012; open daily till 2100.

Central Glasgow

3

Central Glasgow

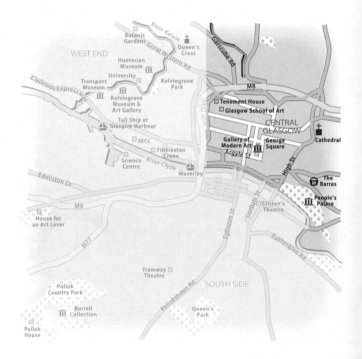

It's no accident that Glasgow was chosen as both City of Culture and, more recently, UK City of Architecture and Design. The city's main attractions are its magnificent Victorian buildings, its museums and its art galleries (most of which are free). Sir John Betjeman, Poet Laureate and architectural enthusiast, described Glasgow as the 'greatest Victorian city in Europe' and many examples of its rich architectural legacy can be found in the commercial centre, stretching from George Square west to the M8.

While **George Square** is the heart of modern Glasgow, the area around the medieval **cathedral** was the heart of the old city. In fact, until the 18th century Glasgow consisted only of a narrow ribbon of streets running north from the river past the Glasgow Cross and up the High Street to the cathedral. Then came the city's rapid expansion west and the High Street became a dilapidated backwater.

To the east of George Square is the **Merchant City**, where the Palladian mansions of the Tobacco Lords have been cleaned up and reclaimed by the professional classes as a fashionable place to eat, drink, shop and play. Further east is Glasgow's **East End**, a traditional working-class stronghold which is gradually giving way to the relentless drive of urban gentrification. Here chic café-bars and art galleries rub shoulders with dilapidated tenements and scruffy markets.

George Square and the cathedral area

George Square The heart of modern Glasgow is George Square, which makes the obvious starting point for a tour of the city centre, as the **tourist information centre** is located here, on the south side of the square. George square was named after George III and laid out in 1781. For several years it was not much more than a watery patch of ground where horses were taken to be slaughtered and puppies to be drowned. The plan was to make it an upmarket, elegant square with private gardens at its centre. However, many of the buildings (designed by the Adam brothers) were never built, while the gardens didn't last long as Glaswegians objected to such an obvious display of privilege and ripped the railings down in disgust. The square only became the heart of the city when the council decided to make it the location for the City Chambers – the most visible symbol of Glasgow's position as Second City of the Empire.

Although there's a statue of Burns in the square, the poet did not have very strong links with Glasgow. On the few times he did come to the city he seems to have gone shopping – buying, on various visits, some books, some cocoa, and some black silk for his wife. Other statues which adorn the square are those of Queen Victoria, Prince Albert, Sir Walter Scott, Sir Robert Peel and James Watt, while the Greek Doric column is dedicated to Walter Scott (1837).

The square is surrounded by fine civic buildings, most notable of which is the grandiose **City Chambers**, which fills the east side, a wonderful testament to the optimism and aspiration of Victorian Glasgow. It was designed in the Italian Renaissance style by William Young and the interior is even more impressive than its façade. The imposing arcaded marble entrance hall is decorated with elaborate mosaics and a marble staircase leads up to a great banqueting hall with a wonderful arched ceiling, leaded glass windows and paintings depicting scenes from the city's history. One wall is covered by a series of murals by the Glasgow Boys (see page 210). ■ *There are free guided tours of the City Chambers, Mon-Fri at 1030 and 1430. T2872000.*

On the northwest corner of George Square, opposite Queen Street Station, is another fine building, the **Merchants' House**, now home to Glasgow Chamber of Commerce. The interior is worth a look as it boasts some beautiful stained-glass windows and chocolate-brown wood panelling. ■ *Free. Entry by appointment only. T2218272.*

The Gallery Just to the south of George Square, facing the west end of Ingram Street, is **Royal**
of Modern Art **Exchange Square**, which is almost completely filled by the **Gallery of Modern Art** (GOMA), yet another example of the city's penchant for setting major public buildings within built-up squares. The building dates from 1778, when it was built as the Cunninghame Mansion, home to one of Glasgow's wealthy Tobacco Lords. It passed to the Royal Bank of Scotland in 1817 and 10 years later the magnificent portico was added to the front and the building then became the Royal Exchange, the city's main business centre. Following a stint as a telephone exchange in the 1920s, it latterly became the local public library, until 1996 when the magnificent barrel-vaulted interior was converted to house one of the city's newest, and most controversial, art venues, drawing the ire of many a critic for its unashamed eclecticism and populism.

The gallery features contemporary works by artists from around the world, displayed on three themed levels: the **Earth Gallery** on the ground floor; the **Water Gallery**; and the **Air Gallery**. It's a bold, innovative art space, making

Things to do in Central Glasgow

- Find out all about the city's fascinating history through the eyes of its people at the People's Palace.
- Take a tour round the School of Art, Charles Rennie Mackintosh's Art Nouveau masterpiece.
- Wander round the Barras market listening to the famous Glasgow East End patter and maybe you'll unearth a hidden treasure.
- Take in the latest arthouse movie at the wonderful GFT and while you're there enjoy a cheap lunch at *Café Cosmo*.
- Get your freak on at the *Arches*, home to some of Glasgow's best club nights.

excellent use of the fabulous original interior. The works you can see are varied and include powerful paintings by **Peter Howson**, the Imperial War Museum's war artist in Bosnia, photographs by **Henri Cartier-Bresson**, and **Beryl Cook**'s jolly work *By the Clyde*. There's also a superb top-floor **café**, with great views across the city's rooftops (see page 57). ■ *Mon-Thu and Sat 1000-1700, Fri and Sun 1100-1700. Free. T2291996, www.glasgow.gov.uk*

In front of the gallery is an equestrian statue of the Duke of Wellington. The Duke can often be seen wearing a traffic cone on his head at a jaunty angle, placed there by over refreshed locals or by students (what is it with undergraduates and traffic cones?). The cone is there so often – and has featured in so many photographs – that the Duke now looks undressed without it.

At the top of the High Street stands Glasgow Cathedral. The rather severe-looking early Gothic structure is the only complete medieval cathedral on the Scottish mainland. It was built on the site of St Mungo's original church, established in AD 543, though this has been a place of Christian worship since it was blessed for burial in AD 397 by St Ninian, the earliest missionary recorded in Scottish history. Most of the building was completed in the 13th century though parts were built a century earlier by Bishop Jocelyn. The choir and crypt were added a century later and the building was completed at the end of the 15th century by Robert Blacader, the first Bishop of Glasgow.

Glasgow Cathedral

During the Reformation, the city's last Roman Catholic Archbishop, James Beaton, took off for France with most of the cathedral treasures, just ahead of the townsfolk who proceeded to rid the building of all traces of 'idolatry' by destroying altars, statues, vestments and the valuable library. The present furnishings mostly date from the 19th century and many of the windows have been renewed with modern stained glass. The most outstanding feature in the cathedral is the fan vaulting around St Mungo's tomb in the crypt, one of the very finest examples of medieval architecture in Scotland. There's also fine work in the choir, including a 15th century stone screen, the only one of its kind left in any pre-Reformation secular (non-monastic) church in Scotland. ■ *Apr-Sep Mon-Sat 0930-1800, Sun 1400-1700, Oct-Mar Mon-Sat 0930-1600, Sun 1400-1600. Free. T5526891, www.historic-scotland.gov.uk*

Behind the cathedral looms the **Western Necropolis**, a vast burial ground overlooking the city from the top of a high ridge. It was modelled on Pere-Lachaise cemetery in Paris. Around 3,500 tombs have been built here and around 50,000 burials have taken place. Most of the burials took place in the 19th century and the ornate nature of many of the tombs makes it appear as if the city worthies buried here really were trying to take their money with them when they died. It's the ideal vantage point from which to appreciate the

George Square, Merchant City & Trongate

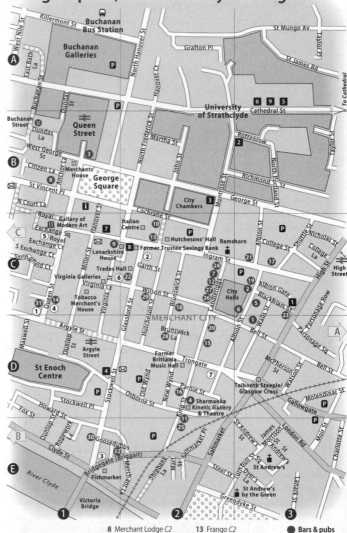

Related maps
A East End,
page 66
B South of the Clyde,
page 106
C City Centre,
page 56

8 Merchant Lodge C2
9 Murray Hall A3

● **Eating**
1 Arta D3
2 Bargo C3
3 Brasserie on George
   Square B1
4 Café Cossachock D2
5 Café Gandolfi C3
6 Caffe Uno C3
7 City Merchant C2
8 Counting House B1
9 Corinthian C1
10 Cuba Norte C2
11 Eat Drink Man Woman D2
12 Farfelu C2

13 Frango C2
14 Ichiban Japanese
   Noodle Café C1
15 Khublai Khan D2
16 Le Bouchon D2
17 Loop C3
18 Mao C2
19 Noah C3
20 Oblomov D2
21 OKO C3
22 Peckham's on Third C2
23 Schottische C3
24 Smiths of Glasgow C2
25 Thirteenth Note E2

● **Bars & pubs**
26 Bar 91 C2
27 Blackfriars C2
28 Mitre Bar D2
29 Rab Ha's C2
30 Scotia Bar E1
31 Strata C1
32 Victoria Bar E1

○ **Entertainment**
1 Archaos C1
2 Bennets C2
3 Clutha Vaults E1
4 Cube C1
5 MAS C1
6 Polo Lounge C1
7 Tron Theatre D2

■ Sleeping
1 Babbity Bowster,
   Restaurant & Pub C3
2 Chancellors Hall B3
3 City Travel Inn Metro B2
4 Express By Holiday Inn D1
5 Forbes Hall A3
6 Garnett Hall A3
7 Jarvis Ingram C1

cathedral in all its Gothic splendour and many of the tombs are well worth a look. The graveyard is overseen by a statue of John Knox, the 16th century firebrand reformer. There's also a monument to William Miller who penned the nursery rhyme *Wee Willie Winkie*. Look out for a monument to Alexander McCall. A Celtic Cross, it's the first solo work by Charles Rennie Mackintosh.

In front of the cathedral is the weetabix-coloured **St Mungo Museum of Religious Life and Art**, which features a series of displays of arts and artefacts representing the six major world religions, as well as a Japanese Zen garden in the courtyard outside – great for a few moments of quiet contemplation. Highlights include **Salvador Dalí**'s astounding painting *Christ of St John of the Cross*, purchased by the city from the artist in 1951. You can also see a Native American ceremonial blanket depicting sacred animals, masks used in African initiation rites, and an Islamic prayer rug. Displays on religion in the west of Scotland cover everything from the Temperance Movement of the late 19th century, to the religious life of the modern city's vibrant ethnic communities. Don't miss the extremely interesting comments on the visitors' board. There's also a bookshop and a café serving hot meals, snacks and drinks. ■ *Mon-Thu and Sat 1000-1700, Fri and Sun 1100-1700. Free. T5532557, www.glasgow.gov.uk*

Cathedral Precinct

Across the street is the **Provand's Lorship**, the oldest remaining house in Glasgow, built in 1471 as part of a refuge for the city's poor and extended in 1670. It has also served as an inn of rather dubious repute in its time. Now it's a museum devoted mainly to medieval furniture and various domestic items. In the grounds is a specially created medieval garden. ■ *Same phone number and opening hours as above.*

Close to the cathedral, at Parson Street, just off the High Street and M8, is one of Charles Rennie Mackintosh's lesser-known works, the **Martyrs' Public School**. Built in 1895, on the very street where CRM was born, this solid red sandstone building is clearly visible from the top of the High Street. ■ *Daily 1300-1600. Free. T2878955.*

Martyrs' Public School

Eating and drinking

The Brasserie on George Square, *Millennium Hotel*, T3073301, Mon-Sun 0700-1000, 1200-1415, 1700-2230. There's a 1930s feel to this brasserie which attracts business diners as well as ladies who lunch. The conservatories overlooking George Sq are a great place for people-watching.

Mid-range
● *on map, page 56*

The Counting House, 2 St Vincent Pl, T2489568, Mon-Sat 1100-2200, Sun 1230-2130, bar open til later. One of those enormous chain bar situated in a former bank, this pub attracts large numbers of office workers who come for a drink and something fast and filling like deep-fried potato skins.

Cheap

Gallery of Modern Art Rooftop Café, Royal Exchange Sq, T2217484. Mon-Sat 1000-1630, Sun 1100-1630. Great city views, but if the weather's dreadful, admire the modern art on show. Lunch menu comprises fairly standard fare of fishcakes and the like. *Caffe Uno*, 18 Royal Exchange Sq, T2217277. New coffee bar convenient for the Modern Art Gallery.

Cafés

The Merchant City

The grid of streets to the east of George Square, stretching as far as the High Street, form the Merchant City, or New Town, is where the Tobacco Lords built their magnificent Palladian mansions. They made Glasgow the most important tobacco trading city in Europe and can also take the credit for it being one of the lung cancer capitals of the world by the mid-20th century. The Tobacco Lords, however, gave way to King Cotton, and by 1820 the area between Candleriggs and Miller Street was largely taken up by the textile industry.

The Merchant City's days as a desirable residential district were numbered when fashionable merchants were lured west by the fine new houses being built on Blytheswood Hill. Banks, markets and warehouses all followed and by the mid-19th century the city's financial heart had been transplanted into the West End. The Merchant City became a wholesale area, largely neglected and under threat of postwar high-rise housing development. Luckily, it escaped, and the return of Glasgow's concert hall to Candleriggs saw the beginning of the regeneration of this area.

Money has been poured into the restoration of its 18th century warehouses and homes in an attempt to revitalize and regenerate the city's old historic core. Though many of the buildings are little more than façades, the investment has succeeded in attracting e xpensive designer clothes shops and a plethora of stylish bistros, cafés and bars, which are packed with the city's young professionals and media types. It's a very pleasant and interesting area to explore, with the advantage that when all that neoclassical architecture gets too much, you can pop into one of the trendy café-bars for some light relief.

A tour of the Merchant City
Like many of the Merchant City's civic buildings, Hutcheson's Hall faces down the street, closing the vista

A good place to start is **Hutchesons' Hall**, at 158 Ingram Street, a distinguished Georgian building which is now the National Trust for Scotland's regional headquarters. It was built by David Hamilton in 1805 in neoclassical style with a traditional Scottish 'townhouse' steeple. It was once home of the Scottish Educational Trust, a charitable institution founded by the 17th century lawyer brothers George and Thomas Hutcheson, which provided almshouses and schools for the city. Their statues gaze down towards the site of the original almshouse in Trongate. Upstairs is the ornate hall where you can see a film on the Glasgow Style, the distinctive style of art that evolved from the works of artists such as Charles Rennie Mackintosh. Downstairs there's an exhibition, also on Glasgow Style, featuring jewellery, textiles, furniture and prints by contemporary Glasgow artists and crafts people. All the works are for sale – for anything from a few pounds to several hundred pounds. ■ *Mon-Sat 1000-1700. Free. T5528391, www.nts.org.uk*

Further west, between South Frederick Street and John Street, is the **Italian Centre** (see page 62), restored by Page & Park from the former Bank of Scotland building, designed by William Burn in 1828. Opposite, at the corner of Ingram Street and Glassford Street is the Edwardian former **Trustee Savings Bank** built in the style of the French Renaissance by the prodigious talent, JJ Burnet in 1900. Further west on Ingram Street, is the lavish, Italianate **Lanarkshire House**, designed by John Burnet in 1876-79 as a refacing of David Hamilton's former Union Bank (1841) which itself replaced Virginia Mansion. Its interior riches have been lovingly restored as *The Corinthian*, a stunning combination of bars, restaurants and meeting rooms. It is particularly impressive at night when floodlit.

In nearby Glassford Street is Glasgow's oldest secular building, the **Trades Hall**, designed by Robert Adam and built in 1794 as the headquarters of the city's trade guilds. It still serves its original purpose. The Grand Hall is an impressive sight, lined with a Belgian silk tapestry depicting the work of a range of former city trades such as bonnetmakers

---

Five of the best: city centre architectural gems

- **Trades Hall** (previous page)
- **St Vincent St Church** (page 70)
- **St Andrew's Church** (page 63)
- **Briggait** (page 63)
- **Gardner's Warehouse** (page 69)

(not much call for them nowadays) and cordiners (bootmakers). ■ *Guided tours by appointment only. Free. T5522418.*

Running south off Ingram Street is Virginia Street, whose name recalls Glasgow's trading links with America. About halfway down, on the left heading towards Argyle Street, is the **Virginia Galleries**, the three-tiered, glass-roofed arcade of the original Tobacco Exchange. Parallel to Virginia Street is Miller Street, originally a street of detached villas which was gradually redeveloped as very grand textile and clothing factories and warehouses. Here you'll find the Merchant City's oldest surviving house (No 42), the **Tobacco Merchant's House**. Designed by John Craig and dating from 1775, it was restored by Glasgow Building Preservation Trust in 1995.

East of Hutcheson's Hall, on Ingram Street, is **Ramshorn Church**, designed by Thomas Rickman in 1826 and one of the earliest examples of Gothic revival ecclesiastical architecture in Scotland. A plaque on the west side of the tower testifies to the church's association with John MacDonald who became the first Prime Minister of Canada. The real delight here lies in the church graveyard, which is well worth a stroll around and offers a quiet picnic refuge in summer. Among the local worthies buried here are David Dale, the pioneering industrialist who helped build New Lanark (see page 159) and John Anderson, founder of Strathclyde University. Also here is the grave of Pierre Emile L'Angelier (his name is not on the tombstone), whose mysterious death led to one of Glasgow's most famous trials (see page 75).

Head south from here, down Candleriggs, and you'll pass the **City Hall**, dating from 1817. This was the first concert hall in the city built specifically for public gatherings and musical performances, and was converted back to a concert hall following the destruction of St Andrews Halls, which once stood on the site of the present-day Mitchell Library (see page 86). The auditorium, designed by George Murray in 1840 (who also designed the Egyptian entrance on Albion Street), was built over the bazaar, itself designed by James Cleland in 1817. The Candelriggs frontage, with its Corinthian pillars, was designed by James Carrick in 1885. This entire block, bordered by Ingram Street, Bell Street, Candleriggs and Albion Sreet, was the site of many of the city's produce markets, including the fresh fruit and flower market, the cheese market and the attractively named dead-meat market. The Bell Street entrance has been completely restored and revamped as a stylish new shopping and restaurant complex called Merchant Square.

At the foot of Candleriggs, look to the right across the Trongate to see the rather shabby exterior of the former **Britannia Music Hall** (1857). Originally the Panopticon, the music hall still survives on the upper floors of this faded Italianate beauty. It has been described by the UK Theatres Trust as the finest surviving early music hall theatre in the UK. It closed its doors in 1938, but during its lifespan has played host to the likes of Stan Laurel, Cary Grant and Harry Lauder.

Central Glasgow

A walk around Glasgow Cathedral and the Merchant City

*From the north side of George Square head up Hanover Street. Turn right onto Cathedral Street, then turn left up Stirling Road. Take the footpath that leads off to the left and have a look at **Martyrs' Public School**, one of the earliest Rennie Mackintosh buildings in the city. Head back towards the High Street to visit the **cathedral** and the **St Mungo Museum of Religious Life and Art**. Then cross over the road to visit the **Provand's***

*__Lordship__, the oldest house in the city. Continue walking down the High Street until you come to Ingram Street and the heart of the Merchant City. Along here is **Hutcheson's Hall**, which houses an exhibition on Glasgow Style. Then go into the **Italian Centre**, where you can shop – or window shop – for designer gear at Versace and Armani and get something to eat in one of the cafés, before walking back to George Square.*

Eating and drinking

Mid-range
● *on map, page 56*

Arta, 13-19 Walls St, T5522101. Wed, Thu and Sun 1700-2300, Fri, Sat 1700-2400; bar open Sun-Wed 1700-2400, Thu 1700-0100, Fri and Sat till 0300. Housed in the Old Cheesmarket, this lavish bar, restaurant and club is sister to *The Corinthian* and currently *the* place to go in Glasgow. Spanish food.

Café Gandolfi, 64 Albion St, T5526813. Mon-Sat 0900-2330. The first of Glasgow's style bistro/brasseries back in 1979, which almost makes it antique by today's contemporary design standards. Still comfortably continental, relaxed and soothing, a good place for a snack or a leisurely late breakfast. Gets busy at lunchtimes so best to book.

City Merchant, 97-99 Candleriggs, T5531577. Mon-Sat 1200-2300, Sun 1700-2300. BYOB. No-smoking area. The best of Scottish meat and game but it's the fish and seafood which stand out. Absolutely superb. It's at the top end of this price range but their 2- and 3-course set menus are more affordable and excellent value (available 1200-1900). Very popular and a good atmosphere.

Corinthian, 191 Ingram St T5521101. Sun-Thu 1200-1500, 1730-2300, Fri, Sat 1200-1500, 1730-2400, bar open daily 1100-0300. There's a sense of occasion about stepping out in this popular spot. There are several bars, a nightclub and private club as well as the restaurant. Food tends to be traditional Scottish with a modern twist and the puddings are very good.

Cuba Norte, 17 John St, T5523505. Mon-Fri 1100-2300, Sat, Sun 1200-2300. As the name suggests there's a Latin American feel here, not just in the food but in the music. There's even dancing every night. Come just for cocktails or for a meal.

Farfelu, 89 Candleriggs, T5525345. Mon-Sat 1200-1400, 1800-2200. A smart and airy place to eat. Chef Kenny Coltman (ex-Malmaison) has a fine pedigree and sources his raw ingredients with care, and with dishes like sea bream with chard and tapenade, puts in no little effort to please. You can dine here for a tenner, so it represents fantastic value.

Frango, 15 John St T5524433. Breakfast from 0900, meals from 1200-2230. There's an all-day menu, with lots of fish dishes such as fish soup, swordfish and fish and chips. Relaxed atmosphere.

Mao, 84 Brunswick St T5645161. Mon-Sun 1200-late. Far Eastern and Oriental food in slick Merchant City outlet.

OKO, 68 Ingram St T5721500. Mon-Wed 1200-1500, 1800-2200, Thu-Sat 1200-1500, 1800-2300. Sushi bar conveyor and hot dishes like tempura, teriyaki, noodles etc.

Khublai Khan, 26 Candleriggs T4008090. Mon-Sun 1730-late. The idea at this

Mongolian restaurant is that you make your own dishes by selecting ingredients from a range of meats, vegetables, herbs and spices. Don't get too carried away with the spices.

Loop, 64 Ingram St T5721472. Mon-Sun 1100-2230. Another trendy Merchant City restaurant, offering quite a few choices for vegetarians. You can also come in for a sandwich during the day.

Five of the best: cool city centre bars

- *Arta* (page 60)
- *Mojo* (page 61)
- *CCA Bar* (page 78)
- *The Arches* (page 79)
- *Spy Bar* (page 80)

Oblomov, 24 Candleriggs, T5524251. Mon-Sun 1100-2030, bar open later. Not surprisingly given the name, this restaurant has an Eastern European theme. Starters like blinis and filling mains served with potato dumplings.

Schottische, 16-18 Blackfriars St, T5527774. Mon-Sat 1230-1530, 1830-2100. Upstairs from the legendary *Babbity Bowsters* (see below). The best of Scottish food at very affordable prices. Leave room for their diet-busting puddings.

Smiths of Glasgow, 109 Candleriggs, T5526539. Tue-Sat 0930-2200, Sun, Mon 0930-1730. There's a French tang to this Merchant City favourite which functions as a café by day and a restaurant by night.

Babbity Bowster, 16-18 Blackfriars St, T5525055. Mon-Sat 0800-2400; Sun 0900-2400. **Cheap** Buzzing café-bar housed in a magnificent 18th century building in the heart of the Merchant City. Traditional Scottish and French dishes served with flair. Outrageously good value. The bar is one of the city's perennial favourites, with a lively atmosphere and wide selection of real ales.

Bargo, 80 Albion St, T5534771. Mon-Sat 1100-2400; Sun 1200-2400. Impressively stylish designer bar serving excellent value bar snacks and meals of superior quality. Definitely a place to be seen in with a high posing quotient.

Ichiban Japanese Noodle Café, 50 Queen St, T2044200. Mon-Wed 1200-1500, 1700-2200, Thu-Fri 1200-1500, 1700-2300, Sat 1200-2300, Sun 1300-2200. BYOB. No smoking. A short walk south of Queen St. Excellent value, healthy Japanese specialities in cool, modern surroundings.

Noah, 84-86 Albion St, T5523044. Mon/Tue/Sun 0900-1900, Wed/Thu 0900-2300, **Cafés** Fri/Sat 0900-2400. Big, bright and popular Merchant City café offering a vast range of coffees and teas and a varied sandwich menu. Pre-theatre or launch specials. Outside seating in the summer.

Peckhams on Third, 65 Glassford St, T5524181. Open Mon-Sat 1000-1730, Sun 1030-1730. Three floors of this food emporium. The basement houses a wine shop, the ground floor a deli, and the third floor a bright, spacious café. Good for a quick bite, great sweets.

Bar 91, 91 Candleriggs, T5525211. Another cool style-bar, but comfortable and relaxed **Bars & pubs** and a good place to eat. Happy hour specials 1700-2000. ● on map, page 56

Blackfriars, 36 Bell St, T5525924. Merchant city favourite which pulls in the punters with its vast range of international beers and lagers. Also a wide range of excellent grub, live music and comedy at weekends and that inimitable Glasgow atmosphere (see also page 129).

The Mitre Bar, T5523764, 12-16 Brunswick St. A great traditional Glasgow pub in the midst of the Merchant City's cool designer bars. Good *craic*, cheap grub and fine ales.

Rab Ha's, T5720400, 83 Hutcheson St. This old Merchant City stalwart still packs 'em in. It has an enviable reputation for its food and is above the restaurant of the same name.

Strata, 45 Queen St, T2211888. Mon-Sun 1200-2400. Another horizontally cool city

**Five of the best:
lunch for under a tenner**

- *Farfelu* (page 60)
- *Babbity Bowster* (page 61)
- *Tempus at CCA* (page 78)
- *Café Source* (page 67)
- *Modern India* (page 78)

bar where you can strut your stuff before heading off to the clubs. Good food (mid-range) served daily 1200-2200.

Shopping

Shopping in the Merchant City translates as 'bring your credit card' as this is the home of the *Italian Centre*, Glasgow's most upmarket shopping area. Created from the husks of abandoned warehouses on Ingram St, the Italian Centre has a rather chilly splendour that successfully deters you from browsing if you're feeling less than chic (not the place to come on a 'fat day'). This is home to *Armani* and *Versace* outlets, as well as some other upmarket shops, cafes and restaurants. There's also a branch of Cruise, at 223-226 Ingram St, T2290000. *Dr Jives*, 111-113 Candleriggs, T5525451, is a great little quality shop selling top brands from Stussy and Silas to APC and Eley Kishimoto. Not cheap but, hey, you're worth it.

Not far away is *Innhouse* on Wilson St, which has lots of contemporary designer homeware by names like Alessi. *Hutcheson's* Hall on Ingram St (see page 58) is a good place for original crafts by Scottish designers.

Trongate to the East End

**Glasgow Cross
& around**

The Merchant City is bounded to the east by the High Street and to the south by Trongate. These two streets meet at Glasgow Cross, once the centre of trade and administration and regarded as the city centre, until the coming of the railway in the mid-19th century. It is now little more than a traffic junction, in the centre of which stands the 126 ft-high **Tolbooth Steeple**, one of only three crowned steeples in the country, and the only remnant of the original tolbooth built in 1626, which housed the courthouse and prison (described by Sir Walter Scott in his novel *Rob Roy*).

The nearby **Mercat Cross** is a 1929 replica of the medieval original, and is notable as the work of Edith Burnet, Britain's first registered female architect. It stands in front of the impressive, though isolated, **Mercat Building**, designed in 1922 by Graham Henderson.

Tron Kirk
*The name comes from
the Public Weighing
Machine – or Tron –
which was located just
outside the church*

Only a few yards west of the Tolbooth Steeple is the **Tron Steeple,** the only surviving part of St Mary's Collegiate Church, dating from 1485 and converted to a civic church in 1586. The original old kirk was accidentally burnt to the ground by drunken members of the aptly named Glasgow Hellfire Club in 1793. After a meeting, they went to the church to warm themselves by a fire, which they built up until it got out of control. It was replaced a year later by a James Adam design. The steeple has since been successfully incorporated into the modern frontage of the **Tron Theatre** (see page 132), and the interior of the replacement church forms the theatre auditorium.

**King Street &
Bridgegate**

Just south of Trongate, around King Street, is a lively area crammed with contemporary art galleries and studios, and laid-back bars and cafés. Most of the galleries are to be found on King Street (see page 68).

An unusual attraction in the same area, is the **Sharmanka Kinetic Gallery and Theatre**, 14 King Street, which puts on performances by mechanical sculptures made from carved wooden figures and old bits of junk. A great place to take the kids. ■ *Performances on Sun at 1500 (short programme for* children) and 1800, Tue 1300, Thu 1900; £3 (£2 children). T5527080, www.sharmanka.co.uk

To the south, on Bridgegate (or Briggait), is the **Merchants' Steeple** (1665), 164 feet-high with details in Gothic and Renaissance style. It is all that's left of the old Merchants' House, built in 1659. The Merchants left this part of the city in the early 19th century to escape the growing squalor, and moved several times before finally settling in George Square in 1877. The old steeple was eventually incorporated into the **Briggait**, built originally as the **Fishmarket** in 1872-73. The huge hall, with its cast-iron galleries, has been beautifully restored and can now be appreciated in all its glory.

The area between the Briggait and the Sheriff Court (see below) is the site of **Paddy's Market**, so named because in the mid-19th century this was where famine-stricken Irish immigrants sold their clothes for money to feed their families. It's a great place for bargain hunters and thrift store aficionados to rummage around to their heart's content.■ *The market is held every weekend 1000-1700.*

Central Glasgow

Sweeping down from Glasgow Cross to the river is the Saltmarket, the city's most 'des res' district in the early 18th century, with its peaceful and secluded riverside location. The arrival of slaughterhouses, bleachfields, the Sheriff Court House (where people may have been tried for bleach of the peace) and, in 1829, the construction of Hutchesons' Bridge, put an end to its secluded status. The late 19th century sandstone tenements which line the street have recently been cleaned up. At the bottom of the Saltmarket is the original court house, whose delicate neoclassical symmetry was in effect destroyed by the building of Hutchesons' Bridge. The new court house building is tucked in behind.

Saltmarket & St Andrew's Square
The Saltmarket, and the streets around it, have recently been given a major facelift and represent a fine example of the East End's ongoing gentrification

Heading back north along the Saltmarket towards Glasgow Cross, St Andrew's street turns right into St Andrew's Square, which is filled by the magnificent **St Andrew's Church**, one of the finest classical churches in Britain and one of Glasgow's hidden gems. Sadly neglected for many years, it has now been restored to its former baroque splendour. It no long functions as a church but has been cleverly converted to house a sleek café (*Café Source*, see page 67) downstairs and a Scottish music venue upstairs. You can go upstairs and see the stunning original stained-glass windows and intricate plaster work. Concerts and ceilidhs are staged throughout the year – tickets are available from *Café Source*, T5486020.

Nearby, on the corner of Turnbull Street and Greendyke Strret, is the Episcopalian kirk, **St Andrew's-by-the-Green**, which aroused the anger of the city's staunch Presbyterians with its sinfully ornate decoration, cushioned seats, and the positively debauched notion of introducing an organ, which earned it the name 'the Whistlin' Kirkie'. The innocent-looking church is a startling example of 18th century Glasgow amidst much 21st century development.

The Barras

The name Barras is presumed to be a corruption of 'the barrows' named after the flea market, but this area was once known as Barrowflats, a name which dates back to the 16th century

East of Glasgow Cross, Gallowgate and London Road lead into the city's **East End**, only a stone's throw from the Merchant City. It may look shabby and run-down by comparison but this is where you can sample a slice of pure Glasgow, especially in The Barras , the famous market which occupies almost the entire area between Gallowgate and London Road, and from Ross Street to Bain Street. Its main entrances are marked by distinctive red, cast-iron gateways which lead you in to a scruffy jumble of tenements, warehouses, sheds and pavements. You could spend days rummaging around through acres of cheap, new and second-hand goods. A lot of it's junk (dodgy computer games, pirate videos etc) but there are plenty of bargains to be found. The real attraction, though, is the atmosphere of the place and wit and repartee of the market traders. This is also the site of the famed Barrowlands dance hall, one of Glasgow's great music venues (see page 129). ■ *The market is held every weekend, 1000-1700.*

Glasgow Green

South of The Barras is the wide expanse of Glasgow Green, said to be the oldest public park in Britain. It has been common land since at least medieval times and Glaswegians still have the right to dry their washing here. Bonnie Prince Charlie reviewed his troops here in 1745 before they were hung out to dry by the English at Culloden. The Green has always been dear to the people of Glasgow and is a vital part of the city's folklore. It served as the very first home of the Glasgow Golf Club, established in the 18th century and was also where the two Old Firm clubs were founded, in the 19th century. Throughout its eventful history, the Green has been the scene of mills, washing houses and abattoirs and the Glasgow Fair was held here for many years (see page 196). Some of the city's major political demonstrators have held meetings here, including the Chartists in the 1830s, Scottish republican campaigners in the 1920s and, the Red Clydesiders who succumbed to flower power when their rallies were disrupted by the authorities planting of strategically placed flower beds. There are various **monuments** dotted around the park, including a 144 ft-high monument to Lord Nelson, erected in 1806, one to James Watt and the 46 ft-high Doulton Fountain, first seen at the 1888 International Exhibition in Kelvingrove and later moved to its present site.

On the edge of the green, opposite the People's Palace, is **Templeton's Carpet Factory**, or Doge's Palace as it is nicknamed. This bizarre but beautiful structure was designed in 1889 by William Leiper in Venetain style and is surely one of the most extravagantly incongruous buildings in the world. Once described as 'the world's finest example of decorative brickwork', it's Britain's best example of polychromatic decoration (in other words, very colourful). The building was converted to the Templeton Business Centre in 1984.

People's Palace

Allow at least an hour, preferably two, to take it all in

On the northern end of the green, approached from London Road, is the People's Palace, opened in 1898 as a folk museum for the East End. The recently refurbished museum is a genuinely fascinating place to visit and gives a real insight into life of this great city and its people from the mid-18th century to the present day. This is very much a social history, told from the perspective of so-called 'ordinary folk', though their ability to survive in often desperate conditions proves just how extraordinary they often were.

How they survived was through their famous gritty humour which has been exported worldwide thanks to comic genius, Billy Connolly, the 'Big Yin'. You can hear him on the audio phones scattered throughout the galleries. These also feature other Glasgow comedians such as Stanley Baxter and

A walk around the East End

Starting at the **Tron Steeple** head east down London Road all the way to the flamboyant **Templeton Business Centre**, a former carpet factory modelled on the Doges Palace in Venice. From here walk back to the **People's Palace**. After you've been round the museum walk across **Glasgow Green** until you come to the main road – Saltmarket. Turn right, then left down Bridgegate and right into **King** **Street**. This is a great street for browsing in as it is lined with contemporary art galleries. Next turn right along Parnie Street, back into Saltmarket. Cross over the road and go down St Andrew's Street (it's just south of London Road) to **Café Source** in the basement of the church, where you can get a drink and something to eat. If you've got time go upstairs to see the original church interior.

Ricki Fulton. The Big Yin's famous banana boots are on display, part of the wealth of artefacts, photographs, cartoons and drawings, in addition to a series of films, music and people's anecdotes. There's a reconstructed 'steamie' (communal laundry) from nearby Ingram Street, brochures extolling the delights of a trip 'Doon the watter' on the Clyde, and video displays on 'the patter' – Glaswegian à la Rab C Nesbitt.

The museum doesn't shrink from covering the less salubrious aspects of city history either. There's a display on 'the bevvy' (drink) which includes a barrow once used regularly by the police to wheel drunks home. There's also a small display on the sectarian divide in city football – evidenced by a t-shirt protesting at Rangers' signing of Mo Johnston (their first Catholic player). A visit to the People's Palace should be on everyone's itinerary, particularly if you're interested in scratching beneath the city's surface and getting to know it better.

When you start to suffer from information overload, take a break in the *Costa* café in the very wonderful **Winter Gardens**, a gigantic conservatory at the rear of the museum, full of exotic plants and without doubt the most relaxing cup of coffee in the entire city. ■ *Mon-Thu and Sat 1000-1700, Fri and Sun 1100-1700. Free. T5540223.*

Eating and drinking

Cantina del Rey, 10 King's Court, T5524044. Sun-Thu 1700-2200, Fri, Sat noon-2300. Large Mexican restaurant where you can fill up with favourites like enchiladas and fajitas.

Mid-range
● *on maps, pages 56 and 66*

Esca, 27 Chisholm St, T5530880. Mon-Fri 1200-1500, 1700-2200, Sat 1200-2230, Sun 1700-2200. Sleek, contemporary restaurant with a friendly, relaxed atmosphere, serving Mediterranean with a strong emphasis on pastas and steaks.

Le Bouchon, 17 King St, T5527411. Mon-Thu 1200-1400, 1730-2400, Fri and Sat 1200-1430, 1700-0100. A genuine Parisian bistro offering classic French dishes at unbeatable value. Their cheap lunchtime set menu is hugely popular with local professionals. They also do a cheap 2-course pre-theatre supper.

The Inn on the Green, 22 Greenhead St, T5540165. Mon-Fri 1200-1430, 1800-late, Sat and Sun 1800-late. A well-establlshed East End restaurant and hotel. Good place for traditional Scottish food, accompanied by piano music at night.

Tron Theatre, Chisholm St, T5528587. Mon-Sat 1200-2200, Sun 1030-1600, 1800-2200. No smoking area. Refurbished restaurant offers a dining experience that's worth applauding. The 2-course set lunch is exceptional value. The effortlessly stylish bar is perfect for that pre-prandial tipple.

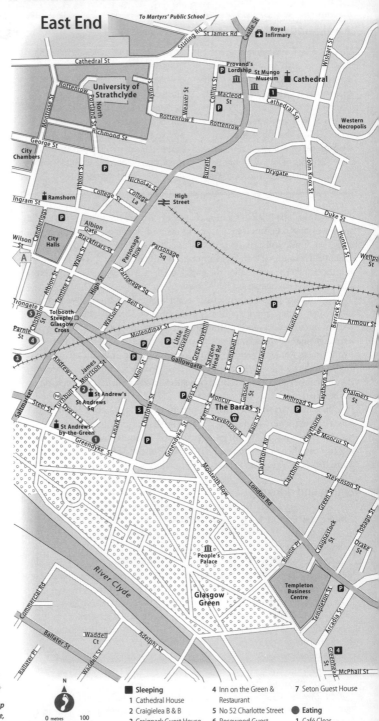

East End

*Related map
A George Square,
Merchant City &
Trongate, page 56*

N

0 metres 100
0 yards 100

■ **Sleeping**
1 Cathedral House
2 Craigielea B & B
3 Craigpark Guest House

4 Inn on the Green &
Restaurant
5 No 52 Charlotte Street
6 Rosewood Guest
House

7 Seton Guest House

● **Eating**
1 Café Clear
2 Café Source

3 Cantina del Rey
4 Esca

● **Bars & pubs**
5 Saracen's Head

○ **Entertainment**
1 Barrowlands

Central Glasgow

Café Cossachock, 10 King St, T5530733. **Cheap**
Mon-Sat 1030-late; Sun 1600-late. Near
the Tron Theatre. Cosy, authentic-feeling
Russian restaurant with a relaxed,
informal atmosphere. Art gallery
upstairs. More than just a good meal, it's
an entire cultural experience.

Café Clear, 51 Greendyke St
T5526454. Tue-Sun 1200-2400. Part of
the Homes for the Future innovative
complex of buildings by Glasgow Green,
this bar/café serves Mediterranean
dishes, sandwiches and soups.

Café Source, 1 St Andrews Sq (in the
church) T5486020. Mon-Fri 1100-2300,
Sat 1100-2400, Sun 1200-2300. Great
contemporary café offering everything
from fishcakes to savoury vegetarian
tart. Or just chill out with a latte and read
the papers. Live music every Wed from
2000.

Eat Drink Man Woman, 34-44 King
St, T5529260. Wed-Thu 1200-2300, Fri,
Sat 1200-2400. Bar/café serving light
snacks. Has jazz every Thu evening and
Sat afternoon.

The Thirteenth Note, 50-60 King St,
T5531638. Mon-Sat 1200-2400; Sun
1230-2330. Cheap and tasty veggie
food upstairs and live indie music downstairs in the sweaty basement (see page
130). Goes without saying (but we're
saying it, anyway), that it attracts a
mixed crowd. Friendly, relaxed atmosphere by day, jumping by night.

Massif, 25 Parnie St, T5527999. Mon-Sun **Cafés**
0830-2400. Trendy black and white
theme to this licensed coffee shop
which also has a take away menu of
bagels and butties.

The Saracen's Head, 209 Gallowgate, **Bars & pubs**
T5529306. Maybe not quite the oldest
pub in Glasgow, but the 'Sarry Heid',
near the Barras market, has a longer, and
more colourful, history than most, dating from the mid 1700s (see above).
Open Fri and Sat 0800-2400, Sun
1230-2400.

The Scotia Bar, T5528681, 112 Stockwell St. This old East End pub also claims
to be the oldest in town, and its low

Central Glasgow

Five of the best: historic pubs

- *Horse Shoe Bar* (this page)
- *Saracen Head* (this page)
- *Curlers* (page 99)
- *Scotia Bar* (this page)
- *Halt Bar* (page 99)

ceilings and wooden beams support a convincing argument. It's also the best place in town for folk music (see page 130), and much-frequented by writers, poets and drinking thinkers (or thinking drinkers).

The Victoria Bar, T5526040, 159 Bridgegate. Real traditional howff in one of Glasgow's oldest streets. Seemingly unchanged since the late 19th century and long may it stay that way. One of the city's great pubs, where entertainment is provided free, courtesy of the local wags. Their bar food is so cheap it's almost complimentary.

Shopping

The art galleries on King St like *Glasgow Print Studio* (see below) are all good places in which to seek out new and original artworks. At No 18 is *Intermedia*, T5522540 (open Mon-Sat 1200-1800), an exhibition space which frequently has works on show by local artists. *Transmission*, at No 28, T5524813 (open Tue-Sat 1100-1700), is a membership gallery exhibiting everything from photography to glass and pottery work. *Glasgow Print Studio Galleries*, on the first floor of No 25, T5520704, www.gpsart.co.uk (open Tue-Sat 1000-1730), are one of the largest publishers of original prints in the UK. They display and sell etchings, lithographs and screenprints by over 300 artists including well known names like Elizabeth Blackadder, Ken Currie, Peter Howson and Adrian Wiszniewski. Next door at No 26 is *Streetlevel*, T5522151 (open Tue-Sat 1000-1700) which specializes in photographic works.

Also have a look upstairs at Café Cossachok (see page 67), a Russian café with a small gallery exhibiting the work of Soviet artists. Many of the works in these galleries are for sale so they're a good hunting ground for original presents. In nearby Parnie Street is *Art Exposure Gallery,* T5527779 (open Mon-Sat 1200-1700), an unpretentious gallery exhibiting the work of Glasgow artists. Also on King St, in Kings Court, is *ESD*, which sells funky ladies clothing and retro designs.

If you fancy a bit of body adornment while you're here, look no further than *Terry's Tattoo Studio*, 23 Chisholm St, T5525740, which has been around since 1965. Around the corner is *The Glasgow Piercing Studio*, 24 Parnie St, T5526655, which offers everything from the tame to the eye watering.

And of course there's *The Barras*, The Barras Centre, London Rd (see page 64), Glasgow's famous East End market with over 1000 traders flogging their wares. Worth coming if only to hear their patter. Also worth a good rummage around is *Paddy's Market*, which is held around the Briggait during the same hours.

Buchanan Street to Charing Cross

Glasgow's commercial heart is the area between Buchanan Square and the M8 to the west. This vast grid-plan – which inspired town planners in the USA – is home to the city's main shopping streets and arcades, as well as its businesses and financial institutions. It is also where you'll find many of its architectural treasures.

At the bottom (south) end of Buchanan Street is St Enoch Square, dominated by the **St Enoch Centre**, a gigantic glass-covered complex of shops, fast-food outlets and an ice rink. Opposite the shopping complex are some notable buildings, such as the Royal Bank of Scotland and the Teacher building headquarters of the whisky maker until 1991. In the centre of the square is the St Enoch subway station, and an attractive little Jacobean pavilion which now houses the SPT Travel Centre.

St Enoch Square looks onto Argyle Street, one of Glasgow's most famous shopping streets. Though its status has been usurped in recent decades by the more fashionable streets to the north, it does boast the **Argyle Arcade**, Scotland's first ever indoor shopping mall, built in 1827 in the Parisian style, at the junction with Buchanan Street.

Argyle Street runs west from here under the railway bridge at Central Station. This bridge has always been known as the 'Heilanman's Umbrella', owing to the local joke that Highlanders would stand under it for shelter rather than buy an umbrella.

Just before Central Station, turn left into Jamaica Street and on the corner with Midland Street is one of the city's most stunning buildings, the former **Gardner's Warehouse**, which was modelled on the Crystal Palace in London and is now a vast pub of the same name. Known as 'The Iron Building' it has variously been described by architectural experts as "one of the great landmarks of Western architectural history" and "one of the most remarkable cast-iron warehouses of its date anywhere in Britain". It certainly matches anything in the Cast Iron district of New York's Soho.

Contuining this theme, opposite the *Crystal Palace* pub is *MacSorley's Bar*, named after the Phillip MacSorley's famous New York bar and originally with the same owner, who imported one of his barmen to run the Glasgow version.

Head back up Jamaica Street, cross Argyle Street into Union Street and on the right you'll see the magnificent **Egyptian Halls** (1871-73), a stunning piece of architectural brilliance from Glasgow's somewhat overlooked genius, Alexander "Greek" Thomson. The fact that this masterpiece lies empty and unused is surely bordering on criminal negligence.

At the top of Union Street, on the corner with Gordon Street, is another of the city centre's great cast-iron buildings the **Ca d'Oro**, designed by James Honeyman in 1872 and modelled on the famous Golden House in Venice. It was originally built as a furniture warehouse and the unusual name comes from a restaurant once housed inside. The building was badly damaged by fire in 1987 but has since been reconstructed in its original form.

Only a few yards away, at 20-26 Renfield Lane, is one of Charles Rennie Mackintosh's lesser-known buildings, the former **Daily Record Building** (1901). ■ *External viewing only.*

Head east on Gordon Street and turn into Mitchell Street. Opposite the car park is Mitchell Lane where you'll find The Lighthouse, another of Glasgow's architectural gems. It was designed by the ubiquitous Charles Rennie Mackintosh in 1893 to house the offices of the *Glasgow Herald*. The *Herald* vacated the premises in 1980 and it lay empty, until its recent transformation into Scotland's Centre for Architecture, Design and the City, a permanent legacy of the Glasgow's role as UK City of Architecture and Design in 1999.

The Lighthouse offers a programme of lively temporary exhibitions associated with architecture and design. In the past these have included an exhibition on the work of Japanese architects and one on Glasgow's favourite

St Enoch Square

Argyle Street, Jamaica Street & Union Street

Central Glasgow

The Lighthouse

Five of the best: places to hear the patter

- In a taxi
- The Barras (page 64)
- In a traditional city pub
- Concourse of Queen Street or Central Stations
- The People's Palace (page 64)

buildings. Situated in the original part of the building is The Mack Room, or **Mackintosh Interpretation Centre**, on the third floor, which features original designs and information on the life and work of the great architect. There are interactive displays telling the story of his life and scale models of his works. From this gallery you can ascend the **Mackintosh Viewing Tower**. Reached by a 135-step spiral staircase, it was part of the original building and offers unbeatable, panoramic views of the city. There are workshops, seminars and events, including a number of activities based on Mackintosh and the Glasgow Style, and specialized tours of the building. There's also a shop and café on the fifth floor (see page 79) and another café on the ground floor. ■ *Mon, Wed, Fri and Sat 1030-1730, Tue 1100-1700, Thu 1030-1700, Sun 1200-1700. £2.50, £2 concession. Tours must be booked in advance (maximum of 20 per tour). For details contact The Lighthouse, Mitchell Lane, Glasgow G1 3NU, T2258414, www.thelighthouse.co.uk*

Buchanan Street
From the Green Room of the Royal Concert Hall there's a great view down Buchanan St

Running all the way north from Argyle Street to Sauchiehall Street is Buchanan Street, perhaps Glasgow's finest street, as much for its variety of retail outlets as for its architectural importance, and now almost completely pedestrianised.

A short walk north on Buchanan Street is **Princes Square**, one of the most stylish and imaginative shopping malls in Britain. Even if you're not buying or looking, it's worth going in to admire this beautifully ornate Art Nouveau creation, or to sit at the top-floor café and watch others spend their hard-earned cash in the designer clothes shops below. A little further north, on the opposite side of the street, is a branch of the famous **Willow Tea Rooms** (see page 71) with replicas of Mackintosh designs. Almost opposite is **Borders Bookshop**, housed in the huge and impressive former Royal Bank of Scotland (1827), which backs onto Royal Exchange Square.

Buchanan Street continues north, crossing St Vincent Street, to reach Nelson Mandela place, which is completely filled by the baroque splendour of **St George's Tron Church**, designed in 1808 by William Stark and the oldest church in the city centre. Opposite is the **Stock Exchange**, designed by John Burnet Senior in 1875 in French Gothic style. A short walk further north, close to Buchanan Street Underground station, is the **Athenaeum**, designed in 1886 by J J Burnet and showing early signs of his later modernism.

St Vincent Street

Running west from George Square, between Argyle Street and Sauchiehall Street, is St Vincent Street, where you'll find one of the city's most unusual buildings, **The Hatrack**, at No 142. Designed in 1902 by James Salmon II, it's 10 storeys high but only 29 ft 6 in wide. It gets its name from the series of projecting finials which once surmounted it and made the building look like an old hat stand.

Further along St Vincent Street, near the intersection with Pitt Street, is one of the jewels in Glasgow's architectural crown, the **St Vincent Street Church**, designed in 1859 by Alexander 'Greek' Thomson, the city's 'unknown genius' of architecture. Much of his work was destroyed in the 1960s and this is his only intact Romantic Classical church, now on the World Monument Fund's

The Sarry Story

Few pubs can have had such an eventful past as the legendary Saracen's Head – or Sarry Heid as it is know in these parts – inthe Gallowgate (see page 67). The present watering hole stands on the site of the original inn, which was Glasgow's first hotel, established in 1755. A sign on the side of the present building tells the story, how it was built from the ruins of the Bishop's Palace on the site of Little St Mungo's Church. Legend has it that St Mungo (officially known as Kentigern) met

St Columba here. You can just imagine them discussing matters spiritual while enjoying a 'hauf and hauf'.

Robert Burns stayed here, as did Johnson and Boswell in 1773 on their grand tour. During their stay Dr Johnson managed to upset political economist Adam Smith, who was thrown out after calling Johnson a "son of a bitch". It is presumed that William and Dorothy Wordsworth didn't resort to such foul language during their visit in 1803.

Central Glasgow

list of the 100 most endangered sites. The Presbyterian church is fronted by Ionic columns like those of a Greek temple and the church also shows Egyptian and Assyrian decoration. The main tower is Grecian in style while the dome could have come straight out of India during the Raj. It's well worth looking inside to see the sumptious colours and ornate decoration.

■ *The church is not open to the public other than during services. For service times, T2211937. Or write to the Alexander Thomson Society at 1 Moray Pl, Glasgow G41 2AQ.*

Around Blythswood Square

Climbing north from St Vincent Street, heading towards Sauchiehall Street, is the grid pattern of streets which composed Glasgow's second New Town. Built in the first decades of the 19th century, the plan was drawn up by one James Craig, coincidentally the name of the architect of Edinburgh's New Town. But though there are similarities between the two designs, there is no conclusive proof that it was the same person. The plan was modified by architect James Gillespie Graham and very much followed the principles of elegant simplicity of the late Georgian period. Over the years the requirements of first Victorian commerce and then 20th century development have intruded on the original look of the streets, though Blythswood Square still hints at the area's original classical beauty.

Worth noting is the door at 5 Blythswood Sq, designed by Charles Rennie Mackintosh for the former Glasgow Society of Lady Artists' Club in 1908

Sauchiehall Street

Further north is Sauchiehall Street, another of the city's main shopping thoroughfares. If there's one thing Glaswegians like to do it's spend money and Glasgow is second only to London in the UK in terms of retail spending. The newest of the city's shopping centres is the upmarket **Buchanan Galleries**, next door to the **Royal Concert Hall** (see page130), at the east end of Sauchiehall Street, where it meets the north end of Buchanan Street.

There are a few notable places of interest on Sauchiehall Street, including Charles Rennie Mackintosh's wonderful **Willow Tea Rooms**, at No 217, above *Henderson's* the Jewellers. This is a faithful reconstruction on the site of the original 1903 tea room, designed by Mackintosh for his patron Miss Kate Cranston, who already ran three of the city's most fashionable tea rooms, in Argyle Street, Buchanan Street and Ingram Street. The tea room was very much peculiar to Glasgow, promoted by the Temperance Movement as a healthy alternative to the gin palaces, popular throughout the country in the late 19th century, and Miss Cranston's were the *crème de la crème* of tea rooms. They offered ladies-only rooms, rooms for gentlemen and rooms

A walk around the City Centre

*Start at the **Tenement House**, the perfectly preserved dwelling that is one of Glasgow's most distinctive attractions. Then walk down Garnet Street and turn left along Renfrew Street until you come to **Glasgow School of Art**, the influential art college that was designed by Charles Rennie Mackintosh. Then continue along Renfrew Street until you reach Rose Street. Turn right down here and you will soon come to Sauchiehall Street, where you are very close to the **Willow Tea Rooms**, also designed by*

*Rennie Mackintosh. Then go down Blythswood Street (it's the continuation of Rose Street) until you come to West Regent Street. At No 93 is **Victorian Village**, a great place to search for bargain antiques and retro clothes. Walk east along West Regent Street until you come to Renfield Street. Turn right down here and you will eventually come to Gordon Street where you can go to **Miss Cranston's tea rooms** for a traditional Scottish tea, with sandwiches, scones and little cakes.*

where both sexes could dine together. In addition, her tea rooms offered a reading room, a billiards room for the gentlemen and a smoking room, not forgetting the unrivalled splendour of the decoration.

Mackintosh had already worked with Miss Cranston on her other tea rooms, but Sauchiehall Street was their *tour de force*. Sauchiehall means 'alley of the willows' and this theme was reflected not only in the name, but throughout the interior. Mackintosh was allowed free rein to design the fixtures and fittings; everything, in fact, right down to the teaspoons. The exclusive Salon de Luxe, on the first floor, was the crowning glory, and the most exotic and ambitious part of the tea rooms, decorated in purple, silver and white, with silk and velvet upholstery. Visitors today can relive the splendour of the original tea rooms as they relax in the distinctive high-backed chairs with a cup of tea, brought to them by the specially selected high-backed waitresses. ■ *The tea rooms are open from 0930 to 1630 (see also page 71). www.willowtearooms.co.uk*

A few yards west, on the opposite side of the street, are the **McLellan Galleries**, another fine example of classical architecture. The galleries are currently closed but when they re-open will host a wide range of touring and temporary exhibitions. ■ *T2872000 to check re-opening date. Opening times and admission charges change with each exhibition.*

Continuing west, Sauchiehall meets Rose Street, which climbs north. On the right is the **Glasgow Film Theatre** (GFT), formerly the Cosmo Cinema, a beautiful Art Deco building which boasts a top programme of arthouse movies and the excellent *Café Cosmo* (see page 79).

Further west on Sauchiehall Street, on the north side, is the **Centre for Contemporary Arts (CCA)**, housed in the elegant Grecian Chambers, a former commercial warehouse designed by Alexander 'Greek' Thomson in 1867-68. The centre opened in October 2001 after a major refurbishment by Page & Park. The original courtyard has been incorporated into the interior and the effect of the stonework enclosed by a modern steel structure is very impressive, creating a light and airy feel. The centre presents a changing programme of contemporary theatre and dance events, as well as art exhibitions, many of the "call that art, my granny could do better" variety. On the ground floor is the excellent *Tempus at the CCA* café-bar and upstairs is the *CCA Bar* (see page 78). There's also a shop on the ground floor. ■ *Centre open Mon-Wed 0900-2400; Thu-Sat 0900-2400; Sun 1200-1900. Galleries open Mon-Sat 1100-1800; Sun 1200-1700. Free. T3327521, www.cca-glasgow.com*

What they said about Mackintosh

"The North façade is one of the greatest achievements of all time, compared in scale and majesty to Michelangelo". Robert Venturi, architect, on Glasgow School of Art, 1985.

"Why is it all white, Dad?" "Because the

man was a genius". Wee boy to his father in Mackintosh House.

"Building in his hands becomes an abstract art, both musical and mathematical". Nikolaus Pevsner, Art Historian, 1935.

A block further west is **Baird Hall**, built in 1938 as the Beresford Hotel for the Empire Exhibition, now part of Strathclyde University and the city's finest example of 1930s architecture. A short distance west, at 518 Sauchiehall Street, is the **Royal Highland Fusiliers Museum,** which details the history of the three regiments from 1678 to the present day. There are medals, uniforms, weapons and musical instruments as well as a wealth of other artefacts on show. ■ *Mon-Fri 0830-1600. Free. T3320961.*

Glasgow School of Art

A very steep walk up from Sauchiehall Street, at 167 Renfrew Street, is the Glasgow School of Art, the city's seminal architectural masterpiece and one of the most prestigious art schools in the country. The building was designed by Charles Rennie Mackintosh, after his proposal won a competition set to find a design for the school, in 1896. It was built in two stages from 1897-1899 and completed in 1907. The school is now regarded as Mackintosh's architectural masterpiece and gives full expression to his architectural ideals: the brilliant use of Scottish vernacular forms and the imaginative and minute interior details which are subtely mirrored in the exterior of the building. Much of the inspiration for his design came from nature and from his drawings of traditional Scottish buildings. He was also influenced by the Art Nouveau style, particularly the illustrations of Aubrey Beardsley.

For more information on the man and his work, contact the CRM Society, at Queen's Cross Church (see page 93)

The building is rooted in tradition, with a thoroughly modern-looking exterior of extreme austerity, and there are medieval, castle-like features such as turrets and curving stair wells. The interior is both spacious and utilitarian and shows perfectly his desire to create a unified and harmonious working environment for both students and teachers. The studio walls and high ceilings are painted white, with huge windows allowing light to pour into the spaces. The corridors and staircases are decorated with glazed, coloured tiles to help guide students and staff around the massive building. The overall effect is part Gothic castle, part museum and part modern functional space, reflecting his blending of creative genius and Scots pragmatist.

The spectacular two-tier library is the *pièce de résistance*. Mackintosh designed everything, down to the light fittings, bookcases and the oak furniture, to create a sense of light filtering through the trees in a forest clearing. There are symbols of nature everywhere throughout the building, used to inspire the students to produce their own works of art. And who could fail to be inspired in such a stunning environment? Several of the city's distinguished writers studied here, including Alasdair Gray and Liz Lochead, as well as dramatist John Byrne and actor Robbie Coltrane, who plays *Hagrid* in the Harry Potter series of films.

★ Five of the best: historic churches

- **St Vincent Street Free Church of Scotland** (page 70)
- **Govan Old Parish Church** (page 104)
- **Glasgow Cathedral** (page 55)
- **Queen's Cross Church** (page 92)
- **St Andrews** Church (page 63)

As it is still a working art school, entry is by student-led guided tour only. The tour visits the main rooms containing many of the well-known pieces of furniture and includes the famous library. The shop on the ground floor, where you collect your tour tickets, has a wide range of Mackintosh paraphenalia.

■ *Tour times Sep-Jun Mon-Fri at 1100 and 1400, Sat 1030 and 1130 and Jul-Aug Mon-Fri 1100 and 1400, Sat, Sun 1030, 1130, 1300. Booking is strongly advised. Closed late Jun for the graduation exhibition and from Christmas through to New Year. £5, £3 students. T3534526, www.gsa.ac.uk*

The Tenement House A few hundred yards northwest of the School of Art, down the other side of the hill, at 145 Buccleuch Street, is the Tenement House, a typical late-Victorian tenement flat. In 1911, 25-year old Miss Agnes Toward and her mother moved into the flat. Agnes, a shorthand typist and spinster, was to live here for most of her life, until she moved out in 1965. During that time, Agnes changed absolutely nothing in her home and it is now a fascinating time-capsule of life in the first half of the 20th century, retaining most of the original features such as the bed recesses, kitchen range and coal bunker. The whole experience is a little voyeuristic, as the flat includes many of Agnes' personal possessions, and in the parlour the table is set for afternoon tea, lending a spooky atmosphere redolent of the *Marie Celeste*. On the ground floor is an exhibition on tenement life. The property is owned by the NTS. ■ *Mar-Oct 1400-1700 daily. £3.50, £2.50 concession. T3330183, www.nts.org.uk*

On the other side of Cowcaddens Road, behind the huge Royal Scottish Academy for Music and Drama, is the **Piping Centre**, at 30-34 McPhater Street. It's kind of a centre for the promotion of the bagpipes and contains rehearsal rooms, performance spaces and accommodation for aficionados of the instrument which divides opinion so sharply. There's also a very fine **café** and a **museum** which features a collection of antique pipes. The museum also has audio visual displays and gives you personal headsets so you can listen to samples of bagpipe music as you go round. ■ *Mon-Sat 1030-1630. Also open Sun in summer. £3, £2 concession. T 3530220, www.thepipingcentre.co.uk*

Continue east along Cowcaddens Road to reach the **Heatherbank Museum of Social Work**, surely one the least appealing-sounding visitor attractions anywhere. Inside are various displays of material relating to social care through the ages. ■ *Mon-Fri 0900-1630. Free.*

Eating and drinking

Expensive *The Buttery*, 652 Argyle St, T2218188. Mon-Fri 1200-1430, 1900-2230, Sat 1900-2230. Victoriana abounds in this old favourite with its clubby atmosphere. Consistently rated as one of the best eateries in the city, with an emphasis on the finest Scottish fish, seafood and game. Good, high-quality wine list. Downstairs is the much cheaper and less formal *The Belfry*, open Mon-Fri 1200-1500, 1700-2300; Sat 1700-2300.

Cameron's, 1 William St, T2045555. Mon-Fri 1200-1400, 1900-2200, Sat 1900-2200. In Glasgow's *Hilton Hotel*. Sublime Scottish cuisine. Pricey but well worth it. No-smoking area.

The Murder Square Mile

The Charing Cross district of Glasgow was christened by local writer, Jack House, "The Square Mile of Murder". This was because four notable murders were committed here between 1857 and 1909. The most notorious of all occurred at 7 Blythswood Square, where Madeleine Smith, daughter of architect James Smith, who designed the McLellan Galleries on nearby Sauchiehall Street, poisoned her lover, Pierre Emile L'Angelier, by lacing his bedtime cocoa with arsenic. At least this is what everyone believed, except the jury who delivered the uniquely Scottish verdict of 'Not Proven', which pretty much means they thought she did it but couldn't prove

it. At 131 Sauchiehall, however, there was no doubt that Dr Edward Pritchard did poison his wife and mother-in-law. As a result, he became the last man in the city to be hanged in public.. Rather less deserving was Jessie MacLachlan of 17 Sandyford Place. She was found guilty of murdering her friend Jess McPherson on the flimsiest of evidence, but at least her death sentence was commuted to life imprisonment. More intriguing still, was the case of Oscar Slater, who was found guilty of murdering Miss Marion Gilchrist at 15 Queen's Terrace (now 49 West Princes Street). He was later reprieved and later still pardoned.

Chardon d'Or, 176 West Regent St, T2483801. Mon-Fri 1200-1430, 1830-2230, Sat 1830-2230. Opulent new venue catering very much to well-lunched businessmen. Head chef was formerly at *Le Gavroche* in London.

Eurasia, 150 St Vincent St, T2041150. Mon-Sat 1200-1430, 1900-2300. Much hyped style restaurant serving fusion food in oh-so-cool surroundings. The place to come when you want a treat.

Gamba, 225a West George St, T5720899. Mon-Sat 1200-1430, 1700-2230. Popular fish restaurant, with dishes often having an Asian flavour.

Groucho St Judes, 190 Bath St, T3528800, Mon-Fri 1200-1500, 1800-2230, Sat 1800-2300; Sun 1800-2230. Bar open Mon-Sat 1200-2400, Sun 1800-2400. Part of the small, chic hotel and opened in partnership with the original *Groucho's* in London. Unlike its southern sister, it is not a members-only club. Anyone can eat, drink or sleep here, though the bar and restaurant are definitely the place to be seen amongst the city's creative and media types. Modern Scottish food with lots of char-grilled fish and meat, and very good puddings.

Ho Wong, 82 York St, T2213550. Mon-Sat 1200-1400, 1800-2330; Sun 1800-2330. BYOB. Tucked away just off Argyle St, this Chinese restaurant doesn't look much from the outside but inside awaits a memorable Cantonese culinary experience and the city's finest Szechuan food. Not cheap but worth every penny.

Quigleys, 158 Bath St, T3314060. Mon-Sat 1200-1430, pre-theatre 1700-1900, 1900-2300. Newly opened restaurant in the old Christie's showroom, offering slick fusion food. Brasserie type food upstairs, more informal food in the bar downstairs,

Rogano, 11 Exchange Pl, T2484055. Mon-Sun 1200-1430, 1830-2230. A Glasgow culinary institution. Designed in the style of the Cunard liner, *Queen Mary*, and built by the same workers. Looks like the set of a Hollywood blockbuster and you'll need a similar budget to pay the bill, but the seafood is truly sensational. Downstairs is *Café Rogano*, which offers a less stylish alternative, but it's a lot easier on the pocket. Sun-Thu 1200-1430, 1830-2230.

Amber Regent, 50 West Regent St, T3311655. Mon-Thu 1200-1415, 1730-2300, Fri **Mid-range** 1200-1415, 1730-2330, Sat 1200-2400. BYOB. Plush and very upmarket restaurant serving classic Chinese cuisine. Those on a tight budget can also indulge themselves, with half-price main courses before 1900 Wed-Sat and all-night Mon and Tue.

Central Glasgow

Axiom, Lancefield Quay, 154 Hydepark St, T2212822. Mon-Sat 1100-2300. Wide-ranging menu featuring contemporary Scottish dishes. Superb value.

Baby Grand, 3-7 Elmbank Gardens, T2484942. Mon-Thu 0730-2400, Fri 0730-0200, Sat 1000-0200, Sun 1000-2400. Chic jazz-café offering good bistro-style food when most other places have shut up shop. Enjoy late-night drinks and food and soothing jazz piano.

Central Glasgow

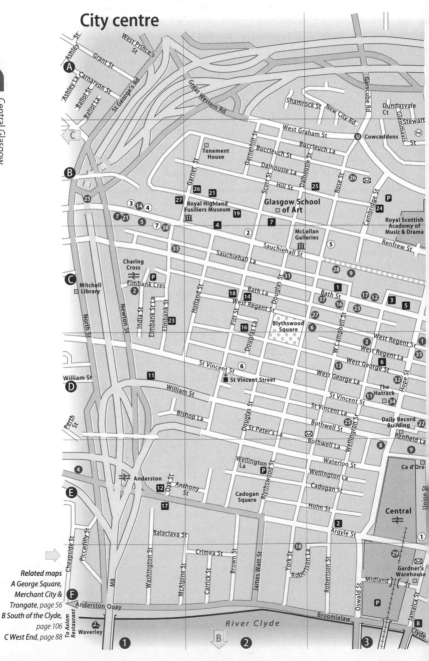

City centre

Related maps
A George Square,
Merchant City &
Trongate, page 56
B South of the Clyde,
page 106
C West End, page 88

Bouzy Rouge, 111 West Regent St, T2218804. Sun-Thu 1200-2130, Fri, Sat 1200-2200. One of a chain offering 2 types of dining – casual and gourmet. Gourmet choices are things like posh Scottish (venison and the like), while casual offers steaks and veggie options. Sleek wooden interior.

Gordon Yuill and Company, 257 West Campbell St, T5724052. Mon-Sat 0800-2230.

Central Glasgow

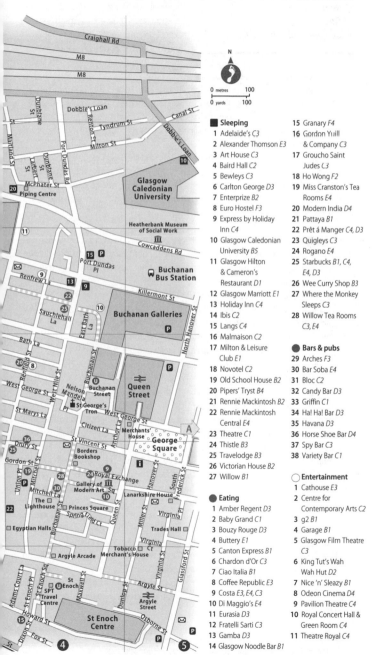

■ **Sleeping**

1 Adelaide's *C3*
2 Alexander Thomson *E3*
3 Art House *C3*
4 Baird Hall *C2*
5 Bewleys *C3*
6 Carlton George *D3*
7 Enterprize *B2*
8 Euro Hostel *F3*
9 Express by Holiday Inn *C4*
10 Glasgow Caledonian University *B5*
11 Glasgow Hilton & Cameron's Restaurant *D1*
12 Glasgow Marriott *E1*
13 Holiday Inn *C4*
14 Ibis *C2*
15 Langs *C4*
16 Malmaison *C2*
17 Milton & Leisure Club *E1*
18 Novotel *C2*
19 Old School House *B2*
20 Pipers' Tryst *B4*
21 Rennie Mackintosh *B2*
22 Rennie Mackintosh Central *E4*
23 Theatre *C1*
24 Thistle *B3*
25 Travelodge *B3*
26 Victorian House *B2*
27 Willow *B1*

15 Granary *F4*
16 Gordon Yuill & Company *C3*
17 Groucho Saint Judes *C3*
18 Ho Wong *F2*
19 Miss Cranston's Tea Rooms *E4*
20 Modern India *D4*
21 Pattaya *B1*
22 Prêt á Manger *C4, D3*
23 Quigleys *C3*
24 Rogano *E4*
25 Starbucks *B1, C4, E4, D3*
26 Wee Curry Shop *B3*
27 Where the Monkey Sleeps *C3*
28 Willow Tea Rooms *C3, E4*

● **Bars & pubs**

29 Arches *F3*
30 Bar Soba *E4*
31 Bloc *C2*
32 Candy Bar *D3*
33 Griffin *C1*
34 Ha! Ha! Bar *D3*
35 Havana *D3*
36 Horse Shoe Bar *D4*
37 Spy Bar *C3*
38 Variety Bar *C1*

○ **Entertainment**

1 Cathouse *E3*
2 Centre for Contemporary Arts *C2*
3 g2 *B1*
4 Garage *B1*
5 Glasgow Film Theatre *C3*
6 King Tut's Wah Wah Hut *D2*
7 Nice 'n' Sleazy *B1*
8 Odeon Cinema *D4*
9 Pavilion Theatre *C4*
10 Royal Concert Hall & Green Room *C4*
11 Theatre Royal *C4*

● **Eating**

1 Amber Regent *D3*
2 Baby Grand *C1*
3 Bouzy Rouge *D3*
4 Buttery *E1*
5 Canton Express *B1*
6 Chardon d'Or *C3*
7 Ciao Italia *B1*
8 Coffee Republic *E3*
9 Costa *E3, E4, C3*
10 Di Maggio's *E4*
11 Eurasia *D3*
12 Fratelli Sarti *C3*
13 Gamba *D3*
14 Glasgow Noodle Bar *B1*

Five of the best: swish restaurants

- *Rogano* (this page)
- *Amaryllis* (page 96)
- *Nairn's* (page 96)
- *Eurasia* (previous page)
- *Ubiquitous Chip* (page 96)

New venture from the Rogano's former manager. Smart Pacific-Rim food and chic looking interior.

Fratelli Sarti, 121 Bath St, T2040440. (Also at 42 Renfield St, T5727000). Mon-Sat 0800-2300, Sun 1200-2300. No-smoking area. Everything you'd expect from a great Italian restaurant, and a lot more besides. Exceptional value food washed down with the best value bottle of wine in the city. No wonder it's always busy.

The Green Room, Glasgow Royal Concert Hall (see page 130), 2 Sauchiehall St, T3323163. Mon-Sat 1200-1430, 1730-2130; also Sun (performance days only). No-smoking area. Much more than a good place to eat before the show. A superb restaurant in its own right where you can indulge in the finest of Scottish produce at reasonable prices. Good vegetarian selection.

Pattaya, 437 Sauchiehall St, T5720071. Mon-Sun 1700-0500. Top-class, well-presented Thai cuisine in calm, casual surroundings. Good value and yes, it really is open that late!

Modern India, 51 West Regent St, T3311980. Mon-Thu 1200-2330, Fri, Sat 1200-0100, Sun 1600-2330. Contemporary Indian restaurant featuring many dishes from Goa. Business lunches are a great bargain.

Cheap   *Café Gandolfi @ Habitat*, Buchanan Galleries, 200 Buchanan St, T3311254. Mon-Sat 0930-1700, Sun 1100-1600. From the people who brought you *Café Gandolfi* (see page 60), a new café-bar made for weary shoppers in Habitat. Quality Scottish ingredients with flavours from around the world.

Canton Express, 407 Sauchiehall St, T3320145. Mon-Sun 1200-0500. No-frills, cheap and filling Chinese fast food at most hours of the day or night.

Ciao Italia, 441-445 Sauchiehall St, T332 4565. Mon-Thu 1030-1500, 1700-2300, Fri, Sat 1030-1500, 1700-2400. Well established Italian restaurant at Charing Cross with an authentic Italian feel. Good business lunch and pre-theatre deals.

Glasgow Noodle Bar, 482 Sauchiehall St, T3331883. Mon-Sun 1200-0500. Oriental fast food eaten from disposable containers with plastic chopsticks or forks. Very cheap chow and great after a heavy night on the town.

The Granary, 82 Howard St, T2263770. Mon-Sat 0900-1730, Sun 1100-1700. No-smoking area. Behind the St Enoch Centre. Serves good, honest and wholesome vegetarian food. Big portions, big value, fast counter service. Popular with office workers and shoppers at lunchtimes.

Tempus at the CCA, 350 Sauchiehall St, T3327959. Mon-Sun 1100-2400 (last order for food 2130). Set in the recently refurbished Centre for Contemporary Arts (see page 72) this effortlessly stylish café/restaurant serves contemporary Scottish dishes. The menu is flexible and you can just drop in for a coffee and a snack if you don't want lunch. Upstairs (also reached via Scott St) is the *CCA Bar* which serves sandwiches and coffees. It is notable for its décor, designed by artist Jorge Pardo, a psychedelic creation with lots of bright colours and carved wood, which has been described as being "like a bad acid trip".

Wee Curry Shop, 7 Buccleuch St, T3530777. Mon-Sat 1200-1430, 1730-2300, Sun 1730-2300. BYOB. Son of *Mother India* (see page 97). Small in every sense except flavour and value. Quite simply the best cheap curry this side of Bombay, in a cosy, relaxed atmosphere. Good vegetarian options and incredible value 3-course buffet lunch.

Cafés   *Borders*, 98 Buchanan St, T2227700. Mon-Sat 0800-2300, Sun 1100-2130. No-smoking area. Inside *Borders* bookshop. Browse while you enjoy some good coffee (free refills) and delicious cakes and scones, a fresh fruit smoothie, or a light snack. Also live jazz bands on Fri nights.

Café Cosmo, 12 Rose St. Mon-Sun 1200-2100. Part of the Glasgow Film Theatre (see page 132) and definitely worth knowing about, even if you're not a movie buff. It's a great cheap lunch venue, especially for vegetarians.

★

Five of the best: late night eats

- *Baby Grand* (previous page)
- *Canton Express* (this page)
- *Pattaya* (previous page)
- *Insomnia* (page 98)
- *Spice Garden* (page 111)

Costa, Royal Exchange Sq. Mon-Sun 0800 till late. Part of the seemingly inexhaustible chain which has several other outlets in the city. Also at 68 Gordon St (Mon-Fri 0700-1900, Sat 0800-1900, Sun 1000-1800) and in *Waterstone's* bookshop, at 153-157 Sauchiehall St (Mon-Fri 0800-2130, Sat 0800-1900, Sun 1030-1800). Other branches are 205 Sauchiehall St, the Buchanan Galleries, and even in the Abbey National Bank on Argyle St.

There are also several branches of *Starbucks* offering tall, skinny caps, lattes and enormous scones. You'll find them at 10 Charing Cross Mansions (by Charing Cross) T3327852 (Mon-Fri 0700-2030, Sat 0830-2000, Sun 0900-2000) and at 13 Renfield St, 27 Sauchiehall St and 33 Bothwell St. The plushest branch of all is at, 9 Royal Exchange Pl, next to *Rogano*. The other main coffee chain in the city is *Coffee Republic*, 13 Bothwell St, T2487152. For take-away sandwiches try *Prêt á Manger*, which has branches at 34 Sauchiehall St and 104 St Vincent St.

Miss Cranston's Tearooms, 33 Gordon St, T2041122. You could miss this traditionally run tea-shop as it's hidden above a baker's shop. This is the place to come for a full-blown afternoon tea with sandwiches, scones, cakes and gallons of tea. *The Doocot Café and Bar*, The Lighthouse, 11 Mitchell La, T2211821. There's a 1950s retro look at this café on the top of the Lighthouse (see page 69). Stop for soups, sandwiches and light meals before immersing yourself in the world of architecture.

Where the Monkey Sleeps, 182 West Regent St, T2263406. Mon-Sat 0700-1900, Sat 1000-1900, Sun 1100-1900. A relaxed exhibition space/café. Good cappucinos and sandwiches, as well as soups from Eurasia (see page 75). Exhibits and sells works of new artists, including graduates of Glasgow and London schools of art.

Willow Tea Rooms, 217 Sauchiehall St, T3320521. Mon-Sat 0930-1630, Sun 1200-1615. No smoking area. A recreation of the original Miss Cranston's Tearooms, designed by Charles Rennie Mackintosh and filled with many of his original features. Most visitors come here for the interior design, but they also offer a good selection of reasonably priced teas, sandwiches, cakes and scones, as well as hot meals. There's also a sister branch at 97 Buchanan St, T2045242, which is licensed.

Bars & pubs

The Arches, 253 Argyle St, T0901 0220300. Mon-Sun 1200-2000 (bar open till 2400). Recently refurbished, this café/bar is now sleek and chic, and offers substantial snacks and sandwiches.

Baby Blue, 214 Bath St, T5724166. Mon-Sat 1130-2400 (food served till 2200), Sun 1400-2400 (food served till around 1900). There's a separate bar and restaurant in this new addition to the Bath St bar scene.

Bloc, 117 Bath St, T5746066. Mon-Thu and Sun 1200-2400 (food served till 1900), Fri, Sat 1200-0200 (food served until late). Another Bath St style bar, with food that's a mix of Eastern European and Far Eastern flavours.

Bar Soba, 11 Mitchell La, T2042404. Sun-Thu 1200-2400 (food until 2200), Fri, Sat 1200-2400 (food until 2300). There's a 1970's feel to this new bar on the ground floor of The Lighthouse. Food is Asian fusion.

The Cask and Still, 154 Hope St. Formerly the *Pot Still* and famous for its massive range of malts (around 500 of them). They also have a selection of cask ales and

Central Glasgow

Central Glasgow

★ Five of the best: places to people watch

- *Borders* bookshop café (previous page)
- Conservatory of the *Millennium Hotel* (page 140)
- Top floor cafés in **Princes Square** (page 70)
- **Kelvingrove Park** (page 86)
- Winter gardens at the **People's Palace** (page 64)

---

decent pub grub.

Candy Bar, 185 Hope St, T3537240. Closed Sun. Billed as one of the city's coolest bars, this is the place to flaunt those new clothes you splashed out on in Princes Sq. A long way from spit and sawdust.

The Gate, 408 Sauchiehall St, T3330250. New addition to the long list of style bars and another popular pre-club place. Cool and intimate at the same time and great value for lunch. Happy hour is 1200-2000 (!) and DJs pump up the volume Thu-Sat.

The Griffin, 226 Bath St, T3315171. Opposite the King's Theatre. Turn-of-the-century pub (not the most recent one) recently renovated but losing none of its style. Still the best place in the city for pie and chips and a drink (only £2.75!). Other traditional dishes, plus vegetarian, at amazing value.

Havana, 50 Hope St, T2484466. Mon-Wed and Sun 1200-2400, Thu-Sat 1200-0100. Is it a bar, is it a restaurant, or is it a club? All three, in fact. Latin grooves, Latin food and Latin spirit, all rolled into one. Coming here is like stepping into a Bacardi advert. Ay, Caramba! (See also page 128).

The Horse Shoe Bar, 17 Drury La, between Mitchell St and Renfield St, near the station, T2295711. Classic Victorian Gin Palace that is still one of the city's favourites. Its much-copied island bar is the longest continuous bar in the UK, so it shouldn't take long to get served, which is fortunate as it gets very busy. Incredibly good-value lunch served till 1430, then all day till 1900 upstairs and perhaps the cheapest pint in town. If you only visit one pub during your stay, then make sure it's this one.

Ha! Ha! Bar, 140 St Vincent St, T2045399. Large city-centre bar that attracts the post-work crowd. Does a popular brunch at weekends.

Mojo, 158a Bath St, T3312257. One of Glasgow's funkiest bars with cool sounds for that pre-club drink. Good food served through the back in a more intimate atmosphere.

O'Neill's, 457 Sauchiehall St, T3530436. Sun-Wed till 0230, Thu-Sat till 0300. Yes, it's another of those dreaded Irish theme bars, but stop and look at the opening hours. This place has a disco licence and you can dance the night away till the wee, small hours. Entry is free Sun-Tue and around £3-4 the rest of the week. There's also a free buffet from 1700 on Fri, be Jaisus!

Spy Bar, 153 Bath St, T2217711. Mon-Sat 1200-2400 (food until 2000). Another sleek style bar on Bath St and popular with a pre-club crowd. Food ranges from sandwiches and soups to more substantial fare.

Variety Bar, 401 Sauchiehall St, T3324449. A strange combination of old-fashioned décor and young, hip clientele. Various drinks promos and happy hours and good music.

Shopping

The possiblities are endless here – and it's all-too-easy to get carried away. You can not only find all the usual high-street stores, but plenty of designer names and some specialist stores. At the top of Buchanan St, just minutes from Queen St Station, is the city's newest shopping centre *Buchanan Galleries*. It's an enormous mall with a good *John Lewis* store and a huge branch of *Habitat*. The other stores major on clothes and range from *Austin Reed* and *Wallis* to *H&M*, *Mango* and *USC Group* which caters for many fashion tastes. There' also a branch of **Ottakars**, the bookshop.

Along Buchanan St itself you'll find plenty of good clothes and shoe shops like Press **and Bastyan**, **Diesel**, **Hobbs** and **Office**. Trendies will also want to check out **Urban Outfitters** which is full of 1970s items and retro gear. There's also a **Fraser's** department store, at No 21, and a large branch of **Graham Tiso**, the outdoor shop, at No 129, which has 5 floors

Five of the best: places to buy a gift

· *Hutcheson's Hall gift shop* (page 58)
· *Great Western Auctions* (page 100)
· *King Street Galleries* (page 68)
· *De Courcey Arcade* (page 100)
· *Whisky shop in Princes Square* (page 70)

Central Glasgow

of boots, waterproofs and anything else you'll need for exploring the hills. If you've set your heart on a kilt, make for **Hector Russell** kiltmakers who also do kilts for hire. Book-lovers won't find any of these shops, however, as they'll be blissfully browsing in the large branch of **Borders**.

Also on Buchanan St is Glasgow's (Britain's?) best shopping centre, **Princes Square**. Housed in a renovated square, with a strong Rennie Mackintosh theme, the *Square* is extremely stylish but never intimidating and has several good cafes and restaurants to collapse in when your feet give out. Clothes and shoe shops include **Karen Millen**, **French Connection**, **Calvin Klein**, **Pied a Terre** and **Phase Eight** for women and **Ted Baker**, **Hugo** and **Lacoste** for men. For unusual gifts there's **Illuminati** and for cosmetics and perfumes there's **Space NK Apothecary** and **Penhaligons**. Off Buchanan St is the **Argyll Arcade** a specialist shopping centre with over 30 jewellery shops.

For more standard high-street chains there is the **St Enoch** shopping centre at the very bottom of Buchanan St, and there's also **Argyle St** which again has high-street stores. At 165 Howard St is the famous and enormous menswear store **Slaters** which has become something of a Glasgow institution.

Along Sauchiehall St you'll find **Geoffrey Taylor**, a kiltmaker who makes an enormous range of kilts and is now producing designer '21st century kilts' too – much to the disgust of some traditionalists. At 153-157 Sauchiehall St is the vast, open plan **Waterstone's**, with a coffee shop on the ground floor for comfy browsing. They also have a branch at 174-176 Argyle St.

Antique hunters should make for West Regent St and **Victorian Village** where a selection of traders sell lovely costume jewellery, antiques and retro clothing. Also on West Regent St are a couple of worthwhile art galleries: **Compass Gallery**, No 178, T2216370. Open Mon-Sat 1000-1730; and **Cyril Gerber Fine Art**, No 148, T2213095. Open Mon-Sat 0930-1730. Farther north, near the Glasgow School of Art is **Fireworks**, 35a Dalhousie St, T3324969, open Tue-Sat 1000-1800, a ceramic gallery and workshop.

For the widest range of retro clothing go to **Saratoga Trunk**, 4th floor, 62 Hydepark St, T2214433, open Mon-Fri only, though do call first. It's an enormous Aladdin's cave of a warehouse stuffed with the most extraordinary range of clothes, from beautiful beaded dresses to swirly 1960s gear. They also have brilliant jewellery and accessories and the staff are very friendly. They supply gear for film and tv crews, which is why you need to check they can see you beforehand. Well worth the journey if you like great vintage clothes. They also have a small outlet in **Victorian Village**.

Fans of American retro and vintage sports gear will head straight for **Flip**, 15 Bath St, T3531634. In the basement is a diverse selection or urban, skate and fetish gear at the Hellfire Club. Cheap and cool.

If you like designer clothing but don't want to pay full price, go to Designer **Exchange**, off 17 Royal Exchange Sq near *Rogano* restaurant. It has loads of nearly new designer clothes, samples and accessories (open Tue-Sat). There are also branches of **T K Maxx** on Sauchiehall St and in the St Enoch Centre, which are great places for seeking out designer goods at very low prices.

West End

4

West End

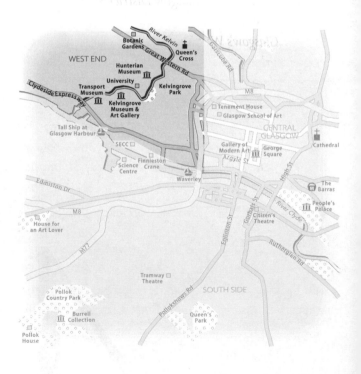

On the other side of the M8 to the city centre is the West End, an area which contains many of the city's major museums, as well some of its finest examples of Victorian architecture. During the course of the 19th century the West End grew in importance as wealthy merchants moved there, away from the dirt and grime of the industrial city. Soon after, in 1870, the university also moved west, to its present site overlooking Kelvingrove Park, and in 1896 the Glasgow District Subway was extended west.

Now, Glasgow's West End is mix of youthful hedonsim and suburban calm. The streets between Kelvingrove Park and the Great Western Road, especially around Hillhead Underground and Byres Road, are alive to the sound of students, shoppers and late-night revellers. Here you'll find some the city's most interesting independent shops, as well as many of the best bars and restaurants. Within a stone's throw is a triptych of great attractions – the **Hunterian Museum**, **Kelvingrove Art Gallery and Museum** and **Transport Museum** – and some dear green spaces, namely **Kelvingrove Park** and the **Botanic Gardens**. Head further along the Great Western Road, however, and the wild west becomes the mild west as you enter the residential districts of Kelvinside, Anniesland and Knightswood, all bywords for genteel respectability.

St George's Cross to Kelvingrove

Mitchell Library

Overlooking the motorway, a short distance west of Charing Cross, is the magnficent edifice of the Mitchell Library, particularly impressive when floodlit at night. Founded in 1874, it is the largest public reference library in Europe, with over 1½ million volumes. The Glasgow Room, on the fifth floor, entered via the south entrance, is a veritable treasure trove of information on the city. The western façade of the building is all that remains of St Andrew's Halls, the city's former concert hall, which was all but destroyed in a terrible conflagration in 1962. It must have been an awesome sight, judging by what's left of it. ■ *Mon-Thu 0900-2000, Fri and Sat 0900-1700. T2872999, www.glasgow.gov.uk/gcl/ref.htm*

The Park Conservation Area

Nearest Underground is Kelvinbridge; from there head down South Woodside Rd into Woodlands Rd

Heading north from the library, or west from St George's Cross Underground station, across Woodlands Road, you enter another world, where elegant classical terraces sweep around the contours of Woodlands Hill, punctuated by the magnificent Romanesque towers of Trinity College. If the sun is shining (yes, it happens occasionally) it is very difficult not to believe you haven't been magically transported from the west coast of Scotland to the Italian region of Umbria. By the middle of the 19th century the Park Conservation Area had been established and was described as one of the finest pieces of architectural planning of the century. The most impressive of all the terraces in the conservation area are **Park Quadrant** and **Park Terrace**, with glorious views across **Kelvingrove Park** and beyond.

Kelvingrove Museum and Art Gallery

Nearest Underground station is Kelvin Hall

Glasgow's greatest art gallery (with the possible exception of the Burrell Collection) is the Kelvingrove Art Gallery and Museum, which stands below the university, on the other side of the River Kelvin, at the most westerly end of Argyle and Sauchiehall Streets, near Kelvingrove Park. This massive sandstone Victorian building houses one of the finest municipal collections of Scottish and European paintings in the country, and should not be missed.

The art gallery and museum was built in 1901 with the proceeds from the hugely successful Glasgow Exhibition of 1888, and housed a second exhibition in the same year. The odd assortment of monuments, fountains and bridges in **Kelvingrove Park** date from the 1888 exhibition.

The museum and gallery can be entered from the 'rear', lending weight to one of Glasgow's most popular urban myths, that it was mistakenly built back to front and when the architect found out he was so distraught that he jumped from one of the towers. It was actually designed by two architects, Sir JW Simpson and Milner Allen, and is a wonderful structure, especially the breathtaking atrium. At one end of the atrium is a huge set of organ pipes, and recitals are still held here.

On the ground floor is the **Scottish Natural History Museum** and, on the opposite side of the main hall, a rather jumbled collection of pottery, porcelain, silverware, costumes and tapestry, and a collection of arms and armour. Some of the specimens in the museum were collected by the explorer David Livingstone, who was a keen naturalist.

But it is the art gallery upstairs which makes this such a fascinating attraction. Displayed in a series of rooms are some superb works, including **Botticelli**'s *Annunciation*, **Giorgione's** *The Adultress Brought Before Christ* and **Rembrandt**'s *Man in Armour*. There are also outstanding examples of French

West End

Things to do in the West End

- Sing a few tunes from 'Meet me in St Louis' as you play on the trams in the Transport Museum
- Browse around the quirky, bohemian shops in Byres Road
- If the weather's fine, take a stroll along the Forth and Clyde Canal towpath, or the Kelvin Walkway
- Don't miss your CRM fix in the Mackintosh House in the Hunterian
- Sample a blast of hot, spicy cooking and jangly music at *Mother India*, one of a clutch of great Indian restaurants at the west end of Sauchiehall Street

Impressionism, Post-Impressionism and Dutch schools, including works by **Degas**, **Monet**, **Turner**, **Bonnard**, **Pissaro**, **Vuillard**, **Braque** and **Derain**. There are also excellent works by many of Scotland's finest artists, including, **Sir Henry Raeburn**, **Horatio McCulloch** and **Alexander Naysmith**. The Glasgow Boys are also well represented, with works by **George Henry**, **Joseph Crawhall**, **Sir James Guthrie** and **Sir John Lavery**. There's also a room dedicated to **Charles Rennie Mackintosh**, featuring a marvellous collection of furniture. Do check that the museum is open before you visit as a lengthy refurbishment is pending – probably starting in late 2002. Plans for the refurbishment include spaces dedicated to hands-on learning, with discovery centres on art, the environment and history. ■ *Mon-Thu and Sat 1000-1700, Fri and Sun 1100-1700. Free. There's a cheap self-service café on the ground floor. Also free guided tours most days from the enquiry desk. T2872699, www.glasgow.gov.uk To get there, take any bus heading for the Dumbarton Rd (Nos 62, 64, 9, 16, 42).*

Opposite the Kelvingrove Museum and Art Gallery, just off Argyle Street, is the huge **Kelvin Hall**, which houses the national indoor running track and sports complex, as well as the Transport Museum. The name may lack appeal but this is one of the city's most fascinating museums. There are collections of trams, trains, motor cars, horsedrawn vehicles, bicycles, motorbikes, as well as a whole room dedicated to models of Clyde-built ships. Everything you ever wanted to know about the history of transport but were too uninterested to ask? Well, this place will change all that. There's also a reconstruction of a 1938 cobbled street, an old Underground station and a cinema showing old films of Glaswegians heading 'doon the watter'. Something for everyone, as they say in the tourist brochures, and a great place for kids, large and small. ■ *Mon-Thu and Sat 1000-1700, Fri and Sun 1100-1700. Free. T2872720, www.glasgow.gov.uk*

Transport Museum

Glasgow University and the Hunterian Museum

The university's roots date back to 1451, when Pope Nicholas V authorized William Turnbull, Bishop of Glasgow, to found a seat of learning in the city. At first there was just an Arts faculty, and lectures were held in the cathedral crypt and neighbouring monastery. In 1660 the university moved to new premises, the 'Old College', in the High Street. This complex of fine buildings, quadrangles and gardens, was sadly demolished in 1870 when the University moved west to its present site, on Gilmorehill, overlooking Kelvingrove Park.

The university building designed by Sir George Gilbert Scott in 1866-86 represents one of his finest achievements, a supremely coherent Gothic

A model of the Old College can be seen in the Hunterian Museum (see below)

West End

West End

To Lock 27, Stazione & Canal Restaurants

To Maryhill Park & Milngavie

Winton Dr

To Lochgilvie House Hotel

To Victoria Park

Kelvin Walkway

Garrioch Dr

Cleveden Gdns

Bellshaugh Rd

Kirklee Gdns

Bellshaugh La

Cleveden Dr

Lismore Rd

Beaconsfield Rd

Devonshire Gdns

Devonshire Terr La

Hughenden Dr

Lancaster Cres La

Julian La

Lancaster Cres

Redlands La

Mirtle Dr

Kirklee Pl

Ford Rd

Wyndham St

Addison Rd

Clouston

Botanic Cres La

Botanic Cres

Kelvin Dr

Hughenden Gdns

Hughenden La

Dudley Dr

Novar Dr

Hayburn La

Montague La

Westbourne Rd

Westbourne Gdns

Kirklee Terr

Kirklee Cir

Kirklee Terr

Kew Terr

Great Western Rd

Botanic Gardens

Buckingham Terr

Hughenden Terr La

Polwarth St

Airlie St

Lauderdale La

Lauderdale Gdns

Kingsborough Gdns

Kensington Rd

Banavie Terr

Horslethill Rd

Huntly Gdns

Grosvenor

Observatory Rd

Vinicombe St

Clarence Dr

Falkland St

Kingsborough La

Prince Albert Rd

Victoria Cir

Dundonald Rd

Bowmont Terr

Athole La

Roxburgh St

Cranworth St

Kersland St

Cecil St

Turnberry Rd

Banavie Rd

Clarence La

Sydenham Rd

Crown Rd N

Prince's Terr

Queen's Pl

Queen's Gdns

Victoria Cres Rd

Ruthven St

Cresswell

Hillhead

Saltoun St

Great George St

Partickhill Rd

Partickhill Ct

Turnberry Rd

North Gardner St

Crown Gdns

Crown Terr

Crown Rd S

Downanside Rd

Highburgh Rd

Havelock St

Downside La

Caledon La

Aston Rd

Byres Rd

Cranworth La

Hillhead St

Great George St

Bute Gdns

Fortrose St

Peel La

Peel St

Hyndland Rd

Gardner St

Westside Gdns

Caird Dr

White St

Lawrence St

Elie St

Lilybank Gdns

Lilybank Terr

University Gdns

Hunterian Art Gallery & Mackintosh House

Lawrie St

Chancellor St

Mansfield St

Stewartville St

Dowanhill St

University Pl

University Av

Glasgow University

Burgh Hall St

Muirpark St

Burgh Hall La

Dumbarton Rd

Anderson St

Purdon St

Walker St

Torness St

Church St

Hunterian Museum & Zoology Museum

Kelvingrove Park

Partick

Beith St

Benalder St

Dunaskin St

Bunhouse Rd

Kelvin Hall & Transport Museum

Old Dumbarton Rd

Blantyre St

Regent Moray St

Argyle St

Kelvingrove Museum & Art Gallery

Castlebank St

Clydeside Expressway

Ferry Rd

Dalnair St

Edmund St

Kelvingrove St

Gilbert St

Gardner St

Yorkhill St

Overnewton St

Lumsden St

Lymburn St

Napier Rd

Napier Terr

Napier Pl

Napier Dr

Govan

Napier St

Clydebrae St

Stag St

Highland La

Yorkhill Par

Carfrae St

Teviot St

Sandyford St

Fattyvale Pl

Haugh Rd

Kelvinhaugh St

St Vincent Cres La

St Vincent Cres

Tall Ship at Glasgow Harbour

Pointhouse Rd

Minerva Way

Broomhilan Rd

Huntra St

Dunsmuir St

Napine St

Orkney St

Vicarfield St

Southcroft St

Elphinstone Pl

Burndyke Ct

Burndyke Sq

Golspie St

Stobcross Wynd

Stobcross Rd

River Clyde

Merryland St

Summertown Rd

Glasgow Science Centre

Scottish Exhibition & Conference Centre

Congress Rd

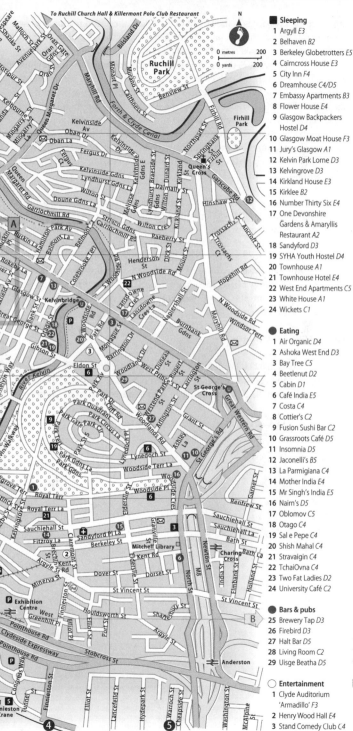

To Ruchill Church Hall & Killermont Polo Club Restaurant

N

0 metres 200
0 yards 200

Ruchill Park

Firhill Park

West End

■ **Sleeping**
1 Argyll *E3*
2 Belhaven *B2*
3 Berkeley Globetrotters *E5*
4 Cairncross House *E3*
5 City Inn *F4*
6 Dreamhouse *C4/D5*
7 Embassy Apartments *B3*
8 Flower House *E4*
9 Glasgow Backpackers
   Hostel *D4*
10 Glasgow Moat House *F3*
11 Jury's Glasgow *A1*
12 Kelvin Park Lorne *D3*
13 Kelvingrove *D3*
14 Kirkland House *E3*
15 Kirklee *B2*
16 Number Thirty Six *E4*
17 One Devonshire
   Gardens & Amaryllis
   Restaurant *A2*
18 Sandyford *D3*
19 SYHA Youth Hostel *D4*
20 Townhouse *A1*
21 Townhouse Hotel *E4*
22 West End Apartments *C5*
23 White House *A1*
24 Wickets *C1*

● **Eating**
1 Air Organic *D4*
2 Ashoka West End *D3*
3 Bay Tree *C5*
4 Beetlenut *D2*
5 Cabin *D1*
6 Café India *E5*
7 Costa *C4*
8 Cottier's *C2*
9 Fusion Sushi Bar *C2*
10 Grassroots Café *D5*
11 Insomnia *D5*
12 Jaconelli's *B5*
13 La Parmigiana *C4*
14 Mother India *E4*
15 Mr Singh's India *E5*
16 Nairn's *D5*
17 Oblomov *C5*
18 Otago *C4*
19 Sal e Pepe *C4*
20 Shish Mahal *C4*
21 Stravaigin *C4*
22 TchaiOvna *C4*
23 Two Fat Ladies *D2*
24 University Café *C2*

● **Bars & pubs**
25 Brewery Tap *D3*
26 Firebird *D3*
27 Halt Bar *D5*
28 Living Room *C2*
29 Uisge Beatha *D5*

○ **Entertainment**
1 Clyde Auditorium
   'Armadillo' *F3*
2 Henry Wood Hall *E4*
3 Stand Comedy Club *C4*

Detail map
A West End detail,
page 90

Related maps
B City centre, page 76
C South of the Clyde,
page 106

structure loosely based on the layout of the Old College and retaining a few fragments from the original, namely the the Lion and Unicorn balustrade on the stone staircase opposite the Principal's Lodging and part of the gatehouse, which forms the façade of the Pearce Lodge. Soaring over all this Gothic glory is the Flemish tower, the university's defining feature, which seems almost omnipresent in the West End. Other notable features worth seeking out are the superb **Bute Hall**, added in 1878, which is now used for graduation and other ceremonies, the **university chapel** and the **Randolph Hall**.

Beneath the Hunterian Museum (see below) is the **University Visitor Centre**, which features interactive displays on the university and a coffee bar. Historical tours are also available. ■ *Mon-Sat 0930-1700; Sun 1400-1700 May-Sep only. Free. T3305511, www.gla.ac.uk*

Hunterian Museum Contained within the university buildings is the Hunterian Museum, named after William Hunter (1718-83), a student at the university in the 1730s. His bequest to the university of his substantial collections led to the establishment of the Hunterian Museum in 1807, Scotland's oldest public museum. It has displays of social history, archaeology and geology and includes Roman relics from the Antonine Wall and one of the largest coin collections in Britain. There's also a **Zoology Museum**, housed in the Graham Kerr Building, a few minutes' walk from the main museum. ■ *Mon-Sat 0930-1700. Free. T3304221, www.hunterian.gla.ac.uk*

Hunterian Art Gallery

Across the road, at 82 Hillhead Street, is the Hunterian Art Gallery, a modern building containing the more interesting part of Hunter's bequest, the fabulous art collection. The gallery holds an important collection of European

West End detail

■ **Sleeping**	● **Eating**	10 Stravaigin 2
1 Bunkum Backpackers	1 Ashoka Ashton Lane	11 Tinderbox
2 Georgian Town House	2 Brasserie Metro	12 Ubiquitous Chip
3 Heritage & Botanic	3 Brel	
4 Hillhead	4 Cul de Sac & The Attic	● **Bars & pubs**
5 Hillview Guest House	5 Deirfiuracha	13 Curlers
6 Kelvin	6 Gong	14 Tennent's
7 Lomond	7 Little Italy	
8 University of Glasgow	8 Puppet Theatre	○ **Entertainment**
	9 Starbucks	1 Grosvener Cinema

0 metres 100
0 yards 100

A walk around the West End

*Start with a visit to **Kelvingrove Museum and Art Gallery**. After you've seen the excellent collections walk right, along Argyle Street into Dumbarton Road, until you come to **Byres Road**, the heart of the West End. There are plenty of shops to browse in here and lots of great cafés where you can get a sandwich and a coffee, or treat yourself to lunch at the 'Chip' – the famous* Ubiquitous Chip *restaurant. If you've got time, go along Cranworth Street (it's off Cresswell Street near Hillhead Station) to see the **Western** **Baths Club**, a well-preserved Victorian bathhouse. Then double back, go up University Avenue (it's south of Hillhead Station) and walk along to the **Hunterian Museum and Gallery** where you can see the recreated Mackintosh House, as well as a great collection of paintings by Whistler. Then continue walking until you come to Kelvin Way, turn right and walk down through Kelvingrove Park and out onto Sauchiehall Street where you can get a bus or walk back into the city centre.*

paintings including works by **Rembrandt**, **Koninck**, **Rubens**, **Pissaro** and **Rodin**, as well as 18th century British portraits by **Ramsay** and **Reynolds**. There is also a fine collection of Scottish 19th and 20th century paintings, including major displays of paintings by the Scottish Colourists, **Fergusson**, **Peploe**, **Cadell** and **Hunter**. The *pièce de résistance* is the huge collection of works by the American painter, **James McNeill Whistler**. There are some 70 paintings and a selection of his personal possessions (including his specially made long-handled paintbrushes) on show, making it the largest display of his work outside the USA. Among the works are many of his distinctive full-length portraits and some moody depictions of the River Thames. The gallery's graphics collection, one of the most important in Scotland, holds 30,000 prints, which can be seen by prior appointment in the Print Room.

Attached to the gallery is the **Mackintosh House**, a stunning reconstruction of the main interiors from 78 Southpark Avenue, the Glasgow home of Charles Rennie Mackintosh and his wife, Margaret MacDonald, from 1906 to 1914. A stairway leads to an introductory display containing numerous drawings and designs, including those for his major buildings, furniture and interiors. From there you are led into the cool, soothing rooms, lovingly reconstructed and exquisitely furnished with some 80 original pieces of his furniture. These give the perfect example of just why this innovative designer and architect is so revered. Among the highlights are the Studio Drawing Room, decorated in white and flooded with natural light, and the guest bedroom, a later commission, with its bold and dazzling geometric designs. When guest George Bernard Shaw was asked if the décor would disturb his sleep, he replied, 'No, I always sleep with my eyes closed.' ■ *Mon-Sat 0930-1700; Mackintosh House closed daily 1230-1330. Free. T3305431, www.hunterian.gla.ac.uk To get there take buses 44 or 59 from the city centre (Hope St), or the Underground to Hillhead and walk. Opposite the entrance is the student refectory.*

Around Byres Road

Heading west, University Avenue meets Byres Road, the bustling hub of the West End, running south from the Great Western Road past Hillhead Underground. It's an area populated mostly by students and full of

West End

**Five of the best:
places for kids**

- **Glasgow Science Centre** (page 118)
- **Transport Museum** (page 87)
- **People's Palace** (page 64)
- **Scotland Street School Museum**
  (page 104)
- **New Lanark** (page 159)

fashionable shops, bars, cafés and restaurants. It's a great place to go shopping on a weekend and ideal for a night out, when it is positively buzzing with energy. Many of the best places are listed on pages 96-100.

Just off Byres Road, and very close to Hillhead Underground is the **Western Baths Club**. It was founded in 1876 and is an original Victorian bath house. The pool still has a trapeze and exercise rings hanging above it, and there is also a gym, sauna, turkish bath and steam room. Temporary membership is available (it costs £15 for a week) and they are also happy to let you have a look around if you just want to see the interior. ■ *T5760294.*

West End

Botanic Gardens

Kids love the insectivorous plants in the greenhouses

At the top of Byres Road, where it meets the Great Western Road, is the entrance to the Botanic Gardens, a smallish but perfectly formed park where you can lose yourself along the remote paths that follow the wooded banks of the River Kelvin (see page 94). The gardens were created to provide medical and botanical students at the university with fresh plant material, but soon became a fashionable place to promenade. There are two large hothouses in the park, one of which is the **Kibble Palace**, built as a conservatory for the Clyde Coast home of Glasgow businessman, John Kibble, and then shipped to its present site in 1873. It was once used for public meetings and British Prime Ministers William Gladstone and Benjamin Disraeli both gave their rectorial addresses here when they became Rectors of the university. The domed glasshouse contains the national collection of tree ferns and temperate plants from around the world. The **main glasshouse** is more attractive and has 11 sections featuring plants such as cacti, palms, insectivorous plants and palms. The collections of orchids and begonias are outstanding. There is also a herb garden with five beds growing medicinal, culinary, dye and scented plants. The central bed has plants that have historically been used in Scotland. Look out for Meadowsweet, used for headaches; Coltsfoot used for coughs and chest complaints; and Yellow Flag iris – the leaves of which give a bright green dye and the rhizomes a black dye which were traditionally used in the Harris Tweed industry. In the Outer Hebrides the black dye was used for the cloth from which suits worn on Sundays were made. ■ *Daily 0700 till dusk. Free. Kibble Palace and all glasshouses open daily 1000-1645 in summer, 1000-1615 in winter.*

North of St George's Cross

Queen's Cross Church
Check out
www.crmsociety.com
for a sneak preview

At the junction of Garscube Road and Maryhill Road is a fascinating piece of architecture, Queen's Cross Church, designed by Mackintosh (his only church) and opened for worship in 1899. It's a little bit out of the way but well worth the effort and has huge secular appeal. Those who have recently plighted their troth will come away thinking "we want to get married there", and possibly even up sticks and move here just for the privilege of doing so.

The distinctive shape of the church and its dark orangey-brown hue can be appreciated all the way from the foot of Maryhill Road, and as you draw nearer you can also see the style reflected in the immediate surroundings. The interior is beautifully simple, with echoes of the symbolism of his other buildings and the characteristically dramatic interplay of light and space. The highlights are the stained glass and relief carving on wood and stonework. The overall effect is impressive yet humble in scale, and the dark woood gives the place a warm feel, unlike many other ecclesiastical buildings.

Five of the best: unusual sights

- **The Necropolis** (page 55)
- **The Tenement House** (page 74)
- **Paddle steamer Waverley** (page 119)
- **Templeton Business Centre** (page 64)
- **Western Baths Club** (page 92)

The church now functions as the headquarters of the Charles Rennie Mackintosh Society. There's an information centre, a small display and a gift shop. The church also plays host to regular jazz concerts. Tickets are £15, which includes wine and nibbles, and programme details are available from the website or by calling the society. ■ *Mon-Fri 1000-1700, Sun 1400-1700. £2, £1 concession. T9466600, www.crmsociety.com Buses 21, 61 and 91 from Hope St (west side of Central Station), or Underground to St George's Cross and 10 mins walk along Maryhill Rd. Entrance on Springbank Rd.*

Nearby is Firhill Park, home to one of Glasgow's *other* football teams, the much-maligned Partick Thistle (though the district of Partick is much further west). Thistle are nicknamed the Jags, though this is not related in any way to the luxury car, as they are more like the Morris Minors of Scottish football. So awful are they, that comedian Billy Connelly once joked that people outside Scotland thought their full name was 'Partick Thistle nil'. Things may be changing, though, as Thistle are experiencing something of a revival and may rejoin the Scottish Premier League soon.

Follow Firhill Road north, across the Forth & Clyde Canal, and you'll reach **Ruchill Park**, from where you get fantastic views across the whole city and surrounding hills.

West of Ruchill Park, and northwest of Queen's Cross Church, is one of Mackintosh's minor treasures, **Ruchill Church Hall.** It was originally built as a church mission amd consists of two halls and two committee rooms, which are still in use. ■ *Mon-Fri 1030-1430. Free. Closed Jul/Aug. To get there head northwest from Queen's Cross Church along Maryhill Rd till you reach the turning for Shakespeare St (10-15 mins walk).*

West of Byres Road

The Great Western Road continues west, straight as a pool cue, until it finally relents and takes a turn around the salubrious district of Knightswood, turning northwest then west to meet the Dumbarton Road, east of Dumbarton (see page 152). The Dumbarton Road, meanwhile, follows the course of the Clyde. On its way, by the junction with Balshagray Avenue (A739), near the north mouth of the Clyde Tunnel, it skirts **Victoria Park**, home of the **Fossil Grove**, which has a glasshouse containing a grove of fossil tree stumps dating back some 350 million years. Information boards provide explanations of the scientific importance of the site. ■ *Apr-Sep, Mon-Sat 1000-1700, Sun 1100-1700. Free. T9592391, www.glasgow.gov.uk Buses 44, 44C and 44D from city centre to park entrance.*

West End

Kelvin Walkway

There are frequent train services to and from Queen St, also bus 119 from Hope St to Milngavie

The Kelvin Walkway follows the River Kelvin from Kelvingrove Park through the northwest of the city all the way to Milngavie (pronounced "Mull-guy"), a distance of eight miles. Along the way, it crosses underneath the Forth and Clyde Canal (see next page) and, with the appropriate maps, you could follow one waterway out and return along the other. The route is flat and fairly easy, though muddy and overgrown in places, so you'll need sturdy footwear.

The route starts on Bunhouse Road, outside the Kelvin Hall, by the bridge on the Old Dumbarton Road, close to Kelvin Hall Underground. Follow the right bank of the river, passing the Hunterian Art Gallery and Museum on the right and the university towering over the scene on the left.

Cross the Kelvin Way, the road which runs through Kelvingrove park, and you enter the park by crossing the footbridge over the river. The path passes under Kelvin Bridge. About 400 yards further on the path re-crosses the river to the left bank and goes under the Great Western Road bridge, by Kelvinbridge Underground, then, a few hundred yards further on, under Belmont Bridge. The path recrosses the river again, where the remains of an old mill can be seen, with the BBC's Queen Margaret Drive studios on the opposite bank. This is the entrance to the Botanic Gardens.

The walkway continues northwest towards Maryhill, passing under the red sandstone Kirklee Bridge and past blocks of high-rise flats on the right. About 500 yards further on it crosses Kelvindale Road and, in another 500 yards, passes beneath the aqueduct that carries the Forth and Clyde Canal above the Kelvin River. You can join the canal towpath here by a path which heads off to the right (see next page).

To continue along the walkway, walk through the arch and under the small bridge (do not follow the track which heads left towards the river). You pass under a another bridge at Skaethorn Road, and follow the river as it curves to the right. Up ahead, on the opposite bank, you'll see a low cliff, and soon after you enter a small wood.

The Kelvin Walkway leaves the riverbank at Dalsholm Road. From the bridge, head up Dalsholm Road, cross Maryhill Road and enter Maryhill Park. From the top of the park there are views across the entire city and east to the Campsie Hills. On the other side of the park, follow Caldercuilt Road back towards the river.

The path then follows the river as it meanders through open countryside. After passing through a wooded area, the path enters an open stretch and heads along the top of an earth flood-dyke, passing a very smelly rubbish tip in the process. Keep going until you reach Balmore Road. Cross the road and continue along the dyke till it reaches the point where the Allander Water flows into the Kelvin.

Here the path leaves the Kelvin and turns northwards to follow the right bank of the Allander back towards Balmore Road. Cross Balmore Road and the B8049 into Bearsden, and rejoin the Allander Water. The path then gently descends towards Milngavie, crossing a footbridge and then joining the Glasgow Road in town. Head up the hill and turn left into Station Road to reach the train station.

A tale of two cities

"The difference between the two cities is that someone of the same age is more worn out in Glasgow than Edinburgh." Dr Graham Watt, The Scotsman 1992.
"It is no cliché to say that Glasgow is a friendly city and Edinburgh a place in which it is hard to make friends."

"Edinburgh is, if not quite a spinster lady, at least a respectable one. Glasgow is no lady." Both Jack McLean, The Scotsman 1997.
"Edinburgh is the receptacle of culture whereas Glasgow is the generator of it." Patrick Robin Archibald Boyle, 10th Earl of Glasgow.

Other walks

Eight miles north of Glasgow city centre, near the select suburb of Milngavie, is Mugdock Country Park. The park is well worth a visit. Here, you can pretend that you're in the country as there are 750 acres of unspoilt grounds and ancient woodlands to explore. As well as some good walking, there are a few sites of historic interest in the park. Near Mugdock Loch is the 13th century **Mugdock Castle**, which was once home to the Graham family, supporters of the king. In 1644 the castle was badly damaged by Covenanter troops sent by the Duke of Argyll and in 1649 James Graham was tried as a traitor and hanged. The castle was in the hands of Argyll, till he himself was executed by Charles II in 1660.

Mugdock Country Park
For a detailed description of a 2-mile walk around the park, see '25 walks in and around Glasgow' by Alan Forbes (HMSO 1997), £8.99

Also in the park is **Craigend Castle**, designed by James Smith in 1818 for the Smith family, lairds of Craigend. Ownership of the estate passed on to Sir Andrew Buchanan, ambassador to the Viennese court. Subsequently, it was owned by Sir Harold Yarrow, the Clyde shipbuilder, and George Outram, one of the former owners of the *Glasgow Herald.*

■ *The park is on Craigallian Rd, 2 miles north of Mingavie. It's open from dawn to dusk every day. T9566100, www.mugdock-country-park.org.uk*

The **West Highland Way** (see page 47), which runs for 92 miles to Fort William, begins in Milngavie, only a few hundred yards from the train station, by Allander Water. You can follow the route as far as Craigallian Road and then enter Mugdock park via the Kyber car park, from where there are great views of the city.

The Forth and Clyde Canal was opened in 1790 and provided a convenient short-cut for trading ships between Northern Europe and North America, linking both coasts of Scotland. The canal became Glasgow's main trading link, until the Clyde was dredged. In 1962 the canal was closed, but was recently granted £32 million of lottery funding for a major regeneration programme and now it is one of the city's best-kept secrets.

Forth & Clyde Canal
For those who wish to combine their walk with lunch, or a drink, the Canal restaurant and Lock 27 pub are recommended (see next page)

The **towpath** starts at **Port Dundas**, just north of the M8 by Craighall Road, and runs to the main canal at the end of Lochburn Road, off Maryhill Road. It then runs east all the way to Kirkintilloch and Falkirk, and west, through Maryhill and Drumchapel to Bowling and the River Clyde. It passes through sections of bleak industrial wasteland, but there are many interesting sights and open, rural stretches along the way.

A series of 'Walk Cards' are available from *British Waterways*, T3326936. Also check www.scottishcanals.co.uk Alan Forbes' *25 walks in and around Glasgow* (see above) provides the details for a 3¾-mile walk along the canal's banks, from Westerton Station to Spiers Wharf.

Eating and drinking

Expensive

Hillhead Underground is the nearest stop for the restaurants around Byres Rd

Amaryllis, 1 Devonshire Gdns, T3373434. Open Sun-Fri 1230-1400, 1915-2200; Sat 1915-2200. No smoking. Part of the luxurious *One Devonshire Gardens* hotel (see page 142). Award-winning restaurant run by celebrity chef Gordon Ramsay.

The Cabin, 996-998 Dumbarton Rd, T5691036. Closed Mon and Sun. BYOB. If you're idea of a good night out is piles of the finest Scottish food followed by a post-dinner cabaret by Wilma, the legendary singing waitress, then this is the place for you. A truly one-off experience and great fun. Not to be missed. The only drawback is there's only one dinner sitting, at 1930.

La Parmigiana, 443 Great Western Rd, T3340686. Open Mon-Sat 1200-1430, 1800-2300. This sophisticated Italian restaurant is one of Glasgow's finest eating establishments. Recommended for a special occasion.

Nairn's, 13 Woodside Cres, T3530707. Open daily 1200-1400, 1800-2200. Much-hyped restaurant run by TV chef Nick Nairn, but deserving of all the praise. Exceptional Modern British cuisine and superb value.

Puppet Theatre, 11 Ruthven La, T3398444. Open Sun and Tue-Fri 1200-1430, 1900-2230, Sat 1900-2300. Very stylish, very intimate dining. Menu is Scottish with an international flavour. Good value set lunches.

Stravaigin, 28-30 Gibson St, T3342665. Open Mon-Thu 1200-1430, 1700-2230, Fri and Sat 1200-1430, 1700-2300; Sun 1700-2230. Hard to define but difficult to resist. An eclectic mix of exotic Asian flavours and prime Scottish ingredients to produce the most sublime results. Expensive but you won't get better value for money in this category and totally justifies its many awards. Upstairs is a café-bar where you can sample some of that fabulous food at more-affordable prices.

Two Fat Ladies, 88 Dumbarton Rd, T3391944. Open Tue-Thu 1800-2215, Fri/Sat 1200-1400, 1800-2215. Fantastic fish and seafood in the humblest of surroundings, tucked away in an unfashionable corner of the West End.

The Ubiquitous Chip, 12 Ashton La, T3345007. Open Mon-Sat 1200-1430, 1730-2300, Sun 1230-1430, 1830-2300. A ground-breaking, multi award-winning restaurant and still the city's favourite place for superb Scottish food, especially venison and seafood. All served in a plant-filled, covered courtyard patio. Upstairs is their bistro, *Upstairs at the Chip*, which doesn't make you feel quite as special but is much easier on the wallet. Open daily 1200-2300.

Mid-range

● on maps, pages 88 & 90

Air Organic, 36 Kelvingrove St, T5645200. Open Mon-Thu and Sun 1100-2300, Fri/Sat 1100-2400. No smoking area. Ultra-cool bistro of the type that could only really exist in Glasgow. Styled on Miami International Airport and serving organic and orgasmic food. Try their Thai or Japanese offerings.

Ashoka Ashton Lane, 19 Ashton La, T3371115. Open Mon-Thu 1200-2400, Fri/Sat 1200-0030, Sun 1700-2400. First-class Indian restaurant, part of the famous west coast chain. Very popular with students and Byres Rd trendies.

Ashoka West End, 1284 Argyle St, T3393371. Open Mon-Thu 1200-1400, 1700-0030, Fri 1200-0100, Sat 1700-0100, Sun 1700-0030. The oldest in this ever-popular chain of excellent Indians. Great value and a vegetarian-friendly menu.

Beetlenut, 142 Dumbarton Rd, T3371145. Open Mon-Sat 1100-0100, Sun 1200-0100. Imaginative, international-flavour food served in a relaxed atmosphere. Good at any time of the day and child-friendly. New addition to the West End's already busy cuisine scene that still manages to fill a gap.

Brel, 39-43 Ashton La, T3424966. Open Mon-Thu and Sun 1000-2300, Fri/Sat 1000-2400. Another stylish continental eating establishment in Glasgow's hippest culinary quarter. This time it's Belgian. Great food and great value, especially during the half-price happy hour (1700-1900).

Café India, 171 North St, T2484074. Open Mon-Thu 1200-2400, Fri/Sat 1200-0030, Sun 1500-2400. No-smoking area. Cavernous Indian restaurant that's big on style and has a deserved reputation for fine food. Good value buffet downstairs.

Cottier's, 93-95 Hyndland St, T3575825. Open Mon-Thu 1700 2230, Fri/Sat 1700-2400, Sun 1200-2230. Very elegant Latin American restaurant housed in a converted church. The food is heavenly and the ambience spiritually rewarding. These dear souls are also great with kids, bless them. Stylish bar and theatre on the ground floor where you can often hear live music (see page 129).

Five of the best:
Indian restaurants

- *Shish Mahal* (this page)
- *Ashoka Ashton Lane* (previous page)
- *Mother India* (this page)
- *Wee Curry Shop* (page 78)
- *Modern India* (page 78)

Cul de Sac, 44-46 Ashton La, T3344749. Open Sun-Thu 1200-2300; Fri/Sat 1200-2400. Enduring West End favourite. Effortlessly fashionable, laid back and oh-so-boho. A great place to sit back, soak up the atmosphere and enjoy good French-style food. Their famous crêpes are half price between 1700 and 1900, as are the tasty burgers and pasta. Good vegetarian choices, too, and it's a great place to work off last night's excesses with a hearty Sunday brunch.

Deirfiuracha, 29 Ashton La, T3373636. Open Tue-Sat 1800-2130. Unusual Gaelic restaurant run by two sisters and very popular with those in the know. The puddings are particularly good.

Fusion Sushi Bar, 41 Byres Rd, T3393666. Open Mon-Wed 1200-1500, 1800-2200, Thu/Fri 1200-1500, 1800-2300, Sat 1200-2300, Sun 1800-2200. Tiny sushi bar offering a good range of Japanese delights. Set lunch is very good value.

Gong, 17 Vinicombe St, T5761700. Open Mon-Fri 1700-2400, Sat/Sun 1200-2400. Sleek new venture housed in an old cinema that is already proving popular with the locals. Lots of sharing platters as well as pizzas and pastas. Brunch served at weekends.

Gingerhill, 1 Hillhead St, T9566515. Open Wed 1200-1500, Thu-Sat 1200-1500, 1930-2130, Sun 1230-1500. No smoking. BYOB (no corkage charge). Well off the beaten track in posh Milngavie, but well worth the trip. By day it's a café and by night one of Glasgow's best seafood restaurants. It's an awfy wee place so you'll have to book well in advance.

Killermont Polo Club, 2022 Maryhill Rd, T9465412. Open Mon-Sat 1200-1400, 1700-2300, Sun 1700-2300. An exclusive, elegant Indian restaurant that offers a genuinely new culinary experience with their astonishing Dum Pukht (slow-cooked) menu. A bit out of the way, but worth it for something out-of-the-ordinary.

Mr Singh's India, 149 Elderslie St, T2040186. Open Mon-Sat 1200-2400, Sun 1430-2400. Imagine good Punjabi cooking brought to you by kilted waiters with a background wallpaper of disco music. If that sounds like your cup of char then get on down here and join in the fun. Many celebs have, so you never know who might pop in for a popadum. Very child friendly.

Mother India, 28 Westminster Terr, Sauchiehall St, T2211663. Open Mon-Thu 1200-1400, 1730-2300, Fri 1200-1400, 1700-2330, Sat 1200-2330, Sun 1700-2300. You can BYOB. Exquisite Indian cooking at affordable prices. Friendly and informal atmosphere. Strong vegetarian selection. Cheap set-lunch and pre-theatre menus.

Oblomov, 372-374 Great Western Rd, T3399177. Open Thu-Sun 1100-2030 (bar open until later). A deliciously decadent slice of Eastern Europe. The dark, sumptuous decor and classic cuisine are enhanced by an accompanying string quartet on Thu.

Shish Mahal, 66-68 Park Rd, T3398256. Open Mon-Thu 1200-1400, 1700-2330, Fri/Sat 1200-1145, Sun 1700-2330. You can BYOB. 'The Shish' has long been a byword for great curry in Glasgow. The food's imaginative and there's loads of choice.

West End

★ **Five of the best:
cheap eats**

- *Sal e Pepe* (this page)
- *Grosvenor Café* (this page)
- *University Café* (next page)
- *Buongiorno* (page 111)
- *Wee Curry Shop* (page 78)

Stazione, 1051 Great Western Rd, T5767576. Open Mon-Fri 1200-1430, 1700-late, Sat/Sun 1200-late. No smoking area. Housed in a converted Victorian train station, this is most definitely the 'rail' thing. Stylish and comfortable, excellent Mediterranean food and great service. Good vegetarian selection too.

Stravaigin 2, 8 Ruthven La, T3347165. Open Mon-Thu 1200-2300, Fri 1200-2400, Sat 1100-2400, Sun 1100-2300. For years this was *Back Alley*, a firm West End favourite famous for its burgers.The burgers still feature, but now it's part of the Stravaigin empire and there are new dishes using fresh Scottish ingredients, like mussels and salmon. The right ambience, good value eclectic menu and child-friendly.

Cheap *The Bay Tree*, 403 Great Western Rd, T3345898. Open Mon-Sat 0930-2100, Sun 1000-2000. No-smoking area. Rather basic self-service café serving rather basic vegan/vegetarian food with a Middle Eastern emphasis.

The Canal, 300 Bearsden Rd, T9545333. Open Sun-Thu 1200-2200, Fri/Sat 1200-2300. Stylish and upmarket American diner beside the Forth and Clyde Canal. Good grub, and beer from its very own microbrewery on the premises.

Grassroots Café, 97 St Georges Rd, T3330534. Open Mon-Sun 1000-2200. Vegetarian and vegan food at this intimate café near St Georges Cross. Lots of soups and salads and filling main courses.

Sal e Pepe, 18 Gibson St, T3410999. Open Mon-Sat 0930-1100, Sun 1200-2300. This little Italian is one of those places you just can't stop talking about (or writing about). It is, quite simply, perfect in every sense. And as if that weren't enough, there are half-price pizza and pasta offers weekdays between 1500 and 1800. What more could you want?

Otago, 61 Otago St, T3372282. Open Mon-Sat 1100-2200. There's a cool, minimalist look to this Mediterranean bistro offering lots of veggie choices. Good selection of wines too.

Cafés *Brasserie Metro*, 8 Cresswell La, T3388131. Open Mon-Sat 0800-1800, Sun 0900-1800.
Caffeine stops include Big and bright West End café/deli just off Byres Rd popular with students. Wide-rang-
a branch of Starbucks ing menu makes it a good, cheap choice for lunch. No smoking area.
on Byres Rd and a *Grosvenor Café*, 31 Ashton La, T3391848. Open Mon 0900-1900, Tue-Sat
Costa on Great 0900-2300, Sun 1030-1730. Behind Hillhead Underground. A perennial favourite
Western Rd with local students who come for the wide selection of cheap food (filled rolls, soup, burgers, pizzas, etc). Cosy and friendly atmosphere. Good Sun brunch, and Thai food in the evenings.

Insomnia, 38-42 Woodlands Rd, T5641700. Open daily. 24-hour café/deli where the menu changes with the mood. Still the best place for late-night refuelling, whether it's a caffeine kick, herbal infusion or a cheap bite to eat. BYOB. No smoking area.

Jaconelli's, 570 Maryhill Rd, T9461124. Traditional Italian café which has featured in a number of films, including *Trainspotting*, and also in the Scottish TV comedy show *Chewin' The Fat*. Closest underground station is St Georges Cross.

Little Italy, 205 Byres Rd, T3396287. Open Mon-Wed 0800-2200, Thu 0800-2400, Fri/Sat 0800-0100, Sun 1000-2200. A convenient and buzzy refuelling stop that never seems to close. Great pizza and strong espresso.

North Star, 108 Queen Margaret Dr, T9465365. Open Mon 0800-1800, Tue-Sat 0800-2000, Sun 1100-1800. Portuguese café/deli that has an extremely loyal following. Good speciality treats.

Tinderbox, 189 Byres Rd, T3393108. Open daily 0800-2200. Coffee shop which looks and feels more like a style bar. Great coffee, good magazines to read and a large no-smoking, child-friendly area.

TchaiOvna, 42 Otago La, T3574524. Open Mon-Sun 1100-2200. Laid back Czech-inspired café, with a huge selection of teas.

Five of the best: cool cafés

- *Tinderbox* (this page)
- *Where the Monkey Sleeps* (page 79)
- *Café Source* (page 67)
- *TchaiOvna* (this page)
- *Little Italy* (previous page)

University Café, 87 Byres Rd, T3395217. Open Mon-Fri 0900-2200, Sat 0900-2230, Sun 1000-2200. A gloriously authentic Italian Art Deco café, where grannies and students sit shoulder-to-shoulder enjoying real cappuccino, great ice cream and good, honest and cheap mince and tatties, pie and chips, sausage rolls, gammon steak and all the other golden oldies.

The Attic, 44-46 Ashton Pl, T3346688. Above the *Cul de Sac* restaurant (see page 97). **Bars & pubs** Stylish designer bar where you can enjoy tasty tapas and a bottle of plonk in cool, calm surroundings. Also good for a sandwich and fresh fruit smoothie at lunchtime.

The Brewery Tap, 1055 Sauchiehall St, T3390643. Classic student haunt, within skiving distance of the university. Convivial atmosphere, cheap food and a good selection of ales on tap are all major attractions, as are the weekday happy hour (1700-1900) and regular live music sessions.

Curlers, 256 Byres Rd, T3386511. One of the city's oldest pubs, if not the oldest. A firm favourite with generations of university students in search of liquid inspiration, and also popular with erstwhile undergrads reliving the past.

Firebird, 1321 Argyle St, T3340594. Yet another of the city's never-ending stream of new style-bars, but this one has the distinct advantage of providing excellent food, especially their pizzas. Happy hour 1700-1900 daily and DJs Thu-Sun.

The Halt Bar, 160 Woodlands Rd, T5641527. This erstwhile tram stop (hence the name) is one of Glasgow's great unspoiled pubs, with its many of the original Edwardian fixtures intact. Also a good place to see live music 2 or 3 times a week (see page 99).

The Living Room, 5-9 Byres Rd, T3398511. Near Kelvinhall Underground. Cool, relaxing space with good music and a wide choice of food throughout the day. Plenty of drinks promos, a happy hour, and DJs 5 nights a week are other reasons to pay a visit.

Lock 27, 1100 Crow Rd, T9580853. If the weather's fine (and it sometimes is), there are few nicer places to enjoy a spot of *al fresco* eating and drinking than this place by the Forth & Clyde Canal in Anniesland. Good food served until 2100 and kids are made welcome. You could take a stroll along the towpath afterwards.

Tennent's, 191 Byres Rd, T3411024. Big, no-nonsense, old West End favourite, serving a range of fine ales to a genuinely mixed crowd. It's also a great place for a chat (no loud music) and some very cheap food.

Uisge Beatha, 232 Woodlands Rd, T3320473. The 'water of life' is one of those pubs you go into for a wee drink and you're still there many hours later, the day's plans in ruins around your feet. Looks and feels like a real Highland hostelry. Cosy and welcoming and serving ridiculously cheap food. Scottish in every sense, right down to the effigy of Mrs T's head strung up by a tartan scarf (if only it were real!).

Wintersgill's, 226 Great Western Rd, T3323532. Nothing fancy or out-of-the-ordinary, but well placed for hostels and B&Bs and one of the few places you can get a decent cheap meal at any time on a Sun.

West End

Shopping

The West End is a great place for browsing as it's full of quirky, off-beat shops that seem to scream 'bargain' at you. You could happily spend a day rummaging through piles of old books, trying on retro clothes, and drooling over the treats in the delis – stopping every so often to re-energize with a strong shot of caffeine in one of the area's buzzing cafés.

For new designer clothes head for *Moon*, 10 Ruthven La, T3392315. It stocks names like Jaspar Conran and Lacroix. There's also *Nancy Smillie* on Cresswell La. If you prefer vintage clothes head for *Starry Starry Night*, 19 Downside Rd, T3371837, which has a brilliant selection of dresses, suits, bags … you name it. There are more second-hand and period delights at *Circa* on Ruthven La.

For kids clothes try *Strawberry Fields* at 517 Great Western Rd. Don't forget the charity shops either. There are plenty in the West End, including two branches of *Shelter* on the Great Western Rd.

There are several good jewellery shops in the West End. *Bethsy Gray* is a jewellery designer with a shop/workshop in *Starry Starry Night* on Dowanside Rd (see above). She specializes is working with silver. *Orro* on Bank St is a sleek contemporary jewellers. You can also find jewellery, as well as antiques, pottery, 'Glasgow Style' artefacts etc in *De Courcey's Arcade* in Cresswell La, which has a brilliant selection of goods from different traders. Here on the top floor you'll find the excellent *Lost in Music*, with an astounding range of new and second-hand Cds.Another good music outlet is Fopp, at 358 Byres Rd, T3570774, which caters for all tastes be it the latest phat underground hip hop or, god forbid, Phil Collins.

If you're a book-lover there are plenty of good second-hand bookshops to explore. *Bookpoint*, 143 Hyndland Rd, T3345522, has lots of books on Scotland and Glasgow. *Voltaire and Rousseau,* 12-14 Otago La, T3391811, is an old established antiquarian bookstore (the oldest in the city, in fact). For academic books there's a branch of *John Smith and Son* on University Av, T3341210. Also worth trying is the *Oxfam* bookshop, at 171 Byres Rd, T3347669.

There are several great delis around here full of treats to help you put together a delicious picnic if the weather's good. *North Star Provisions*, on Queen Margaret Dr, has Portuguese specialities, while *Ian Mellis*, on Great Western Rd, is a wonderful cheese shop full of unusual varieties of cheese ranging from strong blues, to creamy bries. A good little deli is *Peckham's*, 100 Byres Rd, T3571454, but even better is the excellent *Heart Buchanan*, 380 Byres Rd, though it's popularity means you often have to queue up. A must for all you detox junkies is *Grassroots*, 20 Woodlands Rd, T3533278, round the corner from the eponymous café (see page 98).

For fresh fruit and veg try *Roots, Fruits and Flowers ,* at 351 Byres Rd and 451 Great Western Rd. For fresh Scottish produce bought straight from the farmer you can also try the *Farmers' Market* held every other weekend (usually on Sat, 1000-1500) in Mansfield Park on the corner of Hyndland Rd and Dumbarton Rd. A good outdoor equipment shop is *Outside Now*, 316 Byres Rd, T3392202. It's small and the staff are just great.

If you're looking for something different to take home, go to *Great Western Auctions*, Otago St. The auctioneer is a woman, the first female auctioneer in Scotland, and she has worked hard to make the auctions accessible to private buyers. Lots of people come just to experience the atmosphere. You can find anything here from jewellery to furniture and sales of paintings are particularly strong. T3393290. Auctions are held every second Sat afternoon.

South of the Clyde

5

South of the Clyde

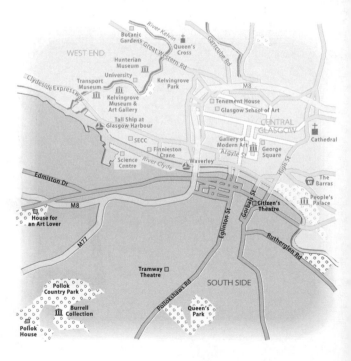

First impressions can be misleading and most visitors' first sight of Glasgow's southern parts will be less than uplifting as they head in from the airport past a great swathe of industrial units and warehouses. South of the River Clyde is a part of Glasgow largely unknown to most tourists, except perhaps for the Gorbals, a name once synoymous with urban violence, but now more likely to enervate rather than inspire fear.

Venture further south and you enter a different world the sedate suburbs and attractive parks of South Side. Here you'll find two of the city's most notable attractions, the **Burrell Collection** and **Pollok House**, both set in the sylvan surrounds of **Pollok Country Park**. There are other reasons to venture south of the river, not least of which is Charles Rennie Mackintosh's **House for an Art Lover** in Bellahouston Park. Further east is another stop on the Mackintosh trail, the **Scotland Street School Museum**, and to the south, in Cathcart, is **Holmwood House**, Alexander 'Greek' Thomson's great architectural masterpiece, which stands overlooking the White Cart, another of the city's bucolic waterways.

Scotland Street School Museum

Directly opposite Shields Road Underground station is another of Charles Rennie Mackintosh's great works, the Scotland Street School, which opened in 1906 and closed in 1979. The entire school has been preserved as a museum of education and offers a wonderfully evocative experience. There's a fascinating collection of school memorabilia and reconstructed classrooms dating from Victorian times up to the 1960s, as well as changing rooms, a science room and headmaster's office (straighten your tie and comb your hair before entering).

This is the most modern of Mackintosh's buildings and is notable for its semi-cylindrical glass stairtowers, the magnificent tiled entrance hall and its customary mastery of the interplay of light and space. The school was recently refurbished and new facilities have been introduced, including a lift, an audio-visual theatre and computer activities for children. There's also a café, but don't worry, they don't serve authentic school food. ■ *Mon-Thu 1000-1700, Fri-Sun 1100-1700. Free. T2870500. Take the underground to Shields Rd, or buses 89, 90, 96 and 97 from the city centre.*

Govan Old Parish Church
Nearby is one of the city's other, main, religious centres, Ibrox, home of Glasgow Rangers

On Govan Road, close to Govan Underground station, is one of Govan's forgotten sights. This old church is worth seeking out. Not only does it stand on an ancient Christian site, it also has a unique collection of carved stones dating back to the 9th century. There's also a sarcophagus which is covered in fine carvings, and a good collection of stained-glass windows. ■ *1st Wed in Jun to 3rd Sat in Sep, Wed 1030-1230, Wed, Thu, Sat 1300-1600, other times by appointment. Free. T4451941.*

House for an Art Lover

A short distance from Ibrox Stadium, across the M8 motorway, is Bellahouston Park, site of the most recent addition to the Charles Rennie Mackintosh trail, the House for an Art Lover. The building was designed in 1901 as an entry to a competition run by a German design magazine, the brief being to create a lavish country house for an art lover. The interior and exterior had to be a coherent work of art. Building never went ahead during Mackintosh's lifetime and it was not until 1989 that construction began, in accordance with his original drawings. The building was not completed until 1996, when it became a centre for Glasgow School of Art postgraduate students, though a number of rooms on the lower floor are open to the public.

Mackintosh worked closely with his wife on the design of the house and there is distinctive evidence of her influence, especially in the exquisite **Music Room** with its elaborate symbolism, particularly the rose motif, which is used throughout. But though the detail is, as ever, intense, the overall effect is one of space and light. The exterior of the house is equally impressive and totally original. On the ground floor is an excellent **café**, which is popular with locals (see page 104). ■ *Apr-Sep Sun-Thu 1000-1600, Sat 1000-1500; Oct-Mar Sat 1000-1500, Sun 1000-1600, call for weekday access times (T3534449). £3.50, £2.50 concession. T3534770. To get there take the Underground to Ibrox station and walk (15 mins), or bus No 9 from Hope St.*

South of the Clyde

Things to do south of the Clyde

- Catch a show at the Citizens' Theatre, home to some of the UK's most exciting and innovative drama
- Relive your childhood at Scotland Street School Museum, another of Charles Rennie Mackintosh's class designs
- Marvel at the genius of Alexander 'Greek' Thomson in Holmwood House, an exquisite architectural gem
- Escape the city traffic with a stroll in Pollok Park or Linn Park
- It doesn't really need saying, but don't miss the outstanding Burrell Collection

The Burrell Collection

Three miles southwest of the city centre is Glasgow's top attraction and a must on any visit, the Burrell Collection, standing in the extensive wooded parklands of Pollock Country Park. The magnificent collection contains some 8,500 art treasures, donated to the city in 1944 by the shipping magnate William Burrell (1861-1958), who sold his shipping interests in order to devote the remainder of his life to collecting art. He began collecting in the 1880s, and in 1917 bought Hutton Castle near Berwick-on-Tweed to house his collection. There it stayed, even after his bequest to the city, as he stipulated that all the works in his collection be housed in one building in a rural setting – since he was concerned about the possible damage caused by the pollution that then blackened Glasgow. It wasn't until the Clean Air Act of the 1960s and the council's acquisition of Pollok Park that a suitable site was found and the modern, award-winning gallery could be built – with £450,000 donated by Burrell. The building opened to the public in 1983.

The collection includes ancient Greek, Roman and Egyptian artefacts, a huge number of dazzling oriental art pieces, and numerous works of medieval and post-medieval European art, including tapestries, silverware, stained glass, textiles, sculpture and exquisitely lit stained glass. The tapestries are particularly fine and date from the late 15th and 16th centuries. There's also an impressive array of paintings by **Rembrandt**, **Degas**, **Pissaro**, **Bellini** and **Manet** amongst many others. Look out too for **Rodin**'s famous sculpture *The Thinker* which, like many film stars and TV personalities you've only seen in pictures, is smaller than you'd expect.

The gallery is a stunning work of simplicity and thoughtful design, which allows the visitor to enjoy the vast collection to the full. The large, floor-to-ceiling windows afford sweeping views over the surrounding woodland and allow a flood of natural light to enhance the treasures on view. Some sections of the gallery are reconstructions of rooms from Hutton Castle and incorporated into the structure are carved stone Romanesque doors. There's also a café and restaurant on the lower ground floor. ■ *Mon-Thu and Sat 1000-1700, Fri and Sun 1100-1700. Free. T2872550, www.glasgow.gov.uk Buses 45, 48A and 57 from the city centre (Union St) pass the park gates on Pollockshaws Rd, also buses 34 and 34A from Govan Underground station. From the gates it's a 10-min walk to the gallery, or there's a twice-hourly bus service. There are also regular trains from Central Station to Pollockshaws West station. A taxi from the city centre costs £6-7. Car parking at the Burrell Collection costs £1.50.*

South of the Clyde

South of the Clyde

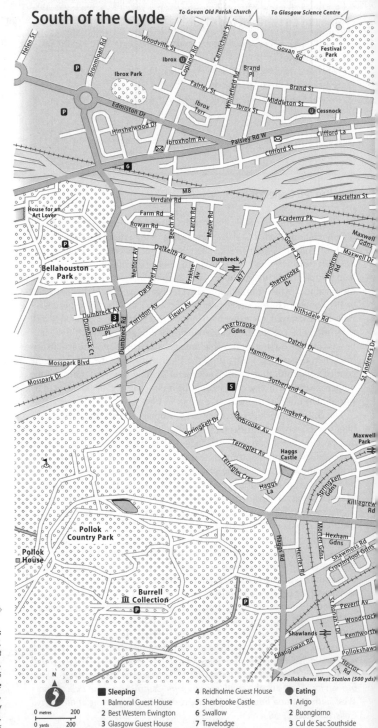

To Govan Old Parish Church   To Glasgow Science Centre

Helen St
Woodville St
Broomloan Rd
Copland Rd
Carmichael St
Govan Rd
Festival Park

P

Ibrox Park

Ibrox

Brand Pl
Brand St

Fairley St
Whitefield Rd
Ibrox St
Middleton St

P

Edmiston Dr

Ibrox Terr

Cessnock

Hinshelwood Dr

Ibroxholm Av
Paisley Rd W
Clifford La

Clifford St

M8

6

Maclellan St

House for an Art Lover

Urrdale Rd
Farm Rd
Beech Av
Larch Rd
Maple Rd
Academy Pk

Maxwell Gdns
Maxwell Dr

P

Rowan Rd

Dalkeith Av

Dumbreck

M77

Gower St
Woodrow Rd

Bellahouston Park

Metfort Av
Dargarvel Av
Erskine Av

Sherbrooke Dr

Dumbreck Av
Dumbreck Pl
Dumbreck Ct

3

Torridon Av
Fleurs Av

Nithsdale Rd

St Andrew's Dr

Dumbreck Rd

Sherbrooke Gdns

Dalziel Dr

Mosspark Blvd

Hamilton Av

Mosspark Dr

5

Sutherland Av

Springkell Av

Springkell Dr
Sherbrooke Av

Maxwell Park

Terregles Av
Terregles Cres

Haggs Castle

Springkell Gdns

Killegrew Rd

Haggs La

Pollok Country Park

Pollok House

Haggs Rd

Mortem Gdns
Hexham Gdns
Shawmoss Rd
Crossmyloof Gdns

Herries Rd

St Roman's Dr

Burrell Collection

P

P

Peveril Av
Woodstock

Kenilworth

Shawlands

Hector Rd

Pollokshaws

To Pollokshaws West Station (500 yds)

Nithsdale Rd
Langowan Rd

N
0 metres 200
0 yards 200

Related maps
A West End,
page 88
B City centre,
page 56
C George
Square,
Merchant City
& Trongate,
page 56

■ **Sleeping**
1 Balmoral Guest House
2 Best Western Ewington
3 Glasgow Guest House
4 Reidholme Guest House
5 Sherbrooke Castle
6 Swallow
7 Travelodge

● **Eating**
1 Arigo
2 Buongiorno
3 Cul de Sac Southside

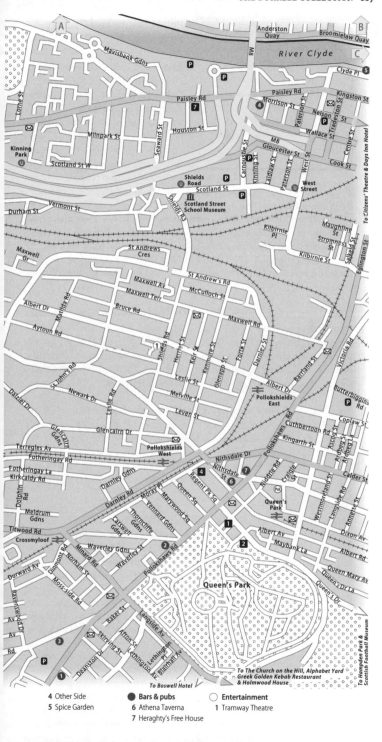

South of the Clyde

4	Other Side	●	Bars & pubs	○	Entertainment
5	Spice Garden	6	Athena Taverna	1	Tramway Theatre
		7	Heraghty's Free House		

Five of the best: exhibits in The Burrell

- *Rodin's The Thinker*
- *Rembrandt's Self Portrait*
- Tapestry of birds and monsters c.1300
- Hutton Castle furniture
- Kangxi period Chinese enamel lantern

Pollok House and Country Park

Also in Pollok Country Park, a 10-minute walk from the Burrell, is **Pollok House**, designed by William Adam and completed in 1752. This was once the home of the Maxwell family, who owned most of southern Glasgow until well into the last century. It contains one of the best collections of Spanish paintings in Britain, including works by **Goya**, **El Greco** and **Murillo**. There are also paintings by **William Blake**, as well as glass, silverware, porcelain and furniture. The most interesting part of the house are the servants' quarters downstairs, which give you a real insight into life 'below stairs' – with rows of bells waiting to summon servants to any part of the house. There's a good tearoom in the old kitchens. ■ *Daily 1000-1700. £4, £3 child/concession; Nov-Mar free.Entry to the park is from Pollokshaws Rd, or Haggs Rd if you're on foot. The house is managed by the NTS (T6166410).*

Walks around the park If the weather's fine, the park is worth exploring. There are numerous trails through the woods and meadows and guided walks with the countryside rangers, who are located in the grounds. Most of the routes start from the free car park at Pollok House. You can wander to your heart's content and eventually you're bound to end up back where you started. There are two golf courses within the park grounds, as well as a herd of highland cattle.

Queen's Park To the east of Pollok Country Park, by Pollokshaws Road, is **Queen's Park**, named after Mary, Queen of Scots, whose reign ended after defeat here by the English, at the Battle of Langside, in 1568. A memorial outside the park marks the site of the battle. It's a pleasant place for a stroll and the views north across the city make it even more enjoyable. ■ *To get there, take a train from Central Station to Queen's Park, then it's a 5-min walk down Victoria Rd to the gates on Queen's Dr.*

Scottish Football Museum
The museum is not signposted from the station, see below for directions

South of Queen's Park, in Mount Florida, is **Hampden Park**, home of Scottish football and once the largest football ground in Britain, with a capacity of 135,000. When full, as was often the case, the famous 'Hampden roar' could be heard for miles around. Nowadays, the capacity is a mere 52,000.

Hampden is also the home of the new **Scottish Football Museum**, which describes the history of the game in Scotland. This may strike some as a rather masochistic idea given some of the more infamous and embarrassing episodes, but there have been highs (Wembley '67 and Lisbon '69) as well as lows (Wembley '66 and Argentina '78). The museum is very large and includes a huge range of football memorabilia. It manages to avoid the obvious pitfall of overloading on Celtic and Rangers to the exclusion of all else and presents a very balanced view of Scottish football through the years. Most interesting are the more obscure details and the audio sets relating strories from players and fans (in particular the one about the Celtic supporters burning parts of their bus to keep warm on the long trip north to Aberdeen). It's all here, from the minutes of the very first meeting of Queen's Park, Scotland's first football club – dated 9th July 1867 – to advertising on team shirts. You can also get a guided tour of Hampden Park. ■ *Mon-Sat 1000-1700, Sun 1100-1700. £5, £2.50 concession. Tour of the ground £2.50 . T6166100, www.scottishfootballmuseum.org.uk Regular trains to Mount Florida station from Central Station; 10 mins, £1.40 return. Turn left out of the station, head down Bolton Dr, cross Cathcart Rd and down Somerville Dr. Buses 12 or 75 from Argyle St and get off on Aikenhead Rd; 31 or 37 to Mount Florida. The museum entrance is at the South Stand.*

Five of the best: Mackintosh sights ★

- **House for an Art Lover** (page 104)
- **Glasgow School of Art** (page 73)
- **The Mackintosh House at the Hunterian** (page 91)
- **The Willow Tea Rooms** (page 71)
- **Scotland Street School Museum** (see page 104)

Holmwood House

South of Queen's Park and Hampden, at 61-63 Netherlee Road in Cathcart, is Holmwood House, designed by Alexander 'Greek' Thomson, Glasgow's greatest Victorian architect, who is now internationally recognised as one of Scotland's most original designers. Thomson was a brilliant exponent of the Greek Revival and his achievement at Holmwood was described thus, by architect Thomas Gildard in 1888: "If architecture be poetry in stone and lime – a great temple an epic – this exquisite little gem, at once classic and picturesque, is as complete, self-contained and polished as a sonnet".

For anyone who appreciates architecture and design, Holmwood is, quite simply, unmissable

The building is a work of genuine originality and has become a monument of international importance, as Thomson was the first modern architect to apply a Greek style to a free, asymmetrical composition. The house also includes features reminiscent of Frank Lloyd Wright, which pre-date the great American architect by some 40 years. Thomson, like Robert Adam before him and Charles Rennie Mackintosh afterwards, exerted complete control over the interiors as well as the exterior. He designed everything in the house and conservation work is revealing very beautiful and elaborate stencilled decoration and friezes with Greek motifs.

The grounds of Holmwood slope gently down to the wooded valley of White Cart Water and are dominated by some magnificent sequoia trees. It's the perfect spot for a picnic. A lovely walk – described below – follows the river as it flows through Linn Park.

Holmwood was built for James Couper, a paper manufacturer, between 1857 and 1858, at a cost of £3,600. It is the most elaborate and sumptuously decorated of all the villas Thomson designed for well-to-do industrialists on the outskirts of Glasgow. After James Couper's death in 1877, Holmwood remained in possession of his trustees until 1909, when it was sold to a Mrs Anne Smith or Simpson. It has had several owners since, the most recent prior to the National Trust for Scotland (NTS) being The Sisters of Our Lady of the Missions, who acquired the house in 1858 and turned it into a primary school. In 1967 the local education authority took over the management of the school, until its eventual closure in 1992. The sisters moved to other premises and granted an option over the property to a developer, who proposed the construction of 93 flats and houses in the grounds. This caused widespread concern and, thanks to the strong opposition of the newly formed Alexander Thomson Society, Glasgow City Council refused planning permission, to their eternal credit. The developer withdrew from their option, thus enabling

A history of Holmwood For more on Alexander Thomson, see page 203

Beyond the pale

Glaswegians may live in one of the wettest cities in the UK, but a sunbed boom is offering some light relief. Gone are the pasty complexions which once characterized its inhabitants. The locals are suddenly looking a lot healthier. The city is basking in the artificial glow produced by more solariums and tanning salons per head of population than any other city in Britain. There are currently 72 such establishments listed in local business directory, only 21 fewer than London, which has more than 10 times as many people. Manchester, Birmingham and even Newcastle all pale in comparison. There may be warnings of the potential dangers of spending too much time under UV light, but Glaswegians are soaking it up and proving that they are no SAD cases.

the NTS to acquire the house in 1994. The Trust embarked on an extensive conservation project, with financial help from various sources, and Holmwood was opened to the public in 1998. Work is ongoing and it will take several years to fully restore Holmwood to its former glory. ■ *Easter-31 Oct, daily 1330-1730, but access may be restricted at certain times; phone in advance (T6372129). £3.50, £2.50 child/concession. Trains every ½ hr to Cathcart from Central Station, or take bus 44A or 44D from Sauchiehall St, or 66 from Argyle St opposite St Enoch Centre, to Cathcart Bridge, next to the train station. From the bridge turn onto Rhannon Rd and walk up it for 10 mins till you see the sign for Holmwood.*

A walk along the White Cart

The grounds of Holmwood look across the White Cart Water, one of the South Side's rural waterways, which flows through the middle of Linn Park. The park gets its name from the linn, or waterfall, over which the river cascades on its route through the lovely wooded glen towards Snuff Mill Bridge. A riverside walkway follows the White Cart through the park and can be joined at several points along its length.

A convenient starting point for those visiting Holmwood is Snuff Mill Bridge, on Snuff Mill Road, which is only a five-minute walk from Cathcart station and can be reached by turning off Rhannon Road.

The picturesque Snuff Mill Bridge dates from the 18th century and at one time was the only crossing of White Cart Water, carrying the main road from Glasgow to Ayr. On the opposite bank is the grain mill, which was built in the 18th century, then switched production to cardboard in 1812, and two years later, to snuff milling. The original mill has long gone and some of the later buildings have been coverted into flats. From the bridge, a flight of steps leads into Linn Park. Follow the path, with the river on your left, then cross Millholm Road and the paths drops closer to the river. Wildlife is abundant here and you're likely to see kingfishers, wood pigeons, chaffinches, grey squirrels, wood mice, kestrels, dippers and rabbits, to name but a few.

The path passes the site of the old Millholm Paper Mill, which was owned by the Robert Couper and his brother James, who had Holmwood House designed for him by 'Greek' Thomson. The path continues through the wooded glen to reach Halfpenny Bridge, passing the linn which can be heard long before it's seen when the river is in spate. Cross the river by the pretty bridge, also called the White Bridge, which is said to get its name from the decorative circular holes in the spans.

Once across the river, head along an avenue of lime trees to reach Linn House, the mansion built as a summer home for the Campbell family. The park's countryside rangers are now based in the house. Head north from here along a tarmac road, with the golf course up on the right. After about 300 yards the road swings round to the right; here you should follow the tarmac path which leads down to the river. The path first runs downhill, then changes to a gravel surface past an open grassy area. It then heads through woods before reaching Snuff Mill Road, which leads you back to Snuff Mill Bridge.

Eating and drinking

Mid-range

● *on map, page 106*

Arigo, 67 Kilmarnock Rd, T6366616. Open Mon-Fri 1200-1430, 1700-2230, Sat 1200-1600, 1700-2230, Sun 1200-1630, 1700-2230. Good Italian restaurant offering high quality fresh food. The sort of place that doesn't need to advertise.

Ashoka Southside, 268 Clarkston Rd, T6370711. Open Mon-Sat 1700-2400; Sun 1700-2300. Small and intimate South Side version of this venerable chain of Indian restaurants.

Cul de Sac Southside, 1179 Pollockshaws Rd, T6491819. Open Mon-Thu 1200-1430, 1700-0100; Sat and Sun 1200-0100. Wee sister to the West End original (see page 97). Same excellent food and atmosphere.

The Cook's Room 205 Fenwick Rd, T6211903. Open Mon-Fri 1800-2130, Sat, Sun 1200-1500, 1800-2130. Good modern Scottish cooking and some great puddings. Sunday brunch is good value.

The Greek Golden Kebab, 34 Sinclair Dr, T6497581. Open Thu-Sun 1700-0100. This place hasn't changed for years – it has no need to as the home-cooked Greek food has a loyal following.

The Other Side, 53 Morrison St, T4294042. Open Mon-Sun 1000-late. Australian restaurant close to the Clyde offering all sorts of unusual 'delicacies' like crocodile, kangaroo and ostrich. Not the most comfortable dining experience for veggies.

Spice Garden, 11-17 Clyde Pl, T4294422. Open daily 1800-0430. There's an enormous choice at this popular Indian restaurant that prides itself on its cleanliness. It's conveniently open all night so good for those desperate for a post-club curry.

The Wok Way, 2 Burnfield Rd, Giffnock, T6382244. Open Tue/Wed 1700-2400, Thu 1200-1400, 1700-2400, Fri 1200-2400, Sat/Sun 1700-2400. Spectacular Chinese cooking in this very popular tiny venue. Gets very lively at weekends! Booking essential at all times.

Cheap

Alphabet Yard, 15 Millbrae Rd, T6496861. Open daily 1200-2145. Harrassed parents love this place as its very child friendly and even has a play barn on the upper floor. Loads of choice on the menu that offers everything from pizza to tempura.

Buongiorno, 1021 Pollokshaws Rd, T6491029. Open Mon-Sat 0900-2300, Sun 1000-2200. Italian family cooking, with cosy ambience to match. They even have occasional 2-for-1 deals! Are they crazy? Simply unbeatable, so book ahead.

Cafés

Art Lovers' Café, Bellahouston Park, Drumbreck Rd, T3534779. Open Mon-Sun 1000-1700; May-Sep, open until 1900. Housed in CRM's exquisite *House for an Art Lover*. A nice place to chill and a good selection of light snacks and hot and cold meals. No smoking.

Chisholm's, 145 Kenmure St, T4201393. Open Mon-Fri 0900-1730, Sat 0930-1700, Sun 1100-1700. No-nonsense traditional caff serving very cheap filled rolls and fry-ups to a grateful public.

South of the Clyde

Bars & pubs   *Boswell Hotel*, 27 Mansionhouse Rd, T6364471. Lively Queen's Park favourite with a good selection of real ales and regular live music sessions. Noted for its good food; also offers accommodation (see page 143).

The Church on the Hill, 16 Algie St, T6495189. Popular Southside bar housed in an old church. Stained-glass windows, beer garden, contemporary menu and DJs preach to the converted at weekends.

Heraghty's Free House, 708 Pollockshaws Rd, T4230380. The best pint of Guinness in Glasgow in an old-style Irish pub with old-style hospitality and old-style prices (no need for happy hours here). And they even have a ladies' toilet, proving that everything comes to those who wait!

Samuel Dow's, 69-71 Nithsdale Rd, T4230107. Or Sammy Dow's as it's known by its many regulars. A friendly South Side local serving good ale and cheap bar food. Also regular live folk music nights.

The Stoat and Ferret, 1534 Pollockshaws Rd, T6320161. No-nonsense real-ale pub also serving traditional food all day.

The Athena Taverna, 778 Pollockshaws Rd, T4240858. Popular South Side venue near the *Tramway Theatre* and Queen's Park. Nice, bright Mediterranean look and feel which extends to their love of kids. Good selection of ales and European beers and good value food, especially their pre-theatre dinner. Next door is a good Greek restaurant.

Shopping

The main shopping outlet on the southside is the enormous *Braehead Shopping Centre*, on King's Inch Rd in Renfrew. It has over 100 high-street names as well as a huge branch of IKEA – said to be the largest in Europe. You can get there on the Clyde Waterbus (see page 119). Out in Shawlands, not far from Pollock Country Park, is *Nuala Ashe*, 168 Kilmarnock Rd, T6323777, hailed as Glasgow's first lifestyle shop, stocked with lots of lovely things you never knew you needed!

Along the Clyde

Along the Clyde

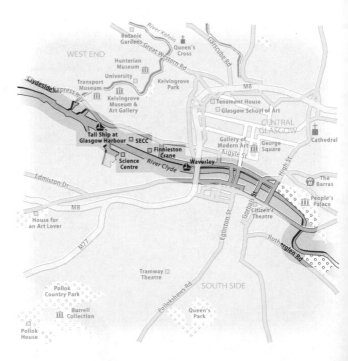

"The Clyde almost runs through my veins"
  Billy Connolly

This chilly grey river has for centuries played a vital role in the life of the city, providing employment and entertainment for generations of Glaswegians. It was on the Clyde that Glasgow's famous shipyards grew and flourished; on the Clyde that goods were transported and unloaded to be traded by the city's merchants; and on the Clyde that poor people escaped from the grime of the industrial city. The Clyde has also always been an important link to the wider world and has helped to give Glasgow its cosmopolitan appeal and restless energy. It was the route taken by thousands of Glaswegians seeking a new life in other parts of the world, and also brought Irish, Italian, Indian and Jewish migrants to the city.

History of the Clyde

The Clyde runs for about 100 miles from its source in the Lanarkshire hills to Greenock. The ancient settlement that became the city of Glasgow grew up at an important crossing point on the river, where the waters were very shallow and could be easily forded. Early settlers certainly used the river, as ancient dugout canoes have been found preserved in riverbank silt. However, as ships became larger and more sophisticated, the very shallowness of the waters made it impossible for them to sail right up to the city, preventing Glasgow from trading as efficiently as, say, London. It was not until after the Act of Union in 1707, when Scotland was united with England, that Glasgow began to look seriously at exploiting the river's potential.

The Union allowed Scotland access to the markets of England's North American colonies – and Glasgow's geographical position on the west coast made it perfectly placed to benefit from this trade. The journey from the Firth of Clyde to North America was a great deal shorter than from southern England, and ships travelling from the Clyde ports could make the journey quicker and more economically. Trade grew quickly, with ships leaving the Clyde laden with goods that the early colonists could not yet manufacture for themselves (like cotton, linen and ironware), and returning with valuable cargoes of tobacco (as well as sugar and rum from the West Indies). These were then re-exported to Europe. Consequently, Glasgow's linen, cotton and iron industries grew rapidly, and the city's merchants, known as the Tobacco Lords, grew extremely wealthy.

At first the shallowness of the Clyde meant that merchants had to unload their cargoes at the Ayrshire ports and then transport them by packhorse to the city. This was an obvious impediment to trade, so the city authorities asked engineers to look at ways of deepening the river. Jetties were built, narrowing the river's channel and increasing the power of the water. The river-bed began to erode and within a few years the depth of the water had risen considerably. The work was refined still further by Thomas Telford in 1805, who effectively turned the upper reaches of the Clyde into a canal. The deeper the Clyde became, the easier it was for ocean-going vessels to sail into the city itself and then be unloaded on the bustling docks. It was this extensive engineering of the river that gave rise to the saying 'The Cyde made Glasgow – but Glasgow made the Clyde'.

Shipbuilding Another important development on the river was that of the shipbuilding industry. In the early 19th century a vessel called the *Comet* was built and launched on the river – it was the first practical sea-going steamer in Europe. It was so successful that demand for steamers grew rapidly and soon Clydebuilt steamships were being sent all over the world.

Shipbuilding became of enormous importance to the city and shipyards opened all along the river. The term Clydebuilt became a by-word for toughness and solid reliability. For generations of Clydeside men, work meant the shipyards. Comedian Billy Connolly was just one of thousands who started his working life in this way.

You don't have to be a naval 'anorak' to recognise the names of some of the ships that were built on the Clyde. There was the clipper *Cutty Sark*, built in Dumbarton and now moored on the Thames at Greenwich; there was the *Lusitania*, which was torpedoed during the First World War with the loss of 1198 passengers and crew; there were the luxury liners *Queen Mary*, *Queen*

Elizabeth, and the *QE2*; and there was even the *Royal Yacht Britannia* – now moored at Leith in Edinburgh. The fact that such well-known ships were built on the Clyde is still a great source of pride to many Glasgwegians.

However, the shipbuilding industry declined rapidly after the First World War and large numbers of workers lost their jobs in the following Depression. Although there was a revival of shipbuilding during the Second World War it was shortlived. To add to the Clyde's woes, new containerised ships reduced the need for dock workers, while the enormous new bulk carriers that came into being after the war, were unable to navigate the upper reaches of the Clyde and unloaded their cargoes at the Ayrshire ports – and later the southern ports – instead. The Clyde became a watery wasteland. Today there are only three shipyards left on the river, but while the great age of shipbuilding may be over, tough-looking Glasgwegians still go misty eyed at its memory.

> ## Five of the best: things to do when it's raining ★
>
> - Go to the **Science Centre** (next page)
> - Go to **Kelvingrove Museum** (page 86)
> - Sit in the winter gardens of the **People's Palace** (page 64)
> - Browse in **Borders bookshop** (page 78)
> - Shop in **Princes Square** (page 70)

'Doon the Watter' The coastal resorts along the Clyde provided a traditional escape for city folk wanting to get away from the filth and grime of the industrial city. Steamships would leave from Broomielaw taking people to places like Dunoon or Rothesay, either for the day or for a holiday. The boats would be packed, full of excitable children and harassed parents. Entertainment was provided, sometimes in the form of a fiddler, harpist or concertina player – sometimes in the form of a band. Unfortunately, it was not always of the highest quality. One letter to *The Glasgow Herald* in 1888 complained of the "torture of having to listen to the terrible musicians". Peak season for a trip 'doon the watter' as it was known, was the Glasgow Fair, the two week period in the summer when most people took their holiday. These trips played an important part in Glasgow life right up until the 1960s – and even today you can take a nostalgic trip on a paddle steamer, the *Waverley* along the Clyde (see next page).

The Clyde Today After the shipbuilding and related maritime industries declined, Glasgow seemed to turn its back on the Clyde and the river became a rather sad, neglected stretch of water. But in recent years the city has turned again to the river and new developments have begun to spring up from the sulky ruins of docks and shipyards. The SECC and Clyde Auditorium (the 'Armadillo') were built on the north bank, followed in 2001 by the futuristic-looking Science Centre on the south. Several types of pleasure craft now offer trips along the river, and new housing and office developments are planned. Life finally seems to be returning to the Clyde.

Along the Clyde

Sights along the Clyde

Glasgow Science Centre

It gets very hot inside so wear layers of clothing that you can remove as necessary

After all the years of neglect, it is good to see that Glasgow's newest, most dazzling development is to be found on the Clyde. The £75 million Glasgow Science Centre, at 50 Pacific Quay, opened in late 2001 on the south side of the Clyde on the former garden festival site. This enormous complex aims to demystify science, bringing it to life with imaginative displays and interactive exhibits covering everything from the human body to the internet. The kids love it – as do their fathers.

The heart of the Centre is the Science Mall, with three floors of themed exhibits. The first floor looks at how we experience the world, the second floor looks at science in action and the third floor looks at how science affects our daily lives. You can find anything here from laboratories where you can study your own skin or hair through a microscope, to an infra-red harp which you play with a beam of light. Two new state-of-the-art facilities planned to open in 2002 are the Scottish Power Space Theatre, which will be Scotland's most modern planetarium, and the Virtual Science Theatre, where you will be taken on a virtual journey around the human body or into space.

Make time to visit the **Glasgow Tower** too, which is the tallest free-standing building in Scotland at 300 ft. Each of its floors has a theme and takes a serious look at aspects of science, from the basic rules of nature to cloning and genetic modification. At the top there's a viewing cabin and great views over Glasgow and the Clyde. Note that the Tower was closed in March 2002, after it was found to have slipped out of alignment because of damage to two bearings in the base mechanism. It is expected to re-open some time in May 2002.

■ *The Centre also contains an IMAX theatre. Science Mall daily 1000-1800; Glasgow Tower Sun-Wed 1000-1800, Thu-Sat 1000-2100; IMAX Theatre Sun-Wed 1100-1700, Thu-Sat 1000-2030 (hours subject to change). Science Mall £6.50, £4.50 concession, family available; IMAX or Glasgow Tower £5.50, £4 concession. Discounts available if purchasing tickets to more than 1 attraction. T4205010, www.gsc.org.uk Arriva buses 23 and 24 go to the Science Centre from Jamaica St, or simply walk across the footbridge from the SECC and Armadillo.*

SECC & Armadillo

Opposite the Science Centre is the **Scottish Exhibition and Conference Centre (SECC)**, built in 1987 on the site of the former Queen's Dock and now the country's premier rock and pop venue. Next door is the controversial **Clyde Auditorium**, known locally as the 'Armadillo', which was designed by Sir Norman Foster and built in 1997. ■ *To get there, take a train from Central Station to the Exhibtion Centre Station(5 mins), otherwise it's a long walk from the city centre.*

Tall Ship at Glasgow Harbour

Further west, also on the north bank of the Clyde, is a romantic-looking sailing ship, the *SS Glenlee* – otherwise known as the Tall Ship at Glasgow Harbour, 100 Stobcross Road. Launched in 1896, this three-masted ship was built on the Clyde and is one of only five Clydebuilt sailing ships that remain afloat in the world. She circumnavigated the globe four times and carried cargo as varied as coal, grain and even guano – which was transported from Chile to the European ports of Antwerp and Rotterdam to be used as fertiliser. The ammonia fumes

Along the Clyde

from the guano were so pungent they corroded the lining of sailor's noses and even killed the occasional ship's cat. The *Glenlee* was saved from the scrapyard in 1992 and has now been restored. Exhibitions on board provide a vivid insight into the daily lives of the sailors and the conditions on-board ship in 1896 (not fragrant – especially when carrying all that guano). ■ *Daily 1000-1700. £4.50, £3.95 concession. T3390631, www. glenlee.co.uk or www.thetallship.com*

Further west still, at Braehead, is Clydebuilt, a museum charting the close rela-   Clydebuilt
tionship between Glasgow and the Clyde. There's an audio-visual presentation on the history of shipbuilding and displays on a whole range of themes related to the river, from the cotton and tobacco trades, to emigration and immigration. There are also plenty of 'hands-on' activities for kids and temporary exhibitions throughout the year. The museum is very close to **Braehead Shopping Centre** which has all the usual high street outlets as well as cafés, and skating and curling rinks. ■ *Mon-Sat 1000-1800, Sun 1100-1700, £3.50, £1.75 concession. Clydebuilt is at junction 25a (westbound) off the M8 or can be reached on the Clyde waterbus (see below). T8861013.*

Trips along the Clyde

At Anderston Quay, east of the Science Centre, is the **Waverley**, the world's last ocean-going paddle steamer. One of a former fleet of pleasure boats that used to take Glaswegians on trips 'doon the watter' to Clyde coast resorts, she was launched in 1947 as a replacement for a ship that was sunk rescuing troops from Dunkirk. Although she fell into disrepair, she has now had a £4 million refit and has been restored to her original glory. You can still take day trips on the Waverley along the Clyde to destinations like Dunoon, Largs, the Kyles of Bute and Arran. ■ *Sailings take place from Easter-mid May and from Jun to late Aug, Fri-Mon. T2218152, www.waverleyexcusions.co.uk Office open summer Mon-Sat 0900-1700, winter Mon-Fri 0900-1700. Trips cost from £10-30.*

Next to the Tall Ship at Glasgow Harbour is **Seaforce**, a company offering high-speed powerboat trips along the Clyde. Trips range from a 15-minute 'taster' (£2.50, £1.50 concession) to a four-hour trip to the village of Kilcreggan (including a chance to visit the village at £30, £15 concession). There's also a mystery tour which goes to, well, it's a surprise.■ *Apr-Sep daily 1300-dusk, Oct-Mar trips can be booked. Office hours 0800-2200. T4007737, www.seaforce.co.uk*

The **Clyde Waterbus**, 'Pride of the Clyde', is a river taxi that runs along the Clyde between Broomielaw and Braehead (where there is the large Braehead Shopping Centre and Clydebuilt maritime museum). ■ *Trips leave from the bottom of Jamaica St under Central Station Bridge every 1½ hrs, Mon-Fri from 1045-1815, Sat from 0945-1715, Sun from 1145-1745. Sailing time 30 mins. £2 one-way, £1.50 child/concession. Price includes a commentary on the history of the river. T7786635.*

The most unusual tour must be that offered by **glasgowDucks**. This company have several brightly coloured amphibious vehicles that take you through the city and along the Clyde. Tours last 90 minutes and start at Pacific Quay, by the Science Centre. The commentary gives an insight into the shipbuilding industry on the Clyde and takes you past the last private shipyard on the river. ■ *Tours operate at Easter holidays and from Jun-Oct; Nov/Dec weekends only. £11.50, £8.50 children, booking recommended. T5728381, bookings T0870 0136140, www.glasgowducks.com*

Clyde Walkway

The Clyde Walkway is a 40-mile walking route which is being developed to link the centre of Glasgow to the Falls of Clyde at Lanark, via the Clyde Valley (see page 160). Sections of the waterfront walk are still rather empty and depressing but the central part, between Victoria Bridge and the SECC, is interesting and takes in some of the more distinguished bridges and much of Glasgow's proud maritime heritage.

Victoria Bridge west to SECC Start the walk at **Victoria Bridge**, built in 1854 to replace the 14th century Old Glasgow Bridge, and continue past the graceful **Suspension Bridge**, built in 1851 as a grand entrance to the 'new town' on the south bank. You can cross from here to **Carlton Place**, whose impressive Georgian façades have been restored and which were designed to front the never-completed 'new town'.

Back on the north bank is **Customs House Quay** and, further west beyond George V Bridge, **Broomielaw Quay**. From here, Henry Bell's *Comet* inaugurated the world's first commercial passenger steamboat service. This was also the departure point for many Scottish emigrants to North America, and, later, for thousands of holidaying locals heading 'doon the watter' to the Firth of Clyde seaside resorts.

Further west, at Anderston Quay, is the **PS Waverley Terminal**. The *PS Waverley* is the world's last sea-going paddle steamer and still operates on the Clyde (see previous page). Between here and the SECC is the huge 175 ft-high **Finnieston Crane**, which was once used for lifting railway locomotives at a time when Glasgow was the largest builder of these in the world outside North America. Close by is the **Rotunda** (1890-96) which was once the northern terminal of the complex of tunnels which took horse-traffic and pedestrians under the river, until the building of a new road-tunnel in the 1960s. The Rotunda has been restored as a restaurant complex. Soon you come to the **SECC** and the **Clyde Auditorium**, or the 'Armadillo', sitting opposite the silvery new **Glasgow Science Centre**. A short distance west is the **Tall Ship at Glasgow Harbour** (see page 118).

Victoria Bridge east to Bothwell Castle
This section of the walkway is about 9 miles long

From Victoria Bridge take a slight detour along Bridgegate, or Briggait (see page 63), then cut back on to Saltmarket and enter Glasgow Green via the huge arch opposite the old Sheriff Court. Head across the Green, under King's Bridge and alongside Fletcher's Haugh, where Bonnie Prince Charlie reviewed his Jacobite troops in January 1746 after their long march north and only a few months before defeat at Culloden. The Walkway then goes under Shawfield Road at Rutherglen Bridge and follows the river. The path begins to narrow then passes under a railway bridge and a road bridge, before following the river in a U-turn, with Celtic Park visible ahead. The path runs in a straight line between the river and the boundary fence of Belvedere Hospital, then reaches more attractive open countryside and runs along the top of a wooded embankment.

As you pass below some pylons, keep to the path as it curves away from the river. It rejoins the river and then crosses the Tollcross Burn before curving round to the right. It goes under a stone railway bridge, then a road bridge and then continues southwards and swings eastwards. The crossing point of the river is now Cambuslang Bridge following the closure of the disused Carmyle railway viaduct. Cross the bridge and turn left along Bridge Street till you reach a roundabout. Go straight across and follow Westburn Road, with the golf course on the right and factories on the left. After 500 yards, past the turning for Westburn Farm Road, Westburn Road branches left. Continue along it for a half a mile further then turn left along Newton Avenue. Follow this road as it crosses Newton Burn and about 400 yards further on, where the road turns sharply to the right, you can rejoin the Walkway, which heads north towards the river.

The path shadows the river for about a mile, then you leave the Clyde where it joins a smaller river, the Rotten Calder. Here the path turns south and follows the Rotten Calder for some 400 yards to where a footbridge crosses it by a railway bridge. Cross a stile and turn right onto a farm road which goes under the railway line, before climbing steadily uphill to join the Blantyre Road (B758).

Turn right and head up this road for 50 yards till you see the path again on the other side of the road. From here the path is easy to follow. About half a mile further on the path rejoins the river. Cross the footbridge into Uddingston and then turn right and follow the path along the riverbank. It heads through a pleasant wooded area for about a mile. As it follows a bend in the river it then climbs to the top of a gorge to reach a gate. Go through the gate and you're at Bothwell Castle, which markes the the end of the walk. There are regular trains from Uddingston station to Glasgow Central station (see also page 158).

Along the Clyde

Along the Clyde

Entertainment & nightlife

7

Entertainment & nightlife

Live music and clubbing

Glasgow comes alive after dark with a buzzing nightlife culture, from live music and bars to cafés and clubs. You will never be stuck for something to do no matter what your taste and preference, whether it is hands-in-the-air dancing, checking out some new bands or catching one of the big names on their world tour. Glasgow definitely has something for everyone.

The city is a hotbed of live music which has gone from strength to strength over the years. In days gone by it was commonplace for people to go to 'the dancin' at the Barrowland Ballroom on a Saturday night, but since then things have changed beyond recognition. There are now more bands than you can shake your booty at and countless live music venues ready to give everyone a stage.

Glasgow's main venue used to be the *Apollo*, which played host to all the big names of the day from *Judas Priest* to *Wham!*. It finally closed its creaking doors in 1985 and was soon replaced as the best gig venue by the reopening of the *Barrowlands*. The *Barras*, with its old-ballroom style décor and incredible atmosphere, has seen an amazing selection of bands over the years including home-grown talent as well as international bands like *Alice Cooper* and *PJ Harvey*. In the same year, the Scottish Exhibition and Conference Centre was built, offering a larger arena-style venue for bigger tours. It is popular with pop bands like *Westlife*, *Hear'say* and *Steps* and rock bands such as *U2* and *AC DC*.

The best places to see smaller gigs are at the *Garage*, *Cathouse*, *King Tuts Wah Wah Hut*, *13th Note* and *Nice'n'Sleazy's*, all of which play host to a fine selection of smaller gigs as well as unsigned talent from Glasgow and further afield. One of *King Tut*'s claims to fame is that *Oasis* were performing there on the night that they were discovered by Alan McGee, boss of record label, Creation records.

With so many venues to play in it is no surprise that Glasgow has produced a mass of excellent bands. The biggest names over the years have included *Simple Minds*, *Wet Wet Wet*, *Travis* and *Texas* as well as the *Delgados*, *Mogwai*, *Urusei Yatsura*, *Belle & Sebastian*, *Teenage Fanclub*, the *Cosmic Roughriders* and *Bis*, to name just a few.

If it's music of a different kind you are looking for there are also a multitude of clubs to choose from, whether it's large underground venues like *The Arches* or smaller spaces such as *Budda* and the *13th Note Club*. Regular nights of house, techno, chart and rock are available as well as major club events, including the ever popular Colours and Inside Out with their celebrity DJs and Glasgow's very own Subculture and Optimo.

One thing's for sure, between the bars, clubs and gigs you won't be stuck in your hotel room with nothing to do all night, and you never know, you may even see the next super group or rub shoulders with some of the best DJs in the world.

Pre-club bars

Glasgow is bursting at the seams with bars, many of which are excellent pre-club venues to get you in the mood for a night's clubbing. The DJs normally start at 2100 and carry on until until 2400 but some start earlier depending on the DJs. Entry is normally free, with some charging after 2300 when they transform into a club.

Ad Lib, 111 Hope St, T2486645. Bar and food by day, bar and club by night. A trendy crowd with good weekend DJs.

Air Organic, 36 Kelvingrove St, T5645201. A popular West End place to be seen in and to enjoy some of the best DJs before you head into town.

Arches, Argyle St, T0901-0220300. This venue is home to both a bar and a club so is

Entertainment & nightlife

Five of the best: city experiences

- Go to a rock gig at the **Barrowlands** and join in the crazy atmosphere in the mosh pit
- See a film at the wonderful **Glasgow Film Theatre**. Choose a film from the current releases, one of the many film festivals or take in a golden oldie
- Put on your stetson and cowboy boots and head on down to the **Grand Ole Opry** for a night of line dancing, country music and quick-draw shoot outs
- Get some retail therapy. Glasgow has the best **shops** outside of London, offering you the opportunity to browse round the big names as well as the smaller independent retro clothing stores
- Get tattooed at **Terry's Tattoo Studio** in the Trongate. The oldest tattoo studio in town and hundreds of tattoos to choose from before going under the needle

the ideal place to get hyped before heading in to one of their many popular club nights.

Bar 10, 10 Mitchell La, T5721448. Set just off Buchanan St, this is a trendy pre-club haunt with DJs at the weekends.

Bar Soba, 11 Mitchell La, T2042404. *Soba* lives in the ground floor of *The Lighthouse* and manages to combine being a bar with a great club feel.

Brel, 39 Ashton La, T3424966. Belgian-themed bar in the West End which has DJs on several nights a week playing laid-back sounds as well as hip hop and soul.

Budda, 142 St Vincent St, T2215660. Situated below *Club Budda* this bar is an ideal place to get ready for a night's clubbing, with DJs to keep you going.

Cul de Sac, Ashton La, T3348899. Situated in the lively Ashton La, the *Sac* is an atmospheric bar where DJs play a wide selection of sounds and styles but all of which are designed to create a good vibe.

Delmonicas, 68 Virginia St, T5524803. A lively and 'up for it', gay-friendly bar with DJs, quizzes and karaoke as well as passes for the *Polo Lounge* club round the corner.

Firebird, 1321 Argyle St, T3340594. A cool place to hang out in the West End and have food, drinks and listen to some of Glasgow's finest DJs on Thu-Sun.

Groucho St Judes, 190 Bath St, T3528800. The haunt of Glasgow's trendy media types with fine cocktails and occasional but top-notch DJs.

McChuills, 40 High St, T5522135. A great place to drink, chat or meet before going to a gig at the *Barrowlands* or pre-clubbing. DJs play everything from hip hop to funk.

McChuills Way Out West, 10-14 Kelvinhaugh St, T5765018. Sister bar to the above, this West End version plays host to a more studenty crowd as well as weekend DJs.

Moda, 58 Virginia St, T5532553. Adjoining the *Polo Lounge* this gay-friendly bar/club has DJs at the weekends for an 'up for it' crowd'.

Moskito, 200 Bath St, T3311777. A relatively new addition to the bar scene in Glasgow, with DJs at the weekends.

Nice 'n' Sleazy, 421 Sauchiehall St, T3339637. A tongue-in-cheek and eclectic mix of people and music, with pre-club DJs such as *Bitch School* who play a mix of rock and metal on Sun afternoons and a more laid back funky feel at other times.

Nicos, 395 Sauchiehall St, T3325736. A well-known and long-standing bar in Sauchiehall St with DJs playing pre-club pop, hip hop and garage at weekends.

Polo Lounge, 84 Wilson St, T5531221. A classy, gay-friendly bar with free entry before 11pm, DJs and the lively Trophy Room downstairs for dancing.

Spy, Bath St, T2217711. A popular pre-club haunt with a trendy crowd wanting jazz, funk, house and soul from Thu to Sun.

Strata, 45 Queen St, T2211888. Busy by day and packed by night with trendy drinkers ready for a night out.

Variety, 401 Sauchiehall St, T3324449. An atmospheric art-deco bar with as varied a crowd as the music policy and DJ sounds.

Yang, 33 Queen St, T2488484. A 3-bar venue with DJs to get you in the mood for *Archaos* next door or for their own bar/club downstairs.

Clubs

Clubbers of all musical tastes and styles are catered for in Glasgow, with rock, techno and chart nights on offer. The dress code changes depending on the venue, whereas opening times are pretty much the same all over with doors opening from 2300 until 0300. Entry costs can vary from £2-5 for the smaller mainstream clubs and £5-10 for the bigger venues, while you can pay up to £20 from some of the special club nights with top class DJs.

Ad Lib, 111 Hope St, T2486645. *Ad Lib* is a bar that changes into a club at 2300 when the DJs take to the decks at the weekends.

Alaska, 142 Bath La, T2481777. A happening club with monthly nights Foot Therapy, Homebass from the Jengaheads and Freelance Science from the Slam boys, Orde Meikle and Stuart McMillan.

Archaos, 25 Queen St, T2043189. A younger, more dressy crowd head out to *Archaos* for house, techno and club classics in this massive venue.

Arches, Midland St, T0901-0220300. This venue is home to some of Glasgow's best club nights including top-notch DJs Paul Oakenfold and Carl Cox at Colours, Judge Jules at Inside Out, and the Slam boys at Pressure, as well as Traxx and the Sunday Social which includes DJs and live music.

Asylum, 70 Cowcaddens Rd, T3320681. This club is set in Caledonian University and as well as being a student union it is also a club with a regular alternative indie night.

Babaza, 25 Royal Exchange Sq, T2040101. An unusual club venue with drapes and booths as well as an 'up for it' crowd who love their R&B and hip hop.

Bennets, 80 Glassford St, T5525761. This is Glasgow's longest-running gay club and continues to offer a great night out 5 days a week. DJs play dance, house and cheesy handbag tunes to a mad, partying, sweaty crowd. They also have a straight night one night a week.

Budda, 142 St Vincent St, T2215660. A small, trendy club with loads of house, garage, soul and funk at the weekends from resident DJs.

CCA, 350 Sauchiehall St, 3524900. The *Centre for Contemporary Arts* mixes music, art and visuals on their popular club nights Future World Funk and Sonic Mook Experiment.

Cathouse, 15 Union St, T2486606. If you like all-things-rock this is definitely the place for you, with two floors devoted to metal, grunge, thrash and a good bit of moshing.

Cleopatras, 508 Great Western Rd, T3340560. This Glasgow institution has been around for years and is well known for its lively clubbers and a jam-packed dance floor for all the chart tunes.

Cube, 34 Queen St, T2268990. A recent change of hands and refit sees this increasingly popular club playing host to a musical mix of club nights 5 nights a week.

Destiny, 18 Cambridge St, T3536555. A dressed-up club for a slightly older crowd wanting to party to the latest dance tracks.

Fury Murrys, 96 Maxwell St, T2216511. A busy club, full of students who like a bit of party and chart music.

g2, 474 Sauchiehall St, T3533111. A weekend haunt for clubbers in search of a good dance to anything from party anthem and disco to funk and soul.

Garage, 490 Sauchiehall St, T3321120. A student 'must' with several club rooms to enjoy the cheap drink, check out the weird décor and dance to chart and dance tunes.

Glasgow School of Art, 167 Renfrew St, T3320691. A venue with a varying club night schedule including the weekly Divine Funk and Northern Soul night as well as the techno My Machines night. Popular nights for students and clubbers young and old.

Havana, 50 Hope St, T2484466. A bar and club playing everything Latin with resident DJs and some fine salsa dancing. They also hold dance classes so you can perfect your club moves.

MAS, 29 Royal Exchange Sq, T2217080. As well as being the temporary home of the Sub Club nights which include the incredibly popular and weekly Sub Culture and Optimo, it is also holds its own nights including a staff night for all hardworking bar and club staff, and hip hop nights.

Polo Lounge, 84 Wilson St, 5531221. This exotic and classy, gay-friendly bar and club offers several rooms to party in with a lively crowd dancing the night away to cheesy chart tunes and dancefloor anthems. Free entry passes can be found round the corner at *Delmonicas* bar.

Privilege, Hope St, T2045233. A crazy club with busy club nights, but none more so than Shagtag – a very appropriately named night with house and trance music and the chance to meet the person of your dreams, or not as the case may be.

Queen Margaret Union, 22 University Gdns, T3399784. A student union that doubles up as a club and music venue. In club terms it is known for its regular nights as well as Glasgow's Bugged Out! Night of techno.

Reds, 375 Sauchiehall St, T3311635. A small but popular club offering a wide range of musical styles at weekends.

Renfrew Ferry, Clyde St, T2275511. As the name suggest this is a ferry which holds one-off club nights, including the fantastically kitsch Vegas night when you can dress up in all your finery, have a go at the gambling tables and dance the night away to some excellent easy listening tunes.

Riverside Club, Fox St, T5697287. Home to hard-core rave club Shake the Disease and electro club Spanner. It also doubles as a ceilidh venue.

Shack, 193 Pitt St, T3327522. This venue is huge, in fact it's an old converted church, which is popular with students and young clubbers alike. Chart and dance tunes abound.

Strawberry Fields, 56 Oswald St, T2217871. A club playing music from the '60s through to present-day chart stuff.

Sub Club, Jamaica St. The '*Subby*' suffered from severe smoke and water damage over a year ago after a fire broke out in the adjoining building. It is undoubtedly one of Glasgow's best-loved clubs and the regulars are eagerly awaiting its return. They will be home again to their popular club nights including Sub Culture and Optimo which are temporarily at *MAS*.

13th Note Club, 260 Clyde St, T2432177. A fine club that not only has two bars over two floors but also holds live music and club nights. A laid-back space with a smorgasbord of musical tastes from electro and hip hop to jazz and indie.

Trash, 197 Pitt St, T5723372. A club made up of several rooms offering a mix of music but mainly focusing on the studenty house and R&B gang.

Tunnel, 84 Mitchell St, T2041000. One of Glasgow's posiest and best-dressed clubs with a regular crowd who know their DJs and their favourite house style.

Velvet Rooms, Sauchiehall St, T3320755. A popular Sauchiehall Street haunt for students and dressed-up drinkers who want to enjoy everything from R&B and soul to more commercial sounds.

Rock, pop, folk, country and jazz venues

Live music is easy to find in Glasgow, from local and unsigned bands playing bars and smaller clubs to international acts playing the bigger venues. The larger and well-known gigs cost anything from £10-25 in the *SECC*, *Barrowlands* and *Glasgow Royal Concert Hall* with the smaller gigs in bars ranging from free entry to about £10 for bigger bands. The bars themselves are open from around 1100-2300 during the week and 1100-2400 on Friday and Saturday, with music-only venues normally opening around 1900 before support bands come on. There is live music on every night of the week so whether you want to sit back in a pub and take a chance with an unknown band or rock out at the *Barrowlands*, it is entirely up to you.

Arches, 253 Argyle St, T0901-0220300. Underneath the railway tracks of Glasgow Central station lies this venue which houses a theatre, bar, restaurant and club. It regularly has live bands either performing a small gig, as part of a festival, or taking part in one of their famous club events such as the Sunday Social.

Barrowlands, 244 Gallowgate, T5524601. The *Barras* is the best place in Glasgow, if not the UK, to see a live gig. It's previous use was as a ballroom so it has everything just right to create a fantastic atmosphere with bands such as *Oasis*, *Motorhead* and *Alice Cooper* having played here in the past year.

Blackfriars, 36 Bell St, T5525924. A Merchant City favourite featuring live jazz in the basement Thu-Sat.

Bourbon Street, 108 George St, T5520141. This bizarre bar and restaurant has live music events which you can enjoy while dining. The bands are normally tribute bands to *Abba*, *The Beatles* and the like.

Cathouse, 15 Union St, T2486606. Glasgow's only rock club also plays host to many a smaller rock gig before the club opens. Ideal for seeing bands before they make it big.

Clyde Auditorium, Finnieston Quay, T2877777. Also known as the Armadillo for obvious reasons, this eye-catching venue looks like a mini Sydney Opera House and tends to feature more highbrow, big-name acts.

Cottiers, 93-95 Hyndland St, T3573868. This converted church in the West End of the city is another mixed venue, with a bar, restaurant and theatre which also puts on live performances.

Clutha Vaults, 167 Stockwell Street, 5527520. One of Glasgow's well known and established pubs which has live music nights from a whole host of local talent.

Fury Murrys, 96 Maxwell St, 2216511. *Fury's* hosts gigs by popular bands before the club opens. Music can range from local rock and pop to small tours.

The Garage, 490 Sauchiehall St, 3321120. This is the place which books you if you're a band that can't quite fill the *Barrowlands* or you are too big for the *Cathouse*. It has seen a whole host of rock stars on their way up as well as on the way down with everything from *Uriah Heep* to *Therapy*. It also doubles as a very busy club later in the night.

Glasgow Royal Concert Hall, 2 Sauchiehall St, 2875511. Just as it's name suggests, the Concert Hall puts on all sorts of concerts from classical to rock and pop. It is a somewhat subdued venue and all-seated, but you can see everyone from Kenny Rogers to Mel C, as well as being the home to the *Celtic Connections* music festival.

Glasgow School of Art, Renfrew St, T3534530. The School of Art sees bands playing a more eclectic mix of music. This venue also holds club nights by night as well as being an art school by day.

Grand Ole Opry, 2 Govan Rd, T4295369. Homage to Nashville in the heart of Govan. Perfect for a fix of C&W and a spot of line dancing.

Halt Bar, 160 Woodlands Rd, T5641527. The Halt is a well-known and long-standing bar in the West End. It offers a mix of musical styles and abilities from local bands as well as an open-stage night for all wannabes.

King Tut's Wah Wah Hut, 272a St Vincent St, 221 5279. Upstairs in *Tut's* is an excellent venue to see live music. It plays host to both signed and unsigned acts and is the place to see up-and-coming bands in an intimate setting. This is a place that most bands have played en-route. There is music on most nights of the week and it's worth a visit on spec to see some new bands.

McChuills, 40 High St, T5522135. Weekends at *McChuills* sees live music from a selection of local bands and all for free.

Nice'n'Sleazy, 421 Sauchiehall St, T3339637. *Sleazy's* is a fantastic bar and music venue with a kitsch art-deco style. Bands play downstairs with everything from indie to rock while upstairs the bar is frequented by muso bods.

Old Fruitmarket, Albion St, T2875511. Underused larger venue which mostly plays host to jazz and blues giants.

Queen Margaret Union, University Gdns, T3399784. Mostly the *QMU* is a university student union bar and club but it is used as a live-music venue by touring bands and is also used as part of the *NME* tour.

The Renfrew Ferry, Clyde Pl, T2875511. The *Ferry* is just that – a ferry, but it is also used as a club and live-music venue for one-off events.

Scottish Exhibition and Conference Centre (SECC), Finnieston Quay, T0870-0404000. The *SECC* is like a big-metal barn but is Glasgow's biggest music arena and has had many a famous name pass through it's dressing rooms. It has played host to all the big UK and international bands from *U2* and *AC/DC* to *Steps* and *Hear'say*.

Samuel Dows, 67-91 Nithsdale Rd, T4230107. This pub is on the south side of the city and is a well-known place to hear local live music including pop and blues as well as a selection of cover bands.

The Scotia, 112-114 Stockwell St, T5528681. The *Scotia* bar is one of Glasgow's 'institutions' alongside its sister bars the *Victoria* and *Clutha Vaults*. It is most familiar as a folky bar but is also known to go a bit more rocky on occasion.

Strawberry Fields, 56 Oswald St, T2217871. An unsigned-band venue, which can be anything from pop to rock. You can also hang around for when it turns into a club later in the night.

Studio One, *Grosvenor Hotel*, Grosvenor Terr, Byres Rd, T3416516. As part of the *Grosvenor Hotel* this is a bizarre place to find live music – but live music it has on several nights of the week. Mainly local talent and covers bands.

13th Note Café, 50-60 King St, T5531638. Downstairs at the *Note* is a superb venue which showcases unsigned bands and new talent. It supports everything from indie to metal and is worth wandering down to in order to sample some new talent, both local and from further afield. Apart from the music it also has an excellent café which serves vegetarian and vegan food.

13th Note Club, 260 Clyde St, T2432177. Like the café the club also plays host to unsigned bands as well as some more well-known names who need a slightly bigger space.

Classical and opera

Glasgow has a number of venues for classical music and opera and is the home of Scottish Opera, the Royal Scottish National Orchestra and the BBC Scottish Symphony Orchestra. The city attracts talent from all over the world, including major stars like Pavarotti. Traditional Scottish music is performed by the Scottish Fiddle Orchestra (www.sfo.org.uk) who perform at various venues in Glasgow to raise funds for a wide variety of charitable causes.

Glasgow Royal Concert Hall, 2 Sauchiehall St, T3538000, www.grch.com Situated not far from Queen Street station and the new Buchanan Galleries shopping centre,

The Empire strikes back

Glasgow Empire, built in Sauchiehall Street, was the city's leading variety theatre. It became know as the "English comic's grave" due to the discriminating audiences. Morecambe and Wise played twice to deafening silence. On their third appearance there was some sporadic applause and a stage-hand told them

"Aye, boys, they're beginning to like you". Eric Morecambe had the last laugh, however, when TV personality Des O'Connor once famously pretended to faint on stage, he was so desperate to get off. The theatre closed, much to the relief of entertainers from south of the border, in 1963.

this sleek venue is the most prestigious in the city. The Royal Scottish National Orchestra, T2263868 (www.rsno.org.uk), frequently performs here, with Proms in June, classical concerts during from October to April, and contemporary concerts at other times of the year. The Glasgow Phoenix Choir (www.phoenixchoir.org), a long-established choir that has made several recordings, has also performed at the Royal Concert Hall, as well as at other venues in Scotland.

City Halls, Candleriggs, T2875024, www.glasgow.gov.uk Another fine concert hall that also hosts the BBC Symphony Orchestra every season. Classical concerts are also occasionally performed here by the Scottish Chamber Orchestra (T0131-5576800, www.sco.org.uk).

Henry Wood Hall, 73 Claremont St, T2253555, www.rsno.org.uk A classical music venue set in a former church that is now home to the Royal Scottish National Orchestra, and also hosts a variety of concerts.

Theatre Royal, Hope St, T3323321, www.theatreroyalglasgow.com Operatic performances generally take place here, the home to Scottish Opera (T2484567, www.scottishopera.org.uk), Scotland's national opera company which stages a number of operas each year, ranging from old favourites like *The Magic Flute* to more contemporary works.

Classical concerts are also sometimes staged at the *Scottish Exhibition and Conference Centre*, on the Clyde, T2483000, www.secc.co.uk

Theatre, cinema and comedy

Theatre

For many years the most famous theatre in Glasgow was the *Glasgow Empire*, a variety theatre whose audience had forthright ways of voicing their displeasure with acts – particularly with comics. These days audiences are more polite and the city has a thriving theatre scene where you have the opportunity to see everything from traditional panto to contemporary plays.

Traditional Theatre

King's Theatre, 297 Bath St, T2485153, www.glasgow.gov.uk The city's main theatre which stages big-name touring musicals, the annual panto and a number of amateur performances.

Theatre Royal, Hope St, T3323321, www.theatreroyalglasgow.com The home of Scottish Opera. It also stages major productions by Scottish Ballet and visiting companies such as the Royal Shakespeare Company and the Royal National Theate.

Citizens' Theatre, 119 Gorbals St, T4290022, www.citz.co.uk famous theatre which has a Victorian auditorium and two modern studio theatres. The resident theatre company present British and European classic plays, as well as popular Christmas shows.

Entertainment & nightlife

Five of the best: city experiences

- See an amazing show at the world-renowned, highly visual **Citizens' Theatre**
- Shop in Glasgow's many **thrift shops**, either at Dumbarton Road, Byres Road or Great Western Road
- Meet the gay man of your dreams in **Revolver Bar**, John Street
- Wander in **Paddy's Flea Market** and purchase bargains for 50 pence a go
- See the whole city spread out in front of you from the flag pole at **Queens Park**, South Side

Pavilion Theatre, 121 Renfield St, T3321846. Victorian theatre continuing the Glasgow tradition of staging variety shows. Seating 1,800, it stages an annul panto, musicals and also hosts an extraordinary range of visiting performers from hypnotists to American wrestlers. Over the years audiences have seen acts as diverse as Lulu, Shania Twain, Billy Connolly, Jim Davidson, Bernard Manning, Ardal O'Hanlon and Roy 'Chubby' Brown. You don't get much more varied than that.

The Royal Scottish Academy of Music and Drama, 100 Renfrew St, T3324101. Has a varied programme of international performances. This is Glasgow's major theatre school and puts on work by its various student companies. Cheap tickets for students.

Contemporary theatre Glasgow also has several venues for more contemporary theatre. There's the recently refurbished *Centre for Contemporary Arts (CCA)*, 270 Sauchiehall St, T3327521, www.cca.glasgow.com, which has regular theatre and dance performances.

Tron Theatre, 63 Trongate, T5524267, www.tron.co.uk is one of Glasgow's leading theatres, presenting a mixed programme of drama, comedy, music and dance. It's also got a trendy bar and restaurant where the city's cool and arty crowd hang out.

Tramway, 25 Albert Dr, T2873900, just off Pollockshaws Rd. After a long period of closure for refurbishment, the *Tramway* has reopened with 3 performance spaces and a café. This is one of Scotland's leading experimental theatres and plays host to international touring companies as well as local acts. You can always expect a challenging and provocative evening here.

Then there's *The Arches*, 253 Argyle St T2214001, box office T0901-0220300, www.thearches.co.uk) situated in a series of Victorian railway arches. It has a resident theatre company and stages works in an innovative and often irreverent way. It puts on modern classics (like *The Crucible* and *The Playboy of the Western World*) and new works, sometimes combining professional actors with volunteers.

G12, 9 University Av, T3305522. Glasgow University's Gilmorehill Centre for Film, Theatre and TV also has its own theatre, housed in a Norman gothic church. It screens short films, stages contemporary dance and also puts on plays such as *The Steamie*, and *Look Back in Anger*.

Mitchell Theatre, 6 Granville St, T2874855, is a theatre that stages some small-scale dramatic productions.

Cinema

There are plenty of cinemas in the city, but the *Glasgow Film Theatre* (*GFT*), 12 Rose St, T3326535, www.gft.org.uk, is in a league of its own. It's city's leading independent cultural cinema, which looks as good inside as it does from the outside . There's always something interesting to see here, from top US indie hits to European cinema, and also a programme of World Film Festivals. *Café Cosmo* by the foyer (see page 79) is a great place for a post-movie discussion or a cheap lunch.

Mainstream films are screened out of town at *Glasgow East Showcase*, Barrbridge Leisure Centre, Langmuir, T01236-438880, at the *Odeon at the Quay*, Springfield Quay, Paisley Rd, T0870-5050007, www.odeon.co.uk and at the *UGC*, The Forge, Parkhead, T0870-1555136. There is also the *IMAX* cinema at the *Glasgow Science Centre*, Pacific Quay, T4205000.

More central mainstream cinemas are the *Odeon City Centre*, 56 Renfield St, T0870-5050007, www.odeon.co.uk, and at the *UGC*, 145 West Nile St, T0870-9070789. There's a small cinema screening less mainstream films at the *Grosvenor*, 31 Ashton La, T3394298.

For something a wee bit spicy, there's the *Bombay Cinema*, 5 Lorne St, Ibrox, T4190722. Some of Bollywood's films are made in Scotland, so it's entirely fitting that there should be a dedicated cinema screening contemporary Bollywood hits.

Comedy

In the city that gave us Billy Connolly, Jerry Sadowitz and Rab C Nesbit, you'd expect a thriving comedy scene. But though the streets of this city are where you can hear the funniest lines (for free), there are also a few clubs where you can sit down in comfort and listen to people who are paid to be funny.

The only dedicated comedy venue is *The Stand Comedy Club*, 333 Woodlands Rd, T0870-6006055, www.thestand.co.uk Here you can see Scottish and international comedy acts every week, from Thu to Sun. It's very popular so you're advised to book in advance.

The State Bar, 148 Holland St, T3322159. Hosts the Madcap Comedy Club every Sat night 2130-2400. You can also sample live blues on Tue and a good selection of real ales. Not a bad pub, actually.

Arta, 13-16 Walls St, T5522101. In the Merchant City. Comedy on Sun nights. Starts at 2100 and costs £5.

Gay venues

Despite its stereotypical hard-man image, there's a thriving gay scene in Glasgow, with numerous bars and several clubs. For details on gay contacts, see page 19.

Café Delmonica's, 68 Virginia St, T552-4803. Mon-Sun 1200-2400. Free. Attracting both gay men and women, Delmonica's is a fun bar . Particularly busy with the young office crowds and late on in the evening when it becomes drunken and defaning. Attracts a young, trendy crowd up for a good time. Activities include DJ,s on Mon, Tue, Fri and Sat, a games night on Wed and quiz night on Thu. **Gay bars**

Candle Bar, 20 Candleriggs, T5641285. Mon-Sat 1200-2400, Sun 12302400. Free. Relatively new to the Merchant City's gay scene, this lively bar has still to assert its identity. Live music , DJ's and karaoke throughout the week.

Court Bar, 69 Hutcheson St, T5522463. Mon-Sat 0900-2400, Sun 1230-2400. Free. Old-fashioned city-centre bar, straighter during the day and becoming increasingly gayer as the day develops. Small and chatty, attracting an older clientele.

LGBT Centre, 11 Dixon St, T4001008. Mon-Sun, 1200-2400. The GLC bar/cafe in the back of the LGBT Centre serves cheap food and drink. Waiters are fast and helpful, and the whole place has a community feel to it. Needs a stronger extractor fan to get rid of frying smells though. Karaoke from Fri to Sun.

Polo Lounge, 84 Wilson St, T5531221. Mon-Thu 1700-0100, Fri-Sun 1700-0300. Free before 2300 Thu-Sun. Beautiful, sumptuous city-centre venue, and the only gay bar which is full of antiques and chaise-longues. Appeals to young, attractive, professionals and their admirers. The sound system can be a bit too loud . Check out the live singing of Marj Hogarth on Tue nights. Extremely busy at weekends.

Revolver, 6a John St, T5532456. Mon-Sat 1100-2400, Sun 1230-2400. Free. Brand-new sexy bar opposite the Italian Centre, run by cheerful gay manager Brendan Nash. Has an amazing free jukebox with over 5,000 top tunes. Attracts men of all ages looking for action! Check out their interesting theme nights.

Sadie Frosts, 8-10 West George St, T3328005. Mon-Sat 1200-2400, Sun 1400-2400. Free. Underneath Queen Street station, is this extremely popular, busy and noisy bar. Cheap food and a whole range of activity throughout the week, including quizzes (Tue and Wed), karaoke (Thu and Sun) and DJs (Fri, Sat and Mon). Sun is women-only in the Blue Room.

Waterloo, 306 Argyle St, T2295891. Mon-Sat 1200-2400, Sun 1230-2300. Glasgow's oldest gay bar has been around forever. Friendly, unpretentious, working-class, it attracts an older clientele. Attitude-free, it becomes incredibly busy and lots of fun late at night.

Clubs *Bennets*, 90 Glassford St, T5525761. 2300-0330. £3-6 (£2-5). Having celebrated its 20th birthday in 2001, Bennets is the longest-running gay club in Glasgow. Attracting a young crowd, ready to whip off their shirts at a moment's notice, it has a new top floor for when it gets busy. At weekends it's packed. With attentive staff, Bennets is open 5 nights a week (Wed to Sun) with student night on Thu. Women-only night is the first Fri of each month on top floor.

Cube, 34 Queen St, T2268990. Daily 2300-0300. £3 (£2 with flyer). Previously known as *Planet Peach*, *Cube* holds gay nights on Mon and Tue only, playing chart music and house.

Polo Lounge, 84 Wilson St, T5531221. Fri to Sun 2200-0300. £5. Free before 2300. Downstairs at the *Polo Lounge*, there's a choice of the main club for harder dance sounds or trashy retro in the wee, intimate Trophy Room. Promos, theme nights, shag-tags a-plenty. Club anthems and chart hits.

Gay culture *The Citizens Theatre*,119 Gorbals St, T4290022. World-class, visually stunning theatre in the heart of the Gorbals, often imbued with a gay sensibility and a certain campness.

GFT, 12 Rose St, T3328128. Glasgow's friendly arts cinema always has a wide selection of movies, often with a gay or lesbian slant. Check their free monthly brochure. Meet in the café before the film.

Glasgay, is Britain's largest lesbian and gay arts festival. See also Festivals (page 135).

The Stand Comedy Club, 333 Woodlands Rd, T0870-6006055. 'OOT in Glasgow' is a gay comedy night, happening the second Sunday of every month. Hosted by the endearing Craig Hill with surprise guests.

The Tron Theatre, 63 Trongate, T5528578. An eclectic programme of theatre and live music, along with three diverse bars makes this an attractive venue for discerning gay folk.

Festivals

For dates, contact Glasgow City Council's events department , T2872000, or visit www.seeglasgow.com

Glasgow doesn't like to be overshadowed by Edinburgh, and has a few notable festivals of its own. Things kick off in the last two weeks of **January** with **Celtic Connections,** Glasgow's annual traditional music festival, now in its ninth year. It features artists from around the world, as well as attracting its audiences from around the globe. Though focussing mainly on folksy music, over the years it has hosted the likes of James Taylor and Van Morrison. It is held in the *Royal Concert Hall*, T3326833.

In the first week of **April** is the **Glasgow Art Fair**, held in George Square over three

Keeping good company

Glasgow is the home to several of Scotland's most important touring theatre companies. Probably the best known is *7:84*, which has provided intelligent and analytical theatre for Scottish audiences since the 1970s. It may have lost its hard, socialist edge, but it still retains an element of social commentary. Another established company is *Bordeline*, which continues to develop

new writing. *Clyde Unity*, meanwhile has been tackling tough social issues for many years with its thought-provoking productions. *TAG* (Theatre around Glasgow) works primarily with young people and provides a large body of outreach theatre. Another experimental, youth-based company is *Raindog*, which can count Robert Carlisle among its high-profile patrons.

---

consecutive days. Art dealers and workshops from all over Britain display and sell works of art.

The city's biggest festival is the **West End Festival**, two weeks of music, theatre, exhibitions and various free events held in early **June**. There also a midsummer Carnival Parade. T3410844. In the last two weeks of **June** is the **Royal Scottish National Orchestra Proms**, held at the Royal Concert Hall. T3538000.

There are several festivals outside the city in **June**. **Lanark Lanimar Day** (T01555-661661) commemorates the checking of the town's boundaries, and dates back to 1140. **Bearsden and Milngavie Highland Games** takes place at Burnbrae in Milngavie, T9425177. **The Shot** is the Renfrewshire Festival, held over three weeks, with a wide variety of performances, exhibitions and participatory events. T8871007.

In the first week of **July** is the **Glasgow International Jazz Festival**, T5523552, held at various venues throughout the city. Also in July is the curiously named **Sma' Shot Day**, at Abbey Close in Paisley, which celebrates the town's proud weaving traditions.

In mid-August is the **World Pipe Band Championships**, T2215414, which is held on Glasgow Green. This prestigious event attracts some 200 pipe bands from around the world.

At the beginning of **September**, in New Lanark village, is the **Victorian Fair** (T01555-661345), featuring street theatre and music. Throughout the month of **September**, at weekends, there are **Doors Open** days, when buildings in the city and beyond, which are not normally open to the public, open their doors. Some offer tours, while others provide music and exhibitions, and it's all free.

Glasgay, Britain's largest lesbian and gay arts festival, runs from **late October** to **early November** at various venues throughout the city. A great outreach programme makes Glasgay felt all over. For information T3347129.

On **5 November**, **Guy Fawkes Night**, there's a spectacular fireworks display on Glasgow Green, with a funfair and live music.

The **Christmas** period is celebrated in style and George Square is transformed into a giant, open-air skating rink. There's also a traditional Christmas market.

Hogmanay celebrations in Glasgow may not be on the scale of Edinburgh's but are impressive nonetheless. Various rock, pop and dance acts perform live at stages across the city centre, and in George Square there's a massive dance party featuring top DJs. For more information visit www.glasgowhogmanay.org

Entertainment & nightlife

Sleeping

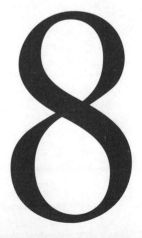

138

Sleeping

Accommodation price codes

Accommodation prices in this book are graded according to the letters below and are based on the cost per person for two people sharing a double room with en-suite bathroom during the high season. Cheaper rooms with shared bathrooms are available in many hotels, guesthouses and B&Bs. Many places, particularly larger hotels, offer substantial discounts during *the low season and at weekends. All places listed are recommended as providing good quality and value within their respective price category.*

L £80 plus	**A** £66-80
B £46-65	**C** £36-45
D £26-35	**E** £16-25
F £15 and under	

Hotels, guesthouses and B&Bs

Glasgow has undergone something of a revolution on the hotel front in recent years and the market is now highly competitive. A large number of big chains have opened up in the city, offering everything from deluxe accommodation to simple, low-cost lodging – meaning that there are often good deals available to travellers prepared to shop around. The city also has several boutique hotels, offering stylish accommodation with more character than the international chains.

At the top end of the scale, there are some fabulously luxurious hotels which offer a chance to enjoy a taste of aristocratic grandeur and style. At the lower end of the scale, there is often little to choose between cheaper hotels and guesthouses or B&Bs. The latter often offer higher standards of comfort and a more personal service, but many smaller hotels are really just guesthouses and are often family-run and every bit as friendly. Rooms in most mid-range to expensive hotels almost always have bathrooms en-suite. Many upmarket hotels offer excellent room-only deals in the low season.

By autumn 2002 there should be two more additions to the Glasgow hotel scene. *Radisson SAS* are opening a 5-star hotel on Argyle St, while the former General Post Office on George Sq is being converted to a luxury hotel and series of apartments to be known as *No1 Glasgow*. The tourist office will have more details.

Guesthouses are often large, converted family homes with up to five or six rooms. They tend to be slightly more expensive than B&Bs and, though they are often less personal, usually provide better facilities, such as en-suite bathroom, colour TV in each room and private parking. In many instances, they are more like small-budget hotels. Many guesthouses offer evening meals, though these may have to be requested in advance.

B&Bs provide the cheapest private accommodation. At the bottom end of the scale, you can get a bedroom in a private house, a shared bathroom and a huge cooked breakfast for around £20-25 per person per night. Small B&Bs may only have one or two rooms to let, so it's important to **book in advance** during the summer season. More upmarket B&Bs have en-suite bathrooms and TVs in each room and usually charge £25-35 per person per night. In general, B&Bs are more hospitable, informal, friendlier and offer better value than hotels. Huge **cooked breakfast**s are a bonus if you're travelling on a tight budget, as you can eat as much as you like at breakfast time and save on lunch because you won't need to eat again until evening.

L *Glasgow Hilton*, 1 William St, T2045555, F2045044, www.hilton.com 319 rooms. Gigantic, futuristic-looking, luxury hotel regarded as one of the city's best. Full facilities include a leisure centre and shopping mall. Their restaurant, *Cameron's*, is also widely held to be one of the finest around (see page 74).

City Centre
■ *on map, page 76*

Sleeping

L-A *Glasgow Moat House*, Congress Rd, T3069988, F2212022, www. moathousehotels.com 283 rooms. Massive glass structure next to the *SECC* and the *'Armadillo'* on the banks of the Clyde. 2 excellent restaurants, *Mariner's* and *Dockside No 1*.

L-B *The Carlton George Hotel*, 44 West George St, T3536373, F3536263, www.carltonhotels.co.uk Established chain with 64 rooms and a rooftop restaurant. Very close to George Sq. Similar is the **L-B** *Thistle Hotel*, 36 Cambridge St, T3323311, F3324050, www.thistlehotels.com which has 300 rooms, and the **L-C** *Glasgow Marriott*, 500 Argyle St T2265577, F2217676, a huge 300-room hotel.

L-B *Langs Hotel*, 2 Port Dundas Pl, T3320330, www.langshotel.co.uk Largest of all the boutique hotels and more of a style hotel, this is far from cheap. Has 110 contemporary bedrooms, a trendy bar and Californian-inspired restaurant.

One of the newest chains to open is the **L-B** *Milton Hotel and Leisure Club*, Argyle St, T0808-1007700, F01786-469400, www.miltonhotels.com It has 136 rooms and aims to cater for those seeking a bit of luxury. There's a pool, sauna and gym, as well as a restaurant and business centre.

L *Malmaison*, 278 West George St, T5721000, F5721002, glasgow@malmaison.com 72 rooms. Best known of the boutique hotels. Sister hotel to the *Malmaison* in Edinburgh and equally chic and stylish. Superior in every way. Their brasserie is also highly recommended.

A *Millennium Hotel*, George Sq, T3326711, F3324264, www.millennium-hotels .com 117 rooms. Huge, 18th-century hotel in the heart of the city, next to Queen St station. Conservatory bar on the ground flr is good for people-watching.

A *Posthouse*, on Bothwell St, T0870-4009032, www.posthouse-hotels.com Huge chain hotel with 247 rooms.

B *Holiday Inn*, 161 West Nile St, T3528300, F3327447, www.higlasgow.com 113 rooms, convenient for the city's theatres. Next door is the more basic **B** *Express by Holiday Inn*, 165 West Nile St, T3316800, F3316828, which offers B&B rather than the full range of hotel facilities.

There's another of these no-frills establishments at **B** *Express by Holiday Inn*, Stockwell St, T5485000, www.hiexpress.com which is convenient for the Argyle St shops. Along the same lines there's the **B-C** *City Travel Inn Metro*, 187 George St, T5532700, F5532719, www.travelinn.co.uk (254 rooms) which is close to Glasgow Cathedral.

Another new, city-centre chain is the **B** *Novotel*, 181 Pitt St, T2222775, F2045438, www.accorhotels.com Similar functional and comfortable accomodation is available at **B-C** *Travelodge*, at 11 Hill St, T3331515, F3331221, www.travelodge.co.uk (95 rooms).

B *Groucho Saint Judes*, 190 Bath St, T3528800, F3528801, www.grouchosaintjudes .com An intimate boutique hotel with only 6 bedrooms and a fine restaurant.

C-D *Adelaide's*, 209 Bath St, T2484970, F2264247, www.adelaides.co.uk 8 rooms. Beautiful 'Greek' Thomson restoration, with 8 rooms in the heart of the city centre.

C *Alexander Thomson Hotel*, 320 Argyle St, T2211152, F2211153, and the **C-D** *Rennie Mackintosh Central*, 59 Union St, T2210050, F2214580, are two, small Glasgow chains exploiting the names of the city's great architects.

C *The Art House*, 129 Bath St, T2216789, www.arthousehotel.com Stylish refurbishment of former education authority building. Inside are some 'interesting' design features, including a waterfall running through the middle and a rickety antique lift. Decadence is what it's all about here. Well located and good value. Features Scotlands's first Japanese teppan-yaki grill.

C *Bewleys Hotel*, 110 Bath St, T3530800, F3530900, www.bewleyshotel.com One of the well-known Irish chain hotels which opened in Jul 2000. 103 rooms all priced at £59 year-round.

C-D *Premier Lodge*, 10 Elmbank Gardens, T2211000. Standard lodge accommodation. 278 rooms.

D *Cathedral House*, 28/32 Cathedral Sq, T5523519, F5522444. 8 rooms. Overlooking the cathedral. Wonderfully atmospheric old building with comfortable rooms and very good moderately priced restaurant (open daily 1030-2400).

Five of the best: luxury hotels

- *One Devonshire Gardens* (page 142)
- *Groucho St Judes* (page 140)
- *Langs Hotel* (page 140)
- *Hilton* (page 139)
- *The Arthouse* (page 140)

   D-E *Ibis*, 220 West Regent St, T225 6000, F2256010. Cheaper lodge hotel, run by French company *Accor*.
   D *Kelvingrove Hotel*, 944 Sauchiehall St, T3395011, F3396566, www. kelvingrove-hotel.co.uk Traditional guest house with 19 rooms.
   D-E *Rennie Mackintosh Hotel*, 218-220 Renfrew St, T3339992, F3339995, www.renniemackintoshhotels.com 24 rooms. A homely guest house offering friendly service and superb value for money.
   D *Theatre Hotel*, 25/27 Elmbank St, T2272772, F2272774, www.theatrehotel .clara.net Characterful hotel which has 52 rooms.
   D-E *The Victorian House*, 212 Renfrew St, T3320129, F3533155, www. hotelsglasgow.com 58 rooms. Large, friendly guest house very close to the art college. Superb location and just about the best value in the city centre.
   There are many other guest houses along Renfrew St, including: **D-E** *The Old School House*, No 194, T3327600, www.hotelsglasgow.com **D** *Enterprize Hotel*, No 144, T3328095 and **D-E** *Willow Hotel*, No 228, T3322332.

E *Greek Thomson* , 140 Elderslie St, T3326556, www.renniemackintoshhotels.com 17 rooms. Named after Glasgow's less-famous architectural son. Good value, city-centre guest house.
   E *Pipers' Tryst Hotel*, 30-34 McPhater St, T3530220, www.thepipingcentre.co.uk Well-established guesthouse situated in the piping centre, with 8 rooms.

A *The Brunswick Merchant City Hotel*, 106-108 Brunswick St, T5520001, F5521551, www.scotland2000.com/brunswick 21 rooms. Chic minimalism in the heart of the Merchant City. Ideal for cool dudes wishing to sample the delights of Glasgow nightlife. Their excellent bar-restaurant boasts style and quality.

Merchant City & East End
■ *on map, pages 56 & 66*

B-C *Jarvis Ingram*, 201 Ingram St, T2484401, F2265149, www.jarvis.co.uk One of the Jarvis chain of hotels. Often does special deals such as shopping breaks.

C-D *Babbity Bowster*, 16-18 Blackfriars St, T5525055. 6 rooms. A local institution and one of the first of the Merchant City townhouses to be renovated. Typical Glaswegian hospitality, a near-legendary pub (see page 61) and an excellent restaurant.

D *The Inn on the Green*, 25 Greenhead St, T5540165, 5564678, www. theinnonthegreen.co.uk Well-established small, hotel featuring hand-crafted furniture and wacky wallcoverings like grass and bamboo. 18 rooms.
   D-E *The Merchant Lodge*, 52 Virginia St, T5522424, F5524747, www. themerchantlodge.sagenet.co.uk 40 rooms. Renovated old building in quiet side-street close to the Merchant City's stylish bars and restaurants. Great value.

Guest houses in the East End area include: **E** *Craigpark GH*, 33 Circus Dr, T5544160; **E** *Seton GH* , 6 Seton Terr, Dennistoun T5567654; **E** *Rosewood Guest House*, 4 Seton Terr,

Sleeping

T5501500; **E** *Craigielea B&B*, 35 Westercraigs, T5543446; and **E** *The Knowes*, 32 Riddrie Knowes, T7705213, www.sol.co.uk/t/theknowes

West End
■ *on maps,*
pages 88 & 90

The West End is very much the studenty/arty part of the city and has plenty of accommodation options, from the swishest hotel in the city to basic B&Bs.

L *One Devonshire Gardens*, 1 Devonshire Gdns, T3392001, F3371663, www.one-devonshire-gardens.co.uk 27 rooms in the original hotel, with 16 more following its merger with the *Devonshire Hotel* next door. Highly acclaimed hotel which is the very last word in style and comfort. There are few, if any, classier places to stay in the country. Each of the rooms is individually designed and many have four-poster beds and porcelain baths so big you can swim in them. Guests have included Tom Jones, Meryl Streep and Robbie Williams. Their restaurant is sensational and is run by celebrity chef Gordon Ramsay (see page 96). At the time of writing, however, the hotel's parent company had gone into receivership, but it is hard to believe that such a superb hotel will not find a buyer.

A-B *City Inn*, Finnieston Quay, T2401002, F2482754, www.cityinn.com Situated on the Clyde and convenient for the *SECC*. 164 rooms all with a contemporary feel. Emphasis is on providing business facilities, with ISDN and modem points in every room.

B *Kelvin Park Lorne Hotel*, 923 Sauchiehall St, T3149955, F3371659, www.regalhotels.co.uk 100 rooms. Dependable old stalwart and well located for galleries, museums etc.
  B-D *Manor Park Hotel*, 28 Balshagray Drive, T3392143, F3395842. 10 rooms. Promotes Gaelic.

C-D *Argyll Hotel*, 973 Sauchiehall St, T3373313, F3373283, www.argyllhotelglasgow.co.uk A traditional hotel in a refurbished Georgian building. 38 rooms.
  C-D *The Belhaven Hotel*, 15 Belhaven Terr, T3393222, www.btinternet.com/-belhaven. 14 rooms, convenient for the Botanic Gardens.
  C-D *The Townhouse*, 4 Hughenden Terr, T3570862, F3399605, www.thetownhouseglasgow.com 10 rooms. Just off the Great Western Rd. Lovely Victorian townhouse offering comfort, hospitality and great value.
  C *Wickets Hotel*, 52 Fortrose St, T/F3349334, www.wicketshotel.co.uk 11 rooms. Overlooking the West of Scotland cricket ground and close to Partick train station and Underground. Family-run hotel with good restaurant and its own beer garden.

D-E *Heritage and Botanic Hotel*, 4-5 Alfred Terr, by 625 Great Western Rd, T3396955, F3371812, www.hotelsglasgow.com 45 rooms. Good value guest house formed from 3 Victorian townhouses linked together. Close to the West End action.
  D-E *Hillhead Hotel*, 32 Cecil St, T3397733, hillhotel@aol.com 11 rooms. Small, friendly hotel ideally placed for the Byres Rd nightlife and close to Hillhead Underground.
  D *Jury's Glasgow Hotel*, Great Western Rd, T3348161, F3343846, www.jurysdoyle.com 136 rooms. Nothing too fancy, but comfortable rooms and good facilities including pool, sauna and gym. Free parking. Very good value.
  D-E *Kelvin Hotel*, 15 Buckingham Terr, Great Western Rd, T3397143, F3395215, www.scotland2000.com/lomondkelvin 21 rooms. Comfortable guest house in lovely Victorian terrace near Byres Rd and Botanic Gardens. In the same terrace, under the same ownership, is the smaller **D-E** *Lomond Hotel*, T3392339, 17 rooms (same website).

Close to Kelvingrove Park and the *SECC* is **D** *Kirkland House*, 42 St Vincent Cres, T2483458, kirkland@gisp.net 5 rooms. A small, family-run guest house with that little bit extra. On the same street are: **D** *The Flower House*, No 33, T2042846, F2265130, www.scotland2000.com/flowerhouse and, at No 36, is **D** *Number Thirty Six*, T2482086, www.no36.gispnet.com

D *Kirklee Hotel*, 11 Kensington Gate, T3345555, F3393828, www.scotland2000 .com/kirklee/ 9 rooms. Lovely Edwardian townhouse with beautiful garden. Close to bars and restaurants on Byres Rd and the Botanic Gardens.

D *Lochgilvie House*, 117 Randolph Rd, Broomhill T3571593, www.lochgilvie .demon.co.uk 5 rooms.

D-E *The Sandyford Hotel*, 904 Sauchiehall St, T3340000, F3371812, www. sandyfordhotelglasgow.co.uk 55 rooms. Comfortable and good value hotel convenient for the *SECC* and art galleries.   **D-E** *The Townhouse Hotel*, 21 Royal Cres, T3329009, F3539604, www.hotels.glasgow.com 17 rooms. Yet another elegantly restored Victorian townhouse (is there no end to them?), set back off Sauchiehall St. Good value and handy for the *SECC* and Kelvingrove Park.

E *Hillview Guest House*, 18 Hillhead St, T3345585, F3533155, kdmcmillan @msn.com 10 rooms. Friendly, good value B&B close to university and Byres Rd.

E *The Georgian Town House*, 29 Buckingham Terr, on the Great Western Rd, T3390008, www.thegeorgianhousehotel.com

Basing yourself South of the river means that, while you've not got the advantages of **South of** being in the heart of the city, you're well placed for exploring attractions like the *Burrell* **the Clyde** *Collection* and *House for an Art Lover*. It's also a quieter part of the city and you're only about 10 mins by car from the centre.

A-B *Best Western Ewington Hotel* , Balmoral Terr, 132 Queen's Drive, T4231152, www.countryhotels.net 43 rooms. Friendly and comfortable hotel in a secluded terrace facing Queen's Park. Their restaurant, *Minstrels*, is superb value and worth a visit in its own right.

A-C *Sherbrooke Castle Hotel*, 11 Sherbrooke Av, T4274227, www.sherbrooke .co.uk A small hotel (25 rooms) with a bit more character than the chains. It's a good base for exploring the attractions of South Side as it's only about a mile from the *Burrell Collection*.

B-C *Swallow Hotel*, 517 Paisley Rd West, T4273146, www.swallowhotels.com This chain hotel is conveniently close to the new Science Centre and has its own pool.

B-C *Travelodge*, on the Paisley Rd, T4203882, www.travelodge.co.uk One of the no-nonsense Travelodge chain with 75 rooms, most of which are suitable for families.

D *Boswell Hotel*, 27 Mansionhouse Rd, T6329812. Just to the south of Queen's Park, off Langside Rd. 11 rooms. Lively and informal hotel better known for its excellent pub where you can hear live folk and jazz.

There's a branch of the American chain **D** *Days Inn*, at 80 Ballater St, T4294233, www.daysinn.com It has 114 rooms and is close to the Clyde.

There are a few more B&Bs and guest houses in South Side worth trying, including: **D** *Balmoral Guest House*, 124 Queens Dr, Queens Park T4018866, www.balmoral.kirion.net **E** *Glasgow Guest House*, 56 Dumbreck Rd, T4270129; **E** *Mrs Bruce*, 24 Greenock Av T6370608; and **E** *Reidholme Guest House*, 36 Regent Park Sq, T4231855. Small, friendly guest house in a quiet side street near Pollockshaws Rd.

Sleeping

Five of the best: cheap places to stay

- *Euro Hostel* (this page)
- *Bunkum Backpackers* (this page)
- *Hillview Guest House* (page 143)
- *Baird Hall* (page 145)
- *The Merchant Lodge* (page 141)

Hostels

For those travelling on a tight budget, hostels offer cheap accommodation. These are also popular centres for backpackers and provide a great opportunity for meeting fellow travellers. Hostels have kitchen facilities for self-catering and some include a continental breakfast in the price or provide cheap breakfasts and evening meals. **Advance booking** is recommended at all times, and particularly from May to September and on public holidays.

The *Scottish Youth Hostel Association (SYHA)* 7 Glebe Cres, Stirling FK8 2JA, T01786-451181, www.syha.org.uk , is separate from the *YHA* in England and Wales. It has a network of over 80 hostels, which are often better and cheaper than those in other countries. They offer bunk-bed accommodation in single-sex dormitories or smaller rooms, kitchen and laundry facilities. The average cost is £9-12 per person per night, and doors are closed as late as 0200.

For Scottish residents, adult membership costs £6, and can be obtained at the *SYHA* National Office, or at the first *SYHA* hostel you stay at. *SYHA* membership gives automatic membership of *Hostelling International* (*HI*). Youth Hostel members are entitled to half-price entry to all National Trust for Scotland properties. The *SYHA* also offers an **Explore Scotland** and **Scottish Wayfarer** ticket, which can save a lot of money on transport and accommodation, especially if you're not a student.

F *Berkeley Globetrotters*, 63 Berkeley St, Charing Cross, T2217880, www.geocities.com/globeberkeley 120 beds. Open all year, very cheap – it can get rowdy. It's just past the *Mitchell Library*, on the other side of the M8 heading west from Bath St. Take a 57 bus from the city centre. It incorporates the *Blue Sky Hostel*, T2217880, next door, which is also open all year.

F *Bunkum Backpackers*, 26 Hillhead St, T5814481, www.easyhostel.com Friendly and cheap hostel in the West End. It has 32 beds and kitchen facilities.

F *Euro Hostel*, 318 Clyde St, T2222828, F2222829, www.euro-hostels.com 364 beds, all rooms with en-suite facilities. It's a huge, multi-storey building overlooking the Clyde. Smartest hostel of them all.

F *Glasgow Backpackers Hostel*, 17 Park Terr, T3329099, www.scotlands-top-hostels.com 12 dormitories, 8 twins and 3 triple rooms. Open 3 Jul-23 Sep. Independent hostel housed in university halls of residence. Very popular, and cheaper than the *SYHA*.

F *SYHA Youth Hostel*, 7/8 Park Terr, T3323004. 150 beds. This former hotel has been converted into a great hostel with dorms for 4-8, all with en-suite facilities. It gets very busy in Jul/Aug so you'll need to book ahead. Open 24 hrs. It's a 10-min walk from Kelvinbridge Underground Station, or take bus 44 or 59 from Central station (or 11 from Queen St station) and get off at the first stop on Woodlands Rd, then head up the first turning left (Lynedoch St).

Campus accommodation

Glasgow's universities open their halls of residence to visitors during the summer vacation (late June to September), and some also during the Easter and Christmas breaks. Many rooms are basic and small, with shared bathrooms, but there are also more comfortable rooms with private bathrooms, twin and family units and self-contained apartments and shared houses. Full-board, half-board, B&B and self-catering options are all available. Prices for bed and breakfast tend to be roughly the same as for most B&Bs, but self-catering can cost as little as £50 per person per week. Local tourist offices have information, or contact the *British Universities Accommodation Consortium*, T0115-9504571 for a brochure.

University of Glasgow, contact the Conference and Visitor Services, 3 The Sq, T0800-027 2030, www.gla.ac.uk/vacationaccommodation   There is a range of **self-catering** accommodation, available Jul-Sep. *Cairncross House*, 20 Kelvinhaugh Pl, off Argyle St near Kelvingrove Park, has rooms to let, and *Kelvinhaugh Gate* and *Murano St Village* have flats and rooms. It also has **B&B** accommodation (**E**) at *Dalrymple Hall* in the West End, available Mar-Apr and Jul-Sep; *Wolfson Hall*, a modern block by Kelvin Conference Centre, available Mar-Apr and May-Sep; and *St Andrews Campus*, 6 miles from the West End, available Apr-May and mid-Jun to mid-Aug.

The *University of Strathclyde*, T5534148, RESCAT@mis.strath.ac.uk www.strath.ac.uk/department/rescat/sales/index.html Has a wide range of **B&B** accommodation available in its various halls of residence across the city, mostly in Jun-Sep, though a few are open all year round. **E** *Baird Hall*, 460 Sauchiehall St. Open all year. 191 rooms (all shared bathrooms). The pick of the bunch. A beautiful art deco, high-rise building in a great location. **E-D** *Chancellors Hall*, Cathedral St (on campus). 218 en suite rooms. **E-D** *Garnett Hall*, Cathedral St (on campus). 124 rooms. Also self-catering, around £260-330 per week. **E-D** *Murray Hall*, Cathedral St (on campus). 70 rooms. *Forbes Hall*, Cathedral St, 20 campus-village flats from £260-330 per week. Farther out of town, but the cheapest of the lot, is **F-E** *Jordanhill Campus*, 76 Southbrae Dr. 189 rooms. More salubrious accommodation is available at the **C** *Strathclyde Graduate Business School*, 199 Cathedral St, T5536000, F5536002, www.sgbs.strath.ac.uk/hotel. 107 en-suite rooms. Open all year.

Alternatively, try *Glasgow Caledonian University*, 218 Dobbies Loan, T3313980, www.caledonian@gcal.ac.uk which has 100 flats – rooms are let singly. Prices from £516-688 per week.

Self-catering and serviced accommodation

There is plenty of Scottish Tourist Board (STB) approved self-catering accommodation available. The minimum stay is usually one week in the summer peak season, or three days or less at other times of the year. Expect to pay from around £200 to over £700 per week in the city. A good source of self-catering accommodation is the STB's guide (£5.95), which is available from any tourist office.

There are also **self-catering** flats (**E-F** per person per night) for 4-6 people, available all year round, at the *YMCA Aparthotel*, David Naismith Ct, 33 Petershill Dr, T5586166, DNC@cqm.co.uk It's a rather characterless tower-block, 3 miles northeast of the city centre.

There is also plenty of more upmarket self catering and serviced accommodation in the city. *Embassy Apartments*, 8 Kelvin Dr, T9466698, F9455377, www.glasgowhotelsandapartments.co.uk 6 apartments in a converted Victorian terrace house in the West End, about a mile from the city centre. All are en-suite and sleep between 1 and 5 people. Weekly rates from £259.

Also in the West End is *The White House*, 12 Cleveden Cres, T3399375, F3371430, www.apartments-glasgow.com This has 32 suites with a country house atmosphere. Weekly rates from £255-550.

West End Apartments, 401 North Woodside Rd, T3424060, F3348159, www.glasgowhotelsandapartments.co.uk Close to Kelvinbridge Underground. Have 4 apartments to let from £259 per week.

Sleeping

The Serviced Apartment Company, SACO House, 53 Cochrane St, T2044610, F2481919, www.sacoapartments.co.uk 12 apartments in the Merchant City. Weekly rates from £420.

Dreamhouse Inc, have several luxury serviced apartments in Woodside Pl, Eldon St and Lynedoch Cres. Weekly rates range from £660-1170. T3323620.

One flat is also available at *Wilton Mansions*, 191 Wilton St, T4021959, www.wiltonmansions.co.uk It sleeps 2-4 and costs from £300 per week.

In the East End, is *Number 52 Charlotte St*, T01436-810264, www.52charlottestreet .co.uk, a former tobacco merchant's mansion now converted into 6 apartments. Weekly rates start at £393.

Camping

The only campsite anywhere near the city is *Craigendmuir Park*, Campsie View, Stepps, T7794159/2973. It's 4 miles northeast of the city centre and a 15-min walk from Stepps station.

Trips from Glasgow

Trips from Glasgow

Glasgow is surrounded by a series of drab satellite towns, once major centres of coal and steel, or shipbuilding, which are struggling to recover their identity. It's tempting to bypass this depressed hinterland, especially as the delights of the West Highlands lie just beyond the city's boundary, to the northwest, but there are some hidden gems waiting for those with the time or the inclination. The 18th-century model community of New Lanark and the spectacular Falls of Clyde nearby are well worth the trip from Glasgow, and there are a couple of interesting historical sights near Hamilton, namely Bothwell Castle and Chatelherault.

Within easy reach of the city, north of the suburb of Milngavie (pronounced 'Mullguy'), is Mugdock Country Park, sitting between Glasgow and the Campsie Fells. It offers some fine walking along marked trails and includes the first section of the West Highland Way, which starts in Milngavie. The 'bonnie banks' of Loch Lomond are also very close to the city and can easily be visited on a day trip, or follow in the footsteps of erstwhile Glasgow generations and take a ferry 'doon the watter' to Cowal or Bute. Still just a day trip away is the historic town of Stirling, famous for its associations with Robert the Bruce and William Wallace, and then, of course, there's that other city, Edinburgh, less than an hour by train but a world away in terms of character and temprament.

Paisley

Phone code: 0141
Population 78,000
Colour map 1,
grid B3
West of Glasgow, close to the airport, is the town that gave its name to the famous fabric design copied from Kashmiri shawls. Paisley grew up around its 12th-century roots and by the 19th century was a major producer of printed cotton and woollen cloth, specializing in the production of the eponymous imitation shawls.

Ins & outs There are frequent **trains** to Paisley's Gilmour St station from Glasgow Central. There are also frequent **buses**, which stop at the abbey. Buses depart from Gilmour St station every 10 mins for Glasgow Airport, 2 miles north of town. The **tourist information centre** is at 9a Gilmour St, and is open Oct-Mar Mon-Sat 0900-1700 (closed 1330-1430), and Apr-Sept Mon-Sat 0930-1730, Sun 1200-1700.

Sights In the town centre, opposite the town hall, is **Paisley Abbey**, founded in 1163 but destroyed during the Wars of Independence in the early 14th century. It was rebuilt soon after, but fell into ruin from the 16th century. Successive renovations took place, ending with a major restoration in the 1920s. The façade doesn't do justice to the wonderfully spacious interior, which includes exceptional stained-glass windows and an impressive choir. Also of note is the 10th-century Barochan Cross, at the eastern end of the north nave. Once or twice a year the 150-ft high tower is open to the public. The views from the top are great. There is also a gift shop and tea room. ■ *Mon-Sat 1000-1530. Free. T8897654. To get there, follow Gilmour St from the train station to The Cross, then turn left into Gauze St and cross the river.*

In the High Street is the **Museum and Art Gallery**, with a huge collection of the world-famous Paisley shawls and an interesting display of the history of weaving. ■ *Tue-Sat 1000-1700, Sun 1400-1700. Free. T8893151.* Also on the High Street is another imposing ecclesiastical monument, the **Thomas Coats Memorial Church**, built by the great Victorian thread maker whose name it bears and one of the grandest Baptist churches in Europe. ■ *Mon, Wed and Fri 1400-1600, May-Sep.* T8899980.

Above the High Street, on Oakshaw Street, is the **Coats Observatory**, which has some interesting displays on climate, seismology and astronomy. ■ *Tue-Sat 1000-1700, Sun 1400-1700. Free. T8892013. Public telescope viewing, Thu 1930-2130 Oct-Mar.* Another interesting sight is the **Sma' Shot Cottages**, in George Place, off New Street. These are fully restored and furnished 18th-century weavers' cottages, with photographs and various artefacts. There's also a tearoom with home baking. ■ *Open Wed and Sat 1200-1600 Apr- Sep. T8891708.* To the south of Paisley is the **Gleniffer Braes Country Park**, which is a great place for a walk in the hills. ■ *To get there, follow the B775 south of town.*

The Firth of Clyde

*West of Glasgow, the banks of the Clyde are still lined with the hulking ghosts of this great river's shipbuilding heritage. West of the **Erskine Bridge**, which connects the north and south banks of the Clyde, is **Port Glasgow**, the first of a series of grim towns which sprawl along the southern coast of the Firth of Clyde. It was developed as the city's first harbour in the late 17th century, but there's little to detain visitors today.*

About 30 miles west of Glasgow, Greenock was the first dock on the Clyde, back in the early 18th century and was the birthplace, in 1736, of James Watt, whose development of the steam engine contributed so much to the Industrial Revolution. Greenock today doesn't look particularly appealing, but it has its attractions. On the quay is the **Customs House Museum**, housed in the 19th-century, neo-classical former Customs House, where Robert Burns and Adam Smith were once employees. The museum charts the history of the Customs and Excise service, which is a lot more interesting than it sounds. ■ *Open Mon-Fri 1000-1600. Free. T881450.* While you're here, you should also visit the **McLean Museum and Art Gallery**, at 15 Kelly St, near Greenock West station. The museum contains a collection of items belonging to the town's most famous son, James Watt, including a precursor to the photocopier which he patented around 1790 and was used in offices right up until the 1940s. There is also an Egyptology collection featuring items brought back from 19th-century explorations. The small gallery on the ground floor has works by the Glasgow Boys as well as Fergusson, Cadell and Peploe. ■ *Mon-Sat 1000-1700. Free. T715624, www.inverclyde .gov.uk/museums*

Greenock
Phone code: 01475
Population: 50,000
Colour map 1, grid B2

A recommended walk near Greenock is to the **Greenock Cut**, a 19th-century aqueduct built to supply water to the town's mills. Follow the A78 south from town and turn off at the sign to Cornalees Bridge Visitor Centre. From the centre walk along the lochside to Overton (3 miles), and the path is signed from here. South of here is **Muirshiel Country Park**, which is a great place to stretch the legs and grab a few lungfuls of fresh air. It's accessed via the A761 south from Port Glasgow, then take the B786 south to Lochwinnoch. It's about 30 minutes drive from the city centre. It covers 102 square miles of land and has walks in woods and over moorland. T01505-842803, www.scottishpark.com Also at Lochwinnoch is an RSPB Nature Reserve. ■ *T01505-842663.*

Eating and transport There are a few decent and cheap places to eat in Greenock itself, including *Morgan's*, at 49 West Blackhall St, and *Aldo's*, at 125 West Blackhall St. You can also try *Rico's*, an Italian place on Tobago St, or *Caravella's*, at 22 West Burn St. There are regular **trains** to Greenock from Glasgow Central and **buses** every hour from Buchanan bus station.

Three miles west of Greenock is the shabby old seaside resort of Gourock. Midway between Greenock and Gourock, on the rail line, is **Fort Matilda** station. It stands at the foot of **Lyle Hill**, which is worth the climb for the fantastic views over the Firth of Clyde.

Gourock
Colour map 1, grid B2

Transport Gourock is the terminal for the *CalMac* **ferry** to **Dunoon**, on the Cowal Peninsula (see page 153). Ferries leave frequently every day on the 20-min crossing. For details call *CalMac* T08705-650000. *Western Ferries*, T01369-704452, also runs a ferry service (every ½ hr) between Gourock and Dunoon. They leave from McInroy's point, 2 miles from the train station, from where *Citylink* buses also depart. *Clyde Marine*, T721281, runs a frequent, passenger-only ferry service to **Kilcreggan** (10 mins) and a less frequent service (40 mins) to **Helensburgh** (see page 152), daily. *Clyde Marine* also run **cruises** on the Firth of Clyde, to Brodick on Arran, Tighnabruaich, or Tarbert on Loch Fyne (June-August). Note that these leave from Victoria Harbour by the station. Gourock train station is next to the *Calmac* ferry terminal. Trains and buses from Glasgow to Gourock are the same as for Greenock (see above).

Trips from Glasgow

Wemyss Bay   Eight miles south of Gourock is Wemyss Bay, departure point for ferries to
Colour map 1, grid B2   **Rothesay**, on the Isle of Bute. Every summer this place used to be packed full
of holidaying Glaswegians heading "doon the watter" to Rothesay, and the
magnificent Victorian train station is a proud legacy of those days. *CalMac*
ferries, T01700-502707, run frequently (see page 154), and trains run every
hour to Glasgow.

Dumbarton   Once the capital of the ancient Britons of Strathclyde, Dumbarton dates back
Phone code: 01389   as far as the fifth century, when it was an important trading centre and of stra-
Colour map 1, grid B3   tegic importance. Today, though, it's a pretty awful place, and of little impor-
tance to tourists.

Ins and outs The **tourist information centre**, T742306, is out of town, on the A82,
which runs north to Balloch and Loch Lomond. It's open daily mid-Oct to Mar
1000-1600, Apr to mid-May 1000-1700, mid-May to mid-Jun 1000-1800, mid-Jun to
late Aug 1000-1900, late Aug to mid-Sept 1000-1800, mid-Sep to Mid-Oct 1000-1700.
Trains to Dumbarton Central and Dumbarton East stations run regularly from Helensburgh and Balloch, and from Glasgow Queen St. Get off at Dumbarton East station for
the castle (see below).

It's best to avoid the town and head straight for the spectacular **Dumbarton
Castle**, perched on top of Dumbarton Rock, which is surrounded by water on
three sides and commands excellent views over the Clyde estuary. This has
been a strategic fortress for 2,000 years, though most of the current buildings
date from the 18th century or later. ■ *Apr-Sep Mon-Sun 0930-1830; Oct-Mar
Mon-Sat 0930-1630 Sun 1400-1630. £2, £1.50 concession. Hours subject to
change. T732167.* If you're interested in shipbuilding then you should visit the
Scottish Maritime Museum, on Castle Street. It has a working ship-model
experiment tank – the oldest one in the world, in fact. ■ *Open Mon -Sat
1000-1600. £1.50. T763444.*

Helensburgh   Twenty-three miles northwest of Glasgow on the A814, overlooking the
Phone code: 01436   Clyde, is the town of Helensburgh, its wide, grid-plan streets lined with ele-
Colour map 1, grid B2   gant Georgian houses. The town boasts a few very notable connections; both
Population: 14,000   **Henry Bell**, originator of the steamship, and **John Logie Baird**, who invented
the television, were born here.

Ins and outs Getting there There is a daily ferry service between Glasgow and
Gourock. There are also 2 train stations: one for Glasgow trains, and the other for trains
to Oban and Fort William (see transport below).
     The **tourist information centre** is in the clock tower on the waterfront, T672642.
Open Apr to mid-May daily 1000-1700; mid-May to Jun daily 0930-1800; Jul-Sep daily
0930-1900; early Oct Mon-Fri 1000-1630, Sat-Sun 1000-1700.

Helensburgh is more famously known for its connection with the great Glasgow architect, **Charles Rennie Mackintosh**. In the upper part of the town, on
Upper Colquhoun Street, is **Hill House**, one of the best examples of Mackintosh's work. The house was designed for Glasgow publisher Walter Blackie in
1902-04, and is now owned by the National Trust for Scotland. The house is a
masterpiece of balanced perfection and artistry and there's much to admire.
The attention to detail, the use of natural light, the symbolism of the floral patterns and use of light and dark, hallmarks of Mackintosh's personal Art Nouveau style, are all very much in evidence. After exploring the house, you can

visit the kitchen, which has been tastefully converted into a tearoom (open 1330-1630). ■ *Daily 1330-1730 Apr-Oct. Adult £6, concession/children £4.50. T673900. To get there from Helensburgh central train station, walk about one and a half miles up Sinclair St, then turn left at Kennedy St and follow the signs. From Helensburgh Upper station (see below) it's a 5-min walk.*

Transport There's a daily, passenger-only *Calmac* **ferry** service from Helensburgh to **Kilcreggan** (30 mins) and **Gourock (40 mins)**, from where there are regular trains to Glasgow Central and other ferries to Dunoon (see below). Helensburgh has 2 **train** stations. The Central station has a regular service (every 30 mins) to and from **Glasgow** (45 mins), while the Upper station serves **Oban** (3 times daily; 2 ¼ hrs) and **Fort William** (4 daily Mon-Sat, 3 on Sun; 3 hrs). For times, contact *Scotrail*, T08457-484950.

Cowal Peninsula

The Cowal Peninsula reaches out into the Firth of Clyde, framed by Loch Fyne and Loch Long. This is the most visited part of Argyll due to its proximity to Glasgow, but, despite the summer hordes, much of it remains undisturbed. Most people head straight for **Dunoon**, the main ferry port and one of the major Clyde seaside resorts, leaving more adventurous souls to enjoy the forests and mountains of **Argyll Forest Park** in the north or the peace and tranquillity of the southwest coastline.

The northern part of the peninsula is largely covered by the sprawling **Argyll Forest Park**, which extends from Loch Lomond south to Holy Loch. This area contains the most stunning scenery in Cowal, and includes the **Arrochar Alps**, a range of rugged peaks north of Glen Croe which offer some of the best climbing in Argyll. The most famous of these peaks is Ben Arthur (2,891 ft), better known as '**The Cobbler**', but this, and the other 'Alps', are only for the more serious hill walker. Rather less imposing are the hills south of Glen Croe, between Loch Goil and Loch Long, in an area known as **Argyll's Bowling Green** (not because it's flat, but an English corruption of the Gaelic *Baile na Greine*, meaning 'Sunny Hamlet'). There are also numerous footpaths and cycle tracks threading their way through the park, and details of these can be found in the Forestry Commission leaflets available at the **tourist office and visitor centre** in **Ardgarten** (T702342), which is open daily April-October 1000-1700, and until 1800 in July and August, and provides useful advice and information on hillwalking and wildlife, as well as organizing various activities.

Transport *Scottish Citylink* **buses** between Glasgow and Oban stop off at Arrochar (1 hr 10 mins to Glasgow; 1 hr 40 mins to Oban), 3 daily in each direction (2 on Sunday). Arrochar shares a **train** station with Tarbet, on the main west-coast line. Trains heading north to Oban (1¾ hrs) or Fort William (2½ hrs) or south to Glasgow (1¼ hrs) stop 3-4 times daily.

The largest town in Cowal, and indeed the largest in Argyll, with 13,000 inhabitants, is Dunoon, one-time favourite holiday destination for Glaswegians, who came in their hordes on board the many paddle steamers that sailed 'doon the watter' from Glasgow. Dunoon still attracts visitors, albeit in much smaller numbers, but the town has fallen on desperately hard times with the recent closure of the US nuclear submarine base on nearby Holy Loch, which was the town's life blood.

Dunoon
Phone code: 01369
Colour map 1, grid B2

Trips from Glasgow

Ins & outs   **Getting there**   The most popular ferry crossing is the *CalMac* car and passenger ferry which makes the 20-min trip daily all year round every 30 mins. The first ferry leaves Gourock at 0620 and the last returns from Dunoon at 2105. There's also a *Western Ferries* service every 30 mins which arrives at Hunter's Quay, a mile north of the town centre, T01369-704452. For times and details of **train** connections from **Gourock** to **Glasgow**, T01475-650100. There are **buses** to **Colintraive** 2-3 times daily Mon-Sat (40 mins), to **Inveraray** (on Tue, Fri-Sat; 1 hr 15 mins) and to **Lochgoilhead** (Mon and Fri; 1 hr 15 mins). For times, contact *Western Buses*, T01700-502076.

Cowal's main **tourist information centre** is on Alexandra Par, T703785. Open Apr Mon-Fri 0900-1700, Sat 1100-1730, Sun 1100-1500; May Mon-Fri 0900-1730, Sat-Sun 1000-1700; Jun and Sep Mon-Fri 0900-1800; Jul-Aug Mon-Sat 0900-1900; Oct Mon-Fri 0900-1730.

Southwest   One of the most beautiful parts of Argyll is the southwest of Cowal, particu-
Cowal   larly the route down to the little village of **Tighnabruaich**. The A8003 runs down the west side of Loch Riddon and there are few lovelier sights than the view from this road across the **Kyles of Bute**, the narrow straits that separate Cowal from the island of Bute. Tighnabruaich gets busy in the summer with visitors who come here to enjoy some of the best sailing on the west coast. Much of the accommodation is booked up by those enrolled at the **Tighnabruaich Sailing School**, T811717, which offers dinghy sailing and windsurfing courses at all levels. There is a bank in the village and buses leave from here to **Portavadie** (one-three times daily; 25 minutes), **Colintraive** (see below) and **Rothesay** (once or twice daily Monday-Thursday; one hour).

Sleeping   The **SYHA youth hostel**, T811622, open Apr-Sep, sits high above the village with great views across the Kyles and is often full. There's also **D** *The Royal Hotel*, T811239, F811300, royalhotel@btinternet.com   on the waterfront, with a multi-gym and sauna and excellent restaurant serving cheap lunches and mid-range to expensive dinners. There are a couple of cheap **B&Bs** in the village, including **E-F** *Ferguslie*, T811414, open Apr-Sep. In neighbouring **Kames**, there's the **C** *Kames Hotel*, T811489, F811283, tcandrew@aol.com   with great views and live music in the bar.

Transport   It's also possible to reach **Bute** (see below) from southwest Cowal.

Isle of Bute

Phone code: 01700   Barely a stone's throw off the south coast of Cowal is the island of Bute,
Colour map 1, grid B1   another favourite holiday destination for people from Glasgow and Ayrshire,
Population 7,500   who come here in droves during the busy summer months. But though the island is small (15 miles long by five miles wide), it's deceptively easy to escape the hordes, who tend to congregate around the east coast resort of Rothesay, leaving the delights of the sparsely populated west coast free for those who enjoy a bit of peace and quiet. Bute has been a popular place since late Victorian times, when a gaggle of Glasgow grannies were to be seen being pushed along the promenade in their bath-chairs under tartan blankets, taking the invigorating sea air. Now, the island is successfully reinventing itself as a haven for walkers and cyclists. Some of the island's walks are described below.

Ins & outs   **Getting there**   Bute is easily accessible from Glasgow. Take a **train** from Glasgow Central to the **ferry** terminal at Wemyss Bay (1 hr 10 mins), and from there it's a 35-min crossing to Rothesay. There are also **buses** to Rothesay from Tighnabruaich in southwest Cowal (see above) once or twice a day Mon-Thu (1 hr). For times, contact *Western Buses*, T502076. **Ferries** sail daily every 45 mins from 0715 till 1945 (later on Fri, Sat and Sun). For times, T502707. The one-way trip costs £3.25 per passenger and £13.15 per car. Bute can also be reached from the Cowal Peninsula. The A8003 turns off the main A883, which runs right down the west of the peninsula and the east side of Loch Riddon to **Colintraive**, at the narrowest

---

Five of the best: trips from Glasgow ★

- Visit **Loch Lomond** (page 160)
- Go to **New Lanark** (page 159)
- Travel on the **West Highland Railway** (page 162)
- Take a trip down the **Clyde**
- Go on a day trip to **Edinburgh** (page 168)

---

point in the Kyles, only a few hundred yards wide. A small car/passenger ferry makes the 5-min crossing from Colintraive to Rhubodach, at the northern end of Bute, daily every 30 mins or hr, from 0530-1955 Mon-Sat and 0900-1955 Sun in the summer (21 Apr-27 Aug). There are buses from **Colintraive** to **Tighnabruaich** (1-2 times daily Mon-Thu; 35 mins), and to **Dunoon** (see previous page).

Buses connect with the arriving ferries at Rothesay and run to: Mount Stuart (hourly; 15 mins), Kilchattan Bay (4 daily Mon-Sat, 3 on Sun; 30 mins) and Rhubodach (1-2 daily Mon-Sat; 20 mins). For **cycle hire** try *Mountain Bike Centre*, 24 East Princes St, Rothesay, T503554, open daily 0800-2000 Apr-Sep, or at *Mount Stuart House*, T502333.   Transport

The Tourist Information Centre has recently moved into The Winter Gardens on the Promenade, in Rothesay, T502151. Open Apr and Oct Mon-Fri 0900-1730, Sat 1000-1730, Sun 1100-1500; May Mon-Fri 0900-1730, Sat-Sun 1000-1700; Jun and Sep Mon-Fri till 1800; Jul-Aug Mon-Sat till 1900; Nov-Mar Mon-Thu 0900-1730, Fri 0900-1700.   Tourist Information Centre

The sole town on Bute is Rothesay, which, like Dunoon, is a hugely popular holiday destination. There the similarity ends, however, for Rothesay is a genteel and tasteful Victorian seaside resort, with its handsome period mansions lining the broad sweep of bay, its elegant promenade lined with palm trees and the distinctive 1920s **Winter Gardens**, now refurbished and housing a cinema and restaurant.   Rothesay

   Rothesay Castle is worth visiting. Built around the 12th century, the castle was attacked by Vikings, before becoming a favourite with the Stewart kings. It fell into English hands during the Wars of Independence and was retaken by Robert the Bruce in 1311. It was also occupied by Cromwell's New Model Army after the Civil War and partly dismantled, but restoration work has helped preserve much of this impressive circular, moated ruin. ■ *Apr-Sep Mon-Sat 0930-1830, Sun 1400-1830; Oct-Mar Mon-Sat 0930-1630, Sun 1400-1630 (closed Thu-Fri afternoon). Adult £1.80, concession £1.30, children £0.75. To get there, follow the signs from the pier.*

   Behind the castle is **Bute Museum**, which features interesting displays covering the island's history, wildlife and archaeology. ■ *Oct-Mar Tue-Sat 1430-1630; Apr-Sep Mon-Sat 1030-1630, Sun 1430-1630. Adult £1.20, children £0.40.*

One of Bute's main attractions is **Mount Stuart**, a Victorian Gothic house set in 300 acres of lush woodland gardens, three miles south of Rothesay. This magnificent architectural fantasy reflects the Third Marquess of Bute's   Around Bute

Trips from Glasgow

Kilchattan Bay to Glencallum Bay walk

The route is waymarked, but if you want to take a map, it's OS Landranger sheet 63. A longer walk is the circular route from **Kilchattan Bay** *south to* **Glencallum Bay** *and back, via* **St Blane's Chapel.** *The walk is five miles in total. Allow about three hours. For buses to and from Rothesay, see previous page.*

Follow the signpost for 'Kelspoke Path' beside Kiln Villas and take the track which climbs steadily before turning sharply back on itself. Go through a gate and shortly before the next gate turn right. Follow the rough track, which swings right, then left over open ground to the ruins of **Kelspoke Castle***.*

Continue along the grassy path, past a reservoir on your right, then cross the stile and go down and across a small burn. Turn left and follow the burn, before heading right to join the shore path and follow this past the lighthouse on your left and around the headland to Glencallum Bay. Continue round the shoreline and at the far end of the bay follow the waymarks as the path climbs to cross the headland. The path then levels out and from here

there are great views across to the mountains of **Arran***.*

The path then reaches the col above **Loch na Leighe***. Drop down to the loch and follow the waymarks south over open ground. Before reaching a farm called 'The Plan', go right over two footbridges, then left below a low ridge. Keep to the right of the buildings, following the waymarks across open ground to the stile that crosses to the ruins of St Blane's Chapel (see above). Leave the chapel by the gap in the boundary wall and go through a gate, turning left onto a clear track that climbs steadily to a stile. Cross the stile and turn right, following the edge of the field down to a gate. Walk uphill on the left side of the field to Suidhe Hill. At the top of the field, cross the fence and keep going, turning right at the corner of the fence. Go through a gate at the next corner and look for a waymark about 100 m downhill. Follow the path steeply downhill, passing through a kissing gate and staying close to the wall. You then reach a drying green at the foot of the hill; turn left and follow a path around the buildings and back onto the road at Kilchattan.*

passion for astrology, astronomy, mysticism and religion and the sheer scale and grandeur of the place almost defies the imagination. This is truly one of the great country houses of Scotland and displays breathtaking craftsmanship in marble and stained glass, as well as a fine collection of family portraits and Italian antiques. Much of the existing house dates from 1877, and was built following a terrible fire which destroyed the original, built in 1719 by the Second Earl of Bute.

Equally impressive are the **landscaped gardens** and woodlands, established by the Third Earl of Bute (1713-92), who advised on the foundation of Kew Gardens in London. It's worth spending a whole day here in order to take in the amazing splendour of the house and to explore the beautiful gardens. And if the weather's fine, why not bring a picnic and enjoy the wonderful sea views.

■ *Easter weekend and 1 May-17 Oct, daily except Tue and Thu. Gardens open 1000-1700; House open 1100-1630. Admission to House/gardens: adult £6.50, concession £5, children £2.50. Gardens only: adult £3.50, concession £3, children £2. T503877, www.Mountstuart.com A regular bus runs from Rothesay to the gates of the House (see previous page).*

South of Mount Stuart and the village of Kingarth is **Kilchattan Bay**, an attractive bay of pink sands and the start of a fine walk down to Glencallum Bay, in the southeastern corner of the island (see box above). There's accommodation at Kilchattan Bay, at **E** *St Blane's Hotel*, T/F831224.

Southwest of Kilchattan Bay is **St Blane's Chapel**, a 12th-century ruin in a beautifully peaceful spot near the southern tip of the island. The medieval church stands on the site of an earlier monastery, established in the sixth century by St Blane, nephew of St Catan, after whom Kilchattan is named. The ruin can be reached by road from Rothesay, or as part of the walk from Kilchattan Bay (see below).

Four miles north of St Blane's, on the west coast, is **Scalpsie Bay,** the nicest beach on the island and a good place for seal-spotting. A little further north is **St Ninian's Point**, looking across to the island of Inchmarnock. At the end of the beach are the ruins of a sixth-century chapel, dedicated to St Ninian.

The Highland-Lowland dividing line passes through the middle of Bute at **Loch Fad**, which separates the hilly and uninhabited northern half of the island and the rolling farmland of the south. The highest point on the island is **Windy Hill** (281 m) in the north, from where there are great views across the island.

A less strenuous walk is up **Canada Hill, a** few miles southwest of Rothesay, above Loch Fad. Walk along Craigmore promenade and turn off at the old pier to Ardencraig Gardens. Then continue uphill along the golf course to the top of the hill for great views of the Firth of Clyde.

Most of the island's accommodation is in and around Rothesay, and the Tourist Information Centre (see page 155) will book your hotel or B&B. Convenient for the ferry is **B** *Cannon House Hotel*, Battery Pl, T502819, F505725, a comfortable Georgian townhouse. Also central is **E** *The Commodore*, 12 Battery Pl, T/F502178, spearcommodore@aol.com one of the nicest guest houses. There are lots of other guest houses and B&Bs on Battery Pl. North of town, in **Ardbeg**, is the **D** *Ardmory House Hotel & Restaurant*, T502346, F505596, ardmory.house.hotel@dial.pipex.com with a restaurant open to non-residents. 3 miles south of town, at **Ascog**, is the excellent value **E-F** *Ascog Farm*, T503372. · **Sleeping**

The best place to eat on the island is the *New Farm Restaurant*, T831646, which is 6 miles south of Rothesay, near Mount Stuart House and Gardens (see previous page). This whitewashed cottage farmhouse is set on a working sheep farm and dairy and uses local produce to great effect. The atmosphere is friendly and informal. Booking is essential for lunch (mid-range) and dinner (expensive). They also offer B&B (**E**, or **D** including dinner). In town, there's *Fowler's*, housed in the Winter Gardens, T500505, offering good value lunches and dinners. It is an absolute culinary must while you are on Bute to sample the superb fish and chips at the award-winning *West End Café*, 1-3 Gallowgate, T503596. It's open for takeaways all year round, and for sit-down meals Easter-Sep 1200-1400 and 1600-2400 (closed Mon). · **Eating**

The island holds its own *Highland Games* on the last weekend in **Aug**. There's also the *Isle of Bute International Folk Festival* and *World Ceilidh Band Championships*, a massive festival of music and dance held on the third weekend in **Jul**, and the *Isle of Bute Jazz Festival*, during the **May** Bank Holiday weekend. · **Festivals**

The Clyde Valley

The River Clyde undergoes a series of changes during the journey from its source, 80 miles southeast of Glasgow, through the orchards and market gardens of pretty Clydesdale and the abandoned coal mines of North Lanarkshire on its way to the former shipyards of Glasgow. The M74 motorway follows the course of the river,

Trips from Glasgow

*straddled by the valley's two largest towns, **Hamilton** and **Motherwell**, the latter still reeling from the recent closure of its steelworks. Sandwiched between them is **Strathclyde Country Park**, a huge recreational area which features a 200-acre man-made loch and is massively popular with water-sports enthusiasts. The M74 then turns south towards the border with England, while the A72 takes up the task of shadowing the river to **Lanark**, the most interesting focus of this area, standing as it does beside the fascinating village of **New Lanark**.*

Blantyre
Phone code: 01698
Population: 18,500
Colour map 1, grid B4

This town, now more of a suburb of Hamilton, is famous as the birthplace of **David Livingstone**, the notable Victorian missionary and explorer, who felt the white man's burden more than most and took off to Africa in 1840 to bring Christianity to the natives. He was born in the humble surroundings of a one-roomed tenement in 1813, and worked in the local cotton mill before educating himself and taking a medical degree. The entire tenement block, at 165 Station Road, has been transformed into the **David Livingstone Centre**, which tells the story of his life, including his battle against slave traders and that famous meeting with Stanley. There's also an African-themed café, gift shop and garden. The centre is a short walk from the train station. ■ *Open Mon-Sat 1000-1700, Sun 1230-1700. £3, £2 child/concession. T823140.*

Southwest of Blantyre is the **Museum of Scottish Country Life**, Philipshill Road, Wester Kittochside, East Kilbride, which gives an insight into the lives of people in rural Scotland. Situated on a 170-acre site complete with Georgian farmhouse, the land was gifted by the Reid family who farmed here for 400 years. The Reids resisted intensive farming methods, so the land is still rich in wild plants that have disappeared from much farming land in Britain. The Exhibition Building has galleries on the environment, rural technologies and people, and has thousands of exhibits, including the oldest threshing machine in the world, dating back to around 1805. The Historic Farm will be worked to demonstrate traditional agricultural methods of the 1950s, and will follow the seasons to show ploughing, seed time, haymaking and harvest. There is also an Events Area where there will be demonstrations of the working collection, plus a shop and café. It's enough to make you start tuning in to The Archers every day. ■ *Daily 1000-1700. £3, £1.50 concession, children free. T01355-224181, www.nms.ac.uk To get there take First Bus 31 from the St Enoch Centre in Glasgow to Stewartfield Way, or a train to East Kilbride.*

A 30-minute walk down the river towards Uddingston brings you to the substantial red-sandstone ruin of **Bothwell Castle**. This is commonly regarded as the finest 13th-century stronghold in the country and was fought over repeatedly by the Scots and English during the Wars of Independence. It has withstood the ravages of time well and is still hugely impressive. You can walk all the way to Bothwell Castle from the centre of Glasgow. For a detailed description, see page 120. ■ *Open Apr-Sep Mon-Sun 0930-1830. £2, £0.75 children. T816894.*

Transport Trains to Blantyre leave from Glasgow Central every half hour. It's a 20-min journey. Buses run regularly from Buchanan bus station; take bus 63 or 67 for Blantyre and bus 55 or 56 for Bothwell.

Hamilton
Phone code: 01698
Population: 51,500
Colour map 1, grid B4

Hamilton has the longest history of any town in the area, with associations with Mary Queen of Scots, Cromwell and the Covenanters, who were defeated by Monmouth at nearby Bothwell Bridge in 1679. The town today is unremarkable, but a mile or so south, at Ferniegair, are the gates to **Chatelherault**, an extensive country park and impressive hunting lodge and summer house, built in 1732 by William Adam for the Dukes of Hamilton. There are ornamental gardens and 10 miles of trails to explore along the deep wooded glen of the River Avon, past the 16th-century ruins of **Cadzow Castle** and into the surrounding countryside. The Ranger service offers guided walks around the park. ■ *Visitor centre open Mon-Sat 1000-1700, Sun 1200-1700. Free. House open Mon-Thu and Sat 1030-1630, Sun 1230-1630. Free. T426213.*

Within the bounds of nearby Strathclyde Park is the **Hamilton Mausoleum**, a huge burial vault of the Hamilton family. It's an eerie place with an amazing 15-second echo: the longest in Europe, Europe, Europe… ■ *Mausoleum tours Apr-Sep on Wed, Sat and Sun at 1500; also at 1900 in Jul and Aug. Tours Oct-Mar Sat, Sun and Wed at 1400. £1.15, children £0.80.*

Lanark and New Lanark

The little market town of Lanark sits high above the River Clyde. Most people come here to visit the immaculately restored village of **New Lanark**, one of the region's most fascinating sights, a mile below the town, beside the river.

Phone code: 01555
Population: 9,000
Colour map 1, grid B5

Lanark is 25 miles southeast of Glasgow. There are hourly trains from Glasgow Central station. There's an hourly bus service from Lanark train station to the village, but the 20-min walk is recommended for the wonderful views. The last bus back uphill from the village leaves at 1700. To book a taxi, call *Clydewide*, T663221. Lanark is home to Scotland's largest residential **horse riding centre**, at the *Race Course Stables*, T01470-532439. There's a **tourist information centre** in Lanark, in the Horsemarket, 100 yds west of the train station, T661661. It's open May-Sep Mon-Sat 1000-1800, Sun 1200-1700, Oct-Apr Mon-Sat 1000-1700.

Ins & outs

The community was founded in 1785 by David Dale and Richard Arkwright as a cotton-spinning centre, but it was Dale's son-in-law, Robert Owen, who took over the management in 1798 and who pioneered a revolutionary social experiment. He believed in a more humane form of capitalism and believed the welfare of his workers to be crucial to industrial success. He provided them with decent housing, a co-operative store (the forerunner of the modern co-operative movement), adult educational facilities, the world's first day nursery and the social centre of the community, the modestly-titled **Institute for the Formation of Character**. Here, in the **Visitor Centre**, you can see an introductory video about New Lanark and its founders, join the Millennium Ride (an atmospheric 'dark ride') and see original textile machinery. In Robert Owen's School for Children, audio-visual technology allows you to see the 'ghost' of Annie McLeod (an imaginary mill girl) on stage, telling you the story of life in 19th-century New Lanark. The programme lasts 15 minutes. There is also a reconstruction of an early classroom. You can wander through the village and see the 1920s shop, a restored mill-worker's house and even **Robert Owen's House**. There's also a tearoom and gift shop. ■ *Visitor centre open daily 1100-1700. Passport tickets to all attractions £4.75, concession, children £3.25. Access to the village at all times. T661345, www.newlarnark.org*

Just beyond the village lies the wooded **Falls of Clyde Nature Reserve**, managed by the Scottish Wildlife Trust (SWT). You can visit the **SWT Wildlife Centre**, housed in the old dyeworks, which provides information about the history and wildlife of the area. ■ *Centre open Easter-Oct Mon-Fri 1100-1700, Sat and Sun 1300-1700; Nov-Dec, Feb-Easter Sat and Sun 1300-1700. £1, £0.50 children. T665262.*

Trips from Glasgow

Walk to the Falls of Clyde

You can walk from the village to the stunning **Corra Linn** waterfalls and beyond. Starting from the village, walk past the SWT centre and up the stone steps into the nature reserve above Dundaff Linn, the smallest of the three waterfalls on the walk. A riverside boardwalk takes you past a 200-year-old weir, and just beyond the end of the boardwalk go right at a junction to pass Bonnington power station.

Steps then lead up to a viewing platform above the dramatic Corra Linn, the highest falls on the Clyde, where the river plunges 90 ft in three stages. Continue up the steps and follow the path through woodlands to reach another set of falls at **Bonnington Linn**.

You can retrace your steps back to the village, or extend the walk by crossing the weir at Bonnington Linn and turning right, down the track on the opposite bank, taking a narrow path on the right after a few hundred yards. Take care here as the path is very close to the lip of the gorge! After about a mile, the path leads you to the crumbling ruin of Corra Castle. To return to Bonnington Linn, retrace your steps for about 100 yds and then follow the vehicle track on the right.

The total distance, including the extension, is about five-and-a-half miles. Allow three to four hours there and back and wear boots or strong shoes as some parts can be muddy.

Eating There are plenty of places to eat in Lanark, including the usual hotels and pubs, cafés, chip shops and Indian restaurants. The best place is *Ristorante La Vigna*, at 40 Wellgate, T630351, a moderately priced Italian restaurant of some renown. It's open daily for lunch and dinner, but is popular, so book in advance. If you're in town on a Mon, which is market day, it's well worth trying the *Market Bar and Restaurant*, at Lanark Market on Hyndford Rd.

Craignethan Castle Five miles northwest of Lanark is the village of **Crossford**, from where you can visit Craignethan Castle, an ornate tower-house standing over the River Nethan. It was built by Sir James Hamilton for James V, in 1530, and was the last major castle to be built in Scotland. Mary, Queen of Scots left from here to do battle at Langside (at Queen's Park in Glasgow), where she was defeated and fled to France before her eventual imprisonment. The castle, like so many others in Scotland, is said to be haunted by her ghost. ■*Apr-Sep Mon-Sat 0930-1630, Sun 1400-1630, Mar and Oct Mon-Wed, Sat and Sun 0930-1630, Thu 0930-1230. £1.50. To get there, take a bus from Lanark to Crossford, from where it's a 15-min walk.*

Loch Lomond

Colour map 1, grid A/B 2/3

Britain's largest inland waterway, measuring 22 miles in length and at certain points up to five miles wide, is one of Scotland's most famous lochs, thanks to the Jacobite ballad about its "bonnie banks". These same banks are now one of the busiest parts of the Highlands, due to their proximity to Glasgow (only 20 miles south along the congested A82). During the summer the loch becomes a playground for day-trippers who tear up and down the loch in speedboats and on jet skis, obliterating any notion visitors may have of a little peace and quiet. In spring 2002 this area will become Scotland's first National Park.

The **west bank** of the loch, from Balloch north to Tarbet, is one long, almost uninterrupted development of marinas, holiday homes, caravan parks and exclusive golf clubs. The most picturesque village on the west bank, **Luss**, is the setting for the Scottish TV soap *Take the High Road*, and is full of visitors buying souvenir tea towels and hoping to catch a glimpse of one of the 'stars'. The **Loch Lomond Authority Visitor Centre**, T01301-702785, next to the large car park in the village, has information on the loch's natural history, flora and fauna. ■ *Easter-Oct daily 1000-1800.*

At the southern end of the loch is the resort town of **Balloch**, packed full of hotels, B&Bs, caravan parks and any number of operators offering **boat trips** around the loch's overcrowded waters. Try *Sweeney's Cruises*, T752376, or *Mullen's Cruises*, T751481, both of which offer a wide range of trips, starting at around £4-5 for an hour. A daily 2½-hour cruise from Balloch to Luss leaves at 1430 (£7). **Loch Lomond Shores**, T721500, is a large visitor centre and orientation centre as you come into town, which operates as the gateway to the National Park. At the 100-acre site you can see a film celebrating the area in addition to shops, restaurants and the restored steamer 'Maid of the Loch'. There are plans to move the tourist office here too. During the early stages of the park's development the old **Tourist Information Centre** near the station, T753533, is also likely to remain open. ■ *Apr Jun, Sep and Oct daily 1000-1700; Jul and Aug 0930-1830.*

North of **Tarbet**, at the narrow northern end of the loch, things quieten down a great deal and the road to **Ardlui**, at the loch's northern tip, is very beautiful and peaceful. The A82 continues north of Ardlui, past **Inverarnan**, to join the A85 at **Crianlarich**. There's a **Tourist Information Centre** in Tarbet (April-October) T01301-702260; and a **Visitor Centre** at Inveruglas, T01301-704392.

Balloch to Tarbet
Phone code: 01389

The tranquil **east bank** of Loch Lomond is a great place for walking. The **West Highland Way** follows the east bank all the way from **Drymen**, through **Balmaha**, **Rowardennan** and **Inversnaid**. Beyond Rowardennan this is the only access to the loch's east bank, except for the road to Inversnaid from the Trossachs. From Rowardennan you can climb **Ben Lomond** (3,192 ft), the most southerly of the Munros. It's not too difficult and the views from the top (in good weather) are astounding. There are two routes: the easier one starts from the car park at the end of the road just beyond the *Rowardennan Hotel*; the other route, known as the 'Ptarmigan Route', starts from beyond the youth hostel. You can also go up by one route and return by the other. Allow about five to six hours there and back.

An easier climb is **Conic Hill**, on the Highland fault-line and very close to Glasgow. The route starts from the Balmaha car park. It takes about 1½ hours to reach the top, from where the views of the loch are stunning.

East bank & Ben Lomond
OS Landranger map 58

Trips from Glasgow

In **Balloch**, the **D** *Balloch House*, T752579, near the A82, has a good restaurant. Best of the B&Bs is the **E** *Gowanlea Guest House*, T752456, on Drymen Rd. There's a good **campsite** at *Lomond Woods Holiday Park* at Tullichewan , T755000, on the Old Luss Rd, where you can hire **mountain bikes**. A few miles further on up the west bank, in **Arden**, is **F** *Loch Lomond SYHA Youth Hostel*, T850226, www.syha.org.uk a grand, 19th-century, turreted mansion complete with the obligatory ghost. A few miles north of Luss, at **Inverbeg**, is the **C-B** *Inverbeg Inn*, T01436-860678, which does good food.

On the **eastern shore** there's an **F** *SYHA Youth Hostel* at **Rowardennan**, T01360-870259, open Feb-Oct. There's also the **C** *Rowardennan Hotel*, T01360-870273, which offers a bit more comfort and serves bar meals. There are a couple of **campsites** on the east bank, at *Milarrochy Bay*, T01360-870236, open end-Mar to Oct, near Balmaha, and the Forestry Commission campsite at *Cashel*, T01360-870234, www.forestholidays.co.uk a few miles further north. On the northeast shore, and

Sleeping & eating
There are numerous hotels and B&Bs in Balloch, Luss, Inverbeg and Tarbet

The rail thing

Running from Glasgow to Mallaig via Fort William, the West Highland Railway is only 164 miles long but is widely acknowledged as one of the most scenic railway journeys in the world. The great thing about this journey is its variety, taking you from the distinctive red tenements of Glasgow and the former shipbuilding areas of the River Clyde, to the windy wilderness of Rannoch Moor and the chilly splendour of the hills. It's about an hour after leaving Glasgow that you get your first taste of Highland scenery when the train hugs the eastern bank of sinewy Loch Long. Then it's on past the 'bonnie banks' of Loch Lomond, Britain's largest body of inland water. It's impossible not to pass this serene loch without thinking of the famous ballad about two Jacobite soldiers captured after the 1745 rebellion. The soldier taking 'the low road' is due to be executed, his companion taking the 'high road' is due to be released.

After Ardlui, at the top of Loch Lomond, the countryside gets more rugged. Wherever you look you see something of interest: a waterfall gushing down a hillside, a buzzard surfing on the breeze – perhaps a herd of Highland Cattle wallowing in a river. The West Highland Way, the long-distance footpath from Glasgow to Fort William, is close to the line now, and at stations such as Crianlarich, Upper Tyndrum and Bridge of Orchy you can often spot footsore walkers with muddy boots who get on the train looking slightly guilty and collapse on their seats with sighs of relief.

The landscape gets wilder and bleaker as the railway crosses the lonely, peaty wastes of Rannoch Moor and on to Corrour, which featured in the film version of Irvine Welsh's cult book Trainspotting.

Then you descend to the lusher countryside around Tulloch, before pulling in to Fort William. This is a popular visitor centre as it's close to Ben Nevis, Britain's highest mountain, and beautiful Glen Nevis, which has featured in films such as Braveheart *and* Rob Roy. *Now comes the most spectacular part of the journey, for the West Highland Line leaves the best till last. Leaving Fort William, the train crosses Thomas Telford's Caledonian Canal - where you can see an impressive series of eight locks known as 'Neptune's Staircase' - hugs the shore of Loch Eil, then crosses the magnificent Glenfinnan Viaduct, a masterpiece in concrete. You soon get superb views of the evocative Glenfinnan Monument that commemorates the start of the 1745 rebellion, before pulling in to Glenfinnan Station. The train now takes you through a landscape of craggy hills and glacial lochs etched with birch and pine trees. You pass Loch nan Uamh, from where Bonnie Prince Charlie fled for France after his defeat at Culloden, then draw in to Arisaig, the birthplace of the man who inspired RL Stevenson's* Long John Silver. *Next is beautiful Loch Morar, Britain's deepest inland loch and home – so legend has it – to a mysterious monster. Soon you get great views across the water to the craggy islands of Eigg and Rhum, before finally pulling in to the port of Mallaig.*

There are 2-3 trains daily from **Glasgow** *to Fort William (3¾ hrs). These trains continue to* **Mallaig** *(a further 1 hr 20 mins) . To do the journey in style, take the* **Jacobite Steam Train** *which runs from Fort William to Mallaig during the summer months. Further details from West Coast Railway Company, T01524-732100,*

only accessible by road via the B829 from Aberfoyle, is the splendidly isolated **D** *Inversnaid Hotel*, T01877-386223.

In **Ardlui**, at the northern tip of the loch, is the comfortable **C** *Ardlui Hotel*, T01301-704243, www.ardlui.co.uk A few miles north, at **Inverarnan**, is the *Drover's Inn*, T01301-704234, the famous Highland watering hole, with smoke-blackened walls, low ceilings, bare floors, open fires, a hall filled with stuffed animals, barman in kilt and a great selection of single malts. The perfect place for a wild night of drinking in the wilderness. It simply doesn't get any better than this.

Scottish Citylink, **buses** run regularly from Glasgow to **Balloch** (45 mins), and on to Luss and **Tarbet** (1 hr 10 mins). Some buses go to **Ardlui** (1 hr 20 mins) and on to **Crianlarich**. There are 2 **rail** lines from Glasgow to Loch Lomond. One runs to **Balloch** every 30 mins (35 mins) the other is the West Highland line to Fort William and Mallaig, with a branch line to Oban. It reaches Loch Lomond at **Tarbet** and there's another station further north at **Ardlui**.

Transport

There's a passenger **ferry service** across the loch between **Inverbeg** and **Rowardennan**, T01360-870273, 3 times daily (Apr-Sep). There are also ferries between **Inveruglas** and **Inversnaid**, T01877-386223. The *Ardleish* to *Ardlui* ferry (Apr-Oct) can be summoned from shore by raising ball up signal mast (0900-1900). Out-of-season by arrangement with Ardlui Hotel (T01301-704243).

The Campsies

Running southeast from Loch Lomond, and bordered by the broad farmlands of the **Carse of Stirling** to the north and the northern suburbs of **Glasgow** to the south, are the **Campsies**. This is an area of gently rolling hills and fertile farmland, comprising the **Fintry, Gargunnock, Strathblane** and **Kilsyth Hills** and the **Campsie Fells**. Other than weekend hikers from Glasgow, the Campsies attract few visitors and their unspoiled peace and beauty is their main attraction. There's a string of picturesque villages nestled in the hills, amongst them **Killearn**, **Kippen**, **Gargunnock** and **Balfron**, birthplace of Alexander 'Greek' Thomson, Glasgow's great Victorian architect (see page203). There's also plenty of good walking to be done here. For details of the **Campsie Fells Trail**, contact the **Stirling Tourist Information Centre**, T01786-475019.

There are several **buses** daily to Drymen from **Glasgow**, via Queen's View. There are also buses through the region from **Stirling**. A **postbus** service, T01752-494527, www.royalmail.com/postbus leaves from **Denny**, 5 miles south of Stirling, to Fintry (Mon-Sat at 0955), from where 2 buses (Mon-Sat) run to Balfron. There are regular buses to Denny from **Stirling** bus station.

Ins & outs

Lying at the heart of the Campsies is the attractive little village of Fintry, at the head of the Strathendrick valley, and regular winner of the 'Scotland in Bloom' competition. Two miles east of the village is the 90-ft-high **Loup of Fintry** waterfall. There are a few places to stay in Fintry, including the wonderful **B** *Culcreuch Castle Hotel*, T860228, www.culcreuch.com a 14th-century castle set in the 1,600-acre Culcreuch Country Park. A cheaper option is the **E** *Fintry Inn*, T860224, which also offers pub food.

Fintry
Phone code: 01360
Colour map1, grid B3

At the western end of the Campsie Fells is the village of Drymen, the busiest of the Campsie villages due to its proximity to the eastern shores of Loch Lomond. Drymen also lies on the **West Highland Way**. There's a seasonal **tourist office** in the library on The Square. ■ *T660068. May-Sep.* There's a decent selection of **accommodation** in Drymen. Best hotel is the **B-C** *Buchanan Arms Hotel*, T660588. There are lots of **B&Bs**, including **E** *Easter Drumquhassle Farm*, T660893, http://members.aol.com/juliamacx on Gartness Road. A highly recommended place to eat is the moderately priced *Clachan Inn*, T660824, on The Square, or you

Drymen
Phone code: 01360
Colour map1, grid A3

can try the Winnock Hotel nearby, T660245. You can rent **bikes** at *Lomond Activities*, 64 Main Street, T660066.

Walks

South of **Killearn** on the A81 is the **Glengoyne Distillery**. ■ *Mon-Sat 1000-1600, Sun 1200-1600; £3.75, £2.75 concession, £10 nosing session. T550254.* It is the starting point for two excellent walks in the Strathblane Hills, to the top of both **Dumgoyne Hill** (1,400 ft), and **Earl's Seat** (1,896 ft), the highest point in the Campsies.

Further west, on the other side of Strathblane, is **Queen's View** on **Auchineden Hill**, from where there are wonderful views up Loch Lomond as far as Ben Ledi. Queen Victoria was particularly impressed with the view – hence its name. The path to the top starts from the busy car park on the A809 Bearsden to Drymen road. It takes about 45-50 minutes each way. From the car park a path also leads up to **The Whangie**, a deep cleft in the rock face with sheer walls rising over 30 ft on either side. A path runs for 100 yds through the narrow gap.

Queen Elizabeth Forest Park
Colour map 1, grid A3

North of the Campsies, bordered by Loch Lomond to the west and the Trossachs to the east, is Queen Elizabeth Forest Park, a vast and spectacular wilderness covering 75,000 acres. The park is run by the Forestry Commission and is criss-crossed by a network of less difficult, waymarked trails and paths which start from the Queen Elizabeth Park **Visitor Centre**, about half a mile north of Aberfoyle on the A821. Available at the centre are audio-visual displays on the park's flora and fauna and information on the numerous walks and cycle routes around the park. ■ *Mar-Oct daily 1000-1800; Oct-Dec 1100-1600 (parking £1). Full details of the park are available from the Forest Enterprise in Aberfoyle, (same tel no). T01877-382258.*

Ins and outs Getting there There are regular **buses** to to the little town of Aberfoyle from **Stirling.** There are also daily services from **Glasgow,** via Balfron. **There's a postbus service**, T01752-494527, www.royalmail.com/postbus from Aberfoyle to Inversnaid on Loch Lomond (see page 161).

The **Tourist Information Centre** is on the main street. Apr-Jun, Sep and Oct daily 1000-1700; Jul and Aug 0930-1900, weekends only Nov-Mar (hours subject to change). T382352.

Sleeping and eating The best place to stay in the area is the **A-B** *Lake Hotel*, in Port of Menteith, situated on the lakeshore overlooking Inchmahome, T385258, www.lake-of-menteith-hotel.com It's stylish, comfortable, very romantic and boasts a fine restaurant (lunch mid-range; dinner expensive). There are dozens of **B&Bs** in and around Aberfoyle. **Camping** is available at *Cobeland Campsite*, T382392, open Apr-Oct, 2 miles south of Aberfoyle on the edge of the Queen Elizabeth Forest Park; and at the excellent *Trossachs Holiday Park*, T382614, open Mar-Oct, set in 40 acres and offering **mountain bike hire**.

There are several decent places to eat in Aberfoyle. The *Forth Inn Hotel*,T382372, and *The Coach House*, T382822, both on Main St, serve good pub food. The best place to eat is the excellent and very popular *Braeval Old Mill*, T382711, a few miles east on the A873 to Port of Menteith.

Stirling

Stirling has a long and fascinating history and is packed with major historical sights. The town is best known for its castle, perched high on a rocky crag above the town and every bit as impressive as Edinburgh's. Then there's the Wallace Monument, a huge monolith high on Abbey Craig to the northeast of town, which commemorates William Wallace, portrayed by Mel Gibson in the movie *Braveheart*. Being so close to Glasgow, the sights of Stirling can be visited in a day.

Phone code: 01786
Colour map 1, grid A4
Population: 37,000

Getting there Stirling is easily reached from Glasgow by regular **bus** and **train** services. *Scottish Citylink* **buses** run at least every hour to and from **Glasgow** (1 hr). There are *ScotRail* **trains,** T08457-484950, every 30 mins (Mon-Sat; hourly on Sun) to **Glasgow** (45 mins). The **train station** is on Station Rd, near the town centre, and the **bus station** is close by, on Goosecroft Rd, behind the Thistle Shopping Centre.

Ins & outs

    Getting around Most of the important sights, except Bannockburn and the Wallace Monument, are within easy walking distance of each other. There's an open-topped 'hop on, hop off' Heritage Bus Tour which runs from Jun to Sep and includes the castle and Wallace Monument. There are tours every 30 mins from 1000 till 1700. A day ticket costs £6.50. Check details at the Tourist Information Centre (TIC).

    Tourist information The TIC is at 41 Dumbarton Rd, in the centre of town. It is the main office for Loch Lomond, Stirling and the Trossachs and stocks a wide range of books, guides, maps and leaflets. It also has information on the various **guided walks** of the town. Open all year Jun and Sep Mon-Sat 0900-1800, Sun 1000-1600; Jul and Aug Mon-Sat 0900-1930, Sun 0930-1830; Oct-May Mon-Sat 1000-1700.

The obvious place to begin a tour is the immensely impressive **Stirling Castle,** which stands 250 ft above the flat plain, atop the plug of an extinct volcano. From the west there's a sheer drop down the side of the rocky crag, making the castle seem a daunting prospect to would-be attackers, and now presenting visitors with fantastic views of the surrounding area. There's been a fortress here since the Iron Age, though the current building dates mostly from the 15th and 16th centuries, when it was the favourite residence of the Stuart kings.

Sights

    On the esplanade is a **visitor centre** which shows an introductory film giving a potted history of the castle. From here you proceed to the **Upper Square**, where you can see the magnificent **Great Hall**, built by James IV and which was recently restored to its original condition. The spectacular **Palace** (1540-42), is the finest Renaissance building in Scotland. This was where the young Mary, Queen of Scots spent much of her life until her departure for France, in 1548.

    The interior of the royal apartments is largely bare but you can still see the **Stirling Heads**, 56 elegantly carved oak plaques which once decorated the ceiling of one of the rooms. Also impressive is the interior of the **Chapel Royal**, built by James VI in 1594 for the baptism of his son. The 16th-century **kitchens** are also interesting and have been restored to recreate the preparations for a royal banquet. ■ *Apr-Oct daily 0930-1800 (last entry 1715); Nov-Mar till 1700 (last entry 1615). £6.50, £5 concession (includes admission to Argyll's Ludging). T450000 (HS).*

    Most of the historic sights are clustered around the medieval cobbled streets of the Old Town, which spreads from the castle down the hill towards the flood-plain of the River Forth. Five minutes' walk downhill from the castle is **Argyll's Ludging** (lodging), the finest and most complete surviving

Trips from Glasgow

example of a 17th-century town house in Scotland. It has recently been restored to its former glory and the rooms are furnished as they would have been in the late 17th century. ■ *Same opening hours as the Castle. £2.80, or included in the price of Stirling Castle ticket. T450000.*

Further down Castle Wynd, at the top of Broad Street, is **Mar's Wark**, the ornate façade of a dilapidated town house, started by the first Earl of Mar, Regent of Scotland, in 1569 but left to fall into ruin following his death two years later. It was further damaged during the 1745 Jacobite Rebellion. A little further down Castle Wynd is the medieval **Church of the Holy Rude**, where the infant James VI was crowned in 1567. The oldest parts, the nave and tower, date from 1456 and the church also features one of the few surviving 15th-century timber roofs.

A short way down St John Street is the impressively refurbished **Old Town Jail**, where the rigours of life behind bars in times gone by is brilliantly brought to life by enthusiastic actors. A glass lift then takes you up to the roof for spectacular views across the town and the Forth Valley. ■ *Apr-Sep daily 0930-1800; Oct daily till 1700; Nov-Feb daily till 1600; Mar till 1700. £3.95, £2.75 concession. T450050.*

Nearby is the **Tolbooth**, built in 1705 as the town's administrative headquarters by Sir William Bruce (who designed the Palace of Holyroodhouse in Edinburgh) and used as a courthouse and jail in the 19th century. It is now a performance venue with a 200-seater theatre and a studio/rehearsal space. At the bottom of Broad Street is **Darnley's House**, where Mary, Queen of Scots' second husband, Lord Darnley, is said to have stayed. It now houses a coffee shop (see next page).

At the bottom of Spittal Street, where it joins King Street, turn into Corn Exchange Road and then head west up Dumbarton Road to reach the **Smith Art Gallery and Museum**, which houses some interesting displays about the town's history and culture, as well as a fine collection of paintings. ■ *All year Tue-Sat 1030-1700, Sun 1400-1700. Free. T471917.*

At the north end of the town, a 20-minute walk from the town centre, is the 15th-century **Old Bridge**, which was the lowest crossing point on the River Forth, and one of the most important bridges in Scotland until Kincardine Bridge was built in 1936. The bridge was built to replace earlier structures, including the famous wooden bridge, scene of the battle in 1297 in which William Wallace defeated the English.

Wallace Monument

A new statue to Wallace located in the car park was decapitated by locals because it bore too strong a resemblance to Mel Gibson

Two miles northeast of the town, near Stirling University and Bridge of Allan, is the Wallace Monument, an impressive Victorian Gothic tribute to Sir William Wallace, hero of the successful but hugely inaccurate film, *Braveheart*. Wallace was knighted by Robert the Bruce for his famous victory at Stirling Bridge, but following defeat later at Falkirk he went off to Europe in search of support for the Scottish cause. During his absence he was betrayed by the Scots nobles and on his return found guilty of treason and cruelly hanged, drawn and quartered in London.

Inside the monument are various exhibits including a Hall of Scottish Heroes and Wallace's mighty two-handed sword (5 ft 4 in long – about the same height as the actor who played him in the film). There are fantastic views from the top of the 220-ft tower – if you can manage the climb up its 246-step staircase. There's a shuttle bus that runs from the foot of the hill up to the tower every 15 minutes. An open-topped **tour bus** runs to the monument from Stirling Castle every half hour (see previous page). ■ *Jan, Feb, Nov and Dec daily 1030-1600; Mar-May and Oct 1000-1700; Jun 1000-1800; Jul, Aug and Sep 0930-1830. £3.95, £2.75 children. T472140.*

A few miles south of Stirling is the site of Scotland's greatest victory over the **Bannockburn** English (no, not Wembley 1967), when Robert the Bruce defeated Edward II's army, on 24 June 1314. It was the **Battle of Bannockburn** which united the Scots and led to the declaration of independence at Arbroath in 1320 (the 'Declaration of Arbroath'). There's not an awful lot to see, but the **Bannockburn Heritage Centre** puts flesh on the bones and brings to life the full scale of the battle. Outside is an equestrian statue of Bruce, on the spot where he is said to have commanded his forces, and the site of the bore stone, where Bruce planted his standard after victory. What's left of the original bore stone is on display in the visitor centre, safe from souvenir hunters. ■ *Site open all year, Heritage Centre open Apr-Oct daily 1000-1730; Oct-Mar 1030-1600; closed Jan, Feb. £2.50, £1.70 child/concession. To get there, take bus No 51 or 52 from Stirling (every 30 mins). T812664 (NTS).*

Mid-range *Scholars Restaurant* at the *Stirling Highland Hotel*, Spittal St, T272727, has **Eating** an excellent reputation for modern Scottish cuisine. *Hermann's*, 32 St John St, T450632, at the Tolbooth on the road up to the castle, is an upmarket choice. It offers excellent Scottish/Austrian cuisine at moderate prices (and a cheap set lunch).

Cheap The best curry in town can be had at the *East India Company*, 7 Viewfield Pl, T471330, with a cheaper pakora snack-bar upstairs. A good Italian restaurant is the busy *Italia Nostra*, 25 Baker St, T473208, which serves cheap to mid-range food daily till 2300; or try *La Ciociara*, 41 Friars St, T451552, which also serves coffees and pastries during the day. On the same street, at No 5, is *Olivia's Restaurant*, T446277, which offers good Scottish food in an informal atmosphere (cheap to mid-range prices, open Mon-Sat 1200-1430 and 1830-2200). *Berties* is a café-bistro in the Albert Hall on Dumbarton Rd, T446930, and a cheap and relaxing place for lunch (open daily 1000-1700). A firm favourite with students is the *Barnton Bar & Bistro*, opposite the post office on Barnton St, T461698. It's cheap, open daily till 2400 (0100 at weekends) and serves great all-day breakfasts. A good place for coffee and a snack is the elegant *Darnley Coffee House*, 18 Bow St, T474468.

Two of the best **pubs** in Stirling are the *Portcullis*, T472268, on Castle Wynd, below the **Bars & pubs** castle; and the *Settle Inn*, further down on St Mary's Wynd, which is the oldest hostelry in town (dating from 1773) and very popular with Stirling's large student population. *Pivo*, on Corn Exchange, T451904, is a trendy Czech bar which also serves light meals. The lively *Barnton Bar & Bistro* (see above) is also a good place for a drink, as is *Whistlebinkies*, on St Mary's Wynd.

Between Stirling and Edinburgh is the pleasant little West Lothian town of **Linlithgow** Linlithgow, home of the magnificent Renaissance **Linlithgow Palace**, one of *Phone code: 01506* the most romantic and impressive historic buildings in Scotland. It's off the *Colour map 1, grid B5* beaten track and relatively little-visited but well worth the detour, for this is a real gem. The 15th-century ruin is set on the edge of Linlithgow Loch and is associated with many of Scotland's main historical players, including James V (1512) and Mary, Queen of Scots (1542), who were both born here. The ruin still conveys a real sense of the sheer scale of the lavish lifestyle of the court, from the ornate fountain in the inner courtyard to the magnificent Great Hall with its massive kitchens. ■ *Apr-Sep daily 0930-1830; Oct-Mar Mon-Sat 0930-1630, Sun 1400-1630. £2.80, £2 concession. T842896.*

Next to the palace is **St Michael's Church**, the largest pre-Reformation church in the country, with its controversial crown and spire, added in 1964. ■ *Oct-Apr Mon-Fri 1030-1500, May-Sep 1000-1630.*

Trips from Glasgow

Eating 2 miles northeast of town, at the junction of the A904 and A803, is the seriously good and seriously expensive **Champany Inn**, T834532, which specialises in beef. Rather more modest is the busy and welcoming **Four Marys**, 65 High St, T842171, which serves cheap bar meals and real ales, daily 1200-1430, 1730-2030, Sun 1230-2030.

Transport Regular **buses** from Stirling stop at The Cross. The **train station** is at the southern end of town. There are hourly **trains** to and from **Edinburgh** (20 mins), **Glasgow Queen Street** (30 mins) and **Stirling** (35 mins).

Edinburgh

*Less than an hour from Glasgow by bus or train is Edinburgh, the country's capital, close enough to make it an easy day trip, though there's an awful lot here to cram into just one day. The best place to start a tour of Edinburgh is in the medieval Old Town, where you'll find most of the famous sights, from the **castle**, down through the **Royal Mile**, to the **Palace of Holyroodhouse**. South of the Royal Mile is the **Grassmarket**, the **Cowgate** and **Chambers Street**, site of the **University of Edinburgh** and two of the city's best museums, the **Royal Museum of Scotland** and the recently opened **Museum of Scotland**. The **New Town** also deserves some serious exploration, in particular the excellent **National Gallery**, **Royal Scottish Academy** and **National Portrait Gallery**. A bit further out from the centre are the **Royal Botanic Garden** and the **Gallery of Modern Art**.*

Ins and outs

Getting there

Population: 440,000
Phone code: 0131
Colour map 1, grid B6

Train All trains to Edinburgh go to Waverley Station, T5562477, off Waverley Bridge at the east end of Princes St. This is where the main ticket booking office is located. Note that during peak periods a wait of 30-40 mins is not unusual. Leave at least 10 mins to buy tickets for immediate travel at other times. Taxis collect passengers from the station concourse, but if the queue is depressingly long, there's another taxi rank on Waverley Bridge. All trains to and from Glasgow, also stop at Haymarket Station. For timetable and ticket enquiries, T08457-484950.

Bus The city's new bus station is under construction so buses currently leave from St Andrews Sq, only a few minutes' walk from Waverley Station.

Getting around

Bus Public transport is generally good and efficient. Two main bus companies operate most services in and around the city: *Lothian Regional Transport* (*LRT*) use maroon and white double deckers, while *First Edinburgh* operate the same routes using green and yellow buses. They also run the so-called 'Barbie' buses, which are pink and more user-friendly for parents with kids and disabled passengers.

Car Edinburgh is one of the least car-friendly cities in Britain. The main routes into town have been turned into 'greenways', which give buses priority, and on-street parking is limited to 10 mins. The centre of town is a complicated system of one-way streets designed to ease congestion. The privatized traffic wardens are ruthless in their dedication to duty. Free parking in most of central Edinburgh is limited to resident- parking permit holders only, Mon-Fri 0830-1800, and the police have powers to tow away illegally parked cars. For details of car rental companies based in Glasgow, see page 37.

On foot Although Greater Edinburgh occupies a large area relative to its population of less than half a million, most of what you'll want to see lies within the compact city centre which is easily explored on foot. The centre is clearly divided in two, with the main thoroughfare, Princes Street, and its gardens, running between them. The **Old Town** is a medieval maze of cobbled streets, wynds and closes on or around the Royal Mile, which runs from the castle down to the palace. The **New Town** is the symmetrical layout of wide streets lined with elegant Georgian buildings which runs north from Princes Street. Though most of the main sights are within walking distance of each other, Edinburgh is a hilly city and a full day's sightseeing can leave you exhausted.

An excellent way to see the sights and avoid wearing out shoe leather is to take one of the city bus tours (Guide Friday or LRT); see below

The city's main **Tourist Information Centre (TIC)** is at 3 Princes St, on top of Waverley Market, T4733800, F4733881, www.edinburgh.org Open Apr and Oct Mon-Sat 0900-1800, Sun 1100-1800; May and Sep Mon-Sat 0900-1900, Sun 1100-1900; Jun Mon-Sat 0900-1900, Sun 1000-1900; Jul and Aug Mon-Sat 0900-2000, Sun 1000-2000; Nov-Mar Mon-Sat 0900-1800, Sun 1000-1800. It gets very busy during the peak season and at festival time, but has the full range of services, including currency exchange, and will book accommodation, provide travel information and book tickets for various events and excursions. They also stock a wide range of guides, maps and leaflets covering all of Scotland. There's also a tourist information desk at the **airport**, in the international arrivals area, T3332167. It's open Apr-Oct Mon-Sat 0830-2130, Sun 0930-2130; Nov-Mar Mon-Fri 0900-1800, Sat 0900-1700, Sun 0930-1700.

Information

The City Council has produced a free map of the different bus routes around Edinburgh. This is available from the TIC or from the **LRT ticket centres** at 31 Waverley Bridge, T2258616 (open Easter-Oct Mon-Sat 0800-1800, Sun 0900-1630; Nov-Easter Tue-Sat 0900-1630), or 27 Hanover St, T5556363 (open Mon-Sat 0830-1800). Both offices sell travel cards. **Traveline** is a public-transport information service for Edinburgh, East Lothian and Midlothian: T0800-232323 (local calls) or T2253858 (national calls), Mon-Fri 0830-2000. Their office is at 2 Cockburn St, near Waverley Station.

One of the best ways to see the city sights is to take a **guided bus tour** on board an open-top double decker bus. These depart from Waverley Bridge every 15 minutes, the first one leaving around 0900 and the last one between 1730 and 2000, depending on the time of year. The complete tour lasts an hour, stopping at the main tourist sights, but tickets are valid for the full day and you can hop on and off any of the company's buses at any of the stops. The *Guide Friday* tours are recommended and cost £8.50 per person (students £7/children £2.50); Guide Friday Tourism Centre, 133-135 Canongate, Royal Mile, T5562244, www.guidefriday.com *Lothian Regional Transport (LRT)* run similar guided bus tours; £7.50 (students £6/children £2.50). Tickets and further information from their city centre offices (see Ins and outs, page 168).

Tours of Edinburgh

The Old Town

The city skyline is dominated by the castle, Scotland's prime tourist attraction and the most visited sight in Britain outside London. The castle sits on top of an extinct volcano, protected on three sides by steep cliffs, and is well worth a visit, if only for the great views over the city from its battlements. You can easily wander round the castle yourself, but for a more colourful introduction to its eventful past, you can join one of the first-rate guided tours.

■ *Apr-Sep daily 0930-1800, Oct-Mar 0930-1700. Last admission 45 mins before closing. £7.50, £2 child, £5.50 concession. T2259846 (HS).*

Edinburgh Castle

Trips from Glasgow

Royal Mile Running through the heart of the medieval Old Town, from the castle down to the **Palace of Holyrood-house**, is the **Royal Mile**, where you'll find a greater concentration of historic buildings than almost anywhere else in Britain. The 1,984 yards of the Royal Mile, from the Castle Keep to the Palace, comprises four separate streets: (from top to bottom) **Castlehill**, **Lawnmarket**, the **High Street** and the **Canongate**. Branching out from these is a honeycomb of wynds and closes, entered via archways known as 'pends'. A close is the entrance to a 'land' or high-rise tenement block, and wynds are the narrow and winding alleyways giving access to the main street. These were the scene of many important – and sinister – events over the centuries and are certainly worth exploring in detail.

The narrow uppermost part of the Royal Mile nearest the castle is known as Castlehill. At the corner of Castlehill and Castle Wynd is the **Scotch Whisky Heritage Centre**, 354 Castlehill, where you can find out everything you ever wanted to know about Scotland's national drink. The best part is the bond bar, where you can sample some of the vast range of malt whiskies on offer before buying a bottle in the gift shop. ■ *Daily Jun-Sep 0930-1800, Oct-May 1000-1730. £5.50, £2.75 children, £3.85 concession. T2200441, www.whisky-heritage.co.uk* Across the street is the **Edinburgh Old Town**

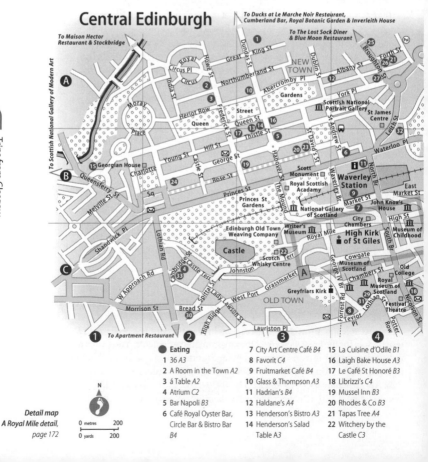

Central Edinburgh

Trips from Glasgow

Detail map
A Royal Mile detail,
page 172

| 0 metres | 200 |
| 0 yards | 200 |

● **Eating**
1 36 *A3*
2 A Room in the Town *A2*
3 á Table *A2*
4 Atrium *C2*
5 Bar Napoli *B3*
6 Café Royal Oyster Bar, Circle Bar & Bistro Bar *B4*

7 City Art Centre Café *B4*
8 Favorit *C4*
9 Fruitmarket Café *B4*
10 Glass & Thompson *A3*
11 Hadrian's *B4*
12 Haldane's *A4*
13 Henderson's Bistro *A3*
14 Henderson's Salad Table *A3*

15 La Cuisine d'Odile *B1*
16 Laigh Bake House *A3*
17 Le Café St Honoré *B3*
18 Librizzi's *C4*
19 Mussel Inn *B3*
20 Rhodes & Co *B3*
21 Tapas Tree *A4*
22 Witchery by the Castle *C3*

Weaving Company, which has a real working mill where you can see tartan being woven and a small exhibition. ■ *Daily 0900-1730. Free entry to mill and a small charge for the exhibition. T2261555.*

A few doors further down, on the corner of Ramsay Lane, is the **Outlook Tower**, which houses a camera obscura. The device consists of a giant camera which sweeps around the city and beams the live images onto a tabletop screen, accompanied by a running commentary of the city's past. There's also an exhibition of photographs taken with a variety of home-made pinhole cameras and the rooftop viewing terrace offers fantastic views of the city. ■ *Daily Apr-Oct 0930-1800 (later in Jul/Aug), Nov-Mar 1000-1700. £4.25, £2.10 children, £3.10 concession. T2263709.*

A little further down, on the opposite side of the street, is the **Tolbooth Kirk**, whose distinctive spire is the highest in the city and a distinctive feature of the Edinburgh skyline. The building was originally intended to house the General Assembly of the Church of Scotland, but they moved across the street in the 1850s. It has recently been converted into **The Hub**, which houses the ticket centre for Edinburgh International Festival (see page174). The Hub also stages various events and is home to the excellent *Café Hub* (see page183).

Here, Castlehill becomes Lawnmarket. At number 477b, is **Gladstone's Land**, the most important surviving example of 17th-century tenement housing in the Old Town, where the cramped conditions meant that extension was only possible in depth or upwards. The magnificent six-storey building, completed in 1620, contains remarkable painted ceilings and was the home of an Edinburgh burgess, Thomas Gledstanes. The reconstructed shop booth on the ground floor has replicas of 17th-century goods and the first floor of the house has been refurbished as a typical Edinburgh home of the period. If you like what you see, then you can also stay here (see page 33). ■ *1 Apr-end-Oct Mon-Sat 1000-1700, Sun 1400-1700. £3.50, £2.50 concession. T2265856 (NTS).*

Further down Lawnmarket, steps lead down to Lady Stair's Close, where you'll find **Lady Stair's House**, another fine 17th-century house, though restored in pseudo-medieval style. It is now the home of the **Writer's Museum**, dedicated to the three giants of Scottish literature, Burns, Scott and Stevenson. ■ *Mon-Sat 1000-1700 and Sun 1400-1700 during Edinburgh Festival only. Free. T5294901.*

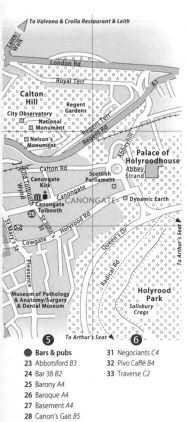

● Bars & pubs
23 Abbotsford *B3*
24 Bar 38 *B2*
25 Barony *A4*
26 Baroque *A4*
27 Basement *A4*
28 Canon's Gait *B5*
29 Iguana *C4*
30 Mondobbo *C2*
31 Negociants *C4*
32 Pivo Caffé *B4*
33 Traverse *C2*

Trips from Glasgow

Across George IV Bridge, at the top of the High Street, stands the **High Kirk of St Giles**, the only parish church of medieval Edinburgh and the home of Presbyterianism, where the firebrand preacher John Knox launched the Scottish Reformation. The Kirk, mistakenly called St Giles Cathedral, was given a major face-lift in the 19th century, covering most of its Gothic exterior, but parts of the original medieval building still survive, most notably the late-15th-century crowned tower. The four huge octagonal pillars which support the central tower are thought to date back to the previous Norman church, built in 1120 and razed to the ground by English invaders in the late 14th century. The highlight is the very beautiful **Thistle Chapel**, the Chapel of the Most Ancient and Most Noble Order of the Thistle (Scotland's foremost order of chivalry), at the rear. The elaborate ornamentation and fine carvings are exquisite (look out for the angel playing the bagpipes). There's a good café in the church crypt (see page 183). ■ *Easter-Sep Mon-Fri 0900-1900, Sat 0900-1700, Sun 1300-1700; Oct-Easter Mon-Sat 0900-1700, Sun 1300-1700. Free (donations welcome). T2259442.*

At the junction of the High Street and South Bridge is the **Tron Kirk**, which houses the Old Town tourist information centre, and recent excavations have revealed sections of Marlin's Wynd, which ran from the High Street down to the Cowgate. On the opposite side of the High Street, in Hyndford's Close, is the **Museum of Childhood**, which is full of kids screaming with excitement at the vast collection of toys, dolls, games and books, and nostalgic adults yelling "I used to have one of those!". ■ *Mon-Sat 1000-1700 and Sun 1400-1700 during the Festival. Free. T5294142.*

Almost directly opposite is the early 16th-century **Moubray House**, thought to be the oldest inhabited building in Edinburgh, but closed to the public. Next door is **John Knox's House**, one of the Royal Mile's most distinctive buildings and dating from the late 15th and early 16th centuries. It's not known for sure whether or not the Calvinist preacher actually lived here, but the house did belong to James Mossman, goldsmith to Mary, Queen of Scots. Today, the house is a rather austere museum devoted to the life and career of John Knox. ■ *Mon-Sat 1000-1700 (in Aug also Sun 1200-1700). £2.25, £1.75 concession, £0.75 child. T5569579.*

The High Street ends at the junction of St Mary's Street and Jeffrey Street,

Royal Mile detail

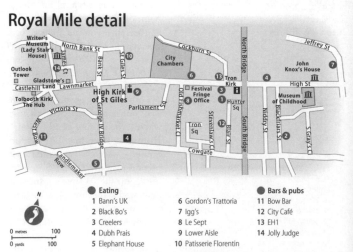

N

0 metres 100
0 yards 100

● Eating		● Bars & pubs
1 Bann's UK	6 Gordon's Trattoria	11 Bow Bar
2 Black Bo's	7 Igg's	12 City Café
3 Creelers	8 Le Sept	13 EH1
4 Dubh Prais	9 Lower Aisle	14 Jolly Judge
5 Elephant House	10 Patisserie Florentin	

24 hours in Edinburgh

For those unlucky enough to have only a day to spend in Edinburgh, the following itinerary should give a taste of why it is the most visited British city outside London.

*Start the day at the **Castle**, after which you'll need a breather and a well-earned coffee break at the **Elephant House**, on George IV Bridge. Afterwards, head across the road to the excellent **Museum of Scotland** in Chambers Street.*

*If you're feeling peckish, take a wee stroll down to **Black Bo's** on Blackfriars Street for a superb vegetarian lunch.*

*Then head down towards Princes Street and pop into the **National Gallery of Scotland**, the city's finest art gallery. If you've still got plenty of energy, head up The Mound and down the Royal Mile to the **Palace of Holyroodhouse**.*

*If the weather's fine, you may fancy a walk up to Calton Hill for the wonderful views, then head down to the nearby **Pivo Caffe** for a drink.*

*Then it's into a taxi and down to Leith for a superb seafood dinner at **Fishers**.*

where the city's eastern gate, Netherbow Port, once stood. The remaining part of the Royal Mile, the **Canongate**, was a separate burgh for over 700 years, taking its name from the canons (priests) of Holyrood Abbey. As it was near the Palace of Holyroodhouse, the area developed as the court quarter with several fine residences being built there. Though the Canongate went into decline once the court moved to London in the early 17th century, it could still boast an impressive number of aristocrats among its inhabitants, even in the late 18th century.

Heading downhill, on the left side is the late-16th-century **Canongate Tolbooth**, the original headquarters of the burgh administration, as well as the courthouse and burgh prison. It now houses **The People's Story**, a genuinely interesting museum which describes the life and work of the ordinary people of Edinburgh from the late 18th century to the present day. ■ *Mon-Sat 1000-1700 and Sun 1400-1700 during the Festival. Free. T5294057.*

The last few yards of the Royal Mile, which forms the approach to the precincts of Holyrood Abbey and Palace, is known as the **Abbey Strand**. Opposite the main gates of the Palace of Holyroodhouse is the site of the new **Scottish Parliament** building, scheduled for completion in Autumn 2002. At present the parliament sits in the Church of Scotland headquarters on The Mound.

At the foot of the Royal Mile is the royal palace, built by James IV at the beginning of the 16th century. The only remaining part of the Renaissance palace is the northwest tower, built as the private apartments of his son James V. Most of the original building was damaged by fire in 1543, and further in 1650 during its occupation by Cromwell's troops.

The present palace largely dates from the late 17th century when the original was replaced by a larger building for the Restoration of Charles II, although the newly crowned monarch never actually set foot in the place. It was built in the style of a French chateau, around a large arcaded quadrangle and is an elegant, finely proportioned creation. Designed by William Bruce, it incorporates a castellated southwest tower that balances perfectly the northwest original.

Inside, the oldest part of Holyroodhouse is open to the public and is entered through the **Great Gallery**, which takes up the entire first floor of the north wing. The **Royal Apartments**, in the northwest tower, are mainly

The Palace of Holyroodhouse

Trips from Glasgow

Festival City

Every year Edinburgh plays host to the world's biggest arts festival when the capital bursts into life in a riot of entertainment unmatched anywhere on Earth.

The Edinburgh Festival is actually a collection of different festivals running alongside each other, from the end of July through to the beginning of September.

The **International Festival** (Box office: The Hub, Castlehill, T4732000, www.eif.co.uk) tends to be a fairly highbrow affair and features large-scale productions of opera, ballet, classical music, dance and theatre performed in the larger venues. It ends with an open-air concert and spectacular fireworks display in Princes Street Gardens. The **Festival Fringe** (Box office: 180 High Street, T2265257, www.edfringe.com) began life in 1947 as an adjunct to the International, or "official" Festival, but has since grown so large that it now overshadows its big brother and is threatening to outgrow the city.

The **International Jazz and Blues Festival** (Box office: 29 St Stephen St, T2252202, www.jazzmusic.co.uk) kicks the whole thing off in July and features some of the world's leading performers, as well as many lesser known ones, playing in just about every pub in the city centre. The **International Film Festival** (Box office: Filmhouse, 88 Lothian Road, T2292550, www.edfilmfest.org.uk) is the UK's most important film festival and screens many brilliant new movies long before they reach London or the rest of the country. It is also the longest continually running event of its kind in the world. The **International Book Festival** (Box office: 137 Dundee St, T2285444, www.edbookfest.co.uk) may look like just a bunch of tents in Charlotte Square, but the marquees are full of some of the biggest names in literature holding readings, discussions, interviews and a whole range of workshops for adults and children. Although it's a separate event, the **Military Tattoo** (Box office: 32 Market St, T2251188, www.edintattoo.co.uk) set against the magnificent backdrop of Edinburgh Castle, is very much part of the Festival. It's an unashamedly kilt-and-bagpipes event, featuring Massed Pipes and Drums, display teams, dancers and bands from all over the world. There's also the **International Science Festival** (box office: Roxburgh's Court, off 323 High St, T2605860, www.sciencefestival.co.uk).

For full information about the International Festival events, and for access to the websites of all the Edinburgh Festivals visit the official festival site: www.go-edinburgh.co.uk

of note for their association with Mary, Queen of Scots and in particular for the most infamous incident in the palace's long history. It was here that the queen witnessed the brutal murder, organized by her husband, Lord Darnley, of her much-favoured Italian private secretary, David Rizzio. He was stabbed 56 times, on a spot marked by a brass plaque and, until it was removed quite recently, by a distinctly unsubtle fake bloodstain.

The later parts of the palace, known as the **State Apartments**, are less interesting, though decorated in Adam Style, with magnificent white stucco ceilings, particularly the Throne Room and Dining room. These are associated with later monarchs, such as George IV, who paid a visit in 1822, dressed in flesh-coloured tights and the briefest of kilts, rather appropriately perhaps, given the length of time he actually spent here. But it was Queen Victoria and Prince Albert who returned the palace to royal favour, as a stopover on their way to and from Balmoral. This custom has been maintained by her successors and the present queen still spends a short while here every year at the end of June and beginning of July. ■ *1 Apr-31 Oct daily 0930-1800; 1 Nov-31 Mar 0930-1630 (by guided tour only). Closed to the* *public during state functions and during the annual royal visit in the last two weeks of Jun and first week in Jul. £6.50, £3.30 child, £5 concession, £16.50 family. T5561096, www.royal.gove.uk*

In the grounds of the palace are the ruins of **Holyrood Abbey**. The abbey was, at its height, a building of great importance and splendour, and this is hinted at in the surviving parts of the west front. Much of it was destroyed, as were many of the county's finest ecclesiastical buildings, during the Reformation. During the reign of Charles I it was converted to the Chapel Royal and later to the Chapel of the Order of the Thistle, but it suffered severe damage once more, this time during the 1688 revolution. Some restoration work was attempted in the 18th century, but this only caused the roof to collapse in 1768, and since then the building has been left as a ruin. In the Royal Vault beneath the abbey are buried several Scottish Kings, including David II (son of Robert the Bruce), James II, James V and Lord Darnley, 'King Consort' to Mary, Queen of Scots.

Edinburgh is blessed with many magnificent green, open spaces, and none   Arthur's Seat
better than Holyrood Park (Queen's Park) – a 650-acre rugged wilderness of mountains, crags, lochs, moorland, marshes, fields and glens – all within walking distance of the city centre. This is one of the city's greatest assets, and it's easy to wander around till you're lost from the eyes and ears of civilization.

The best walk in the city is to the summit of **Arthur's Seat**, from where you get the very best view of the city, as well as of the Pentland Hills to the south, the Firth of Forth and of Fife to the north, and, on a clear day, the Highland peaks, 70 or 80 miles away. The walk to the top is a popular one, and easier than it looks. If you want to avoid the crowds during summer, then make an early start before breakfast and watch the sun rise over East Lothian.

There are several different routes, all of which take less than an hour. One starts opposite the palace car park and winds up by the foot of Salisbury Crags. This is the **Radical Road**, which traverses the ridge below the crags and continues on grass through 'Hunter's Bog' and up to the summit. You can also walk along the top of the crags, though there is no path.

South of the Royal Mile

Holyrood Road runs from the palace back to the Old Town, running parallel to and south of the Canongate. Close to the palace is one of the city's newest attractions, and now one of its most popular, **Dynamic Earth**. The visitor is taken on a fascinating journey of discovery from the very beginnings of time right through to the future. Using the state-of-the-art technology and special effects, you'll experience every environment on Earth and encounter many weird and wonderful creatures. An absolute must if you've kids in tow and you're guaranteed to find out things about our planet that you never knew. ■ *Apr-Oct daily 1000-1800; Nov-Mar Wed-Sun 1000-1700. £6.95, £3.95 child/concession, T5507800, www.dynamicearth.co.uk*

Holyrood Road continues west till it's crossed by the Pleasance and becomes the **Cowgate**, one of Edinburgh's oldest streets and once one of its finest. In recent years the Cowgate has become one of the city's best night-life streets, with many good pubs and clubs, but it attracts few tourists, and remains a spooky place to wander in alone after dark.

The Cowgate passes beneath George IV bridge to become the Grassmarket, a wide cobbled street closed in by tall tenements and dominated by the castle looming overhead. The Grassmarket, formerly the city's cattle market, has been the scene of some of the more notorious incidents in the

Trips from Glasgow

city's often dark and grisly past. At the west end, in a now vanished close, is where **Burke and Hare** lured their hapless murder victims, whose bodies they then sold to the city's medical schools. The gruesome business finally came to an end when Burke betrayed his partner in crime, who was duly executed in 1829. Today, the Grassmarket is one of the main nightlife centres, with lots of busy restaurants and bars lining its north side.

At the southwestern end of George IV Bridge, at the top of Candlemaker Row, is the statue of **Greyfriars Bobby**, the faithful little Skye Terrier who watched over the grave of his master John Gray, a shepherd from the Pentland Hills, for 14 years until his own death in 1872. The little statue, modelled from life and erected soon after his death, is one of the most popular, and sentimental, of Edinburgh's attractions, thanks to a number of tear-jerking movies of the wee dog's life.

The grave that Bobby watched over is in the nearby **Greyfriars Kirkyard**, one of Edinburgh's most prestigious burial grounds.

Greyfriars also has its its sinister tales. Some of the memorials are protected with metal lattices. This was to defeat the efforts of body-snatchers. One woman was buried here while in a trance and awoke when body-snatchers tried to remove the rings from her fingers. Greyfriars is particularly associated with the long struggle to establish the Presbyterian Church in Scotland. The kirkyard was the first place where the National Covenant was signed, on 28 February 1638. Later, in 1679, over 1,200 Covenanters were imprisoned by George 'Bloody' Mackenzie, former Lord Advocate, in a corner of the kirkyard for three months, and many died of exposure and starvation. The prison, known as the 'Black Mausoleum', behind the church on the left, is said to be haunted by Mackenzie's evil presence. **Greyfriars Kirk,** somewhat overshadowed by the graveyard, dates from 1620 and was the first church to be built in Edinburgh after the Reformation.

The Museums & around the University

Across the road from Greyfriars Bobby, running between George IV Bridge and South Bridge, is Chambers Street, home of two of the best museums in Scotland. On the corner of Chambers Street and George IV Bridge is the **Museum of Scotland**, a striking contemporary building housing a huge number of impressive Scottish collections. The museum is a veritable treasure trove of intriguing and important artefacts, including Roman gold and silver, Pictish and Gaelic carved stones and medieval armour. The museum also contains an excellent rooftop restaurant, *The Tower* (see page 180). ■ *Mon-Sat 1000-1700 (Tue till 2000), Sun 1200-1700. Free. Full disabled access to all floors. Free guided tours at 1415 (and 1800 on Tue). T2474422, www.nms.ac.uk*

Further east along Chambers Street, on the same side, is the **Royal Museum of Scotland**. The extensive and eclectic range of collections on display include everything from Classical Greek sculptures to stuffed elephants, from whale skeletons to Native North American totem poles. It's all here, beautifully presented in a wonderful Victorian building. Of particular note is the largely hands-on technology section which features a dazzling collection of machinery of the Industrial Revolution. The magnificent atrium soars high above and makes a very impressive entrance to what is probably the most complete museum in the country. To cap it all, there's a great café (see page 183). ■ *Same opening hours as the Museum of Scotland. T2257534.*

Alongside the Royal Museum is the earliest surviving part of the **University of Edinburgh**, the **Old College**, built between 1789 and 1834, whose main courtyard is reached through the massive arch on Nicolson Street.

Edinburgh University is the largest in Scotland, founded in 1582 (the oldest is St Andrews). The finest section of the Old College is the **upper library**, a magnificent architectural achievement, which is now used for mainly ceremonial occasions, but can be viewed by guided tour in summer. The upper museum hall, once housed the Royal Museum before it moved to its present site, and now is the home of the **Talbot Rice Gallery**, which features the university's collection of Renaissance European painting as well as several temporary exhibitions every year. ■ *Talbot Rice Gallery open Tue-Sat 1000-1700 (daily during the Fesitval). Free. T6502210. There are also free lunchtime guided tours of the Old College 19 Jul-28 Aug, Mon-Sat, starting at 1300 in the reception, T6506379. For more details T6502252.*

Almost opposite the Festival Theatre, at 18 Nicolson Street, is the Royal College of Surgeons, which houses the **Museum of Pathology and Anatomy**, a gruesome freak show of various diseased and abnormal body parts. ■ *Open only by booking well in advance and to groups of at least 12. T5271649.* Hidden behind the Royal College of Surgeons, at 19 Hill Square, is the **Sir Jules Thorn Exhibition of the History of Surgery and Dental Museum**, a bit of a mouthfull but a hidden gem which outlines the history of surgery in the city since the early 16th century. It's all a bit ghoulish but great for kids. ■ *Mon-Fri 1400-1600. Free. T5271600.*

The New Town

The neoclassical New Town, one of the boldest schemes of civic architecture in the history of Europe, is what makes Edinburgh a truly world-class city, every bit as impressive as Paris or Prague, Rome or Vienna.

The southernmost terrace of the New Town plan was never intended to be the most important, but **Princes Street** has developed into the city's main thoroughfare and principal shopping street. It is also one of the most visually spectacular streets in the world, because the south side has remained undeveloped, allowing superb uninterrupted views of the Castle Rock, across the valley now occupied by Princes Street Gardens. Princes Street may be Edinburgh's equivalent of Oxford Street in London, but at least the magnificent view makes walking its length a more pleasant experience.

Running along most of the south side of Princes Street are the sunken **Princes Street Gardens**, which are a very pleasant place to sit and relax during the summer. Standing in East Princes Street Gardens, is the towering **Scott Monument**, over 200 ft high and resembling a huge Gothic spaceship, and built in 1844 as a fitting tribute to one of Scotland's greatest literary figures. Beneath the archway is a statue of Sir Walter Scott, and there are also 64 statuettes of characters from his novels. The monument is open to the public, and a 287-step staircase climbs to a platform near the top of the spire, from where you get wonderful views. ■ *Mar-May and Oct Mon-Sat 0900-1800, Sun 1000-1800; Jun-Sep Mon-Sat 0900-2000, Sun 1000-1800; Nov-Feb 0900-1600. £2.50.*

A little further west, Princes Street gardens are divided in two by **The Mound**, a huge artificial slope that runs from George IV Bridge in the Old Town down to Princes Street. At the junction of The Mound and Princes Street are two of Edinburgh's most impressive neoclassical public buildings, the **Royal Scottish Academy** and the **National Gallery of Scotland**, both designed by William Playfair between 1822 and 1845 in the style of Greek temples. The oldest of the two is the Royal Scottish Academy, which presents an annual exhibition by its members from April to July and special exhibitions during the Festival. To the rear of the RSA, the National Gallery of Scotland houses the largest permanent collection of Old Masters outside London, many of which are on loan from The Duke of Sutherland. Around the galleries is a wide space which has long been used as Edinburgh's version of Hyde Park Corner. ■ *National Gallery of Scotland: Mon-Sat 1000-1700, Sun 1200-1700. Free (charges sometimes for loan exhibitions). T6246200, www.natgalscot .ac.uk The RSA is closed for refurbishment and due to reopen in 2003.*

Running to the north and parallel to Princes Street is **George Street**, a bustling thoroughfare of upmarket shops, banks, offices and fashionable bars and restaurants. At the western end of the street is **Charlotte Square**, designed by Robert Adam in 1791. It is now the heart of the city's financial community, home to bankers, investment-fund managers, stockbrokers, corporate lawyers, accountants and insurance executives. Charlotte Square has long been the most prestigious address in the city, particularly the **north side**, the oldest part and the best preserved. Number six is the official residence of the Secretary of State for Scotland. The upper floors of number seven are the official residence of the Moderator of the General Assembly of the Church of Scotland, while the lower floors are open to the public as the **Georgian House**, which gives a fascinating insight into how Edinburgh's gentry lived in the late 18th century. The house has been lovingly restored by the National Trust for Scotland and is crammed with period furniture and hung with fine paintings. The NTS has its head offices on the south side at number 27. ■ *1 Mar-31 Oct Mon-Sat 1000-1700, Sun 1400-1700; Nov-Dec Mon-Sat 1100-1600, Sun 1400-1600. £5, £4 concession . T2263318.*

Parallel to George Street, and slightly downhill from it, is **Queen Street**, the most northerly terrace of James Craig's New Town plan, bordered by Queen Street Gardens to the north. The only public building of interest here is the **Scottish National Portrait Gallery**, at the far eastern end of the street, a huge late-19th-century red sandstone building, modelled on the Doge's Palace in Venice. The gallery contains a huge range of pictures of notable Scots from the 16th century to the present day. It also has a good café (see page 183). ■ *Mon-Sat 1000-1700, Sun 1400-1700 (till 1800 and from 1100 on Sun during the festival). Free. T6246200.*

Calton Hill   From the east end of Princes Street rise the slopes of Calton Hill. The summit is covered with many fine buildings, which probably earned Edinburgh the epithet 'Athens of the North'. The climb to the top is via the stairs at the east end of Waterloo Place. The views from the top are simply stunning, especially up the length of Princes Street and the sweep of the Forth Estaury.

On the west side of the hill, overlooking the St James Centre, is the old **City Observatory**, built by Playfair in 1818 for his uncle, a renowned mathematician and philosopher. It was abandoned in 1895 when light pollution became too great and relocated to Blackford Hill in the south of the city. The observatory equipment is still used by students and the small, domed pavilion now houses the **Edinburgh Experience**, a 20-minute 3-D presentation of the city's history. ■ *Apr-Oct daily 1000-1700. £2, £1.20 child.* The observatory complex also contains the **Old Observatory**, a fantasy Gothic castle and the last surviving building of James Craig, the designer of the New Town.

Calton Hill is full of monuments of all shapes and sizes. Southwest of the observatory is the **Monument to Dugald Stewart** (1753-1828), a Playfair construction commemorating an obscure University professor. A little further south, overlooking Regent Road, is **Nelson's Monument**, a 108-ft tower built in 1816 to commemorate Nelson's victory at the Battle of Trafalgar. It's a strange-looking structure, built in the shape of an upturned telescope, and every day, at precisely one o' clock, a large ball is still dropped from the mast at the top to mark the time for ships in the Firth of Forth. It's worth climbing to the top of the monument, for the panoramic views are even better. ■ *Apr-Sep Mon 1300-1600, Tue-Sat 1000-1600; Oct-Mar Mon-Sat 1000-1500. £2.* Standing beside Nelson's monument is the **National Monument**, an over-ambitious project begun in 1822 by Playfair as a memorial to those who fell in the Napoleonic Wars. The intention was to build a replica of the Parthenon in Athens, incorporating catacombs for the burial of Scotland's greatest figures, but the money ran out and it never got further than what you can see today – 12 huge columns which have come to be known as 'Edinburgh's Disgrace'.

Further north, beyond the northern boundary of the New Town and the Water of Leith, is the district of Inverleith, where you'll find Edinburgh's gorgeous **Royal Botanic Garden**, on Inverleith Row. Contained within its 72 acres is a mind-boggling variety of plants and trees, as well as walkways, ornamental gardens, various hothouses and huge open spaces, with not a dog poo in sight. Many of the exotic species you can see were discovered by Scottish collectors during their expeditions around the globe. At the southern end of the gardens, at the highest point, is **Inverleith House**, a fine Georgian mansion which stages a changing programme of exhibitions. The Terrace Café is a good place for lunch (see page 183), with stupendous views across the New Town to the castle. ■ *Nov-Feb daily from 1000-1600; till 1800 Mar-Apr and Sep-Oct; till 2000 May-Aug. Free, but voluntary donations welcome. Take buses 8, 17, 23 and 27 from city centre. T5527171.*

North & west of the New Town

From the west end of Princes Street, Queensferry Street runs all the way to the Forth Road Bridge. Only 10 minutes from Princes Street it reaches the wooded valley of the **Water of Leith**, the little river which flows from the Pentland Hills to the port of Leith where it enters the Firth of Forth. The road crosses the steep valley along the 100-ft-high **Dean Bridge**, a remarkable feat of engineering, built by Thomas Telford in the 1830s.

About 10 minutes' walk from Dean Bridge, set in spacious wooded grounds along Belford Road, is the **Scottish National Gallery of Modern Art**, which is definitely worth visiting. It opened to the public in 1984 as the first ever gallery in Britain devoted to 20th century art. The hugely impressive permanent collection features everything from the Impressionists to Hockney and is now second in Britain only to the Tate Museums in London. There are also frequent temporary exhibitions, and don't miss the excellent café, especially if the sun is shining on the terrace. Across the street is the new **Dean Gallery** (same opening hours as above and also free), featuring the work of Edinburgh-born artist **Sir Eduardo Paolozzi**. It also houses a major Dada and Surrealist collection and exhibitions of contemporary art. ■ *Both galleries open Mon-Sat 1000-1700, Sun 1400-1700. Free. A free bus leaves the National Gallery and visits the Portrait Gallery then these galleries. It leaves the National Gallery at 1100 and every hour on the hour till 1600. For more details T6246200.*

Three miles west of the city centre, is **Edinburgh Zoo**, by far the largest in Scotland, set in 80 acres on the side of Corstorphine Hill. Whatever you think of zoos, this one is highly respected for its serious work as well as being an enormous amount of fun. There are over 1,000 animals from all over the world, but the zoo is best known for its penguins – the largest breeding colony of Antarctic penguins anywhere outside Antarctica itself. You can watch the

Trips from Glasgow

famous penguin parade at 1400 daily (March-October weather permitting) and see them swimming underwater in the world's largest penguin pool. ■ *Apr-Sep daily 0900-1800; Oct-Mar 0900-1630. £7, £4 child. T3349171, www.edinburghzoo .org.uk There are numerous buses from Haymarket and Princes St.*

Leith

Leith Walk leads from Princes Street down to the old port of **Leith**, which has a distinct flavour all of its own. Millions have been spent on restoring many of its fine historic buildings, and it is now one of the best parts of the city for eating and drinking, with scores of fashionable restaurants, bistros and bars (see below. At the same time private developers have been converting old warehouses and office buildings into expensive dockside flats.

Leith's main attraction is the **Royal Yacht Britannia**, which is now moored at its own purpose-built Ocean Terminal, complete with swanky restaurants, bars and shops. The old ship is well worth visiting, despite the rather steep entrance charge, and a genuine and fascinating insight into the lives of the royals. It's like stepping into a 1950s time warp and you'll be amazed (or appalled) at the sheer ordinariness of it all. ■ *Mon-Fri 1030-1630, Sat/Sun 0930-1630; till 1930 fri-Sun in Aug. £7.75, £5.95 concession, £3.75 child. To pre-book tickets T5555566 (daily 0900-1730) or at the Tattoo Office, 32 Market St. Guide Friday and LRT buses (No X50) run a shuttle bus to and from Waverley Bridge every 20 mins from 1010 (0950 Sat/Sun Mar-Oct) till 1605 Mon-Fri and 1650 Sat/Sun (till 1910 Fri-Sun in Aug).*

Eating and drinking

Expensive **Old Town** *The Atrium*, 10 Cambridge St (same building as the Traverse Theatre), T2288882. More Lothian Rd than Old Town. Award-winning Scottish cooking in elegant modern surroundings. This outstanding restaurant is one of the best in town, but by no means the most expensive. Open Mon-Fri 1200-1430, 1800-2230, Sat 1800-2230. Upstairs is its stylish sister bistro, *blue*. *Iggs*, 15 Jeffrey St, T5578184, a superb Spanish restaurant which has recently expanded to include a new tapas bar, Barioja, next door. Serves the best tapas in town at lunch, then in the evening changes into a contemporary Scottish restaurant with a formidable reputation. Open Mon-Sat 1200-1430, 1800-2230. *Librizzi's*, 22a Nicolson St, T6681997. At the lower end of this category and great value. If you like Italian food, especially fish, there are few, if any, better places to eat. Open Mon-Sat 1200-1400, 1730-2300. *The Tower*, Museum of Scotland, Chambers St, T2253003. Still the place to be seen amongst the corporate set, and recent reports of pretentious service can't detract from superb Scottish menu and magnificent views across the city skyline from the rooftop terrace. No smoking. Open daily 1200-2300. *The Witchery by the Castle*, 352 Castlehill, T2255613. Dining doesn't get much more atmospheric than here in one of Edinburgh's finest, on the Royal Mile. Downstairs, in a converted schoolyard, is the impossibly romantic *Secret Garden*, a real hidden gem. Both restaurants share the same glorious Scottish menu. This was formerly a meeting place for Satanists, so go on, be a devil. Open daily 1200-1600, 1730-2330.

New Town *Café Royal Oyster Bar*, 17a West Register St, T5564124. An Edinburgh institution and much-loved by numerous celebrities. The ornate tiles and stained-glass windows create an atmosphere of Victorian elegance and opulence – just make sure you look at the prices first! There are better seafood restaurants in town but none are as classy. Open daily 1200-1400, 1900-2200. The adjoining bar is just as impressive (see page 184). *Duck's at Le Marche Noir*, 2-4 Eyre Pl, T5581608. Classic French provincial cooking (perhaps Edinburgh's finest) in sumptuous surroundings. Complemented by an extensive wine list. Open Mon-Fri 1200-1400, 1900-2200, Sat 1900-2230, Sun 1830-2130. *Haldane's*, 39 Albany St, T5568407. Smart Scottish country house cuisine in the centre of town. Excellent value set lunch. No smoking. Open Mon-Thu 1200-1400, 1800-2130, Fri till 2200, Sat 1800-2230, Sun 1800-2130. *Hadrian's*, 2 North Bridge (under the *Balmoral Hotel*), T5575000. Excellent modern Scottish cuisine with nouvelle-ish tendencies, soothing and well-designed modern surroundings. Superb value for money. Open daily 1200-1430, 1830-2230 (Sun 1230-1500). *Le Café Saint-Honoré*, 34 Thistle Street La, T2262211. Tucked away in a little side street, this place couldn't be any more French. An authentic corner of Paris in the heart of Scotland's capital. The food is seriously French, too, and seriously priced, but seriously wonderful. Seriously! Open Mon-Fri 1200-1415, 1900-2200, Sat 1900-2200 only. *36*, 36 Great King St, T556-3636. Basement restaurant of the *Howard Hotel*. One of the places to eat in the capital. The very best of modern Scottish cuisine in contemporary, minimalist surroundings. Open Sun-Fri 1200-1400, 1900-2200, Sat 1900-2200. No smoking.

Leith *Fishers*, 1 The Shore, T5545666. This is one of Edinburgh's finest fish restaurants, in an area packed full of them. It's housed in the tower at the end of The Shore. Open daily 1215-2230. *(fitz)henry*, 19 Shore Pl, T5556625. This stylish warehouse brasserie is one of only two city eateries to receive a Michelin Red M (the other is *The Atrium*) for its genuinely original and excellent Scottish cooking. Open Mon-Thu 1230-1430, 1830-2230, Fri/Sat till 2230. *Restaurant Martin Wishart*, 54 The Shore, T5533557. French-influenced cuisine at its finest from the renowned chef. Unfussy decor for a memorable meal. Open Tue-Fri 1200-1400, 1900-2200, Sat 1900-2200. *Skippers*, 1a Dock Pl, T5541018. Many in-the-know would say this is the best place to eat seafood in town. This nautical bistro is small and intimate, and very popular, so you'll need to book. Open Mon-Sat 1230-1400, 1900-2200. *The Vintners Rooms*, 87 Giles St, T5546767. These former wine vaults dating from the 17th century now house a restaurant and bar, both lit by candlelight and oozing historic charm and romance. The food is French provincial and excellent, as is the service. Meals in the bar at lunch-times are cheaper. Open Mon-Sat 1200-1400, 1900-2230.

Old Town *The Apartment*, 7-13 Barclay Pl, T2286456. South of the Old Town is Edinburgh's most talked-about new eating establishment. A hip and happening place where the portions are as big as the owner's personality. A truly different eating experience with dishes divided into 'CHLs' (Chunky Healthy Lines), 'Slabs', 'Fish Things' and 'Other Things'. All in all, a great night out. Open Mon-Fri 1800-2300, Sat/Sun 1200-1500, 1800-2300. *Bann's UK*, 5 Hunter Sq, T2261112. Just off the Royal Mile by the Tron Kirk. A popular street performance place during the festival so perfect for an al fresco lunch. Busy but laid-back and offering an adventurous range of dishes. Great value. Open daily 1000-2300. *Black Bo's*, 57-61 Blackfriars St, T5576136. Vegetarian restaurant that is one of the city's truly great culinary experiences. So good even the most fanatical carnivore might even give up meat. Supremely imaginative use of various fruits gives the exotically delicious dishes a real splash of colour. Their lunch is superb value at under £10. The bar next door serves the same food. Open Mon-Sat 1200-1400, 1800-2230, Sun 1800-2230. *Creelers*, 3 Hunter Sq, T2204447. Wonderfully fresh seafood and a great location beside the Tron church, with outdoor seating in the summer. You can push the boat out in the more formal restaurant at the rear or save your pennies in the busy bistro at the front, where the cheap 2-course lunch is great value. Open Mon-Thu 1200-1430, 1730-2230, Fri/Sat till 2300, Sun 1730-2230. *Dubh Prais*, 123b High St, T5575732. Small basement restaurant in the heart of the Royal Mile offering

Mid-range

Trips from Glasgow

the best of traditional Scottish cooking, as well as more contemporary innovations. Dinner is à la carte, but you can enjoy a two-course set lunch for a tenner. Open Tue-Sat 1200-1400, 1830-2230. *Le Sept*, 7 Old Fishmarket Close, T2255428. Down a steep, cobbled close off the High Street below St Giles. This lively little restaurant is famed for its superb crêpes but also has a 3-course set menu offering good French bistro-type food. Separate no-smoking room. Open Mon-Thu 1200-1345, 1800-2200, Fri 1200-2300, Sat 1200-2230, Sun 1200-2130.

New Town *A Room in the Town*, 18 Howe St, T2258204. Excellent-quality Scottish produce presented with flair and imagination in a friendly atmosphere. Exceptional value. BYOB. Open daily 1200-1500, 1730 till late. *The Lost Sock Diner*, 11 East London St, T5576097. Relaxed by day and buzzing by night, this bistro offers a huge range of dishes at unbeatable value. Open Mon 0900-1600, Tue-Sat 0900-2200, Sun 1000-1700. *Maison Hector*, 47-49 Deanhaugh St, T3325328. Described as Stockbridge's answer to Central Perk, this is one of Edinburgh's original bistros but still one of the best. Restaurant serves a fine Scottish/French menu while the café-bar area is just brill for weekend brunch. Open Mon-Wed 1100-2400, Thu/Fri till 0100, Sat 1030-0100, Sun 1030-2400. *The Mussel Inn*, 61-65 Rose St, T2255979. What could be better than a huge pot of steaming fresh mussels and a bowl of fantastic chips? Not much, judging by the popularity of this place, in the heart of pub-land. A must for seafood-lovers. Open Mon-Thu 1200-1500, 1800-2200, Fri/Sat 1100-2200. *Rhodes & Co*, 3-15 Rose St, T2209190. Recently opened by TV celebrity chef Gary Rhodes. Very retro (food and decor), serving British standards as you've never tasted before. Open Mon-Sat 1200-1430, 1800-2230, Sun 1200-1430. *Tapas Tree*, 1 Forth St, T5567718. This Spanish restaurant, has built up a reputation for excellent food and service. Their tapas are good value, particularly the lunch-time specials, and they even offer a vegetarian selection. Booking advised at weekends. Open daily 1100-2300.

Leith *Malmaison Brasserie*, 1 Tower Pl, T468-5000. Attached to the acclaimed *Malmaison Hotel*. They serve excellent French brasserie food in stylish surroundings. Open Mon-Fri 0700-1000, 1200-1400, 1800-2230 (Sat from 0800, Sun till 2200). *The Shore*, 3-4 The Shore, T5535080. One of the city's best fish restaurants with a real fire and huge windows overlooking the Water of Leith. No smoking. You can eat from the restaurant menu in the adjoining bar. Open Mon-Sat 1100-2400, Sun 1230-2300. *The Waterfront*, 1c Dock Pl, T5547427. Great for fish or just for a relaxing drink. Seating in the conservatory or cosy booths. Open Mon-Thu 1200-2300, Fri/Sat till 2400, Sun 1230-2230.

Cheap **Old Town** *Gordon's Trattoria*, 231 High St, T2257992. Great-value Italian food, which is why it's so popular. Great for people-watching in summer when tables spill out onto the street. Open Sun-Thu 1200-2400, Fri and Sat till 0300.

New Town *à table*, 4 Howe St, T2205335. Eating here is like sitting in someone's French farmhouse kitchen. There's one huge table in the middle where you're served with healthy continental dishes made from organic produce. Open Mon-Fri 0830-1730, Sat 1000-1800, Sun 1000-1600. *Bar Napoli*, 75 Hanover St, T2252600. Basic Italian which offers much the same as the others in the street but which has the added advantage of offering the best-value set lunch and it stays open late. Open Mon-Thu and Sun 1200-0200, Fri/Sat 1200-0400. *Henderson's Salad Table*, 94 Hanover St, T2252131. This basement vegetarian self-service restaurant is the oldest in the city and still one of the best. It can get very busy but manages to combine efficiency with comfort. Excellent-value 2-course set lunch. Open Mon-Sat 0800-2230. Upstairs is their deli and takeaway, and round the corner, at 25 Thistle St, is *Henderson's Bistro*, T2252605, which provides the same excellent food but in more intimate surroundings, with table service and at only slightly higher prices. *La Cuisine D'Odile*, 13 Randolph Cres, T2255685. Hidden away in the French Institute, this is genuine quality French cuisine at amazingly low prices. Great views from the terrace in the summer. Open Tue-Sat 1200-1400 only.

Old Town *Café Couronne*, Royal Museum of Scotland, 2 Chambers St, T2474111. Elegant pâtisserie in the museum foyer serving good coffee and great cakes and pastries. No smoking. Open Mon-Sat 1000-1600, Sun 1200-1600. At the back of the museum, next to the Lumière cinema, is *Petite Couronne*, a self-service café-bar offering good-value snacks. No smoking. Open Mon-Thu 1000-1630, Fri/Sat 1000-1630, 1700-2030, Sun 1200-1630, 1700-2030. *Café Hub*, Castle Hill, T4732015. Coffee drinking doesn't get any more stylishly laid-back than this. The food on offer is tasty, inventive and available all day and evening, and there's seating outside on the terrace in summer. The Hub plays host to the Festival Club, as well as housing the ticket centre for the International Festival (see page 174). No smoking. Open daily 0930-2300. *Café Lucia*, Festival Theatre, 13-29 Nicolson St, T6621112. Light, airy and contemporary café with a relaxed feel. Usual array of light snacks on offer. No smoking. Open from 1000 till half an hour after the show (from 1600 on Sun). *City Art Centre Café*, 1 Market St, T2203359. Good coffee and cakes and an affordable selection of main dishes in a spacious environment with helpful staff. No smoking. Open Mon-Sat 0830-1700, Sun (only during exhibitions) 1100-1700. *Elephant House*, 21 George IV Bridge, T2205355. Very studenty – a great place to linger over coffee and bagels or one of many cheap snacks and main courses. Mellow vibe and lots of elephants (on the walls, not at the tables). Café bar by evening with live music. Open Mon-Fri 0800-2300, Sat/Sun 1000-2300. *Favorit*, 19-20 Teviot Place, T2206880. Café/bar/deli with an Italian-American look. A cool place to stop for a quick coffee and sandwich at any time of the day or night. Open daily 0830-0300. Also at 30-32 Leven St. *Fruitmarket Café*, Fruitmarket Gallery, 45 Market St, T2261843. One of the coolest cafés in town with windows large enough to guarantee being seen. A great place for a quick, cheap and tasty lunch, or just for coffee and a chat. No smoking. Open Mon-Sat 1100-1700, Sun 1200-1700. *The Lower Aisle*, St Giles Cathedral, High St (entrance via Parliament Square), T2255147. This self-service café underneath the cathedral is popular with the legal profession. Good for a cheap light lunch. Open Mon-Fri 0930-1630, Sun 0900-1400. *Patisserie Florentin*, 8 St Giles St, T2256267. Large and lively place to stop for a coffee, a filled croissant and a generous slice of Edinburgh life. Open Sun-Fri 0700-2100, Sat 0700-2200.

New Town *Blue Moon*, 1 Barony St, T5562788. Gay café in the city's 'pink triangle'. Good selection of cakes, also snacks and meals. Gets busy later in the evening with pre-clubbers. Open Mon-Fri 1100-0030, Sat/Sun 0900-0030. *Glass & Thompson*, 2 Dundas St, T5570909. Coffee shop and deli with the emphasis on quality food. Popular with local residents who know a good thing when they see (and taste) it. Open Mon-Fri 0830-1830, Sat 0830-1730, Sun 1100-1630. *The Laigh Bake House*, 117a Hanover St, T2251552. Downstairs from the hustle and bustle is a quiet little corner of the Orkneys and Edinburgh's oldest coffee house. The food is made from purely organic ingredients. Open Mon-Sat 0830-1700. *The Queen Street Café*, The Scottish National Portrait Gallery, 1 Queen St, T5572844. The best scones and caramel shortcake in town, not to mention excellent value snacks and light meals, served in grand surroundings. No smoking. Open Mon-Sat 1000-1630, Sun 1400-1630. *Terrace Café*, Royal Botanic Garden, Inverleith Row, T5520616. Set in the grounds next to Inverleith House, this is little more than a school canteen, but the views of the castle, Old Town and Arthur's Seat take some beating. No smoking. Open daily 0930-1800. *Valvona & Crolla*, 19 Elm Row, top of Leith Walk, T5566066. More authentically Italian than almost anything you'd find in New

Cafés

Trips from Glasgow

York. Great home cooking and the best cappuccino in town. Needless to say, somewhere this good is very, very popular. No smoking. Open Mon-Sat 0800-1700.

Bars & pubs **Old Town** *The Bow Bar*, 80 West Bow (halfway down Victoria St), T2267667. No nonsense, no frills pub for real ale enthusiasts and those who long for the days before mobile phones and sun-dried tomatoes. A dependable pint in an ever-changing world. Open Mon-Sat till 2330, Sun till 2300.*The Canon's Gait*, 232 Canongate, T5564481. Worth a stop, especially around lunchtime for its excellent-value food. *City Café*, 19 Blair St, T2200125. Style bar done out like an American diner with chrome-topped bar and booth seating. Still the busiest and most vibrant pre-club bar. Set on two floors with a large bar area with pool tables to the rear on the top floor and smaller bar where funky House/Garage DJ's play at weekends. Open daily till 0100. *EH1*, 197 High St, T2205277. Attracts workers from the High Street area during the week and popular with tourists sitting in the sun. In the vicinity of the main clubs which are situated around the Cowgate/Royal Mile area and is a modern furbished bar with a small area at the back where DJ's play on Fri-Sat nights. Open daily 0930-0100. *Iguana*, 41 Lothian St, T2204288. Next door to *Negociants*. Refurbished from old student haunt the *Bristo Bar*. Smart deco and DJ's Fri/Sat night. Large video screens. Can be too noisy to maintain any form of conversation. Popular with clubbers going to *Potterrow* which is a student venue. The food is excellent and the menu imaginative, but it gets busy at night, so book if you want to be sure of a table. Open daily 0900-0100. *Jolly Judge*, 7 James Court, T2252669. Turn off the High Street just down from the castle, down a narrow close, then down the stairs to reach this cosy, intimate wee place. Live folk music and good-value bar food. Open Mon/Sun till 2300, Tue-Sat till 2400. *Mondobbo*, 34 Bread St, T2215555. Part of the supremely stylish *Point Hotel*, and don't it show. Popular with local office workers for a sophisticated light lunch or after work for happy-hour cocktails. Open Mon-Thu and Sun till 2400, Fri/Sat till 0100. *Negociants*, 45-47 Lothian St, T2256313. Is it a bar, is it a bistro? Both, actually. Great for a relaxing lunch-time beer or coffee and popular with students and professionals alike. At night it's a fave late-night watering hole with DJs and dancing downstairs. The menu is international in flavour, excellent value and available till 0230. Good place for a relaxing Sun brunch. Open daily 0900-0300. *Traverse Bar Café*, Traverse Theatre, 10 Cambridge St, T2285383. Very stylish bar that's popular with luvvies, suits and students. Excellent and affordable food served at all times and regular special drinks offers. Open Mon till 2300, Tue-Thu and Sun till 2400, Fri/Sat till 0100.

New Town *The Abbotsford*, 3 Rose St, T2255276. Big, old reliable pub in a street that's largely lost its drinking appeal. Good, solid pub lunches and a restaurant upstairs that's open in the evenings. Open Mon-Sat till 2300. *Bar 38*, 126-128 George St, T2206180. Large, elaborately decorated and popular with the after-work, young professional crowd. And, yes, those toilets are worth checking out! Open Mon-Sat till 0100, Sun till 2400. *Barony Bar*, 81-85 Broughton St, T5570546. Stylish and lively place where you won't feel like you've gatecrashed your young nephew's party. Very busy at weekends. Good bar food. Open till 2400, weekends till 0030. *Baroque*, 39-41 Broughton St, T5570627. Brightly coloured décor that's not quite as loud as the young party lovers who frequent this popular bar. Usual range of trendy grub and a great selection of juices. Open daily till 0100. *The Basement*, 10-12a Broughton St, T5570097. This Broughton Street original feels like it's been around for ever and is just as hip and happening as ever. Good bistro food with a mainly Mexican flavour. Open daily 1200-2400. *Café Royal Circle Bar*, 19 West Register St, T5564124. You can't help feeling spoiled in these elegant and civilized surroundings. Adjacent to the famous *Café Royal Oyster Bar* (see 'page 180). Treat yourself to the seafood menu while enjoying the sumptuous splendour. Open Mon-Wed 1100-2300, Thu till

2400, Fri/Sat till 0100, Sun till 2300. Next door upstairs is the *Café Royal Bistro Bar*, a big favourite with the rugger fraternity. *The Cumberland Bar*, 1 Cumberland Street, T5583134. Classic New Town bar that oozes refinement and respectability. Fine selection of real ales, a beer garden and some decent nosh. A good place to kick back and while away an hour or several. Open Mon-Wed till 2330, Thu-Sat till 2400, Sun till 2200. *Pivo Caffé*, 2-6 Calton Rd, T5572925. At the top of Leith Walk opposite the St James Centre. Czech-themed bar offering a thick slice of Prague. Very good Czech beer and huge portions of grub.

Background

10

Background

History

There's an old saying that Edinburgh is the capital but Glasgow has the capital. This dates back to the late 19th century, when Glasgow was known as the 'Second City of the Empire'. It was a thriving, cultivated city grown rich on the profits from its cotton mills, coal mines and shipyards, and a city that knew how to flaunt its wealth. The heavy industries have long gone, but Glasgow has lost none of its energy and excitement, and its people possess a style and swagger that makes their Edinburgh counterparts look staid and stuffy by comparison.

Despite the fact that Glasgow really made its mark on the world from the mid-18th century onwards, the city has a long, eventful history that dates back to the very origins of Christianity. By 1175 Glasgow had been granted burgh status (the Scottish equivalent of a borough to chartered town) and the establishment of a cathedral in the 12th century and Scotland's second university in the 15th century brought added status to the city. It was made a royal burgh in 1611, and continued to expand until by the end of the 17th century it had become second only to Edinburgh in terms of size and commercial importance.

In the beginning

The city's exact origin, like so much else here, is a matter of some conjecture. There is no doubt that there was a Roman presence here in the first and second centuries AD, evidenced by the proximity of the Antonine Wall to the city boundary. This wall was built by the Romans between the Firths of Clyde and Forth in order to stem the flow of nasty northern tribes southwards. The Roman invaders eventually left for home when their sun tans began to fade, but their religious influence remained when in the fifth century Glasgow received more visitors, in the shape of the Roman-educated Christian missionary St Ninian and his sidekick St Kentigern, or Mungo as he affectionately became known.

Mungo it was who established an episcopal church somewhere near the site of the present city, though its precise location is unkown, some time towards the end of the sixth century. Legend has it that he did this at the request of Rydderch Hael, King of Strathclyde, though bearing in mind that Mungo is claimed to have assisted the king's wife in her adulterous ways, this was perhaps more out of guilt than generosity.

As the years passed a cult grew up surrounding Mungo and his mother, St Thenew (or Thaney), attracting pilgrims to the fledgling community from near and far. Intertestingly enough, Mungo's mother name evolved to become St Enoch, and her memory has been preserved in the shape of a huge glass-covered shopping mall. Mungo, meanwhile, became the patron saint of Glasgow, no less, and he is seen on the civic coat-of-arms, together with two salmon (see box on next page), a tree, a bird and a bell. The bird represents the robin redbreast which he brought back to life, while the tree was originally a hazel branch which Mungo miraculously caused to burst into flame. Sccoridng to legend, the bell is the hand-bell used by the saints of the Celtic Church to call their flocks to worship. The city's motto, 'Let Glasgow Flourish' is meant to represent Mungo's ability to work for the common good.

Glasgow had been part of the Kingdom of Strathclyde, but following the death of King Owen in 1018 it became embroiled in the dynastic struggles of the emerging Scottish kingdom. Not much is known of this period until the establishment of a bishopric in 1114 under direct papal authority. This led to the construction of the

A fishy tale

It's not every day you hear about a saint colluding in an act of adultery, but trust Glasgow to come up with an example of such an unsaintly act.

Though it is many years since salmon were caught in the Clyde, two appear in the city's coat of arms. Each fish has a ring in its mouth, recalling an old local legend.

Queen Languoreth of Strathclyde was given a ring by her husband, King Rydderch Hael, but then promptly gave it to her lover.

The king found the lover wearing the ring as he slept beside the Clyde. He took the ring and threw it into the water, and then went to his wife and asked her to show it to him. The Queen prayed to St Mungo for help, and immediately one of her servants miraculously found the ring in the mouth of a salmon he had caught. The king then had to accept his wife's pleas of innocence, despite knowing something fishy was going on.

cathedral, on the Molendinar burn, which was the spiritual centre of a diocese stretching all the way to the Solway Firth. The cathedral was dedicated in 1136 by King David I of Scotland and in 1175 Glasgow was granted burgh status by Bishop Jocelin at the behest of King William the Lion. This gave Glasgow certain trading priviledges, such as the right to hold a weekly market. Soon after came the granting of an annual fair, an event that is still celebrated to this day as a public holiday in mid-July, though the commercial aspect has long gone (see box on page 196).

The original cathedral was destroyed by fire in 1190, but was quickly rebuilt on a much grander scale, making it the second largest Gothic church in Scotland after St Andrews, the ecclesiastical capital. From 1492 the first archbishop, Robert Blacader, initiated a series of improvements to the cathedral, but before this Glasgow had gained significant academic kudos with the founding of the university in 1451.

Glasgow's ecclesiastical standing, however, far outweighed its economic and political significance. The town played little part in the political or economic history of medieval Scotland. It was largely ignored during the bitter wars with England and most of the country's trade was with the Low Countries via the east coast ports. Despite this, though, the burgh developed and the population more than doubled between the mid-15th century and the Reformation in 1560. During this time, the town grew along the present route of the High Street, from the cathedral south to Glasgow Cross, where the first Tolbooth was built. Also, the first stone bridge was built over the Clyde, which helped improve communications and thus boosted trade.

Glasgow was slowly catching up with the more important east coast burghs such as Aberdeen and Edinburgh, and in the west was second only in status only to Ayr. The 15th century saw the rise of the merchant class, culminating in the granting of a royal charter in 1490 which secured the right to export goods, namely cured salmon and herring to European ports. Glasgow may not yet have been a royal burgh but it was being effectively recognized as one, with representation at the Scottish Parliament.

Post-reformation Glasgow

Post-reformation Glasgow saw an increasing shift of power away from the church towards mercantile interests as Presbyterianism took hold. And though the archbishop, James Beaton, fled to France, taking most of the cathedral's valuables with him, Glasgow largely escaped the ravages of Protestant iconaclasm, which is rather ironic given the city's more recent reputation for sectarianism.

Despite the subsequent political turmoil caused by Mary Queen of Scots' short reign, the new Protestant religion grew in strength and influence following her

What's in a name

The roots of the city's name are difficult to pin down and have become enmeshed in the city's folklore. The earliest records state that St Kentigern, or Mungo, set up his church in a place called deschu *(later changed to* glaschu*), which translates as* 'dear place'. *Another theory is that the name is derived from two gaelic words,* glas *meaning 'green' and* cau *meaning 'hollow' or 'valley'. Over the years these explanations have been amalgamated to from 'Dear Green Place'.*

defeat in 1568 at the Battle of Langside, not far from the town, and only six years later a Presbyterian principal, Andrew Melville, was appointed to the university. Glasgow continued to thrive; its population rose to around 7,000 by 1600 and it was considered the most important trading market in the west of Scotland. The town had established trading links with Ireland and the western Highlands, as well as with France, Spain, Flanders and the Netherlands, and some of the city's merchants were now making a small fortune from import and export. This allowed them to diversify into property as the church's grip on its considerable lands weakened.

Though it was becoming established as a merchant town with a broad manufacturing base, Glasgow did not become a royal burgh until 1611, during the reign of King James VI. His son, Charles I, did much to alienate Protestant opinion by attempting to reform the hard-fought gains of the Protestant religion. In 1638 the cathedral was the setting for a meeting of the General Assembly of the Church of Scotland, which had been sanctioned by the king in the arrogant belief that he would encounter little opposition to his proposed changes. But he was sorely mistaken. The Assembly defiantly voted to endorse the National Covenenant, a document which asserted parliament's authority over the crown. This led to the so-called 'Bishops' Wars' in which the forces of Presbyterianism took on the king's armies in defence of the Covenant and won.

Throughout the 17th century Glasgow's importance as a commerical burgh was greatly enhanced. The Union of Crowns in 1603 led to an increase in trade with England, especially in linen cloth and yarn, which helped establish a base for manufacture in the town. At the same time, King James sought to quell rebellion in Ulster by transplanting thousands of Scots there from the west coast. This proved advantageous to Glasgow as it strengthened existing trading links with Ireland. Trading links were also established with Norway and Baltic States, for timber, flax and iron ore, then, in 1647, a Glasgow ship brought a cargo of tobacco from the French Caribbean island of Martinique, setting a trend which would eventually change the face of Glasgow. By the latter half of the 17th century, Glasgow had risen to become Scotland's second most important town behind Edinburgh.

Despite the years of war and English occupation, Glasgow experienced dramatic changes in the years which followed the restoration of King Charles II. The Gothic and Renaissance styles of the Tolbooth serve to indicate the town's growing prosperity. Although the main building was demolished in 1921, the steeple still stands at Glasgow Cross. Then came the university, or college, rebuilt between the 1630s and 1650s near the cathedral in the High Street (till its move across the city two centuries later), followed by Hutcheson's Hospital in Trongate and the Merchant's House in Bridgegate. Though two great fires, the first in 1652 and the second in 1677, were a major setback to the city's architectural progress, the town's population grew steadily, reaching 15,000 by the 1690s.

The expansion of transatlantic trading opportunities continued throughout this period, despite the imposition of English navigation laws in 1660, designed to prevent Scots from dealing directly with English colonies. This inevitably led to the

Background

growth of smuggling as a means of circumventing the restrictions. Such was the burgh's determination to capitalize on these properous new trading links that the Town Council built a large harbour nearly 20 miles down river and called it Port Glasgow.

This growth in trade continued against the backdrop of political tensions as the restored episcopal church of Charles II faced the wrath of Presbyterian opposition. In 1679 a Presbyterian insurrection was suppressed at Bothwell Bridge, on the outskirts of Glasgow, leading to the ruthless government repression of dissidents. The accession of the more tolerant King James VII did little to dampen criticism of crown and clergy, and there was minimal support for the new monarch when he was ousted in 1689 by his Protestant daughter Mary and her husband William of Orange (who also happened to be James' nephew). This date is still celebrated by some in the city, especially at Old Firm football matches.

The 18th century

The years following the Act of Settlement in 1688-90 were crucial in the development of Glasgow as a merchant city. The 1707 Union of Parliaments with England allowed Glasgow's merchants access to English colonial markets and paved the way for the tobacco trade, which transformed the city into a truly international trading centre, and by the 1800s Glasgow had grown to become one of the largest cities in the British Isles, with a population of over 77,000.

Towards the end of the 17th century tobacco and sugar were becaming profitable commodities for Glasgow merchants, despite the constraints of English navigation laws. Free trade was in the interests of the city's merchants and to that end they supported commercial union with their southern neighbour. However, that idea soon gave way to the Scots' desire for a colonial enterprise of their own. In 1695 the 'Company of Scotland Trading to Africa and the Indies' was set up, with a third of the total investment – some £56,000 – coming from Glasgow. The plan was to establish a colony at Darien, in Panama, one of the most inhospitable regions of the world, but it failed miserably, thanks to pressure from the Spanish and English. The Scots were forced to withdraw, incurring massive financial loss in the process.

The disastrous Darien Scheme was a huge blow to Scotland's commercial credibility and confidence, and was in no small part responsible for the willingness of many Scottish nobles and merchants to enter into negotiations with England for political and economic union. Many felt that political freedom would have to be sacrificed for the economic benefits of a common market with their wealthy and powerful southern neighbour. This was a view endorsed by Glasgow's merchants who stood to gain massively from a share in England's colonial markets in America.

Union with England alone did not ensure Glasgow's trading success. A combination of its location on the west coast, alllowing faster sailing times to the tobacco colonies in the Americas, and considerable business acumen meant that by 1771 Glasgow had risen to become the most important tobacco port of the United Kingdom (two hundred years later it would also become the lung cancer capital of Europe).

But trouble was brewing. American colonists rebelled against British rule in 1775 and the ensuing War of Independence had a devastating effect on the tobacco trade. The trading monopoly was broken and imports plummeted. Yet, despite this, Glasgow's economy survived. This was partly due, in the short term at least, to importers taking advantage of shortages by raising prices, but more fundamental was the ability of the tobacco merchants, or Tobacco Lords as they became known, to diversify into other profitable areas such as land and industry. Linen manufacture was one of these areas. Like transatlantic trade in tobacco, the linen trade had

Science in Glasgow

It was while walking across Glasgow Green that James Watt got the idea that revolutionized steam power and made it possible to build powerful engines that could be used in mines, factories and ships. Watt worked at Glasgow University and has been described as 'the inventor who made the Industrial Revolution possible'.

Glasgow has long had an important place in the history of science. It was here, in the Royal Infirmary, that Joseph Lister pioneered the use of antiseptic in surgery – at a time when gangrene and blood poisoning were killing many patients after surgery. Lister discovered that carbolic acid could keep wounds free of germs. It was also in Glasgow that William MacEwan developed antiseptic surgery, eliminating bacteria from operations altogether by boiling instruments and bandages, and making staff 'scrub up' before surgery. The Royal Infirmary was also a leading hospital in the development of the diagnostic use of X-rays in the late 19th century.

It was a Glasgow scientist, Peter Low, who wrote the first English language text on surgery. And he who, in 1599, when operations were often carried out by barbers, pressed for a charter preventing anyone but doctors from performing surgery – a charter that was responsible for the establishment of the Royal College of Physicians and Surgery.

One of Glasgow's greatest scientists was William Thomson, Lord Kelvin, who was Professor of Natural Philosophy at the university. Kelvin combined theoretical and practical science to extraordinary success. Among his achievements was propounding the Second Law of Thermodynamics, inventing many types of electrical equipment and proposing the Kelvin (Absolute) temperature scale. He was also one of the first people in the world to have a house lit by electricity. In the mid-1950s a Glasgow obstetrician, Ian Donald, pioneered the use of ultrasound (then used for checking the quality of welding in ships) in medicine. In 1957 he was able to show that a woman thought to have cancer in fact had a cyst. The woman was treated and recovered, following which the use of ultrasound in medicine developed rapidly.

benefitted from union with England. There was also a long-standing tradition of handloom weaving in the region, and the outlying communities of Calton and the Gorbals were developing as weaving centres by around the beginning of the 18th century. Furthermore, the focus of trade was shifting towards the West Indies, in sugar and spice and something that would prove to be a very nice little earner in the near future – cotton.

The legacy of Glasgow's extravagant energy and entrepreneurial past is all around: in the beautiful City Chambers in George Square; in the elegant neoclassical townhouses of the Merchant City; in the sweeping terraces of the West End. It was during the course of the 18th century that Glasgow began to be known and praised for its fine buildings. There was also a desire amongst the mercantile elite to show off their vast wealth. After all, what is the point in having lots of money if no one else knows about it?

The Tobacco Lords spent their cash on building and furnishing their magnificent mansions in what is now called the Merchant City. Virginia Street, for example, is a name that harks back to tobacco wealth. Property development really took off from around 1770 when wealthy merchants began to move west of the then city centre. Glasgow's New Town was built around George Square and quickly became the most *des res* address. Merchants, clergy and the professional classes all had townhouses in the New Town and many of the public buildings here, notably the Trades Hall and the Assembly Rooms, were designed by the

Adam brothers, two of Scotland's greatest architects, who remain the only ones in Britain to have a style of architecture named after them. By the 1790s the population of the city and suburbs was around 66,000, making Glasgow one of the fastest-growing towns in the UK.

The 19th century

By the end of the 18th century the textile industry was already established in Glasgow, mainly through the small weaving communities in what is now the East End and South Side of the city, but it was the coming of the Industal Revolution, sparked by the invention of the steam engine, that really moved Glasgow's economy into another gear and saw it transformed into one of the great urban economies.

It is entirely appropriate then, that James Watt, the inventor of the steam engine which did so much to drive forward the Industrial Revolution, was a Glasgow man, educated at the city's university. Glasgow's University, or College as it was then, was key to the Scottish Enlightenment of the mid- to late-18th century. This was a great movement of ideas, powered by such giants of philosophy as David Hume, but infused with a peculiarly Scottish practicality. Without the Enlightenment there would have been no Industrial Revolution, and the uniquely Glaswegian combination of great scientific minds and the mercantile wealth and business acumen to invest in such ideas was what sealed the city's destiny as the Tobacco Lords gave way to King Cotton.

Many of the pioneers of the cotton-spinning industry were from a weaving background – men such as Charles Tennant, who ran the massive St Rollox chemical works in the north of the city, and David Dale who built the cotton mill at New Lanark (see page 159). And, of course, another major factor in Glasgow's cotton boom was the city's existing trading links with the Caribbean and Americas, the sources for the imported raw materials.

Glasgow's development as a major centre of industrial capitalism may have been healthy for the entrepeneurs who invested in and profited from the new industries, but far from healthy for the poor workforce as health and safety took a back seat to productivity. An unfortunate truism of industrial capitalism is that the rich get richer and the poor get poorer, and in Glasgow this was an even crueller fact of life. There was a relatively high percentage of children employed in the textile industries, and the ratio of women employed was also high. There was a simple reason for this – women and children could be paid much less. Consequently, in the 19th century Glasgow became characterized as a low-wage city.

But the cotton boom was short-lived. By the 1830s the city was losing out to the more efficient and productive techniques of the Lancashire mills. It clung on until the end of the century, specializing in fine muslins, but increased competition from Europe and North America eventually hammered the last nails into King Cotton's coffin.

Once again Glasgow had to redirect her energies into alternative sources of income. Shrewd textile families had already been looking elswewhere for profits and by the 1830s the emerging iron industry was showing potential. And, once again, Glasgow was able to take advantage of that serendipitous mix of exisiting resources and technical genius. The city's hinterland of Lanarkshire was rich in mineral resources, particularly coal and ironstone, and in 1828 James Neilson's revolutionary 'hot blast' process, which enabled furnaces to boost temperatures for smelting, meant that Lanarkshire could produce higher quality iron. As the 1830s progressed and transport became revolutionized by the coming of the railway, worldwide demand for Scottish pig-iron grew.

Demand also grew domestically as work began on the rail line between Glasgow and Edinburgh, and the 1840s became something of a golden era for the city's financial sector with unprecedented levels of economic activity and investment. In 1844 Scotland's first formal stock exchange was opened, a major coup for the city.

Glasgow's location in the Clyde valley, surrounded by developing coalfields and with deep-water docks only 20 miles from the sea, had ensured its development in the aftermath of the Industrial Revolution. The city grew rapidly, with an influx of immigrants, mainly from the surrounding areas and West Highlands, to work in the cotton mills. The deepening of the Clyde up to the Broomielaw, near the heart of the city, the creation of extensive canal routes and the coming of the railway in the 19th century, all helped transform the city into one of the great industrial centres of the world.

Glasgow continued to expand rapidly between the late 18th and early 19th centuries, growing five-fold in only 50 years, and by the mid-19th century its population had reached nearly 400,000. It had now usurped Edinburgh as Scotland's largest city.

A large proportion of this population increase consisted of Irish immigrants, who had fled their homeland in 1846 to escape famine and to seek work. At the height of the famine, in 1848, it was estimated that around 1,000 Irish immigrants were moving into the city each week, mostly settling in the poorer parts, namely the East End.

At around this time there was an outbreak of cholera, which reached its peak between 1845 and 1849, and which was initially blamed on the 'growing evil of uncontrolled Irish immigration'. But this did at least highlight the growing problems of extreme poverty and overcrowding in the slum districts of the city. One social commenator described the conditions in the Trongate and Saltmarket area thus:

"I have seen human degradation in some of the worst places, both in England and abroad, but I can advisedly say, that I did not believe, until I visited the wynds of Glasgow, that so large an amount of filth, crime, misery, and disease existed on one spot in any civilised country."

Part of the problem was the drive by unsrupulous property speculators to provide accommodation for increasing numbers of newcomers, thus reducing the amount of space available for living. Rows of sub-standard tenements were built in what had been the gardens of the mansions of the Tobacco Lords, the original inhabitants having long since departed for more salubrious surroundings. Landlords were also keen to maximise their profits by renting out as many individual homes as possible, cramming families into tiny, one-roomed dwellings. By the middle of the 19th century the authorities considered overcrowding a threat to the social fabric of the city, a health hazard and a stain on their self-image as urban progressives. There was, of course, a financial incentive for initiating a programme of urban regeneration. It made economic sense to clear the inner city districts in order to make space for the developing railway network. But it was essentially a second cholera epidemic, in 1848, that finally motivated the authorities to act, both out of a sense of moral duty and the desire to exert more social control over the lower classes.

By this time there was a growing social polarisation in Glasgow between the poorer districts of the East End and middle-class West End. Glasgow's second New Town had been built west of the burgh, on Blythswood Hill, but by the 1830s the demands of business for office space forced the middle classes to migrate even further west, a move facilitated by improved transport links. The construction of two major thoroughfares were key to the development of the West End as a middle-class enclave; firstly Argyle Street (originally called Yoker Turnpike), and later, in 1841, the Great Western Road, which runs straight as a pool cue for over a mile to the very exclusive suburb of Kelvinside. The development of the West End

Background

It's no fair

Glasgow Green will always be associated with the city's annual fair. Initially established as a trade fair in the 12th century, by the early 19th century it had evolved into a giant carnival, held in mid-July when most of the working population was on holiday.

It soon earned something of a reputation for excessive drinking and such offensive activities as spontaneous dancing, and was frowned upon by the more temperate sectors of society. There were also professional entertainers, mostly of the freak-show variety, and what were known as 'penny theatres', which many considered lewd and subversive.

Basically, the Glasgow Fair was an opportunity for the low-paid and oppressed Glasgow working-class to let off steam, and this worried the authorities who saw it as a threat to the city's moral welfare. The arrival of cheap holiday excursions resulting from the expansion of the rail and steamship network brought a collective sigh of relief from the city's moral guardians.

continued throughout the 19th century and, as transport facilities improved, middle class suburbs such as Pollokshields grew up south of the river. A sign of the aspirations of those decanting to the southern suburbs can be seen by the fact that many of these South Side villas were designed by none other Alexander 'Greek' Thomson, Glasgow's brilliant Victorian architect (see page 203).

Another architectural visionary of the time was Charles Wilson, who wanted to build a public park in the West End. This new West End Park, which later became Kelvingrove Park, proved an expensive business and provoked much criticism, and though its defenders pointed to the health-giving benefits of such a fine green space, the real reason behind its existence was to stimulate more building in the West End. Wilson achieved the desired result and went on to produce his plan for the stunning Park District which overlooks the park today. Kelvingrove Park came to symbolize the aspirations of the West Enders, in the same way that Glasgow Green, in the East End, was associated with the city's working classes.

Glasgow's immigrants

Background

Most of Glasgow's new arrivals were from rural parts of Scotland, coming in search of work and looking for a better life, and from Ireland following the terrible potato famine there. But like most large industrial port cities, Glasgow acted as a magnet for economic migrants from all parts of the globe.

Jewish immigrants Glasgow's large Jewish population grew substantially over the course of the 19th century, mirroring the city's own dramatic growth. A permanent settlement of Jews in Glasgow first appeared around the 1820s, mainly made up of traders and merchants, many of whom were from Holland and Germany. In the latter part of the 19th century, however, there was a large influx of Jews from Russia and Poland. This was partly due to the rise of anti-Semitism in Russia, as well as the recruitment of Jewish tailors from London by one of the city's largest warehouse businesses. The increasing numbers of Jewish settlers led to a greater demand for places to worship and to this end Scotland's first purpose-built synagogue was built in the Garnethill district, north of the city centre, and was consecrated in 1879.

Between the end of the 19th century and the outbreak of the First World War, the Jewish population of Glasgow increased from around 2,000 to almost 6,000, most of the new arrivals coming from Eastern Europe. Whereas the earlier immigrants had settled on the north side of the river, the latter moved into the Gorbals,

Arrivederci Barga

A wet winter's day in Glasgow feels like a world away from sunny Rome or Florence, yet the city has very strong links with Italy and the 'Glasgow Italians' have made a huge contribution to the life of the city. The majority of the Italian community in Glasgow originate from the beautiful hilltop town of Barga, not far from Lucca in Tuscany. The Italians migrated to Glasgow for a variety of reasons. Some came to the city while selling plaster religious statues, others were said to have arrived by ship – apparently mistaking Glasgow for New York. Still more came seeking work in the mines and shipyards. Whatever the reason, the Barghigiani who settled in Glasgow liked it and told their families and friends, many of whom came to the city in

their turn. To make a living, many of the Italians began to make ice cream and to fry fish and chips – and with their entrepreneurial skills they were soon able to open cafes throughout Glasgow and down the Clyde coast. Today you can still find many of these original cafes (like Nardini's in Largs) as well as many excellent Italian-run restaurants and fish and chip shops. Other notable west coast 'Italians' include the actors Peter Capaldi ('Local Hero' and 'It's a Wonderful Life'), Daniella Nardini ('This Life') and Tom Conti. And if you go to Barga in August you will find it full of Glasgow-Italians visiting friends and family. In fact, links with Glasgow are so close that Barga even has an annual fish and chip festival.

south of the Clyde, and by the early 20th century the district was beginning to show signs of this influence, with Yiddish names appearing in shop windows and a proliferation of Jewish bakers and butchers.

Gradually, as the century progressed, Jewish incomers moved further south, first into Govanhill and then into Queen's Park. After the First World War this migration south continued, and by the 1980s there was hardly a Jew left in the Gorbals and not a single Jewish building. Newton Mearns, several miles south of the city, is now the main Jewish community in the west of Scotland, though the Garnethill synagogue still attracts worshippers from the western part of the city.

Glasgow's trade with the East Indies brought Asians to the city, mainly as servants or seamen, throughout the 19th century, but it wasn't until the 1920s that larger groups began to arrive, mostly unemployed Muslim males from the Punjab, coming in search of work. They quickly found a niche for themselves as hawkers, visiting various parts of the city selling clothes. Their success as street traders brought others and by 1940 the Indian community had grown large enough to be able to establish a permanent religious centre, the Muslim Mission, in Gorbals Street. The following year the Sikh Association was established with a temple in South Portland Street, another example of the Asian community occupying the parts of the Gorbals which had been vacated by the Jewish community.

Asian immigrants

After the Second World War the number of immigrants from India and Pakistan grew rapidly because of high unemployment at home, and wives and children also began to move in, helping to form more permanent roots. Street peddling continued to be the most common way to earn a living for Asian immigrants throughout the 1950s, but as the influx increased, with many unemployed English Asians moving north, many found work elsewhere, generally at the bottom of the social ladder.

Employment patterns began to change after the 1962 Commonwealth Immigration Act, which effectively ended emigration from the Indian subcontinent. As the community began to thrive, peddling became less of an acceptable job and many found alternative work as drivers and conductors on the city's buses and trams. By

Background

Red Clydesiders

Glasgow had long been a city of low-paid workers, and though trade union activism was high, there was no tradition of worker militancy. But all that changed in the years immediately preceding the outbreak of war in 1914, when trade union militancy reached unprecedented levels. This became known as the period of Red Clydeside, when ecomomic factors combined to change the direction of politics in the city. The industrial slump of 1908 led to high unemployment and increased job insecurity in shipbuilding and engineering. The fact that a Liberal government was in power only heightened the sense of frustration at rising prices and falling living standards and there followed a wave of industrial action over wages and conditions.

This growing industrial militancy came to a head in 1918, after the general election, when the engineering workers went on strike for a 40-hour working week. A trade union delegation went to meet with civic leaders but in the meantime a riot had broken out outside the City Chambers. The authorities took swift action, fearing civil unrest in the wake of the Bolshevik revolution in Russia, and jailed the alleged ringleaders.

The incident did little to damage the reputation of the Labour Movement, however, and in the 1922 general election the more passionate and direct campaigning methods of the Red Clydesider activists seemed to strike a chord with people. The Labour Party won 10 out of 15 Glasgow seats, radically changing the colour of the city's political map.

the late 1960s most of the Asian community were earning their living from some form of shopkeeping. More recently, an increasing number of Asian doctors and nurses have been employed to make up the shortfalls in the NHS.

In 1984 the Central Mosque (Scotland's first mosque) opened on the south bank of the Clyde, as the Asian community doubled in size, with the majority living in and around Glasgow. But though overt expressions of racism are mercifully rare in Scotland, due no doubt to the small numbers invloved, signs of tension are beginning to show as young Asians increasingly assert their rights to an equal place in society.

The city's **Chinese** community are mainly Hong Kong Cantonese who came to Glasgow in the 1950s at the request of the City Corporation. They originally found employment in the city's hospitals but now mostly work in catering.

Towards the 20th century

In the second half of the 19th century and into the 20th century Glasgow once again changed direction and profited from its natural resources and the innovation of its entrepreneurs. From 1860 till the end of the First World War, Glasgow became known as the shipbuilding capital of the world. This was a time best summed up by the popular refrain, 'Glasgow made the Clyde and the Clyde made Glasgow'. (A more detailed explanation of the history of the Clyde can be found on page 116).

The city benefitted from the abundance of coal and iron supplies in the west of Scotland, which were key to the success of shipbuilding on the Clyde, but there were other factors, such as the knowledge and experience of marine engineering firms who had been involved in shipbuilding since the days of Henry Bell's *Comet* in 1812 (see page 116). With typical entrepreneurial flair, Glasgow's shipbuilders quickly took the proverbial bull by the horns when the opportunity presented itself and during the 1850s and 1860s Clyde shipbuilders produced 70% of all iron-built ships launched in Britain. The district of Govan in particular became associated with shipbuilding, as firms set up outside the city centre where the water was deeper.

Such optimism, however, was tempered by the growing realization that in a volatile market bust quickly followed boom. The Clyde may have become identified with the city's prosperity by the beginning of the 20th century, but there were also times when shipyards were struggling for survival and were forced to take on unprofitable contracts simply to stay open.

Furthermore, there were still problems with a lack of harbour space, and, as a result, there began a major programme of expansion. Kingston Dock and the huge Queen's Dock were opened. These developments, coupled with navigational improvements, allowed Glasgow to become established as a shipowning port and, along with shipbuilders, the shipowners became a symbol of the city's wealth and commercial prowess in the 19th century.

This vast commercial wealth is what made Glasgow a centre for the arts. It was the great ship owners whose collections filled the Kelvingrove Art Gallery and the Burrell Collection and paved the way for the city's proudest moment, when it was chosen as European City of Culture, in 1990. The ship owners also built beautiful mansions in the West End and South Side of the city, many of which lay unnoticed until 1999, when Glasgow was chosen as the European City of Architecture and Design.

By the beginning of the 20th century Glasgow could justifiably call itself the 'Second City of the Empire' in terms of its commercial and industrial success, but its civic leaders were also aware of its image as a place of overcrowded slums and poor health. They embarked on a programme of slum clearance and expanded the city's boundaries to absorb the surrounding communities and by 1912 the population had risen to over a million. Improvements in health and housing continued after the First World War, but the onset of depression from the 1920s and through the 1930s meant that much of the postwar reconstruction had to be abandoned. With the depression came massive unemployment and a whole new set of social problems that would blight the city for much of the 20th century.

No mean city

Glasgow's economic fortunes went into a downward spiral from the end of the First World War. When worldwide demand for shipping fell drastically after the war Glasgow experienced economic recession and by the 1930s the worldwide depression had begun to hit hard. Things improved briefly during the Second World War but despite attempts to introduce new industries the city seemed to be in terminal decline. Since the Second World War and the decline of shipbuilding and heavy industries, Glasgow's population has fallen from over a million to less than 700,000 – the result of planning policies designed to decant its population from slum tenements into 'new towns' such as East Kilbride and Cumbernauld outside the city.

In the 1970s it was said that the milk bottles in Glasgow had a shorter lifespan than those in any other city in Britain. Statistics like this seem to sum up Glasgow's notoriously tough image. For years the very name 'Glasgow' seemed to be a sort of shorthand for violence and poverty – it was known as a macho, hard-drinking city – a place to be avoided.

The city's problems had really begun in the 19th century when dirt and pollution from the mills and factories covered the city in grime, and when factory workers were crammed together in cheap, unsanitary housing. Glasgow's slums grew even worse when the heavy industries went into decline, with thousands of people living in extreme squalour. By the 1920s and 1930s gang warfare had also become part of city life, with 'razor gangs' scrapping for territory and superiority on the streets. It was an aspect of the city that was graphically depicted in the novel *No Mean City*, published in 1935. It was also an image that was extremely

Background

Gangland

Glasgow's Gorbals was a breeding ground for street gangs in the 1950s. The Hammers, the Skulls, the Clatty Down and the Cumbie fought fiercely over territory using hammers and razors. The Cumbie branched out into burglary, protection and racketeering, and by the 1960s had intensified their activities as each mob struggled for supremacy. The Cumbie, under the guidance of Jimmy Boyle, Willie Smith and John McCue, achieved their objective, becoming Glasgow's top outfit. Unfortunately for them, they also spent a lot of time behind bars.

hard to shake off . Billy Connolly once said that documentary film makers: "when short of evidence of marauding gangs terrorising the wide-eyed and innocent populace, were not above slipping some unemployed youths a couple of bob to impersonate the same".

However, in the early 1980s Glasgow made an heroic effort to change its image and make itself attractive to tourists. With its customary energy and wit, the city launched the 'Glasgow's Miles Better' promotional campaign in 1983, with Mr Happy as its mascot. Buildings that had become blackened by grime were cleaned, derelict areas were cleared and redeveloped, and tenements were renovated. In the 1990s, when Glasgow was chosen as European City of Culture, the city began to regain its confidence and rediscover its many architectural and cultural assets. Creative energy flourished once again, and smart shops, cafes and restaurants opened up. Today Glasgow still has its problems – like any big city – but it doesn't shy away from them, and its warmth and energy make this one of the most vibrant cities in Europe.

Glasgow Today

Glasgow today is among the coolest of cities – and that's not just because it stands at the same latitude as Moscow. The cappuccino capital of Scotland, it's full of lively bars and restaurants, great museums and galleries, and sleek designer stores. The home of Scottish Opera and Scottish Ballet, this is the place to come if you want to check out the contemporary art scene in Scotland, stock up on *Armani* clothes or just chill out for a few days.

The city has an energy and exuberance that is simply not found anywhere else in Scotland. It even looks different to other Scottish cities, which tend be dominated by buildings made of sober grey stone, giving them a restrained, slightly austere appearance. Glasgow, by contrast, is a cheery blend of old red sandstone and quirky ironwork, laced with glinting contemporary glass and steel. It's a place where testosterone architecture flourishes and is often described as Scotland's most European city. That's probably true. However, it also has an air of Celtic edginess like Liverpool, a distinctive city swagger like London, and a lingering sense of Victorian civic pride like Manchester. In fact, Glasgow (whisper it) is really rather English. It is also a city that does not take itself too seriously, or at least cannot be serious for very long. Humour is integral to life here and Glaswegians find it in everything (particularly in people from Edinburgh, who they traditionally see as cold, humourless and full of their own importance).

Today Glasgow is one of the most interesting cities to visit in Britain. Yet for most of the 20th century people would have laughed if anyone had suggested visiting it for pleasure. The city had a reputation for both violence and poverty, and the conditions in its sprawling slums (ironically a legacy of the very industries that had made the city wealthy) were amongst the worst in Britain. It's a reputation that has been slow to shift. As late as 1996 a survey by *The Scotsman* newspaper asking residents of Edinburgh (only 40 miles away) what they associated with Glasgow, came up with: deep fried pizzas, rickets, Rangers and Celtic, Irn Bru and Billy Connolly. Hardly a ringing endorsement.

It's true that the city's renaissance suffered a few blows in the late 1990s when its great rival Edinburgh was announced as the permanent home of the Royal Yacht Britannia – a ship that had been built on the Clyde and that would have provided a welcome boost to the city's tourist industry. This was followed by the announcement that Edinburgh would also be the site of the new Scottish parliament and – even worse for Glasgow's fashionistas – would be the location for Scotland's first branch of *Harvey Nichols*. It would be much harder now for Glasgow cabbies to happily dismiss Edinburgh as 'one street and a castle'.

However, the city has refused to give in. An enormous shopping centre, the Buchanan Galleries, recently opened in the city centre, and a gleaming, futuristic Science Centre has been built on the banks of the Clyde. New homes, offices and hotels are currently being built on derelict land along the river. Of course the city still has its social problems and areas of deprivation – what city doesn't – and also true that not everyone in Glasgow wears designer clothes (thank goodness) or eats in trendy restaurants. But the city no longer has to prove itself, it knows that it can now compete with the best in Europe, and while it has gained a new confidence in recent years, it hasn't lost its irreverent sense of humour along the way. Glaswegians might drink cappuccino now – but they'll soon spot if its got too much froth on top.

Culture

Architecture

Glasgow is unusual among great cities in that it has no single defining monument: no Eiffel Tower; no Trafalgar Square; no Empire State Building; or Edinburgh Castle. Ironically, though, this city – the world's first successful post-industrial city – has picked itself up from the near terminal trauma of economic wipe-out, dusted itself down and re-invented itself as a major European tourist attraction, thanks mainly to its buildings. Glasgow may not have been the architect of its own downfall, but its great architects have risen from beyond the grave to breathe new life back into the city; their monuments standing as testimony to the city's former glories as the 'Second City of Empire'.

Very little of medieval Glasgow remains. The Provand's Lorship, opposite the cathedral, is the oldest standing building in the city, which, at that time, consisted of little more than a single street running from the cathedral south to Glasgow Cross. Even by the mid-18th century, it had only extended east along the Gallowgate and west along Trongate. It was the prosperity which came with the tobacco trade that first started Glasgow's rise to become a giant of urban architecture. The Tobacco Lords built streets of detached Palladian mansions, the best examples of which were in Virginia Street, Miller Street and Queen Street, in what is now known as The Merchant City. Their like had never before been seen in Britain and efforts are being made to preserve what is left of them (see page 58).

It was around this time that the unique Glasgow square began to appear. This is a tightly enclosed urban square with a church or prominent civic building in the centre, unlike the more bucolic squares of Edinburgh or London. The best examples

Background

of these are St Andrew's Square just off the Saltmarket, St George's Square on Buchanan Street and Royal Exchange Square, between Queen Street and Buchanan Street. As well as these distinctive squares, Glasgow also differs from other British cities in its street plan. This is best seen in The Merchant City, where the streets are laid out with prominent buildings facing down the streets and closing off the vistas, for example on Candelriggs, which is closed off by the Ramshorn Kirk.

With the Industrial Revolution came heavy industry, aided and abetted by the ready availability of mineral resources in the Lanarkshire hinterland. The city began to spread west and the grid-like street network extended across Blythswood Hill. This time it was an open-ended grid, more redolent of American cities, and when the city centre buildings were rebuilt ever higher in the 19th century after the invention of the mechanical lift, Glasgow began to resemble a young Chicago or New York.

Glasgow grew phenomenally through the 19th century to emerge as the 'Second City of the Empire'. While acres of tenements housed artisans and middle class families, older Georgian suburbs were abandoned for commodious villas further west by the prosperous, in areas like Kelvingrove. Many of these villas, especially on the South Side, were designed by Alexander 'Greek' Thomson using Classical Greece and Egypt as inspiration (see below). Meanwhile, conditions in the old city centre worsened until the Second City of Empire became known as Cancer of the Empire. Public shame coupled with fear of disease and social unrest led to the demolition of the ancient heart of the city, replaced with City Improvement Trust tenements.

By the end of the 19th century, Glasgow could boast some of the most exciting architecture in Europe. While Gilbert Scott's Glasgow University on Gilmorehill was inspired by Flemish cloth halls, new banks were modelled on Renaissance palazzos. Thomson designed Egyptian-style warehouses, and John Burnet in the 1890s returned from New York to design tall, narrow-fronted buildings with steel frames. The forward-looking Beaux Arts rationalism of Burnet and company was challenged by Traditionalists reacting against an aggressive modernity, advocating traditional building materials and craftsmanship, and referring back to 16th- and 17th-century vernacular architecture. Charles Rennie Mackintosh was a leading, if not independent, exponent, as exemplified by Hill House in Helensburgh (see page 152).

In contrast, Art Deco was favoured by architects such as Jack Coia and, by the mid-20th century, Basil Spence was a champion of Modernism. His Luma building (which can be seen on the cover of this book) provoked as much controversy as any.

Economic depression and dramatic social change brought an urgent need for solutions to urban overpopulation and decay. A desperate need for housing resulted in massive building projects from the postwar period into the 1970s. Many historic buildings were demolished and the city centre gutted in an effort to remedy post-war dereliction. The first residential tower blocks, the epitome of a modern functionalist 'Brave New World', appeared, most notoriously in the Gorbals. Urban over-spill was rehoused in New Towns such as East Kilbride and Cumbernauld, which, although internationally acclaimed in the 1960s, was unpopular with the inhabitants.

At one point in the late 1950s civic leaders even proposed to flatten the entire city centre and start again. The inner ring road was carved right through Anderston Cross, Charing Cross and St George's Cross, creating a division between the city centre and the West End. It all could have gone horribly wrong. Glasgow might have ended up as some nightmarish futuristic disaster – a hideous meeting of Blade Runner and Milton Keynes – but it didn't. It survived, in true Glasgow fashion.

Charles Rennie Mackintosh

To say that Barcelona has Gaudí and Glasgow has Rennie Mackintosh is not over-stating the case. He is not only one of Scotland's most celebrated architects, but also one of the creative geniuses of modern architecture.

Charles Rennie Mackintosh was born in Glasgow in 1868 and at the age of 15 began work as a draughtsman with a local firm of architects. At the same time, he continued to pursue his studies at the Glasgow School of Art where his talent as an artist soon earned him recognition, and his experimental, decorative style brought him into contact with kindred spirits Herbert MacNair and two sisters, Frances and Margaret MacDonald. They became known as 'The Four' and together they developed their unique form of art and design, which became known as the 'Glasgow Style'.

Mackintosh was as much an artist and interior designer as an architect but he saw no conflict in this. He considered architecture to be, "...the synthesis of the fine arts, the commune of all the crafts", and he used his diverse talents to great effect, designing every detail of a building, down to the furniture, carpets and decoration. This can be seen to greatest effect in his new **Glasgow School of Art** (see page 73) building, one of the most important buildings in the city, if not the entire country.

In the late 1890s he began his Argyle Street tea room project for Miss Cranston, and developed his distinctive, elegant high-backed chairs, for which he is probably best known today. In 1900 he married Margaret Macdonald (Herbert MacNair and Margaret's sister were married the previous year) and they began to design the interior of their own flat, creating their distinctive colour schemes of white and grey, pink and purple, and the light and dark interiors representing the masculine and feminine.

Throughout his career, Mackintosh's talents were far better understood abroad than at home, where his designs were often criticised as being iconoclastic and too modern. He was forced to leave Glasgow in 1914 due to lack of work and soon became depressed and alcoholic, and though his fortunes improved after moving to London, he died, a tragic but romantic figure, in 1928.

It is only in the past few decades that his genius has been fully recognised and serious efforts made to preserve his artistic legacy. The restoration of the **Willow Tea Rooms** (page 71), **Scotland Street School** (page 104), **Queen's Cross Church** (page 93) and the **Mackintosh House** at the Hunterian Art Gallery (page 91), as well as **The Hill House** in Helensburgh (page 152), are all testimony to his prodigious talents.

Before visiting the Mackintosh sights listed here, it's a good idea to first visit **The Lighthouse** (page 69), the state-of-the-art design and architecture centre housed in CRM's former Glasgow Herald building, where you can enjoy an introduction to the man's life and work. And even before setting off for Glasgow, you can visit the CRM Society website, at www.crmsociety.com

Alexander 'Greek' Thomson

Alexander Thomson was the greatest architect of Victorian Glasgow, who did as much to shape the city as the famous Charles Rennie Mackintosh. In the middle of the 19th century, when Glasgow was a growing, dynamic place, he brought a distinctive flair to all manner of buildings – warehouses and commercial premises, terraces and tenements, suburban villas and some of the finest Romantic Classical churches in the world.

Background

Alexander Thomson, the 17th child of John Thomson, a devout Presbyterian bookkeeper, was born in Balfron, Stirlingshire, in 1817. After his father's death, he moved to live near Glasgow. He began work in a lawyer's office, aged 12, and in 1834 attracted the attention of architect, Robert Foote, who took him on as an apprentice.

During his training he studied the principles of Classical architecture and his belief that the style of the ancient Greeks could be the basis of modern architecture earned him the nickname 'Greek' Thomson. Yet, despite his nickname, he never visited Greece and was not a conventional Greek Classicist. In fact, he thought the architects of the Greek revival had failed: "...because they could not see through the material into the laws upon which that architecture rested. They failed to master their style, and so became its slaves". Instead, Thomson evolved a distinctive manner of building using a Greek style but in an unconventional way and incorporating modern inventions such as iron beams and plate glass. Thomson was struck by "the mysterious power of the horizontal element in carrying the mind away into space and into speculations on infinity". This dominance of horizontality has led to comparisons with Frank Lloyd Wright, though Thomson predates him by 40 years.

In 1847 Thomson married Jane Nicholson, daughter of London architect Michael Angelo Nicholson and granddaughter of the architect and writer, Peter Nicholson, who designed Glasgow's Carlton Place (1802). In 1848 Thomson set up a partnership with his wife's brother-in-law, John Baird, and after it was mutually ended in 1856 he went into business with his brother George as A & G Thomson. It was during this period, between 1854 and 1857, while living in Hutchesontown near the Gorbals, that four of Thomson's children died of cholera. The family then moved to Shawlands, and, later still, into 1 Moray Place, a house he had designed himself.

In the mid-19th century, as Glasgow developed rapidly into an industrial giant, Thomson's prolific output not only reflected the city's booming confidence but also helped establish its growing reputation. Yet this truly original and brilliant architect was shamefully neglected after his death in 1875. In the 1960s, in a frenzy of destruction, the city planners did their best to wipe out this man's amazing achievements completely. Finally, though, the city paid tribute to one of their most talented sons with a major exhibition about his work as part of the City of Architecture and Design year in 1999.

Thankfully, some of Thomson's great buildings still exist. Among the most impressive are **Holmwood House**, near Cathcart in the South Side (see page 109), which is owned by the National Trust for Scotland, the glorious **St Vincent Street Church** (see page 70), and the Grecian Chambers, now beautifully restored as the **Centre for Contemporary Arts** (see page 72).

People

The driving force of Glasgow is its people, with their distinctive mix of guts, determination, energy and humour. Glaswegians seem to thrive on adversity (which is a good thing, as they've had plenty of it) and have made their mark all over the world. The city also once had a reputation for nurturing some colourful eccentrics. Many of these were poor street people who came to Glasgow in the Industrial Revolution.

There was Blind Alick, a talented fiddle player who earned a living playing at ceilidhs and weddings in the city and who preferred to be paid in drink rather than cash. There was Robert Hall, also known as Rab Ha', the Glesca Glutton, who had such a huge appetite that people would place bets on his ability to eat. He was apparently only beaten once, by a dish of oysters, cream and ground sugar. Another 'character' was Wee Willie Wilson, a blind street musician who used to play the tin whistle. He was so popular that when he died his admirers paid to have him buried in the Southern Necropolis and had his gravestone decorated with a carving of his tin whistle.

A more recent eccentric (who died in 1964) was AE Pickard, an engineer by trade and a highly successful businessman who became a millionaire. He bought a number of small theatres in Glasgow – including the Britannia Music Hall in Trongate where Stan Laurel made one of his first stage appearances. Pickard used to sit in the wings throwing screws at rowdy members of the audience. If he didn't like a particular act he would drag them off by the neck using a long pole with a hook on the end. He had the distinction of being the first man in Glasgow to be booked for a parking offence – he'd parked his car on the platform at Central station as he was late for his train. And during the war he built an air raid shelter in the garden of one of his mansions and decorated it outside with neon lights.

One of Glasgow's most famous characters is fictitious, but has done more than any other to bring the reality of life in the city's faceless council housing estates to the attention of the outside world. We are, of course, talking about the one and only Rab C Nesbit. Rab, alias Gregor Fisher, was first unveiled on BBC2's *Naked Video* sketch show and instantly became a huge hit, evoking the pain and humour in a city rendered bankrupt by successive Thatcher governments. The irrepressible working-class bard soon had his own series, which is now sadly missed. In one particularly poignant moment from the series, Rab drags his eldest son down to the local boozer for his first ever drink in a rare instance of father and son bonding. "What'll ye have, son?" asks Rab, proud as a Highland chieftain. "Ah'll have half a snakebite an' seven aspirins, Da", comes the reply. A clip round the ear quickly follows.

The biggest of Glasgow's characters towers over the city's cultural landscape like a colossus. Billy Connolly's influence on Scottish comedy and the portrayal of working-class attitudes cannot be overestimated. The Big Yin, as he is affectionately known, first came on the scene in the 1970s with his trademark black-and-white striped suit and big banana boots (which are now on display in the People's Palace). The sheer comedic genius of this former shipyard welder soon transcended national boundaries and he is now recognized internationally, not only as a great comedian but also as an actor of considerable talent. With typical modesty, he once claimed that there were many funnier men than he working at the shipyard. If that was the case, then it's nothing short of a miracle that any work was ever done. And, despite his success on the big screen, most notably when he teamed up with Dame Judy Dench as Queen Victoria's faithful ghillie, John Brown, in the hit film, *Mrs Brown*, Billy is equally humble about his acting ability. He once said that while acting opposite Judy Dench he didn't know when many of the scenes had started or finished.

It's difficult to imagine it now, but Billy Connolly was not always loved by everyone. He often upset the more sensitive sectors of society with his 'flowery' language and no-holds-barred attacks on religious hypocrisy. In the late 1980s, while a row was raging over his increasing use of bad language, the Big Yin walked onstage in Glasgow and said: " I've been taking a bit of stick for using bad language. Me, can ye believe it?" The audience, mostly middle-class suburban folk, laughed uncomfortably. He went on: "I'll try not to upset anyone tonight, and if I do, I apologise in advance. If, on the other hand, you don't like the language, yez can just **** off!" Nearly a third of the audience got up and walked out in disgust. This uncompromising, take me or leave me attitude is pure Glasgow.

Background

A few Glasgow words

Bahookie	*backside, bum*
bampot	*idiot*
boggin	*smelly*
boufin	*stinking*
cludgie	*toilet*
dog	*to play truant*
dowt	*cigarette butt*
gallus	*cocky or flash*
ginger	*any type of soft drink*
gub	*mouth*
hoachin	*full of or infested with*
honk	*to vomit*
knock	*steal*
mingin, manky, mockit	*filthy*
messages	*food shopping or groceries*
mental	*insane, enraged*
molocate	*to batter or destroy*
pochle	*to get something by cheating*
see	*to pass, as in 'see me ower thon hammer'*
stoatir	*a desirable girl, as in 'she's a wee stoatir'*
tube	*idiot*
wallies	*false teeth*
weans	*young children*

Language

Background

In his book *Notes from a Small Island* Bill Bryson describes the difficulties he experienced in understanding the often inpenetrable Glasgow accent. "I don't speak Glaswegian" he complains worriedly. Many visitors experience the same problems, for not only do Glaswegians speak very quickly, they also have a rich variety of local words and phrases, and a distinctive way of expressing themselves. It's known as 'the patter' – the equivalent of London's cockney. The most famous exponent of this is TV's Rab C Nesbitt who introduced audiences throughout Britain to this colourful vernacular.

Some aspects of the patter are down to pronunciation, such as '*whit*' for what, '*herr*' for hair and '*flerr*' for floor. Many Glaswegians also flavour their sentences with words like 'see', 'pure' and 'but' (as in '*I'm no' goin' but*'). The word 'see' is commonly used as an emphatic pointer, for example, '*see him, see his wee brither, thur baith mental*' – both he and his little brother are unhinged. Some examples of Glasgow grammar include the use of '*am ur*' for I am. '*Amurny goin*' is I'm not going, and '*amur so*' is I am indeed. Also '*gony no dae that*', means please don't do that.

Then there's the use of 'belong' instead of own, as in '*who belongs tae this dug?*' – whose is this dog? A few other examples are '*mines*' for mine and '*hing*' for thing, and '*youse*' for the plural of you. Women may find themselves addressed as '*Missus*' – or even worse, '*Missus Wumman*' by strangers – and there's also the term '*wifie*' used to describe a middle-aged or older woman. Glaswegians also have some

Dug-out heroes

The west of Scotland has produced some world-class footballers over the years – most notably Jim Baxter (Rangers) and Kenny Dalglish (Celtic and Liverpool. This deep well of talent appears to have dried up recently, but the region's influence on the British game is strong as ever. The most successful British football club manager of all time, Sir Alex Ferguson of Manchester United, hails from Govan and was a former Rangers player. Two other legendary football managers from the west of Scotland were Sir Matt Busby, who reigned supreme at Manchester United in the 1960s, and Bill Shankly, who has practically been deified at Anfield, home of Liverpool Football Club.

wonderfully expressive words, though these are constantly changing and growing. A few examples are given in the box above.

The best thing about the patter, though, is its humour – and the classic way Glaswegians have of delivering a put down to someone they think has got a bit above themselves. Scottish comedian Andy Cameron once recalled a woman coming up to him in Glasgow and saying, "See compared tae Robert De Niro, by the way, you're shite". That's Glasgow patter.

The use of the Glasgow dialect can be traced back to before the First World War in JJ Bell's humorous tales of a Glasgow boy, *Wee Macgreegor* (1902). The first use of Glaswegian in a serious work of literature is probably Alexander McArthur's *No Mean City* (1935), but its regular written use dates from the 1970s. As it is essentially a spoken dialect it is well represented in a number of plays such as *The Sash* (1974) by Hector MacMillan and *The Slab Boys* (1978) by John Byrne. Several poets, including Tom Leonard and Tom McGrath, have used it as their authentic voice, while it appears as a matter of course in the novels of James Kelman and Alan Spence, among others (see page 213).

Football

Background

The late Bill Shankly, former manager of Liverpool FC, once famously said that football's not a matter of life and death – it's more important than that. This may seem fatuous to some, but to the supporters of Glasgow's two big clubs, Celtic and Rangers, collectively known as the 'Old Firm', he was talking their language. There is no greater rivalry in world football than that which exists between Glasgow's two main teams. AC Milan and Inter? Real Madrid and Barcelona? Forget it. Parkhead or Ibrox on derby day is a seething cauldron of passion and hatred that makes the San Siro or Bernabau seem like a Sunday village cricket match by comparison.

Yet neither Celtic not Rangers were the first football team to be formed in the city. That was Queens Park, formed in 1867, in the South Side suburbs by members of the Glasgow YMCA. Six years later, Queens Park, along with eight other clubs (Clydesdale, Dumbreck, Vale of Leven, Eastern, Third Lanark Rifle Volunteers, Rovers and Granville) set up the Scottish Football Association.

Around this time another two momentous events took place in the history of Glasgow football. In 1872, a team was formed on Glasgow Green calling themselves Rangers, then, in 1888, a Roman Catholic priest formed a football team called Celtic in an effort to alleviate poverty in the East End. The next development was the setting up of a Scottish League in 1890-91, in which both clubs played an important part, followed by the introduction of professionalism into the game in 1893, a move opposed by Queens Park who still remain an amateur club to this day.

Fever pitch

No football fixture has a worse reputation than Rangers versus Celtic, where passions run so high it can be positively scary, even for the most experienced of football spectators. But crowd violence at this most fiercely contested of games is nothing new. Almost a century ago, a cup tie at Parkhead had to be abandoned, with Rangers leading 2-0,

when the sending off of a Celtic player provoked the home supporters into invading the pitch. They tore up the surrounding fence and then proceeded to remove the spiked metal palings, presumably to use as spears. The poor referee was saved from the fans' wrath only by the timely intervention of the Celtic captain.

Celtic and Rangers both took full advantage of the creation of a professional league and adopted a businesslike approach to their development. By the end of the 19th century, they were becoming the biggest names in the city and beyond. Their first meeting was in 1894 when Rangers defeated Celtic 3-1. They worked together to ensure they could get the most lucrative fixtures, and as a large percentage of their revenue came from playing each other, both quickly realised there was money to be made from exploiting their religious and ethnic differences, with Rangers in blue representing the Protestant community, and Celtic in green the Catholic Irish.

Throughout the 20th century, football has stirred powerful emotions amongst the supporters of both clubs. George Blake, in his 1935 novel *The Shipbuilders*, called the Old Firm players "peerless and fearless warriors, saints of the Blue and Green". Though bitter sectarianism grew in the 1920s and 30s and went on to scar the image of the Old Firm, football at least provided an escape for both sets of supporters from the deep insecurities of the depression.

During the inter-war years, Rangers dominated the Scottish League, winning the old first division 14 times, but, under the brilliant guidance of Jock Stein from 1965, Celtic went on, not only to dominate the domestic game, but also to conquer Europe by becoming the first ever British club to win the European Cup, in 1967, defeating the highly-fancied Inter Milan 2-1. The famous Lisbon Lions – as the Celtic side became known – were all the more remarkable as the entire squad were born and lived within a 35 mile radius of the city centre, a quite inconceivable notion today.

Big changes took place in Scottish Football in the 1970s, which raised the stakes for both clubs. Rangers brought Graeme Souness from Liverpool and he revolutionized the club by making big-name international signings and raising their profile considerably. But, at the same time, Rangers realised they had to lose their sectarian image in order to attract the best players and to this end they broke their policy of never employing a Roman Catholic player in 1989 and signed Maurice Johnston. This shook the very foundations of football in the city but paved the way for a long period of total domination by Rangers, broken only recently by a rejuvenated Celtic under the shrewd guidance of Martin O'Neill.

Of course there's more to Glasgow football than Celtic and Rangers. Two other senior teams are still based in the city. Queens Park continue to defy logic by existing as an amateur club, the only one in Britain large enough to remain so. Since 1903 they have played their games at Hampden Park, the national stadium, which at the time was the finest football stadium in the world. Across the city, in Maryhill, Partick Thistle serve as a refuge for those who are turned off by the Old Firm domination and the ever-present shadow of sectarianism. Glasgow's other club, Clyde, now play at Cumbernauld.

Glasgow on screen

"Glasgow's citizens are larger than life. They live life as though it was a movie…" So said one commentator on the city and he certainly had a point. Glasgow's gritty history, and the strong character and sense of humour of its people, has provided plenty of potential for film-makers in recent years – and the city has recently witnessed something of a renaissance in film-making. Although it must be said that films tend to focus on the darker side of Glasgow life – even comedies, such as Bill Forsyth's 1984 film, *Comfort and Joy*, which dealt with the city's famously violent ice-cream wars. Films set in Glasgow are inclined to have a hard edge, as if film makers cannot, or do not want to, forget the city's old 'razors and rivets' image.

It was the shooting of *Shallow Grave* in 1993 that really put Glasgow on the movie map. This film, in which a group of flatmates try to dispose of a dead body, was not only filmed on location in Glasgow but also launched the career of Ewan McGregor. It was a commercial and critical success and encouraged investment in more films set in the city. Since then there have been several films made in Glasgow including *Small Faces* (1996), *The Slab Boys* (1996) which was filmed entirely in a disused warehouse in the heart of the city, *Ratcatcher* (1999), and *My Name is Joe* (1998), Ken Loach's acclaimed film in which a recovering alchoholic Joe (played by Peter Mullan) struggles to stay on the wagon, while combining his involvement with a young social worker, and the worst football team in town. Other Glasgow films have included *The Acid House* (1998), the film adaptation of Irvine Welsh's novel, and *Carla's Song* (1996). One of the latest films to be set in the city is Peter Capaldi's *Strictly Sinatra* (2001), which stars Ian Hart, Kelly Macdonald and Brian Cox.

On the small screen Glasgow is probably most famous for the long-running TV detective series *Taggart*, in which the police deal with a seemingly inexaustible number of grisly murders and brutal crimes. It has done nothing to dent the city's tough image.

The city's distinctive mix of flamboyant Victorian buildings, rundown high-rise flats, derelict industrial sites and acres of green parks and gardens, means that Glasgow is not only a suitable subject for a film, it also has plenty of suitable locations for film-makers. *Regeneration*, the First World War film based on the novel by Pat Barker, was filmed in Glasgow, and the Glasgow to Dumfries railway line featured – unlikely as it may seem – in the Hollywood blockbuster *Mission Impossible*. The city also doubled as Moscow in the 1983 film *Gorky Park*, while film crews on *The House of Mirth* (2000) used several places in Glasgow: Kelvingrove art gallery and museum was used as a train station, and the City Chambers became an apartment foyer. The City Chambers also featured in *Heavenly Pursuits* (1985); doubling as, of all things, the Vatican – which can't have pleased the 'blue-nosed' elements of the population, who still detest all things Catholic.

Glasgow and the Clyde towns have also produced an extraordinary number of famous actors. As well as Ewan Macgregor, there are people like Tom Conti, Kelly Macdonald, Alan Cumming, Daniella Nardini, and Billy Connolly, the comedian whose first big screen role was as Queen Victoria's devoted servant in *Mrs Brown*. Then of course there's Robert Carlyle, who has a string of big-screen successes like *Trainspotting* and *The Full Monty*, and Robbie Coltrane – who played Hagrid in *Harry Potter and the Philosopher's Stone*. With major stars like these, and any number of talented directors, designers and technicians based in the city, it looks likely that Glasgow will feature in plenty more films in the years to come.

Background

Art

Billy Connolly once told a story about a friend of his who went into a café which had a garish mural painted on one of the walls. The owner asked him what he thought of it, but when his friend politely mumbled "very nice", another customer, who appeared to have been sleeping in a corner, sat up and said loudly: "Very nice? Ye call that a muriel? Christ, Venus de Milo would turn in his grave if he'd seen that!"

Many Glaswegians certainly have a robustly irreverent approach to art, but that has not prevented the city from developing a thriving visual arts scene. In fact it is possibly this very irreverence that has prevented Glasgow artists from becoming too hidebound by tradition, and has meant that many contemporary local artists have gained international respect and recognition.

With the coming of the industrial age, Glasgow had grown rapidly from a small, provincial town into a large city. This sudden growth in size and wealth led to the beginnings of the famous and long-standing rivalry between Glasgow and Edinburgh, and, by the 1880s, to a new departure from the cultural mainstream. It was this forthright rejection of the conventional that led to the growth of the group of artists known as the 'Glasgow Boys' around the 1870-1880s, comprising **James Guthrie**, **Joseph Crawhall**, **John Lavery**, **George Henry** and **EA Hornel**.

They rejected the contemporary Scottish trend for painting historical melodrama, sentimental 'poor but happy' cottagers and grandiose visions of the Highlands inspired by Sir Walter Scott, referring to these paintings as 'gluepots' for their use of megilp – a treacly varnish that lent the paintings a brown patina of age. They began to experiment with new techniques and methods they had come across on trips to Paris, Japan and London. This not only shocked and offended the genteel Edinburgh art establishment, but also scandalized their fellow citizens. Many of their works can be seen today in the Kelvingrove Art Gallery. These include *A Galloway Landscape* by **George Henry**, which has an almost unfinished effect, and *The Druids – bringing in the mistletoe*, by **Henry** and **Hornel**. This painting is strong on symbolism and introduced new elements to Scottish painting such as a flattened picture space and use of gold leaf.

The Glasgow Boys left Scotland to study in Paris, where their work met with great acclaim. Subsequently, their art began to fetch high prices from the new rich of Glasgow, eager to buy status through cultural patronage. But once the group had achieved the artistic respect and commercial success its members craved, they sadly lost their freshness. The influence of the Glasgow Boys, however, cannot be underestimated. They shook the foundations of the art establishment and were the inspiration for the next generation of great Scottish painters, known as 'The Colourists'.

A number of the Glasgow Boys had been trained at Glasgow School of Art, which was established in 1840, with the initial aim of training textile designers for the city's thriving textile industry. As the trade in textiles declined, the art school diversified and began to train students in a wide variety of artistic disciplines – from painting to embroidery. It was another group of students associated with the school who were responsible for developing the distinctive Glasgow Style in the late 19th century. This was a Scottish response to continental Art Nouveau, as well as to William Morris's Arts and Crafts movement. Members of the group included **Charles Rennie Mackintosh** (its most famous exponent), the designer George Walton and book illustrator Jessie M King.

The Glasgow Style was characterised by the use of elongated motifs taken from nature, such as roses or leaves, or slender human shapes. The colours used were soft shades of purple, pink and green. Perhaps the best example of Glasgow Style to be seen today is the school of art itself (which was designed by Mackintosh). However, if you look carefully you will also see similarly distinctive stained-glass windows and glazed tiles decorating old houses and tenement closes (known as 'wally' closes) all around the city.

For a number of years Glasgow seemed obsessed by Rennie Mackintosh and his imprint was seen everywhere, from the design of the Princes Square shopping centre, to the mugs, jewellery, scarves and greetings cards that were to be found in every gift shop. His distinctive style is still very popular and you can still find plenty of these goods today.

However, contemporary art and design in Glasgow has managed to move on. During the 1980s a number of new artists – **Peter Howson**, **Adrian Wiszniewski**, **Ken Currie** and **Steven Campbell** – known as the 'new Glasgow Boys', appeared on the scene. Also trained at Glasgow School of Art, their imaginative and angry works soon gained widespread recognition. Howson, for instance, was the Imperial War Museum's official war artist in Bosnia, painting works dealing with machismo, patriotism and xenophobia. Some works by these artists can be seen in the Gallery of Modern Art in Royal Exchange Square, off Queen Street.

Today, Glasgow School of Art trains students in a huge range of artistic fields, from painting, architecture and sculpture to ceramics, silversmithing and interior design. There is also a new digital design studio that enables students to work with the latest design technologies. The school's annual Degree Shows in late June are open to the public and are a great opportunity to see the best examples of contemporary art and design. There are also plenty of galleries exhibiting and selling contemporary art. *Where the Monkey Sleeps*, a small gallery/cafe has recently shown works ranging from charcoal drawings, prints relating to the troubles in Ireland, photographs of navels, illustrations and installations. Then there's *The Arches* which regularly exhibits experimental works of art. In the past some of these works have involved actors working together with sound, light and film to create sensory effects.

Glasgow Print Studio is also a good place to see a variety of new arts and crafts. Past exhibits have included paintings, prints and drawings by figurative painter John Bellany; etchings and screenprints by Alan Beveridge, inspired by his memories of shipbuilding on the Clyde; and colourful contemporary jewellery by Katie Clarke. Not far from the *Print Studio* is *Street Level*, a gallery which specialises in photo-based art and new media. Many other places in the city also display contemporary works of art. The People's Palace, for instance, has a gallery for temporary exhibitions. Works shown here are varied and have recently included the disturbing and atmospheric artworks of **Frank McNab**. McNab photographs and makes drawings of Glasgow tenement 'closes', or stairways, from which he produces works in chalk and charcoal. Another, more widely known, artist working in the city today is **Avril Paton**. Her paintings of tenements are extremely popular, as they have the appeal of the familiar. One of her works *Windows in the West*, hangs in the Gallery of Modern Art, and also appears on greetings cards and in numerous print shops.

Books

Literary Glasgow, like so much else in the city, is largely a product of the late-Victorian era. One of the few notable examples of 18th century Glasgow is in **Walter Scott**'s *Rob Roy* (Constable, 1817) in the shape of Bailie Nicol Jarvie, seen as the archetypal Glasgow merchant. Perhaps the best-known evocation of Victorian Glasgow is **Guy McCrone**'s *Wax Fruit* (Constable, 1947), in which the matriarchal Bel Moorhouse is something of a prototype of the strong Glasgow women who would come to characterize many Glasgow novels.

Another well-known novel of this period, *The Beggar's Benison* (Cassell, Petter and Galpin, 1866), by **George Mills**, is one of few which focussed on the problem of the city's notorious slums which mushroomed during the rapid industrial expansion of the late 19th century. Today, it seems astounding that the whole issue of industrialisation, growing social division and immigration was not irresistible to most writers of the late 19th and early 20th centuries, but a common criticism of the time was the relative absence of such novels. Rather than explore the vexed issues of poverty, class division and the growing Celtic influence, most writers belonged to the 'Kailyard School', which presented a romantic, sentimental and completely unrealistic image of Scotland, perhaps reflecting the overwhelmingly middle class background of novelists at that time.

In the wake of the First World War, and the beginning of Glasgow's terminal industrial decline, a new breed of novel emerged, the 'Gangland School'. This type of novel, the most famous (or infamous) of which is *No Mean City* (Longmans, Green, 1935) by **Alexander McArthur**, could not have depicted a more different picture of life in Glasgow, featuring as it did the violence and alienation of life in the Gorbals, the city's most notorious slum. This novel has, more than any other before or since, (dis)coloured most people's perceptions of the city, and it is only since the 1990s that this image has been successfully dispelled. In its own way, *No Mean City*, could be criticised for presenting a one-dimensional view of life in Glasgow.

Despite its failings, *No Mean City* was important as a precursor to the realistic Glasgow novel. This phase of literature began in the 1920s and was inspired by one of the greatest novels to emerge from Scotland, **George Douglas Brown**'s ground-breaking *House of the Green Shutters*, which destroyed the bucolic escapism of the Kailyard School. Perhaps the most acclaimed example from this period is *Open the Door!* (Andrew Melrose, 1920) by **Catherine Carswell**.

The 1930s saw the dramatic rise of the 'proletarian' novel, whose greatest exponent was George Blake. His *Shipbuilders* (Faber and Faber, 1935) is seen as the definitive portrayal of Glasgow during the Depression.

It was the postwar period that really saw Glasgow emerge as a city of true literary credentials. The seeds were sown with Clifford Hanley's *A Taste of Too Much* (Hutchinson, 1960) and unprecedented perspective of life through the eyes of an adolescent boy on a council housing estate, and **Archie Hind**'s *The Dear Green Place* (Hutchinson, 1966), but it was **Robin Jenkins**, hailed as the Scottish Thomas Hardy, who put the city firmly on the literary map. His most Glaswegian of novels, *A Very Scotch Affair* (Gollancz, 1968), is still regarded as a highpoint in pre-1970s Glasgow fiction.

One of the best novels to come out of the 1960s was by one of the city's greatest writers, **George Friel**: *Grace and Mrs Partridge* (Calder and Boyars, 1969) is a humorous portrayal of tenement life, and a lot more besides. Around this time another literary talent was emerging – **William McIlvanney**. Though he had already published two Glasgow novels in the 1960s, it was the following decade which saw him emerge as one the city's greats. In *Laidlaw* (Hodder and Stoughton, 1977), McIlvanney explored Glasgow's seedy, criminal underbelly through the eyes of the eponymous police Detective-Inspector, who became as much a part of the city as Ian Rankin's Rebus has become a part of Edinburgh. Two subsequent crime thrillers featuring Laidlaw, *The Papers of Tony Veitch* (Hodder and Stoughton, 1983) and *Strange Loyalties* (Hodder and Stoughton, 1991) helped McIlvanney transcend the crime novel genre, in the same way that Ian Rankin has done today. Another notable novelist who emerged in the 1970s is **Alan Spence** whose *Its Colours They are Fine* (Collins, 1977) which follows the path of a Glasgow hard man from adolescent delinquency to macho 'maturity'.

If the 1970s were good for the image of Glasgow literature, then the 1980s were nothing short of earth-shattering. In 1981 **Alasdair Gray's** totally original debut novel, *Lanark* (Canongate, 1981), changed everything. It single-handedly raised the profile of Glasgow fiction. Suddenly, the outside world stood up and took notice.

Since then, Glasgow's writers have gone from strength to strength, most notably with **James Kelman**, a giant on the Glasgow literaty scene, whose brilliant fourth novel, *How Late It Was, How Late* (Secker and Warburg, 1994), won the Booker Prize. A one-time bus conductor, Kelman is a committed and uncompromising writer whose use of dialect has attracted as much criticism from the literary establishment as it has praise from fellow writers at home. When some reviewers accused him of insulting literature, he retorted that "a fine line can exist between elitism and racism. On matters concerning language and culture the distinction can sometimes cease altogether."

Kelman has revolutionized Scottish fiction by writing not just dialogue but his entire novels in his own accent, and the debt owed to him by young contemporaries is immense. Writers such as Duncan Mclean, Alan Warner and Irvine Welsh all cite Kelman as a major influence on their writing. Cairns Craig, who has written widely on the modern Scottish novel, states that Kelman's real importance lies in his original use of the English language. "He can be seen as a post-colonial writer who has displaced and reformed English in a regional mode". Among Kelman's finest is his forst novel, *The Busconductor Hines* (Polygon Books, 1984) and *A Disaffection* (Secker and Warburg, 1989). Kelman's most recent work, *Translated Accounts* (Secker and Warburg, 2001) is his most 'difficult' to date. One literary critic claimed that, while it took Kelman three years to write, it might take the reader three years to understand it.

There are many other notable Glasgow novelists who began to make their name from the 1980s onwards. Jeff **Torrington**, the Linwood car-plant shop steward who was discovered by Kelman, won the Whitbread Prize for his debut novel *Swing Hammer Swing* (Secker and Warburg, 1992), which is set in the Gorbals of the late 1960s. **Janice Galloway** received much praise for her first novel, *The Trick is to Keep Breathing* (Vintage, 1990), which was on the short-list for Whitbread First Novel, and followed it up with an excellent collection of short stories, *Blood* (Secker and Warburg, 1991). Another brilliant collection of mostly Glasgow short stories is **AL Kennedy**'s *Night Geometry and the Garscadden Trains* (Edinburgh: Polygon, 1991), while *So I am Glad* (Jonathan Cape, 1995) is Glaswegian take on Magic Realism. Also worthy of mention is **Christopher Whyte**'s humorous and scathing *Euphemia McFarrigle and the laughing virgin* (Gollanz, 1995).

For an overview of Glasgow writers and the Glasgow novel, see *The Glasgow Novel* by **Moira Burgess** (3rd edition, Scottish Library Association, 1999). Another book about Glasgow fiction, is *Imagine a City*, by **Moira Burgess** (Scottish Arts Council, 1998). For a short literary tour of the city, see *Reading Glasgow* by the same author (Book Trust Scotland, 1996).

Further reading

The best general overview of Scottish social history is given by **Professor Chris Smout** in his excellent *A History of the Scottish People (1560-1830)* and *A Century of the Scottish People (1830-1950)*. A worthy new contender is *Scotland A New History*, by **Michael Lynch** (Pimlico, 1999). Also, *Scotland the Story of a Nation*, by **Magnus Magnusson** (Harper Collins, 2000) is a mighty tome, and after reading it you're unlikely to pass on any questions on Scottish history. All have substantial sections on Glasgow's history. Two new additions are *The New Penguin History of Scotland*, edited by **RA Houston and WWJ Knox** (Penguin, 2001), and *The Oxford Companion to Scottish History*, edited **Michael Lynch** (OUP, 2001).

Local history & folklore
For an in-depth exploration of the ciy's history, look no further than **Irene Maver**'s superb *Glasgow* (Edinburgh University Press, 2000). A detailed study of Glasgow's great river is given in *The Clyde: The Making of a River*, by **John Riddell** (John Donald, Edinburgh, 2000). For a selection of Glasgow folk tales, read **John Burrow**'s *Great Glasgow Stories* (Mainstream, 1998).

Art & Architecture
Two good books on Charles Rennie Mackintosh are *Charles Rennie Mackintosh* by **Alan Crawford** (Thames and Hudson, 2000), and *Charles Rennie Mackintosh Synthesis in Form*, by **James Steele** (Academy Editions, 1994), which is a glossy coffee-table book with excellent photographs. Those who wish to read up on Alexander 'Greek' Thomson should get hold of *'Greek' Thomson* by **Gavin Stamp and S McKinstry** (Edinburgh University Press, 1994). For the best overall study of Glasgow's buildings and architectural development, see *Central Glasgow: An Illustrated Architectural Guide*, by **Charles McKean**, **David Walker** and **Frank A Walker** (The Rutland Press, 1999). For a thorough, but not too weighty, look at the history of Scottish art, see *Scottish Art* by **Murdo MacDonald** (Thames and Hudson, 2000).

Travelogues, memoirs & biographies
If you only read one general Scottish travelogue, then make it **James Boswell** and **Samuel Johnson**'s *A Journey to the Western Islands of Scotland* (Penguin). For a selection of the bestof travel writing on Scotland, including Daniel Defoe, Edwin Muir and Jan Morris, there's *The Road North - 300 years of Classic Scottish Travel Writing*, edited by **June Skinner Sawyers** (The Inn Pinn, 2000). For an insight into the deep, dark recesses of Glasgow and its greatest comedian check out *Billy*, a biography of the Big Yin by his wife, **Pamela Stephenson** (Harper Collins, 2001).

Food & drink
Those wishing to bone up on their malt whiskies should refer to the *Scotland and its Whiskies,* by **Michael Jackson**, a beautiful journey through the water of life. Fans of the ale, meanwhile need to get hold of *The Scottish Beer Bible* by **Gavin D Smith** (Mercat Press, 2001). An excellent Scottish recipe book is the *Claire MacDonald Cookbook*, by **Lady Claire MacDonald** (UK Bantam) who runs a hotel on Skye. Also good is *Scots Cooking* by **Sue Lawrence** (Headline, 2000) and *Scottish Cookery* by **Catherine Brown** (Mercat Press, 1999).

Genealogy
The Collins pocket guides to *Clans and Tartans*, *Scottish Surnames* and their *Scots Dictionary* are handy and informative. For more detailed genealogical study, look at *Tracing your Ancestors*, by **Cecil Sinclair** (HM Stationery Office). Also worth a look are *The Search of Scottish Ancestry*, **Gerald Hamilton-Edwards** (Phillimore, 1983), and *Scottish Clans and Family Names*, **Roddy Martine** (Mainstream, 1992).

Footnotes

12

Footnotes

Index

Q

Queen Elizabeth Forest Park 164
Queen's Cross Church 92
Queen's Park 108
Queens Park Football Club 208

R

radio 39
rail passes 37
railcards 30
Ramshorn Church 59
Rangers Football Club 207
Red Clydesiders 198
religion 34
responsible tourism 34
River Clyde
  history of 116
  trips along 119
Rothesay 155
Rowardennan 161
Royal Concert Hall 71
Royal Highland Fusiliers
  Museum 73
Ruchill Church Hall 93
Ruchill Park 93

S

safety 34
Saltmarket 63
Sauchiehall Street 71
Scotland Street School
  Museum 104
Scott, Walter 211
Scottish Exhibition and
  Conference Centre (SECC)
  118, 130
Scottish Football Museum 108
Scottish National Gallery of
  Modern Art 179
Scottish tourist board 17
self-catering 145
Sharmanka Kinetic Gallery and
  Theatre 62
shipbuilding 116, 198
shopping 43
  City Centre 80
  Merchant City 62
  Trongate 68
  West End 100
sleeping 35,137
Snuff Mill 110
South of the Clyde 101
Spence, Alan 212
sports centres 48
St Andrew's Church 63
St Andrew's Square 63
St Andrew's-by-the-Green 63
St Enoch Centre 69
St George's Cross 86
St George's Tron Church 70
St Mungo (Kentigern) 189

St Mungo Museumof Religious
  Life and Art 57
St Vincent Street 70
St Vincent Street Church 70
Stirling 165
  Stirling Castle 165
student travellers 20

T

Tall Ship at Glasgow Harbour 118
Tarbet 161
tax 24
taxi 36
telephone 39
Templeton's Carpet Factory 64
Tenement House 74
theatres 131
Thomson, Alexander 'Greek'
  109, 203
Thomson, William, Lord Kelvin 193
Tighnabruaich 154
time 32
tipping 34
Tobacco Merchant's House 59
tobacco trade 192
Tolbooth Steeple 62
Torrington, Jeff 213
tour operators 14
tourist boards 17
tourist information 17, 32
tours 16
Trades Hall 59
trains 30
transport 35
  air 26
  bus 29, 35, 37
  information 35
  road 29
  sea 30
  train 30, 37
  underground 36
Transport Museum 87
travellers' cheques 25
Trips from Glasgow 147
Trongate 62
Tron Kirk 62
Trustee Savings Bank (former) 58
TV 39

V

value added tax 24
Victoria Bridge 120
Victoria Park 93
Virginia Galleries 59
visas 23

W

Wallace, William 166
Watt, James 193
Waverley, Paddle Steamer 119
websites 18
weights and measures 32
Wemyss Bay 152

West End 83
West Highland Railway 162
West Highland Way 47, 95, 161
Western Baths Club 92
Western Necropolis 55
whisky 42
White Cart Walkway 110
Whyte, Christopher 213
Willow Tea Rooms 70, 71
Winter Gardens 65
Wiszniewski, Adrian 211
women travellers 22
working in Scotland 23

Map index

Shorts

Five of the best boxes

Footprint travel list

Footprint publish travel guides to over 120 countries worldwide. Each guide is packed with practical, concise and colourful information for everybody from first-time travellers to travel aficionados. The list is growing fast and current titles are noted below. For further information check out the website **www.footprintbooks.com**

Andalucía Handbook
Argentina Handbook
Bali & the Eastern Isles Hbk
Bangkok & the Beaches Hbk
Barcelona Handbook
Bolivia Handbook
Brazil Handbook
Cambodia Handbook
Caribbean Islands Handbook
Central America & Mexico Hbk
Chile Handbook
Colombia Handbook
Costa Rica Handbook
Cuba Handbook
Cusco & the Sacred Valley Hbk
Dominican Republic Handbook
Dublin Handbook
East Africa Handbook
Ecuador & Galápagos Handbook
Edinburgh Handbook
Egypt Handbook
Goa Handbook
Guatemala Handbook
India Handbook
Indian Himalaya Handbook
Indonesia Handbook
Ireland Handbook
Israel Handbook
Jordan Handbook
Laos Handbook
Libya Handbook
London Handbook
Malaysia Handbook
Marrakech & the High Atlas Hbk
Myanmar Handbook
Mexico Handbook
Morocco Handbook

Namibia Handbook
Nepal Handbook
New Zealand Handbook
Nicaragua Handbook
Pakistan Handbook
Peru Handbook
Rajasthan & Gujarat Handbook
Rio de Janeiro Handbook
Scotland Handbook
Scotland Highlands & Islands Hbk
Singapore Handbook
South Africa Handbook
South American Handbook
South India Handbook
Sri Lanka Handbook
Sumatra Handbook
Syria & Lebanon Handbook
Thailand Handbook
Tibet Handbook
Tunisia Handbook
Turkey Handbook
Venezuela Handbook
Vietnam Handbook

Also available from Footprint
Traveller's Handbook
Traveller's Healthbook
Traveller's Internet Guide

Available at all good bookshops

Glasgow by cuisine

A quick reference guide to help you locate a restaurant to suit your taste and budget near to you. Further details can be found by turning to the page ▸▸

Codes are: **£** under £10; **££** £10-20; **£££** over £20.

Australian

South of Clyde	*The Other Side*	**££**
	T4294042	▸▸ 111

Belgian

West End	*Brel*	**££**
	T3424966	▸▸ 96

Brasseries/Bistros

Central	*Baby Grand*	**££**
	T2484942	▸▸ 76
Central	*Brasserie on George Square*	**££**
	T3073301	▸▸ 57
Central	*Café Gandolfi*	**££**
	T5526813	▸▸ 60
Central	*Café Gandolfi @ Habitat*	**£**
	T3311254	▸▸ 78
Central	*The Counting House*	**£**
	T2489568	▸▸ 57
Central	*Smiths of Glasgow*	**££**
	T5526539	▸▸ 61
West End	*Air Organic*	**££**
	T5645200/5201	▸▸ 96

Chinese

Central	*Amber Regent*	**££**
	T3311655	▸▸ 75
Central	*Canton Express*	**£**
	T3320145	▸▸ 78
Central	*Ho Wong*	**£££**
	T2213550	▸▸ 75
South of Clyde	*The Wok Way*	**££**
	T6382244	▸▸ 111

Eastern European

Central	*Oblomov*	**££**
	T5524251	▸▸ 61
West End	*Oblomov*	**££**
	T3399177	▸▸ 97

Fish and seafood

Central	*Frango*	**££**
	T5524433	▸▸ 60

Fish and seafood cont.

Central	*Gamba*	**£££**
	T5720899	▸▸ 75
Central	*Rogano*	**£££**
	T2484055	▸▸ 75
Central	*The Buttery*	**£££**
	T2218188	▸▸ 74
West End	*Gingerhill*	**££**
	T9566515	▸▸ 97
West End	*Two Fat Ladies*	**£££**
	T3391944	▸▸ 96

French

Central	*Babbity Bowster*	**£**
	T5525055	▸▸ 61
Central	*Chardon d'Or*	**£££**
	T2483801	▸▸ 75
Central	*Le Bouchon*	**££**
	T5527411	▸▸ 65
South of Clyde	*Cul de Sac Southside*	**££**
	T6491819	▸▸ 111
West End	*Cul de Sac*	**££**
	T3344749	▸▸ 97

Fusion

Central	*Eurasia*	**£££**
	T2041150	▸▸ 75
Central	*Quigleys*	**£££**
	T3314060	▸▸ 75
West End	*Stravaigin*	**£££**
	T3342665	▸▸ 96

Greek

South of Clyde	*The Greek Golden Kebab*	**££**
	T6497581	▸▸ 111

Indian

Central	*Modern India*	**££**
	T3311980	▸▸ 78
Central	*Wee Curry Shop*	**£**
	T3530777	▸▸ 78
South of Clyde	*Ashoka Southside*	**££**
	T6370711	▸▸ 111

Indian cont.

South of Clyde	*Spice Garden*	££
	T4294422	▸▸ 111
West End	*Ashoka Ashton Lane*	££
	T3371115	▸▸ 96
West End	*Ashoka West End*	££
	T3393371	▸▸ 96
West End	*Café India*	££
	T2484074	▸▸ 97
West End	*Killermont Polo Club*	££
	T9465412	▸▸ 97
West End	*Mother India*	££
	T2211663	▸▸ 97
West End	*Mr Singh's India*	££
	T2040186	▸▸ 97
West End	*Shish Mahal*	££
	T3398256	▸▸ 97

International

Central	*Babbity Bowster*	£
	T5525055	▸▸ 61
Central	*Eat Drink Man Woman*	£
	T5529260	▸▸ 67
South of Clyde	*Alphabet Yard*	£
	T6496861	▸▸ 111
West End	*Beetlenut*	££
	T3371145	▸▸ 96
West End	*Gong*	££
	T5761700	▸▸ 97

Italian

Central	*Ciao Italia*	£
	T3324565	▸▸ 78
Central	*Fratelli Sarti*	££
	T2040440	▸▸ 78
South of Clyde	*Arigo*	££
	T6366616	▸▸ 111
South of Clyde	*Buongiorno*	£
	T6491029	▸▸ 111
West End	*La Parmigiana*	£££
	T3340686	▸▸ 96
West End	*Sal e Pepe*	£
	T3410999	▸▸ 98

Japanese

Central	*Ichiban Japanese Noodle Café*	£
	T2044200	▸▸ 61
Central	*OKO*	££
	T5721500	▸▸ 60
West End	*Fusion Sushi Bar*	££
	T3393666	▸▸ 97

Latin American

Central	*Cuba Norte*	££
	T5523505	▸▸ 60
West End	*Cottier's*	££
	T3575825	▸▸ 97

Mediterranean

Central	*Café Clear*	£
	T5526454	▸▸ 67
Central	*Esca*	££
	T5530880	▸▸ 65
West End	*Otago*	£
	T3372282	▸▸ 98
West End	*Stazione*	££
	T5767576	▸▸ 98

Mexican

| Central | *Cantina del Rey* | ££ |
| | T5524044 | ▸▸ 65 |

Middle Eastern

| West End | *The Bay Tree* | £ |
| | T3345898 | ▸▸ 98 |

Modern British

Central	*Bargo*	£
	T5534771	▸▸ 61
Central	*Café Source*	£
	T5486020	▸▸ 67
Central	*Corinthian*	£
	T5521101	▸▸ 60
Central	*The Counting House*	£
	T2489568	▸▸ 57
Central	*Farfelu*	££
	T5525345	▸▸ 60
Central	*Frango*	££
	T5524433	▸▸ 60
Central	*Loop*	££
	T5721472	▸▸ 61
Central	*Tron Theatre*	££
	T5528587	▸▸ 65
South of Clyde	*Alphabet Yard*	£
	T6496861	▸▸ 111
West End	*Amaryllis*	£££
	T3373434	▸▸ 96
West End	*The Canal*	£
	T9545333	▸▸ 98
West End	*Nairn's*	£££
	T3530707	▸▸ 96

Mongolian

Central	*Khublai Khan*	££
	T4008090	▸▸ 60

North American

West End	*The Canal*	£
	T9545333	▸▸ 98

Oriental

Central	*Glasgow Noodle Bar*	£
	T3331883	▸▸ 78
Central	*Mao*	££
	T5645161	▸▸ 60

Pacific Rim

Central	*Gordon Yuill and Company*	££
	T5724052	▸▸ 77

Russian

Central	*Café Cossachock*	£
	T5530733	▸▸ 67

Scottish

Central	*Axiom*	££
	T2212822	▸▸ 76
Central	*Bouzy Rouge*	££
	T2218804	▸▸ 77
Central	*The Buttery*	£££
	T2218188	▸▸ 74
Central	*Cameron's*	£££
	T2045555	▸▸ 74
Central	*City Merchant*	££
	T5531577	▸▸ 60
Central	*The Green Room*	££
	T3323163	▸▸ 78
Central	*Groucho St Judes*	£££
	T3528800	▸▸ 75
Central	*The Inn on the Green*	££
	T5540165	▸▸ 65
Central	*Schottische*	££
	T5527774	▸▸ 61
Central	*Tempus at the CCA*	£
	T3327959	▸▸ 78
South of Clyde	*The Cook's Room*	££
	T6211903	▸▸ 111
West End	*The Cabin*	£££
	T5691036	▸▸ 96
West End	*Deirfiuracha*	££
	T3373636	▸▸ 97
West End	*Puppet Theatre*	£££
	T3398444	▸▸ 96

Scottish cont.

West End	*Stravaigin 2*	££
	T3347165	▸▸ 96
West End	*The Ubiquitous Chip*	£££
	T3345007	▸▸ 96

Spanish

Central	*Arta*	££
	T5522101	▸▸ 60

Thai

Central	*Pattaya*	££
	T5720071	▸▸ 78

Vegetarian

Central	*The Granary*	£
	T2263770	▸▸ 78
Central	*The Thirteenth Note*	£
	T5531638	▸▸ 67
West End	*The Bay Tree*	£
	T3345898	▸▸ 98
West End	*Grassroots Café*	£
	T3330534	▸▸ 98

Will you help us?

We try as hard as we can to make each Footprint Handbook as up-to-date and accurate as possible but, of course, things always change. Many people email or write to us – with corrections, new information, or simply comments. If you want to let us know about your experiences and adventures – be they good, bad or ugly – then don't delay; we're dying to hear from you. And please try to include all the relevant details and juicy bits. Your help will be greatly appreciated, especially by other travellers. In return we will send you details about our special guidebook offer.

email Footprint at:
sco2_online@footprintbooks.com

or write to:
Elizabeth Taylor
Footprint Handbooks
6 Riverside Court
Lower Bristol Road
Bath   BA2 3DZ
UK

What the papers say

"I carried the South American Handbook from Cape Horn to Cartagena and consulted it every night for two and a half months. I wouldn't do that for anything else except my hip flask."
Michael Palin, BBC Full Circle

"The titles in the Footprint Handbooks series are about as comprehensive as travel guides get."
Travel Reference Library

"If 'the essence of real travel' is what you have been secretly yearning for all these years, then Footprint are the guides for you."
Under 26 magazine

"Excellent, best buy whether travelling independently or with a tour operator."
Adventure Travel

"Footprint can be depended on for accurate travel information and for imparting a deep sense of respect for the lands and people they cover."
World News

"Footprint Handbooks, the best of the best."
Le Monde, Paris

Mail order
Available worldwide in bookshops and on-line. Footprint travel guides can also be ordered directly from us in Bath, via our website **www.footprintbooks.com** or from the address on the imprint page of this book.

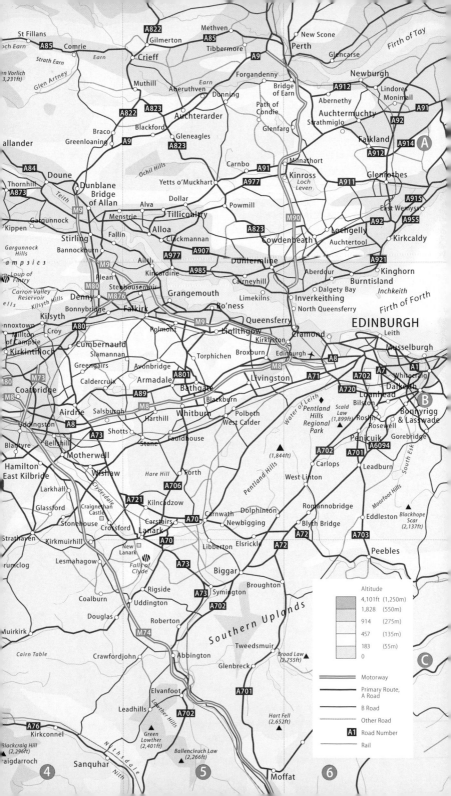

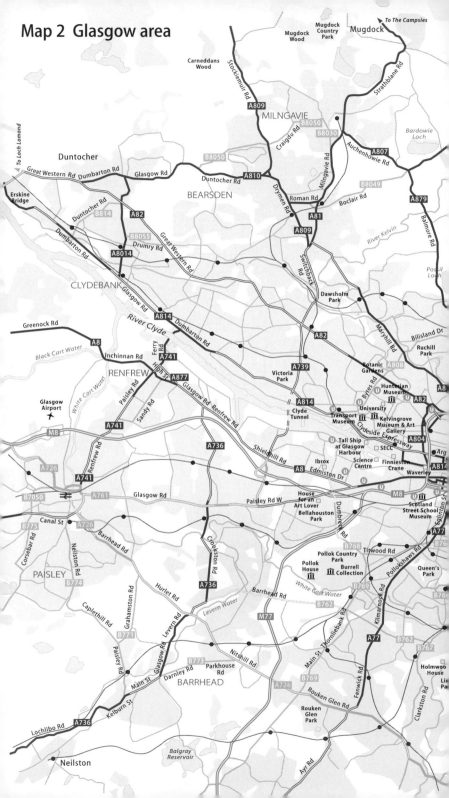

Map 2 Glasgow area

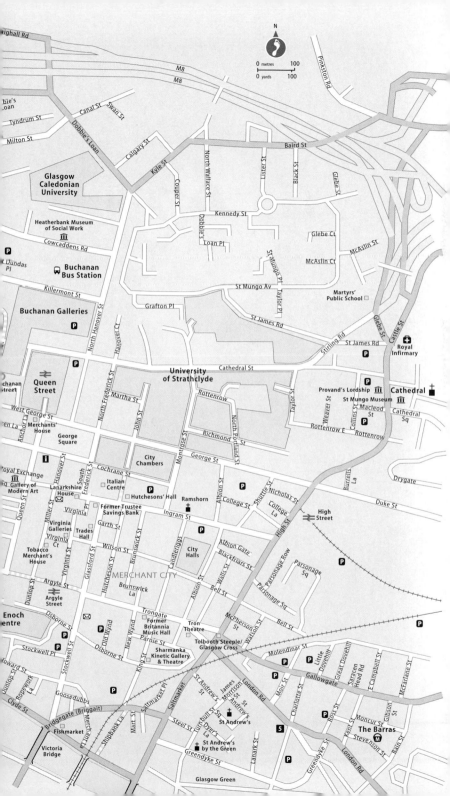

www.footprintbooks.com
A new place to visit

Acknowledgements

Alan and Rebecca would like to thank Moira Dyer at Greater Glasgow & Clyde Valley Tourist Board for her invaluable help and support throughout the entire project. Thanks to Jane Hamilton and John Binney for their knowledge, advice and contributions to the Entertainment and nightlife chapter, Gay and lesbian travellers section and also for giving us the benefit of their 'city experiences'. Thanks also to the National Trust for Scotland, the Charles Rennie Mackintosh Society, the staff at Holmwood House, Richard McPherson at Strathclyde Passenger Transport, Ged O'Brien at the Scottish Football Museum, and all the friends who chipped in with information on their favourite restaurants, bars and shops.

A big thank you to all those at Footprint, especially Ian Emery and Stephanie Lambe.

About the authors

Born and raised in Fife, **Alan Murphy** then moved to Dundee to begin a career in journalism. Ten years later he swapped shorthand notebook for a rucksack and escaped to the relative obscurity of Bolivia, where he wrote for an English language newspaper, taught English and helped out in a home for orphaned street children. After brief stints as a guinea pig farmer, a performing condor in local Carnivals and a professional llama-wrestler, Alan suffered terrible injuries in a freak accident with a howler monkey. Many months later, after recuperating in the home of an Andean witchdoctor, Alan turned up in London, where fate played her propitious hand and introduced him to the editor of the legendary South American Handbook. The rest, as they say, is history. Alan now lives in the southwest of England with his wife, Philippa and daughter, Rosa. As well as co-writing the Glasgow Handbook, he has written Footprint guides to Scotland, Edinburgh, Highlands and Islands, Bolivia, Ecuador, Peru and Venezuela.

A graduate of St Andrews University, **Rebecca Ford** worked in public relations and advertising for several years, before becoming a full-time travel writer and photographer. Her travels now take her all over the world, although she specializes in writing about the British Isles and Italy. Her work has appeared in newspapers such as The Guardian, the Daily Express and Scotland on Sunday and she also writes and contributes to many other guidebooks.